THREE DAYS AFTER

ARPress
45 Dan Road Suite 5
Canton MA 02021

Hotline: 1(888) 821-0229
Fax: 1(508) 545-7580

Ordering Information:
Quantity sales. Special discounts are available on quantity purchases by corporations, associations, and others. For details, contact the publisher at the address above.

Printed in the United States of America.
ISBN-13:   Paperback   979-8-89356-007-7
              eBook   979-8-89356-008-4

Library of Congress Control Number: 2024902594

Contents

"Intense, calculated and riveting. *Three Days After* will keep you wanting for more."

"Three Days Later gives us a glimpse of what would have happened had Ludlum collaborated with LaHaye and Jenkins"

"A powerful page-turner, Ribble will have you questioning if we are currently in the End Times"

- Scott Budweiser

"Fiction? Too close to reality...maybe, just maybe, this author knows more than he's telling..."

"First-rate storytelling, a spy novel wrapped in biblical mystery, where the truth of it... looms over our heads at this very moment!"

"Wow, this story sticks with you...be prepared!"

-Tom D Hughes

Relatable, suspenseful and yet utterly refreshing, *Three Days After* will reel you in with its character descriptions and then fully captivate you as each character's role spirals unpredictably before bringing you to an unparalleled ending.

Taking a step out and putting a fictional voice behind taboo topics, *Three Days After* combines worldwide politics and biblical theory to entrance its readers into questioning the often avoided "what ifs" of whether the prophesied end times could be happening among us today.

Ribble ingeniously uses a fictional stance to address taboo topics within worldwide politics and biblical theory. *Three Days After* entices readers to question the all-too-often avoided topic of whether the prophesied end times could be happening among us today.

-Heather Anders

The perfect mix of action and suspense. I didn't want to put it down. Vivid details immerse the reader, making them feel as though they are part of the story.

-Nicole Jonas

Preface

"Eric come here," his Dad calls out to him. "It's time to go to church. You are ready." His voice made it sound like a question with only one proper response.

"Course Dad, but why do I have to go? It's just a bunch of mythological mumbo jumbo. You know what my teacher says about this garbage?"

"Don't know, don't care," responds his Dad.

"Look, I can understand if you want to participate in this stuff, but why do you have to make me? I'm never going to buy into this stuff again. I bought it when I was a little kid, but those days are long gone."

"If they've been gone so long, how come I still feed, cloth and put a roof over your head? In my estimation, you still qualify as a kid until you can support yourself financially. And that, we both know, is a few years away. While we're waiting for that day to arrive, you can humor me by going to church with the family." His Dad had developed a reluctant acceptance to his son's perpetual complaints regarding church.

- - - -

The pastor has been preaching from the last book in the Bible. He's been stuck on this topic for some time now, and Eric is questioning if it ever will make sense. For the last few weeks, he's been telling the congregation why he believes we're in the 'end times.' Wars, the EC, meteorological catastrophes and a host of other reasons. Last week he even decided this garbage with President Clinton was additional proof. Today he's talking about the Antichrist. The Antichrist is supposed to fool the world into believing he is the real Messiah. The one Christians believe was Jesus Christ, and the one Jews have been waiting for six thousand years. Give me a break, Eric thinks.

Interesting concept though, Eric continues. If in fact this person could exist, and he really could convince people throughout the world that he had some magical power, the possibilities would be limitless.

But in order for this to come true, the guy would have to have something more than charisma working in his favor. He'd need a whole network of truly loyal followers, the kind that could look past all his frailties and see the power. The power a properly managed image could wield over the world, he thought.

"The exact time the Antichrist comes to power is unknown," the pastor was saying. "The Bible gives very limited information about the man, himself. But he is clearly defined by his position during the Tribulation. Some Biblical scholars have claimed that the tribulation cannot begin until this man has acceded to a position of at least world influence and more likely actual control. I am not convinced…"

The Tribulation is the last seven years before the 'end of the world,' as we know it, Eric remembered. It's times like these that years of rigid attendance in church pays dividends, he thought. He vaguely remembered something about the first half of the seven years was supposed to be a period of unprecedented peace. "Daniel, I believe, is where that can be found in the Bible," he says to himself in imitation preacher mode. Then, if he remembered properly, the second half of the seven years is followed by---What did they call that again? Oh, yeah, Armageddon. Why they come up with these obtuse names is a mystery to me, he thinks.

Eric's thoughts returned to the Antichrist. What kind of person could command this type of support? The man would obviously have to be charismatic. But that wouldn't be enough to keep him in power, or really even put him there. Let's face it, there are a lot of people that have generated a following based primarily on this trait, but it is usually restricted to a given country or nationality. Hitler, Stalin, Napoleon; they obviously had a charismatic component to their personality, but they came to power by knowing how to manipulate the system. Kinda' like Reagan and Clinton, he chuckled to himself. Wouldn't that blow more than just a few minds if this Antichrist didn't even turn out to be a Jew?

Unlike them, this person has to gain control over more than a single country. Not, he thought, without a lot of help. He would have to appeal to a population base that had a common interest across a wide range of countries. Somehow, they will have to cross not only physical boundaries with their influence, but cultural and societal boundaries. This includes societal variations within and between countries. They will also have to manage vastly different political landscapes both within and between countries.

Eric was still deep in thought considering the necessary character traits the Antichrist would need to be effective when the Music Director managed to break through his thoughts by telling everyone to turn to page 423 in their hymnal.

As they filed out of the sanctuary, Eric decided he needed to become better versed in this topic. He vowed to listen to the Pastor's sermons during the next few weeks and whenever a special speaker was in the area preaching on the 'end times', he'd be there. Maybe it's time to take some of this mythology serious, he thought.

- - - -

Six years later, Eric received a bachelor's degree from the University of Minnesota in Police Science. As with any student that excels in this field of study, he regularly received inquiries from the CIA regarding job interests. With graduation behind him, he decided to see the world at the U. S. government's expense.

-A poor yet wise man is better than an old and foolish king who no longer knows to receive instruction

The light of the new day had just begun to cast shadows. It was only three in the morning, but this far north the sun rose early. He had been living here for just over a year and had already become accustomed to the early summer mornings. It was the long winter nights that still caused concern. Still, it was a better life that he had found, or so he hoped. This morning was unusually cool considering the time of the year. The air here was fresh, no pollutants, and peacefully quiet. No smog to breath, no traffic jams to fight, no one to take orders from. That was why he was here in the first place; he wasn't very good at taking orders.

The nearest city, Red Deer, was about a hundred and fifty miles southeast of here. The trick was knowing which combination of unmarked gravel roads would get you there, or grid roads as they were referred to by the locals. Using a compass would help you find the way, just not in a reasonable amount of time and probably after traveling twice the distance. That was another thing he liked about living here. The only visitors you'd see were people with a reason to be here. Tourists seldom found the area and even if they did, they wouldn't stay long. The area was too desolate for most. A few people did live here, but most kept to themselves. It seemed if you stayed here long enough, you'd become a type of hermit. Not to imply that the population consisted of so many hermits, but it did help to be able to get along with yourself, as well as by yourself.

This morning Eric had placed himself at the edge of a small cropping of pines about forty yards south of the lake. The lake was no more than three miles long and barely eight hundred yards wide at the center. Most maps didn't even identify it, but locals called it Shinnebeg. There was supposed to be a story that went with the name, but Eric hadn't had much luck finding out what it was. He was still considered a tourist to the few people he had become acquainted with since he first arrived. And unless you lived here all your life, the natives would always consider you a tourist. "Just visiting?" they'd ask.

A small river, more like a creek, fed the lake along with a couple springs, as a result, water temperature never got much above forty-five degrees all year around. Pan fishes were plentiful, and trout were a regular catch in the creek, but today Eric had come to hunt.

He had seen an elk drinking at the edge of the lake on a frequent basis. He usually wanders in during the first two hours after sunrise and sometimes he'd come back about an hour before sunset. It had been three weeks since he'd finished eating the last of his meat and the idea of buying more in town was not very appealing. He'd heard elk was almost like beef, just a little sweeter, and he was hoping to try some. He was tired of fish, and since he was supposed to be self sufficient, at least according to the U. S. Government, he felt a driving need to get this elk. In theory, he had been trained to live off the land indefinitely, albeit for a completely different purpose. But now, it's more a matter of pride than survival that drives him to live this way.

Patience is the most important attribute a successful hunter can have, and Eric had the time, so Eric had the patience. Most people think the ability to fire a rifle accurately or track a kill or even locate game is more important. But if you can't wait for the game to come to you, you'll blow opportunities for a kill that you never even knew you had.

Maybe some things the government had taught him were worthwhile, Eric thought, but it was the way they wanted him to use that knowledge that he had come to hate. Here alone, he could put that knowledge to use in a way that didn't hurt anyone, especially himself. The healing had finally begun, the hate he had held inside for so long was starting to dissipate, and it was days like this that was making the difference. The Doc had said, "The only thing that'll help this boy is time. What he went through, by rights, should have put him in the mental ward." Sometimes, Eric thought, he'd be better off if that's where he had ended up.

But now looking out over the south end of the lake, all he cared about was getting that elk. Scanning the edge of the woods he thought he saw something move. Just to the right of a lone maple tree there appeared to be movement. Slowly he brought the rifle up to look through the scope. There was something there all right, but he couldn't quite make out what it was. Keeping the animal in sight through the scope, Eric decided to wait him out. It wasn't long before the animal cleared the base of the maple tree. Now it was completely visible, and Eric could tell it wasn't the elk. Walking on hind legs and black as night; it was a bear. Definitely a worthy target he decided.

Bringing the crosshairs of the scope to the center of what was the bear's chest, Eric prepared to fire. There was a little bit of brush in the way, so he couldn't aim directly at the heart. He took one last deep breath, held it, steadied the rifle, and slowly squeezed the trigger just as he had done so many times before. Only this time the target wasn't human. Immediately the bear reeled backwards, stumbled, then charged off into the woods. "Damn, I should'a waited for a better shot," Eric mumbled. He knew he should have waited until a kill shot was a sure bet, because now he would have to track it. Eric thought tracking any wounded animal was a sign of failure. "You're only supposed to need one shot," he repeated an oft heard admonition from his mentor. Besides, the thought of having to waste time looking for the bear, was not his idea of a relaxing day.

Eric began the walk of about one hundred seventy-five yards to the place the bear was when he shot. A couple of times during the walk he would stop to listen for the bear, as soon as he heard it, he would continue on his way. The third time he stopped he couldn't hear any-thing. In fact, it seemed a little bit too quiet, there weren't any sounds. Then he heard a bird chirp and the wind rustling through the trees and everything seemed more or less back too normal again. Too quiet made Eric nervous, even up here where quiet was a way of life. Eric stopped about thirty yards shy of the spot to listen again. He thought he heard something move. It sounded as if it was straight back in the pines, but it was so soft he couldn't be sure. It certainly didn't sound like a wounded bear, he thought.

Upon arrival at the base of the maple tree, it quickly became apparent that Eric's shot had hit its mark. In fact, judging from the amount of blood, the slug had hit a spot much better than the one he had aimed for. This explains why I didn't hear much activity in the woods, he reasoned. Relieved that the tracking was going to be relatively easy, Eric decided to relax with a cup of coffee. He took off his thermos, which was latched to his belt and looked at it for a moment. A wonder of old-time science that works like a charm to keep things hot or cold, he thought, then poured himself a cup. He decided he could muse about the social benefits of a thermos another time, so with cup in hand, he started the short walk to breakfast, lunch, and dinner for the next few weeks.

The tracking was easy, every few feet there were large blotches of wet blood. In between the blotches was a steady path of droplets. By the time Eric reached the bear, not more than two hundred yards inside the woods, the bear had mercifully died. Another shot would not be necessary.

It didn't take long to dress it out once he got going but getting the carcass back to the cabin would take some innovative thinking. Quartering the beast would make it easier to handle and require the least amount of physical effort. However, that also meant leaving a sizable portion of food for critters to nibble on. Eric gave this some thought and decided most of the meat would be safe if he could hang it high enough in the air. The maple tree back at the lake had some branches that would work perfectly, he thought. Four trips later and using all the rope he had brought with him, one front quarter and a hindquarter were swinging in the breeze. As he started to throw the last of his rope over a branch to pull the next quarter up, he heard what he thought, were horses approaching. He stopped to listen, just then the wind picked up and all sound was lost in the rustling of the leaves and branches brushing against each other.

He tossed the rope toward the branch but missed. It was three more tries before he was successful. Then tugging on the rope, he lifted the last quarter, and tied it off. This wasn't the best way to hang meat, but this isn't like hunting with your buddies at home either. Out here there isn't time to hang the carcass whole, skin it, then butcher it in a nice, neat pattern. Here, one has to protect the kill first or there won't be anything left to butcher.

With the three quarters now safe from scavengers, Eric set the remaining quarter behind his saddle. He quickly checked the three quarters swinging in the tree, making sure they were securely fastened. Satisfied, he climbed onto his horse and headed back to the cabin.

The cabin was situated on the lower portion of a mountain that climbed just over 6,500 feet at its peak. For the most part it was surrounded by scotch, spruce and white pines scattered among each other. There was no more than a twenty-five-yard clearing between the cabin and the trees on both sides and the rear. In front of the cabin there was an open space that curved out away from the cabin in a ragged arc.

The cabin was nothing more than a handmade wood framed structure, with half logs on the exterior to give the impression it was a full-fledged log cabin. In reality, it was someone's attempt at a log cabin without the backbreaking work of full-sized logs.

Whoever built it, although not a carpenter, was fairly handy with tools. The construction was better than average, particularly for something this far from civilization. One could see where the miters were occasionally gapped, and the counters had just the slightest tilt back toward the walls. Other than that, and a few other minor shortcomings, Eric felt the cabin had been an excellent buy.

He was able to purchase the cabin with just over two acres of pretty much useless land around the cabin, for $25,000. Since the man who sold him the cabin and the Canadian government were the only other landowners in the area, those two useless acres grew to just over fifteen thousand acres. Not a bad little deal, Eric thought.

The cabin had a kitchen, two bedrooms and a living room all neatly furnished in late 1950 furniture. All the walls were covered with knotty pine tongue and groove panel boards stained slightly darker than their natural color. The living room had a sofa, two chairs and an assortment of electronic gadgetry: a computer, TV wired to a satellite dish, standard AM/FM radio and a two-way radio. Electricity was supplied by a 25 hp., gas fueled, electric generator. The front room extended the length of the cabin and had one large picture window that overlooked the clearing in front. There was also one standard sized double hung window at each end of the room.

The kitchen was sparse, containing a small wooden table with two accompanying chairs. Cabinets lined the wall from the rear door to the corner of the room, except where the three-foot-wide slide by window was located over the sink. A refrigerator, sink and four feet of counter completed the room. On either end of the kitchen was a bedroom. Each bedroom was a perfect ten by ten square and contained one old bed with matching sagging mattresses. A single double hung window on the side wall of the cabin provided the main source of light into each bedroom. Almost all of Eric's possessions were stored in one of the bedrooms.

As Eric rode up to the cabin, but before he entered the clearing surrounding it, he sensed something was wrong. He dismounted from his horse, and quietly tied the animal to a tree. He began walking around the cabin in a large circle. He stayed five or six yards inside the perimeter of the woods, and as he walked, he would look, first at the cabin, then the ground near him, then finally into the woods. Completing the front side of the cabin, the east side started to come into view. As he worked his way farther around, he came upon the tracks of two horses.

Keeping an eye on the cabin and woods, he followed the tracks around to the rear of the cabin where they headed back into the woods. Following the tracks, he went another two hundred yards into the woods, before he came to the horses. They had been tied up and muzzled as an extra precaution against making noise. He examined the horses looking for clues to the owners but found nothing. The saddles were generic and there were no markings or brands on the horses that were local enough for Eric to recognize.

Eric started back to his horse, the whole time he racked his brain trying to figure out who he would find inside the cabin. Once back at his own horse, he sat down inside the woods where he could watch the cabin, while he developed his plan.

After ten or fifteen minutes he noticed someone walk past the picture window toward the kitchen. The man looked to be about six feet tall, solid build, and blonde hair. Eric didn't recognize him. A minute later the same man returned, then a very familiar figure walked into view and stood talking to him. As they talked, the man used his hands constantly, then pointed out the window as if to acknowledge Eric was outside watching them. He continued using his hands as he talked as if his hands could somehow communicate more intimately than his words. Whatever he was saying, he was saying in his typically animated and energetic fashion. It was exactly that trait that had drawn Eric into doing this man's bidding in the first place. He came across so honest, so sincere, that almost no one refused his requests, particularly Eric.

Well, this time, Jim was in for a surprise, Eric thought. Not only was his request going to be denied, but also the delivery of the message would convince him once and for all to: Leave Eric alone! Eric was out of the business, finished, permanently retired, whatever description you wanted to use didn't matter, because Eric was not available. Just the sight of Jim inspired Eric's plan.

It was five in the afternoon, so he had about five hours of daylight left, more than enough time to emphasize his point. Jim, and whoever was with him, couldn't watch all four sides of the cabin at once, and Eric knew Jim couldn't watch any side for more than thirty seconds before losing interest so this should be easy. Eric lined up with the northwest corner of the cabin, just inside the woods, where he could make out the window on the side and monitor the rear door as well. One of the two men would have to be positioned in the southwest corner of the living room and look out at just the right time in order to see him as he crawled to the cabin. While crawling, he grabbed any stones he could find and stuffed them in his pockets. As Eric expected, getting to the cabin was easy.

With his rifle slung over his shoulder, Eric began the tedious job of scaling the log cabin wall and climbing onto the roof. The rake at the eave was just over nine feet from the ground. If noise hadn't been an issue he could have jumped up, grabbed the eave then climbed on the roof. Instead, he scaled the wall. Then taking hold of the rake, he continued climbing the wall until his body matched the pitch of the roof. Now he simply rolled onto the roof without making a sound. Once on the roof, he took a well-deserved rest while he considered his next move.

Quietly Eric worked his way to the ridge of the roof, then back down the front side of the cabin. When he was midway down the slope, he stopped, removed his rifle from his shoulder and sets it down next to him. Taking one of the stones he had gathered on his way to the cabin, he estimated how much plastic explosive he would need to cover it. He began kneading the explosive until he had a thin sheet roughly the size of the stone. When finished, he set the stone in the center of the sheet of explosive, then wrapped it around the stone. When the entire surface of the stone was covered, he set the stone behind his rifle. He repeated the process until all four stones were neatly coated with the explosive.

Now it was time to find out what Jim wanted.

Eric took three of the stones and put them in the left breast pocket of his shirt, then picked up the rifle and the last stone. He slung the rifle over his left shoulder. To make sure Jim was provided the best view possible for the show, he threw the stone out toward the edge of the woods directly in front of the picture window. Immediately after the explosion, which sprayed some sand and very little else, he heard footsteps inside the cabin rush to the front window to see what happened. Before they could react, he threw the second stone just out of sight on the East side of the cabin. The footsteps immediately ran to that side of the cabin to look out the window. Then Eric sat down on the chimney and waited for one of them to venture out to investigate. Knowing Jim, the other man would be sent out soon as the guinea pig.

It didn't take long before the man with the blonde hair came flying out the rear door, did a somersault, rolled once, came up running and disappeared into the woods. While this was going on, Eric slid behind the chimney. He watched the front of the cabin as well as the man running to make sure Jim wasn't doing the same thing out the front door. As Eric considered his next move, he saw the man in the woods approach the edge and begin walking the perimeter of the open area surrounding the cabin. The man stayed about two yards inside the woods but remained visible the entire time. Not once did he look up at the roof of the cabin. As he walked the perimeter, Eric kept the chimney between himself and the man in the woods. This is going to be easier than I expected, Eric thought.

Just as Eric was preparing to climb down the roof and surprise Jim, he heard the front door slam against the wall. Turning to look, he saw Jim running toward the woods. With his third stone, he took aim and threw it so that it would land somewhere between the two men. At the sound of the explosion, they both fell to the ground covering their heads with their hands. Eric quickly came around the chimney, and while sliding the rifle off his shoulder, rushed to the eave of the roof. Then, without aiming, he shot twice at the base of a tree near the man in the woods. As expected, Jim froze at the sound of the gunshots. The man with the blonde hair started to get up when Eric yelled, "Move an inch and you're history." He froze as well.

"What's on your mind Jim?" Eric asked. "And don't bother getting up to answer," he added.

"I'm sorry to bother you Eric, you know I wouldn't risk coming here unless it was an emergency," Jim replied.

"Your definition of an emergency usually doesn't even warrant a response with most people, so don't feed me any stories. Just tell me what you want, I'll say no, and you can be on your way."

"Look, I didn't come all this way to talk to the ground, can I at least stand up while we talk?" Jim asked.

"I can't see why that is necessary. Just state your business."

"I know who killed your wife."

Eric was stunned. He hadn't thought about her for the last year and wasn't sure he wanted to reopen that part of his life. The healing hadn't begun until he had given up on getting revenge. Evening the score at this point wouldn't help anyone.

"I don't care who killed her," responded Eric. "Now I think it's time for you and your boyfriend to head back home."

"I can't leave until you've at least heard me out, Eric. Can't you give me a chance to state my case?" he pleaded.

Eric shot one more time. The bullet came within inches of the other man's feet. "Your friend better not move again, because that's the last warning anyone's going to get," Eric yelled at Jim. "Now I don't know why I should give you, or anyone like you, the chance to talk. Unless there is some pressing reason, I'm not aware of, you're going to hav'ta leave," Eric finished.

"Eric, we need your help. We talked it over and we all agreed. You're our only chance on this one. Even Tom had to agree,"

"Gee, I feel honored. Even Tom agrees. What's the matter? Tom's fair-haired boy fall off his pedestal? That still doesn't tell me why I should have to waste my time with you or him."

"Tom's 'boy' as you say, was killed three days ago trying to do the job I wanted you for. We don't know how, but it appears his cover had been compromised, leaving him exposed so to speak. Tom's acknowledged that he shouldn't have been sent in the first place because he didn't have the right connections. But it's too late for that now. We haven't been able cultivate any reliable sources in that area since you quit, and Tom's finally realized we don't have the time or resources to try again without you."

Eric sat down on the roof, laid the rifle across his legs, then looked out at Jim and his unknown friend. The two men were lying on their bellies, looking so pathetic; like children caught in the act of doing something they knew was wrong. Eric couldn't keep from smiling. There weren't any good reasons he could think of to listen to Jim, but remembering Jim used to be his friend, he decided to give him the opportunity to state his case.

Jim was reaching the age where retirement should be his primary objective, but the thought rarely, if ever, crossed his mind. He always placed the Agency's work above all else, and that's probably why all three of his marriages failed. No person or cause had ever supplanted the Agency's work in his life. He approached work much as an Israeli zealot might approach fighting for the Holy Land, with the unquestioning conviction that what he was doing was the only acceptable course of action. No other method, no other ideology, no other cause could be as important or as just, than what the Agency decided was important and just. It was men like Jim that perpetuated the belief, within Agency employees, that they could never rightfully be accused of any wrongdoing.

Jim was an administrator and communicator for the Agency. He was a poor tactician, as demonstrated by his earlier action of charging out the front door during Eric's assault. As a consequence, he was usually confined to his office, except when details or assignments had to be communicated directly to the people in the field. Then, with reservations, he would be sent out.

His communication skills made him the ideal candidate to explain orders to personnel. The agents listened to him and respected him, as well as protected him. His less than intimidating stature heightened his effectiveness as the courier because no one would suspect him to be tied to the Agency. Unfortunately, his longevity with the Agency had ultimately diluted this benefit.

In cowboy boots, which were favorites of Jim, he had to lie to say he was five feet four inches tall. His shoulders were rounded from being hunched over a desk too many hours a day, and his stomach gave the impression he was permanently five months pregnant, due solely to his propensity for beer. Gray was the dominant color in his hair, but there were still a few streaks of the shiny black hair he once had. He was not particularly strong, nor had he ever been. Exercise was not considered a worthwhile activity to him, and his body was an excellent example of what happens when one doesn't exercise.

The need to ride horseback to Eric's cabin also gave Jim the excuse he needed to dress the way he preferred. He wore a plaid, black and red flannel shirt, blue jeans and of course the cowboy boots that had become his favorite footwear outside the office. While Eric watched, he saw Jim shift every so often trying to keep the pistol inside his shirt from poking him. Eric decided it was time to disarm them. He knew Jim was not a real threat, but the blonde was still an unknown. Eric removed the rifle from across his knees, aimed at a spot two inches away from the blonde man's feet, then fired once again. Jim jumped as if he'd been shot, but the man Eric meant to intimidate didn't even move. This man should be watched closely, Eric thought. He obviously has been brought along in case Jim needed help. And at first glance he certainly appears capable.

"It's time to get undressed boys." Eric continued not giving Jim a chance to protest. "Jim, you go first, your friend can wait a minute. Throw the gun over there," Eric pointed to a spot midway between the men and the cabin.

Once Jim was down to his underwear, Eric told him he could stop. "Jim pick up your clothes, and move away from the boy, but not toward your gun."

"Now tell your friend to toss his gun over by yours and begin getting undressed, too. Only he should throw his clothes over by the guns, one at a time. And tell him not to do anything foolish."

Jim relayed the message, as if his partner hadn't already heard Eric, and the process started all over again. Except this time, with the removal of each piece of clothing, he paused to throw it over by the guns. It wasn't very long before both men were standing dressed only in their underwear. "Turn around," Eric ordered. As they began to turn around, Eric jumped off the roof. "You can turn back now," he said as he walked over to the pile of clothes near the guns. At the pile, he reached down and picked up the two guns. Next, he gathered the clothes to himself, and began to meticulously inspect each piece of clothing. Other than a piece of wire, whose purpose was obvious, Eric didn't find anything else. After he was sure there wasn't anything left in the clothing that could be used as a weapon, he stood up. Stepping back from the pile of clothes, he began talking.

"I'm not convinced I shouldn't just send the both of you on your way, but I've decided to hear you out Jim. But before you start, I want to lay down some ground rules. First and foremost, I don't want my wife's death used as a bargaining chip. That part of my life is best left alone by you and everyone else. I don't need your help deciding what needs to be done about it. Second, give me the facts and keep the editorializing down to a minimum. I realize that this is going to be difficult for you, since you have an opinion on everything. And finally, you can start by explaining who your friend is and why you brought him along."

Jim and his companion walked over to their clothes and started getting dressed. "My friend, as you call him, is the best trainee we've had since you," Jim began. "He was brought along for two reasons. We didn't, or I should say Tom didn't, think it was safe to come looking for you without some protection. He thought you might still be angry enough to do something foolish. I tried to convince him you weren't one to lose control and I'd be perfectly safe coming here alone, but he didn't accept that. Also, whatever the outcome of our conversation, he has a job to do. He may do it alone, or under your direction. That's for you to decide. Just for the record, his name is Steve Monroe."

"He's been with the Agency now for two years. As I said earlier, he's probably the best recruit to come along since you. He has the same natural instincts you have."

"I don't ever remember being taken quite so easily as **he** was today," Eric cut in.

"No," there was a long pause as if Jim was thinking how to respond. "I warned him that the best way to approach you, if you were hostile, was to get caught and do as we were told. Just like you used to do, he listened well. What I didn't need was one of you killing the other one before we had a chance to talk. When the explosions started, I knew right away it was you and it was just a matter of getting caught in an acceptable manner. By acceptable I mean no one getting hurt.

You must have known we weren't too dangerous when you saw we weren't heavily armed. Anyway, before I sent him out the rear of the cabin, I told him if he made it to the woods without being shot, to begin circling around to the front of the cabin making sure he was close enough to the edge to be seen. I didn't know where you were, but I knew your vantage point would allow you to see him. Then it was a simple matter for me to wait a little while, then come out and get caught. I was fairly confident you wouldn't kill me on sight. I figured you'd allow me the opportunity to provide you justification before you actually killed me. It was a calculated risk, but remember I'm paid to think, not fight. And that is exactly what I did. What can I say?"

"I never knew you were paid to think," Eric jabbed back. Without waiting for a response, he added. "If you would like, we can finish this conversation inside. I have the feeling it's going to be a long story."

The three men walked back to the cabin without saying anymore to each other. Once inside, Eric returned their emptied guns and offered them each a cup of coffee. Eric wasn't surprised that a hot pot of coffee was ready. He had expected Jim would have made himself comfortable while waiting for Eric in Eric's own cabin. The coffee was a nice homey touch, he thought. One had to admit Jim had a certain way about him that allowed him to get away with these types of intrusions. As soon as Eric handed Jim the cup of coffee, he started talking.

"Have you been able to keep up with world events out here? Judging by your collection of electronic equipment, you certainly have the capability."

"I manage to maintain a vague understanding of current events, if that's what you mean," Eric answered.

"Then you're aware of Sheik Omani's ever-increasing circle of influence, or more accurately his rise to power," Jim stated.

"I know a year ago no one had heard of him and today he's involved with almost every major event that takes place in the Middle East whether of Arab or Israeli origin. I know that he consults with not only recognized governments in the Middle East, but with many of the smaller factions, including terrorist organizations. I know he seems to have gotten a little too much power, or influence if you prefer, and fast enough he must have someone's help. However, everything he has done so far has resulted in the peaceful reconciliation of some rather sensitive situations, as opposed to the old method of survival of the fittest, which usually resulted in far too many innocent people paying the price," Eric explained.

"You're right on a couple points, but there is considerably more you need to be aware of. To date, the Agency hasn't been able to determine who or what group is responsible for his rapid rise to prominence. We have narrowed it down to three very different groups and are continually gathering new information. For now, I'll just give you a brief description of each group."

"The first is the unlikely Israeli based Zealots; they have supported every major settlement Sheik Omani has suggested, including the splitting of Jerusalem, similar to Berlin after WWII. They are supporting his position of returning half the city to Arab control. The Arab half will encompass the entire old city that contains the site of Solomon's Temple. Needless to say, this raised more than a few eyebrows of leaders around the world. It was at this point that President Harris made this our number one priority. There are other indications that the Zealots have been included in secret meetings with Sheik Omani; the only Israeli group to be included in such meetings.

"The second group is as unlikely as the first. The terrorist group led by Jihad Nadu, which we believe was responsible for starting the recent rash of terrorist activities. We have confirmed that they were the group that bombed the restaurant across from Harrods, killing General Gage, his wife Naomi, two upper-level officers, their wives and twelve Brits. It has been surmised that General Gage was the target due to something he did or said while he was stationed in Beirut, as an advisor with the U. N. security forces. Most likely it was a name and face easily recognized by Nadu's people, and since he was an American military officer, he became the perfect target. Nadu hasn't claimed responsibility or accepted any of the Sheik's proposals publicly, but where he has previously been a very vocal critic, of any and all peace proposals, regardless of origin. Lately he's been so quiet that some people actually began theorizing he had died. We know that's not true. Also, he's been seen entering a building that Sheik Omani was known to be in at the same time."

"The last group is an anomaly. It is a consortium of wealthy oilmen throughout the world. Actually, none of them are the recognized head of any oil company, but all are major stockholders in various companies. This information was acquired through some excellent detective work by Eddie. You remember Eddie, don't you Eric?" Jim asked.

"Wasn't he the bookworm responsible for most of the research into public domain type documents? The one the majority of us thought had the most boring job and probably the best-looking wife. She had been a model or actress or something like that. Anyway, we became fairly dependent on him for supplying us with information we could use freely because it was public knowledge. He also was responsible for identifying a few connections that existed on the business level that may have taken an agent years to figure out because traditional contact between the parties was nonexistent; they communicated through reams of lawyers. Yea . . . I remember, he was indispensable."

"Well, Eddie has been able to connect six of these oilmen through various documents, that prove beyond any doubt, they are major stockholders of some of the most prestigious oil companies in the world. The lists of companies include Standard, Exxon, Texaco, British Petroleum, and a few others. As you can see their sphere of influence exceeds the Middle East and complicates matters considerably if they are involved. And we think they are."

"Eddie says it was the most convoluted trail he had ever tried to trace. Each name was hidden behind a trail of phantom holding companies. One person was ten levels deep before Eddie could confirm the connection. However once identified, the task of determining their collective influence on the companies became relatively easy. You see the group feels they are so well hidden and unknown, that they meet publicly every three weeks at various locations throughout the world. A simple well-placed bug has provided us with a dearth of valuable information."

"If we can come to an agreement, and I'm sure we will, you'll be provided a dossier on each and everyone of them. You'll also receive Eddies 'Prophetic Report,' this is a document you may not be familiar with. We've never provided it to a field agent before, but we've come to depend on it at HQ when we put together any strategic plans. We figure you will need this and once you've read it, you'll see why. I'm sure you'll use it extensively in your own planning."

"Anyway, back to the oilmen. If we were only dealing with the likes of the first two parties, although the reason for their connection wouldn't be obvious, at least it would be somewhat consistent with the geopolitical situation over there. The oilmen really don't fit the scenario very well. But both radical factions have been tied to the oilmen through financial contributions they've received for their respective causes. We haven't been able to pinpoint the exact reason they are supporting both sides, but it's a fairly common practice within governments and we assume the same reasons apply. Our own government has done it in the form of arm sales during almost every war since our inception and the support actually increases during times of peace in the form of dollars. Granted we claim to do it for the noble purposes of making large profits, but we feel confident it buys us an edge at the bargaining table if or when the time comes. On the surface these appear to be the only reasons for their assistance. In either case, we're not particularly fond of the idea of so-called private citizens becoming involved in this type of activity. The Armand Hammers of the world make great copy if you're in the newspaper business, but they create nothing but headaches for governments.

"The most important find of Eddie's research was each of the six men, and their respective oil companies, were the only sources of financial support for Sheik Omani during the first nine months of his rise to prominence. We can not find any evidence linking other groups or individuals or governments backing the Sheik prior to three months ago. Now, as with so many other things, people can't jump on the bandwagon fast enough.

"As I said earlier, we bug every one of their meetings, or at least we think it's every one of their meetings. The last meeting provided some rather curious information, and this is why we **need** your help," Jim emphasized the word need. "It seems this group of oilmen have decided to eliminate the Sheik. I know it doesn't make sense to essentially create the man, then turn around and destroy him, but that's what they intend to do, or so we think. And that's why we suspect we're missing some critical bit of information, or possibly, there are still more, yet to be identified, players in the game.

"Also, we haven't been able to connect the oilmen to the sheik in any other fashion than financial support. There has been absolutely no physical or verbal contact between this group and the Sheik or this group and the Zealots or Jihad Nadu. That's why we think there is still at least one more person or group involved that we haven't identified. We're investigating every possible avenue, but until we can determine who they are and their motivation, we remain vulnerable.

"Tom's 'fair haired boy,' as you called him, has already become a casualty in this activity. We can't be sure, but we suspect it was this fourth party that caused his premature demise. He was neutralized by a hired assassin, and here's where you might be particularly interested; the assassin was Jacque the Frenchman. Probably the single best assassin in Europe, and as you know, the man responsible for your wife's death," Jim paused to give Eric a chance to absorb this twist.

Eric thought he could compartmentalize this part of his life and leave it forever unfinished. But the rush of hatred that supplanted all other emotions at the moment made him realize just how deeply he had been affected by his wife's death. When he'd left the Agency, he was confident it could never lure him back, but this changed everything. At that moment, Eric knew he was going to accept one last assignment. However, this time it wouldn't be for the patriotic causes that Jim had become a master at espousing. Nor would it be for the money that could provide for almost any lifestyle he chose. No, it would be for the revenge that Eric had so proudly denied needing. It would be to finish that unfinished portion of his life that he thought he had so neatly tucked away in a corner of his mind. He would accept the assignment of terminating his wife's killer, but not become involved with the politics of the situation. His decision was made. He could achieve the objective for the Agency, avenge his wife's death and stay completely removed from any further involvement.

"I'll do it," Eric said curtly.

"Wait a minute, there is more to it than just 'I'll do it'," Jim responded. "First, we figured you might be inclined to take the assignment just to neutralize Jacque, then consider your job done. That would fulfill your needs, but not all of ours. Our solution to that is to require you take Steve with you. It will be his job to help you in any way you deem necessary, as well as learn from your techniques and ensure all our objectives are met. You can consider it a training exercise for him, and insurance for us.

"He will also be responsible for collecting and forwarding to us, any information the two of you might dig up. That will help fill in the blanks, particularly with respect to the unknown entity. Knowing how single minded you might be on this; we want you to know this point is not negotiable. You will take Steve with you," Jim demanded.

"I will decide what's negotiable," Eric countered. "Before I take anyone with me, they'll have to demonstrate their creativity, so to speak. I won't accept someone that can't take care of himself. Steve will be tested, and if he doesn't make the grade, I'll be on my own."

"That depends on the test, what does he have to do?" Jim asked.

"You wouldn't give a student the test questions ahead of time, would you? Likewise, I have no intention of providing him with that information. The test will be of my choosing and you're just going to have to trust me to be fair," Eric answered.

"I'll agree to that as long as we can replace him with someone else if he fails."

"We've got a deal."

"One last thing," Jim said. "We don't want to communicate with you directly while you're in the field. Steve has been supplied a list of contacts that the two of you can report to. All communication will be channeled, through Steve, to one of them. If you try to make direct contact to any of us at the Agency, access will be denied. At this point in time, we can't risk anyone becoming aware of our involvement. If things change, and direct contact is not detrimental, we'll let you know. Eric, if you'll accompany me out to the horses, I have a dossier on Sheik Omani that you may find helpful."

Eric and Jim left the cabin. Steve, recognizing he had not been included with Jim's invitation, remained seated. He watched as both men walked outside in the direction of the horses.

"Files on each of the oilmen and Eddie's 'Prophetic Report' will be provided to you along with airline tickets to wherever you decide to start your quest," Jim continued as they approached the horses.

Jim lowered his voice as if the forest around them might hear what he was about to say next. "There's something I think you should know about Steve before you head out," he began. "I helped Tom pick Steve for this job, however, unknown to me at the time, Tom had already chosen Steve for this assignment. He just let me believe I had a part in the decision. Also, I found out the two of them have had a number of unscheduled meetings that have purposely excluded me. Tom used the 'don't have a need-to-know excuse,' but since I'm the primary source on this project, it's inconsistent with the Agency's policy. And with me reporting to Tom these days, my hands were tied. I can't be sure, but I think you need to be careful with what you say or show Steve. I'm not convinced he's here entirely for your benefit," Jim finished,

"I appreciate the warning Jim, and just to repeat what I told you when I left: I don't blame you for anything. Tom, on the other hand, may not have survived if he had been sent here instead of you."

"Put the files and at least $50,000 to start in a lockbox at the airport," Eric abruptly changed topics. "You can send the airline tickets and the key to the Hotel Concorde in Calgary. I want tickets to London, either Gatwick or Heathrow. It doesn't matter. You'll need to setup an account in a Swiss bank for an extra $50,000 and get the account number to me by the time I leave the plane in London," Eric rattled off the orders. "As far as Steve's concerned, if the plan was put together by Tom, it will probably fail anyway. If Steve becomes too much of a problem, he'll probably get lost along the way."

Jim handed the dossier to Eric, then climbed onto his horse. Eric turned and began heading back to the cabin. Steve, who was frantically searching the cabin, noticed Eric approaching. He stopped and quickly returned to his seat. When Eric came to the door of the cabin he stood for a moment and glanced back at Jim as he rode off. Entering the cabin, Eric grabbed their two empty coffee cups and walked back to the kitchen. He put Jim's in the sink and grabbed a clean one for himself. After filling both cups, he returned to the living room, handed Steve his cup and sat down.

"Enjoy the coffee, because when you're done, we'll be going for a ride," Eric said. Eric sat back in the chair and began to evaluate the man sitting across from him, the warning from Jim fresh on his mind. Steve was a little taller than Eric, maybe six feet tall give or take an inch. Even with the loose-fitting clothing he wore, one could tell he was in great shape. He couldn't be described as husky, but his solid build gave the impression he was bigger than he really was. His face had nice clean features, no scars, no uniquely identifying marks. Obviously, a face that either hadn't seen many fights or hadn't lost too many, Eric thought. His hair wasn't really blonde, but it had that indistinguishable color somewhere between blonde and light brown. His eyes were a bright blue. They gave him an eerie, dangerous appearance. The kind you'd associate with a blue-eyed Siberian husky.

Eric noticed Steve staring back but said nothing. He knew Steve should be doing the same thing to him, evaluating, critiquing, appraising his newfound partner. It was expected.

Eric broke the silence as he set his empty cup down on the table. "Are you prepared to spend the night in the woods?" Eric asked. "Because your evaluation will begin there."

"Whatever or wherever you want," Steve replied.

"Good, let's get going." Eric stood up and Steve followed his lead. They exited the cabin through the front door. "Go get your horse and bring him around front," Eric said as the door slammed shut behind him.

Both men met at the front of the house with their horses. "I've changed my mind about the ride. Get off your horse and take whatever you don't need out of the backpack. We'll be taking a little nature hike," Eric added.

As soon as Steve indicated he was ready, Eric started jogging toward the woods, Steve picked up his backpack and followed him. For the next five miles neither one said anything, the sound of their feet landing on leaves or breaking twigs was the only sound they heard. As they approached the end of their seventh mile Steve's breathing had gotten noticeably strained. Eric, who wasn't carrying anything, knew his lack of load gave him the advantage and he intended to make the most of it. The next three miles would take them part way up the mountain and should finish the job, Eric thought.

Steve surprised him, it was six winding miles up the mountain before Eric was satisfied that Steve had tired sufficiently. The last mile, Eric started searching for an outcropping of large rocks that would provide some protection for Steve. When he spotted one, he stopped and had Steve put his backpack underneath it. Eric waited until Steve bent over while stuffing his pack up underneath the rocks. Then he clasped his hands together and in one swift motion, raised them over his head and then brought them crashing down on Steve's back, just below the neck. He didn't want to maim Steve, just immobilize him for a few hours. Steve's body fell forward from the force of the blow. His head glanced off the edge of one of the rocks in the outcropping as he fell to the ground.

Eric quickly grabbed his shoulder and rolled him over to see how badly he had been hurt. Steve was unconscious. Eric pulled the body farther underneath the overhang and began rifling through the backpack. Eric searched for anything that would give him an insight into Steve, the man or the agent. He also checked for anything that might give Steve an advantage for his journey back. Eric came up empty in both regards. Satisfied with the search, Eric sat down and wrote him instructions.

Steve,

As you are painfully aware, your test has begun. You have the simple task of meeting me at the Hotel Concorde in Calgary within 48 hours. The time at the tone is 8:25.

Eric

Eric pinned the note to Steve's shirt, admired how peaceful he looked, turned, and began the long run back. Sixteen miles was not going to be easy, but then he had no intention of taking the long way back. Heading in a relatively straight line back to the cabin, he should be back in a little over an hour, and still have some natural light to help square things away in the cabin. If Steve is smart, Eric thought, he won't start back 'til the morning.

Once back at the cabin Eric began preparing the place for an extended vacancy. Knowing there weren't too many people that would happen upon the cabin unexpectedly, he still felt a need to protect some of his more prized possessions. It was about one in the morning when he finally placed the last box in the closet. Closing the door and locking the padlock completed his effort to protect everything of value. He knew this didn't offer any real security, but it was meant more as a deterrent than anything else.

Eric poured a cup of the coffee he had recently brewed, grabbed the file on Sheik Omani and sat down to learn more about the man who's life he was supposed to save. To say he was disappointed with Eddie's research effort was an understatement to the nth power. Eric couldn't believe what he saw, exactly two pages of double-spaced information. None went back beyond one year ago when this whole charade began.

About the only thing worthy of Eddie's reputation was the detailed description of the man's physical features. He had even succeeded in identifying a one-inch mole on his left buttocks. Eric felt confident he could recognize the Sheik anywhere after reading the file. "Eddie I'm disappointed with you," Eric said aloud. "I may be able to recognize him, but I still don't know him."

Eric got up from the sofa with the file in hand, then went outside. He located the generator and flipped the switch to turn it off. The cabin went dark. Next, he tied his horse to the rear of his Toyota 4-Runner and headed for his nearest neighbor's. He wanted to be certain the animal was properly cared for while he was away.

2

- He who watches the wind will not sow, and he who looks at the clouds will not reap.

Eric approached the desk at the Hotel Concorde, as would any typical American tourist, somewhat hesitantly, as if he were unsure, he was in the right place. While registering, he asked the receptionist to check for any messages he might have. She returned a few minutes later carrying a thick manila envelope and handed it to Eric. "I hope you enjoy your stay with us," she said as she handed Eric the room key and a receipt. "Do you need any assistance with your bags?" she asked, then volunteered, "I could get a bellboy if you'd like." Eric just shook his head no, turned and walked away.

Once he was situated in his room, he sat down and began reading the local newspaper he had picked up while in the lobby. He just started to read the front section when he realized his message light was on. Reaching over to the phone, he dialed the front desk. The same girl that checked him in answered. "We've just received another letter addressed to you Mr. Dent. Would you like me to send it up to your room?" She asked. Eric told the girl it wouldn't be necessary; he'd pick it up next time he was downstairs.

Wanting to make sure he had received everything, he opened the thick manila envelope and quickly thumbed through the contents. All the files he expected were there, as well as the airline tickets and the key to the lockbox at the airport. Then his thoughts turned to the newly arrived letter. He realized that whoever sent it may still be around, and decided it was time to do a little sightseeing in the hotel and on the way, pickup the envelope.

In the lobby Eric strolled around looking at everything. He made sure to look impressed with his surroundings just in case anyone was watching him. As he inspected items in the gift shop, he would discreetly let his eyes wander throughout the shop and through the open door to the lobby. He was alone in the gift shop except for the salesclerk, but he could see three people in the lobby beside the receptionist. Two were an older couple just checking in. The other, a somewhat dowdy looking younger woman, was leaning against the wall reading a copy of Ms. magazine. She was wearing a waitress uniform and looked like she had just finished work and was waiting for a ride.

Eric walked out of the gift shop and began walking around admiring the interior design of the hotel lobby. The decorations were an overdone attempt by the designer to give an old-world motif to the hotel. Eric had seen too many versions of the real thing to be fooled by poor imitations made with modern construction materials. Although they looked very authentic, they were too new, too clean, and too sharp in their appearance. They lacked the character that only time can give to a well maintained building as it ages. As he walked out of the shop, he spotted an obviously very old gentleman. He was sitting on the sofa looking out the window watching pedestrians pass by. Eric studied him for a moment before he decided the man, really was old. And he probably was here simply to pass the time.

Stepping through the lobby doors, Eric walked out into the bright sunlight on to the sidewalk. Continuing his charade as a curious tourist he casually strolled first to one corner, then turning around, he walked back to the other corner. There was no one actually standing on the sidewalk. Everyone was busy going about their daily activities, hustling to and fro. He couldn't see into the buildings across the street because the sun was reflecting back off the windows. So, Eric decided to cross the street and inspect the buildings over there. After he completed a similar inspection of this side of the street, he was satisfied everything was normal and returned to the hotel lobby.

Inside the lobby, he immediately noticed the same waitress he'd seen earlier had taken a position near the windows and was staring at the activity outside. As he walked past her, he studied her more fully. Nothing new was readily apparent. She looked to be an authentic waitress, but one never knew. He decided to sit down next to the old man on the sofa and watch her for a little while. No more than ten minutes after he sat down, the waitress dashed out the front door as if her ride had just arrived. She turned right immediately out the door and Eric quickly lost sight of her.

Deciding he should keep track of her, he got up, and trying to look as normal as possible, hurried across the lobby floor to see where she went. By the time he got to a window with a view of that side, she was gone. Eric was not sure if she was anything to be concerned about, so he filed her away in his memory.

- - - - -

The man walked into the room with the air of unquestioned authority that comes with being in control of every circumstance your entire life. The four other men in the room quietly watched and waited trying to interpret what their commander would have them say or do. He walked around the small wooden table at the end of the room and sat down in the vinyl covered kitchen chair. Putting his elbows on the table and clasping his hands together, he looked over at each man in turn.

The four men were his closest friends, assuming you could make the jump from compatriot to friend. These were the children of his youth. They had been called the "Gang of Five," because as kids they had been inseparable. Also, they were as ruthless as their namesakes in China. Each had experienced the devastation of this religious battle firsthand. Each had personally felt the loss of at least one loved one: Credited to Israeli commando attacks or air strikes from Israeli fighter pilots. Each hated the Jew as completely as the other.

It was a natural evolution that the "gang of five" should grow from a common street gang to one of the most effective terrorist groups to enter the Arab Israeli War. Granted this wasn't a declared war as defined by western thinking, but this was war as defined by the common denominator, loss of human life. Both sides had experienced the decimation of entire families. Generations cut off, effectively truncating a family tree. They experienced the burden of caring for maimed family members made more difficult by the fact that only remnants of the original families still existed. Remnants so small they were almost incapable of even caring for themselves. Each of these men had seen enough, and experienced enough, to become desensitized to their own acts of terrorism, as well as those of their enemies.

Jihad spoke in a soft, almost apologetic manner, "As you are aware, Jacque has neutralized the oppressor. However, as we suspected, another has been chosen to take his place. A message has been delivered to him advising him it would be better to remain in his tranquil home, than to enter a battle where he does not belong. I suspect he will not listen." Lack of sleep was evident in his voice, but he continued his explanation.

"Early yesterday morning a waitress was chosen and today she was to deliver the message to his hotel. Because of the time difference, we have not been able to confirm it has been delivered and received. We expect to have that information shortly."

"This man who is to replace the other, will he listen to the warning, or will he also need to be neutralized?" asked one of the four.

"It is doubtful this man will accept the message in the spirit it is given. He is reputed to be the best the CIA has to offer, and he is motivated not unlike our own to succeed. However, he has been in a self-induced state of retirement due to his disdain for this type of work. We are unprepared for his response. Therefore, we will proceed as if he can not be convinced." Turning to the man on his left, Jihad asked, "Can you contact Jacque again and inform him of this new development?"

"Yes. What information can I supply him?" he responded.

"Tell him the man's name is Eric Dent. And he will arrive at Heathrow International Airport in the morning, day after next, on SAS flight 011. From there we do not know what his plans are."

"By the time I get this to Jacque, this man Eric will have already left. Will we be able to supply him anymore information by then?" The man acting as the messenger asked.

"The man will be isolated, he can send information through specified channels, but can not communicate directly with his superiors. Therefore, we do not expect to be able to furnish more before the man arrives in London. From what we have been able to learn, we may not be able to track him at all once he arrives. This is not important; Jacque knows this man and his abilities better than any of us. Tell him he will receive the same fee as last time." Jihad paused, then added, "If there is nothing else, you may go." As if ordered, the men immediately turned and left the room.

Jihad looked at the three remaining friends and thought, this is my family, this is my destiny. With these we will return peace to our countrymen. We will live free of the Jewish curse. Once all Arabs unite in the final push, the Israelis will have but one choice; to die or return Arab land to Arabs and go back to where they came. It is for eternal peace that we must kill today.

"We will have a visitor tonight," Jihad started in. "Our finances are being replenished once again. It seems our benefactors are aware of this Eric Dent as well. They are concerned that he may not be handled quite as easily as his predecessor. As a result of their concern, they have generously offered to provide us with a rather large stipend to ensure that this man does not reach Jacque. They also believe it would be wise to hire another to assist Jacque. It is their concern that Jacque's primary objective may be compromised if he is distracted. We will not inform them that Jacque has already been retained to neutralize Eric. They are not well educated in things of this nature and do not understand the need of someone like Jacque to handle these things his own way. Therefore, it is important that we employ a second assassin to give the impression to our benefactors that we are doing as they have asked." Jihad looked at all three men waiting for a response.

After a little while, one of the three remaining men responded, "I believe there is one called the Snake who might prove useful. He has been hired to do this type of work in the past, although on a much less important scale. He is your basic hoodlum, capable of killing a man for money. His past experience could be checked and verified. If we don't want him to get in Jacque's way, we could tell him it is his job to give chase throughout Europe until further notice. He would not need to know why or even who. Then when Jacque has disposed of this Mr. Dent, we could end the charade."

Jihad thought about what had been suggested. The biggest concern he had was not with the plan, but rather with the person chosen. "No," Jihad stated simply, "the person must have sufficient reputation for this type of work to convince them. The plan is perfect in all other facets, except the Snake, as you call him, is inadequate. Manuel, the Portuguese, would be a better choice. His reputation is international in scope and would convince everyone that we have chosen a viable assassin. He will be more expensive, but if for some reason Jacque failed, we could also have him step in to assassinate Sheik Omani as well as Eric Dent. Does everyone agree?" Jihad asked. All three men shook their heads yes. "Jamaal, you have relatives in Lisbon, don't you?" Jihad asked one of the three. "Can you or one of your relatives take care of hiring Manuel?" Jihad added.

"I will leave tonight," Jamaal stated simply. "It would be best if I handled the negotiations personally. And if he accepts, I can make the initial payment, ensuring that Manuel begins the assignment as soon as possible."

- - - - -

The men entered the room single file, each representing a controlling interest in at least one of the major oil companies throughout the world. Standard Oil of Ohio was Howard's contribution to the group. He had managed to accumulate almost eighteen per cent of the available stock through various holding companies. When he notified the Securities and Exchange Commission of his intent to go over the fifteen per cent limit, they were horrified. "How had he been able to purchase that much stock without them becoming even remotely aware of it?" They had asked. Howard had informed them that it was not his responsibility to teach them how to do their jobs, he was simply notifying them, as per the law.

Howard was a small, compact man. He felt that the body, just like a business, must be treated with respect. As a result, that small man was in the best physical shape of anyone in the room. Everyone there respected Howard's physical prowess and business acumen, an unexpected accomplishment for one so young and from such lowly beginnings. Howard had come from a broken home, the only memories he had of his father were the regular beatings he had given his mother. His father deserted them when Howard was six, and his mother, having no work experience, took to the streets to support Howard and herself.

The beatings of his mother didn't really stop, the face of the perpetrator just changed more frequently. For many children this would have doomed them to a never-ending cycle of poverty, crime, and death. Howard was not like many children. By the time he was twelve years old, he had a work force of ten other kids delivering newspapers for him. If any of the kids got wise and threatened to leave and get their own route, Howard would encourage them to do just that. Then Howard would quietly find out what paper route and offer to buy the route from its present owner. The other kid couldn't match Howard's offer and would ultimately become a delivery person for Howard once again, only at a slightly reduced wage.

The newspaper business instilled in Howard the desire to make money because he learned that power belonged to the person with the most money. It was the power of money that allowed him to protect his investment by buying new newspaper routes, as circumstances would dictate. Howard's next venture into the world of capitalism was a result of great timing. Before Howard had a driver's license, he bought an old pickup and hired two high school dropouts to drive around town collecting newspapers and cardboard boxes. He would split the earnings fifty/fifty with them after subtracting all the costs of operating the truck and charging a small rental fee to the two boys for the use of his truck. It wasn't long and this business began to grow.

Other unemployed high school dropouts heard about Howard's arrangement with these two, and they would approach Howard about the same type of deal. In order for Howard to provide honest work for these new employees, he began to expand to include other types of recyclables. By the time Howard turned eighteen he had incorporated and was pulling down almost $10,000 per month in earnings. It seemed like everything Howard got involved with from a business standpoint was a success, and this continued as Howard entered adulthood. He was so successful, that at the age of twenty-eight, he was offered a position in this unique collection of businessmen.

The second man through the door, Jason, was the complete opposite of Howard both physically as well his family background. Jason came from a wealthy family that experienced poverty through reading National Geographic. As a family, they had never been exposed to real life poverty; they could always choose to ignore it by never placing themselves in contact with the people or property of poverty. Granted the family owned many parcels of real estate that could only be described as being part of a slum. However, one can own the property without ever going near it. And that was the philosophy Jason grew up espousing. Power was money and money was land, it didn't make any difference where that land was located. If its location wasn't pleasant, you simply avoided it.

Jason felt all sports were for entertainment only. The thought of actually participating in a sport was foreign to him. That thought simply had not ever crossed his mind, and his body paid the price. Underneath the obese exterior there may have been a finely tuned instrument at one time in its life, but shortly after birth it was hidden behind a layer of fat. Jason was taught early in life that exercise was a form of forced labor and should be avoided at all costs. Jason not only came to believe this precept, but he also defined it. If a tool existed or person could be paid to do it, Jason found it, bought it, or employed it. Regardless, Jason was able to avoid burning any unnecessary calories except those needed to sustain life. The result was obvious, where Howard was five feet five inches small and one hundred forty-five pounds of solid muscle; Jason was six feet two inches tall and two hundred eighty-two pounds with limited muscle.

Jason did have some redeeming qualities as far as this group was concerned. He was responsible for the Texaco portion of this consortium. He was also the only one that owned the stock in his own name. Jason had received the 4.25 per cent ownership of Texaco when he turned twenty-five from a trust fund set up for him by his grandfather.

In the ensuing twenty-one years he had increased his ownership to fourteen per cent. At that point, he felt comfortable demanding a seat on the board of directors---a demand the rest of the board felt obligated to satisfy. He had enough power that he could have replaced the existing CEO. But he wanted control without the notoriety of that position.

The third man to enter the room was a Brit. and he carried himself as if that mere fact would demand respect. He was British in every aspect of his life; from his need for tea every afternoon, to his habit of never fully recognizing the United States as being anything but a British colony. One would think this fact alone would be a cause for contention between him and the Americans, Howard, and Jason, but they accepted Seymour's eccentricity for just that. They recognized his contribution to the group for its significance and ignored the man. He, on the other hand, considered them British subjects, thereby bestowing on them some semblance of old-world respectability. Seymour brought with him the connection to British Petroleum. When the government sold BP in their attempt to return capitalism to the forefront of the British economy, Seymour was first in line to purchase as much as he could afford. At the time, that meant almost twelve per cent.

One of Seymour's eccentric tendencies was his desire to be viewed by the public as a member of the idle rich. Consequently, his purchase of BP stock had been camouflaged. As with most of the other members of the group, he was a major shareholder without the extra baggage associated with visible ownership. This made Seymour a perfect addition to the group: he had influence yet could remain obscure.

Seymour was raised under the influence of British aristocracy. His father had been knighted for his contributions to Britain's effort during WWII. His mother could trace her heritage back to a remote line that diverged from the Royal line in the late eighteenth century. Both families were wealthy in their own right and brought the trappings of that wealth to their union. Seymour was one of the recipients of this wealth, along with his three brothers. All of them received the guidance of a nanny while growing up and attended some of the best private schools in all of England. Seymour excelled at academia and was invited to attend Oxford. Upon graduation, he joined his father in the family business.

As with education, Seymour exceeded everyone's expectations for him as a businessman. However, when he was thirty-five and his father was making the final preparations for him to take total control of the business, Seymour made an unexpected announcement---He was not interested in following in his father's footsteps. It was at this point Seymour decided to step out from under the overshadowing control of his father and venture out on his own. Without a word of explanation to his father or anyone else in the family, Seymour severed all connections to the family and the business.

He quickly presented an image to the public of a totally hedonistic lifestyle. But hidden safely behind that image, he became obsessed with accumulating wealth. He also became very good at it. His name disappeared from the original twelve per cent, safely camouflaged behind reams of legal documentation. Then the twelve per cent grew to nineteen per cent. His empire expanded into the banking industry, and soon his circle of influence was as strong there as well. It was also just as well hidden. Although he had become one of the wealthiest men in England, he was able to maintain a public image that was not associated with power. His behavior made him an enigma, but also provided the impetus for his inclusion in this group.

The fourth man entered the room and immediately walked over to the table to pour himself a drink. He was a harsh, strong willed, powerfully built German. His name was Toomas, and he looked like the perfect specimen for Hitler's Aryan race. He was a tad over six feet tall, with a strong, muscular build---A body usually the result of expensive steroids, but not his. He condemned the use of steroids by anyone. He considered those who used chemicals to achieve what God had not given them naturally, and those who were incapable of achieving it on their own, to be reprobate. His blonde hair was rapidly turning white with age, and his steel blue eyes had been tempered with years of hard dealing.

Although his father fought with the French resistance during WWII, and hated the German military for what it defined, he instilled in Toomas a strict, militaristic approach in the business world. That approached proved its usefulness many times over.

In some ways Toomas was a combination of the excellent education found in Seymour, and the self-made man experiences of Howard. His home environment had been stable, albeit on the poorer end of the social ladder. From a very early age in life his father taught him the importance of not only achieving academic recognition through formal education, but also acquiring and developing the skills necessary to apply that education. Even today his father's words would echo in his head, "Toomas, intellect can not be judged by academic achievement, for any plodding fool can eventually succeed in academia. It is imperative that formal education be augmented continually through the practical education of life. True learning is the accurate assimilation of empirical data into the theoretical world. Never be satisfied with what you know. Learning must never stop. And knowledge in and of itself is useless, even dangerous if one does not gain the wisdom to use it properly."

This instilled a healthy skepticism in Toomas as he listened to teachers, professors or proclaimed experts. He would be the one student, in all his classes that asked the instructor the difficult questions. Add to this his ability to ask questions that often unearthed contradictions in the lesson, and Toomas became less than the ideal student in the eyes of many of his teachers. They often shared notes on how best to defend against "his attack" but were seldom successful.

The other students found solace in Toomas' ability to make the instructors squirm, elevating him to leadership status. If it wouldn't have been for his disdain of student organizations, he could have picked the cause or group he wanted and become President of any of them. Toomas felt student led organizations lacked the influence to accomplish very much. They wasted energy fighting for or against causes that had little impact on the world as a whole. It was his premise; if the students were truly committed to any cause, that cause would dictate the direction of their entire lives. They would direct their studies to the field that offered the best chance to have impact, excel, then move into an appropriate job after graduation. At that point, they could effect change or be swallowed up by the organization they chose and allow their ideology to be modified, reflecting the status quo.

Toomas chose the oil industry in Europe, because with the loosening trade restrictions across European borders through the European

Community, otherwise known as the EC, the opportunity for a new company would never be better. As a student, he developed the plan and began soliciting political support and investors while still in school. Prior to graduation and the official beginning of the EC, he had completed his support structure. Even though his investment amounted to little more than the idea and the sweat equity to develop it and make it work, he was able to maintain control of an unheard of thirty-six per cent through shrewd negotiations that played each investor against each other. He remained forever, in the eyes of his financial benefactors, precariously caught in the middle.

Five years after graduation he had adequate investor support to open a single petrol station in the largest city of each of the participating countries. During the first few years he had trebled many times over his petrol stations through shrewd acquisitions of weak or failing stations and sophisticated and innovative business approaches. During that same time frame, he purchased an old, unused oil refinery in North Africa, refurbished it, then began refining his own crude oil. Now he was able to limit his purchase of refined oil on the spot market to less than five per cent annually. He also managed to accrue enough wealth and power to force the largest investor to sell his entire holdings in the burgeoning business to Toomas, for what appeared to be a fair price. This effectively gave Toomas absolute control at forty-one per cent.

He named the company Deutsche Euroil, to reflect his heritage, and his homeland. He coined the word "Euroil" to mollify those that might be offended by a new German company excelling in an "open European market."

The last to enter the room was Sergei. He was the only member of the group representing a government. Although the Soviet Union had passed by the wayside a few years back, the superstructure of the old guard still existed sufficiently to hinder progress every step of the way. Communism may be dead according to the world's media, but it was still very much alive and thriving behind the scenes in the various "independent states". A poorly defined, loosely knit government subculture continued to direct the most important industries.

Sergei had the delicate task of satisfying those in control of this delicate, anti "independent states", old Soviet, government-controlled industry. The Russian president Slatin felt all critical industries should remain under total government control while privatization was taking place in less important industries. Sergei had the unenviable task of keeping traditional communists, who were still powerful, and the new regime, which was powerful but fragile, satisfied.

Meanwhile, he had to protect and increase his own power in this position. He had to recognize and act on opportunities as they became available without offending either side, at least until one side was able to demonstrate real strength.

He was approached to join the group because the vast reserves available in the old Soviet Union could not be allowed to be used against the other five men in their plan. Since the focus of the plan was the Middle East, and the group could not be perceived by the Arab or Israeli communities as being unfairly sympathetic to one side at the expense of the other, it became necessary to include the only other major oil reserve source. This consortium, when in agreement, had control over a much larger portion of the world's oil supply then OPEC ever did. This consortium would make OPEC a two-bit player in the world oil market.

Sergei was a communist when convenient and a capitalist when appropriate---A true political survivor. With Sergei, they manage to, at best, influence the direction of Soviet oil policy, and at worst, have no impact whatsoever. It was a calculated risk, and the group as a whole felt it was well worth it. He had risen in the communist party through the erratic and uncontrolled era of Khrushchev, the sedate almost boring eras of Brezhnev and Gromyko, and the dangerous unsettled era caused by the social and political reforms of Gorbachev and Yeltsin. When Gorbachev was exiled due to his slower then desired move toward reform, Sergei, recognizing the need to espouse the benefits of Soviet styled capitalism, became a reformer of unmatched fervor.

He climbed from relative party obscurity to a position reporting directly to the Minister of Energy. When the Minister was killed in an explosion at an oil refinery, Sergei was given the opportunity to oversee the first privatization of the Soviet oil industry. Only now he was doing it for a poorly defined group of independent states. Regardless of who he was working for, he was in a position that allowed him the luxury to purchase the maximum amount of stock a Russian citizen could own in any publicly owned company, four per cent. Although this made Sergei the single most powerful man in the new coalition's oil policy, his first priority was to protect Russian interests, and his own.

Russian interests were not always in tune with this group's interest. It was important that if they could not solicit the outright support of the coalition's policy makers, they must ensure its policy was neutral with respect to any plans they had. That was Sergei's charge. That was why he was invited to join this group.

The sixth man never entered the room. Antonio had been their South American connection. He was the least liked by the entire group, but originally it had been thought he was necessary. Antonio was like so many of the men in power in South America. They either attain positions of prominence financially through drug deals, or they rose politically, often through the military, and then solidify their position through drug deals. The group's total disdain for gaining wealth through drugs precluded them from ever fully accepting Antonio, the man.

The other five men could not or would not see that their methods often caused as much pain and ruined as many lives as Antonio's. It was so much easier, like society in general, to hold drugs up as the cardinal sin. As the crime everyone could hate. It was easy to rationalize their methods as much more humane, when in fact they were not. None of the five could ever be accused of putting individual human rights or needs ahead of a business decision. It is understood that because they were just making a "business decision" that all actions that follow are somehow justified by that fact. This was all that was necessary for them to assuage their consciences, ignore their indiscretions, and decree Antonio was more morally corrupt than they were.

Antonio's connection to the Venezuelan oil supply was viewed as more important than his connection to the Venezuelan drug cartel---The crime they all claimed was repugnant. This should have told the other five something about themselves, but it didn't. They simply chose to ignore it like anything else that caused their conscience to stir. Of course, through the years items that elicited a response from their individual consciences had become almost nonexistent. So, they invited Antonio to join their group regardless.

When the men received word last week that Antonio had been killed in a feud with a rival drug cartel from Colombia, no one felt a need to mourn. None of them felt it warranted an emergency meeting either, although most assumed that it would be the central topic of this meeting. In any event, the six oilmen, at present, were only five.

Toomas had called for the meeting only yesterday. It was unscheduled, and although the group as a whole tried to limit these types of meetings, Toomas informed each of them personally this one was necessary. He selected a hotel called Le Seine. It was frequented by tourists who were more concerned with finances than proximity to the attractions of Paris. Toomas, at the dismay of most of the men in the group, was not prone to extravagant hotels.

This was particularly evident by his selection this time. The hotel was a converted warehouse on the outskirts of Paris, just off the trans Europe Highway 1. The building offered little in appearance and less in amenities. Each room consisted of the bare essentials, a bed, and a bathroom. Total living area couldn't have been more than one hundred and fifty square feet. The rooms were just wide enough to accommodate a bed, single, and a small imitation desk. Walking between the two usually resulted in bumping your shins against one or the other. Every other room had the luxury of a window that opened up to a view of a wall. The wall belonged to the warehouse still in use next door. Activity at the warehouse began to slacken around six in the evening, and by nine had ceased completely. By six in the morning workers would begin arriving to start a new day.

Sitting at a table, in the center of the room that the hotel designated as its convention hall, was Jason. He looked up at Toomas who was standing next to the conference table and sarcastically said. "Couldn't you have found a more remote, Spartan hotel, possibly in Germany? I wouldn't have believed the French had anything like this."

Toomas ignored the question, and turning to Sergei, asked if he had any difficulty getting away under such short notice. "No," Sergei replied. "However, in the future we should have available for me a method to make my voice heard without having to be here. It cannot be guaranteed that I will always be able to leave on such short notice, and without explanation. As we approach more critical milestones, it will become essential that I -- we be kept informed and have a mechanism for making decisions that doesn't require a formal meeting," Sergei added.

Toomas, who usually acted as the moderator at these meetings, agreed and asked everyone to provide and maintain a secure telephone number for the sole purpose of conducting business. "Since reform has not spread to the KGB," Toomas said. "We will have to rely on a messenger in your case. Naturally this can only apply in cases where time is not an issue. In that event, you will either have to meet with us or accept our decision. Can you think of any other alternatives, Sergei?"

"It would appear you are correct. However, that may make it more difficult for me to direct Russian policy toward our objective. Regardless, if you insist, it is a risk we must take."

Before continuing with the meeting, Toomas took the time to greet everyone individually. This provided everyone the opportunity to talk with each other for a few minutes and relax. Toomas knew the importance of allowing friendships to develop among the members of the group. In this way it became more than just a business meeting. Contrary to standard business practices, where it was believed that friendship created difficult decisions where none existed; Toomas believed it strengthened alliances and created the opportunity for unity where chaos might normally exist.

It was these little, almost unnoticeable, novel approaches to everyday situations that allowed Toomas to rise to the top of any group. Even in a group such as this, where egos could dictate decisions, and each man had become accustomed to complete control, Toomas had managed to rise to the position with the most impact. To an outsider he would be perceived as the unofficial, unchosen and to some degree, the unrecognized leader. Since the group was made up of men essentially equal in most aspects of life and business, leadership was more a function of who mediated their meetings. That task was most often performed by Toomas, and without dissent from anyone else in the room.

Anyone was capable of calling a meeting. In the past that task usually meant sending out notices by special delivery or overnight mail. On rare occasions it could have demanded direct phone calls to the participants, however that had never been done. Up until recently, time had not been an issue and did not require quick responses. Their efforts had been directed more toward positioning themselves for this occasion, rather than meeting the needs it would require.

Toomas directed their attention back to the purpose of the meeting. "We have two rather important items to address today. As you are aware, Jacque was able to identify and eliminate the person that was following him. As soon as I was notified of this, I put in motion a plan that needs your approval, or we must stop it immediately. To help increase the chance that Jacque does not get killed before the assassination, I've asked Jihad to hire someone else to help protect Jacque. This person will be responsible for killing the CIA's replacement, Eric Dent. Does everyone concur?" Toomas asked.

Toomas looked at each person in turn. They were all nodding yes, so Toomas continued. "Jacque was not able to determine how much the CIA knows about his assignment, or more importantly us, before he killed his attacker. We must presume they understand what Jacque has been hired to do, or they would not have tried to kill him. All of us need to use our connections as best we can to determine the extent of their knowledge. Also, we must assume that if the Americans know about Jacque, others may know."

Toomas paused again before he offered his suggestion, unsure of how each of the men sitting at the table might react. "I think it would be wise to have an alternative to Jacque. If Jacque should be killed before he is able to assassinate the Sheik, we will have to start the process all over again setting our schedule back considerably. Add to this the fact that each day increases the chance that we might be discovered, and it provides even greater incentive. What I am proposing to do is hire a second person to assassinate the Sheik. We will work the hiring of this man through the Zealots, this will provide some unusual benefits."

"When I first thought of this my intent, as I just mentioned, was to protect our interests and keep our timetable. But by using the Zealots as our intermediary we receive a certain level of protection similar to why we are using Jihad and his band of ruffians as our channel to Jacque. Second, and even more important, if both are able to participate in the assassination, we can control that information. We can choose to leak their names and their association with the two groups at the right time or to the right people and maximize the impact of the assassination. We can control who knows what about who did what, to whom. We control information, a special form of power we should all be familiar with."

Sergei's immediate response was an emphatic and loud, "Brilliant Toomas. You have the makings of a truly great Russian."

Howard, in a much more reserved voice, asked, "Did you have anyone in mind? Or were you going to rely on the Zealots to choose him?"

"My research indicates a Portuguese named Manuel might be the best choice. He is considered on the same level as Jacque in expertise, similar styles, comparable reputation, and we can expect to pay him a like amount. He is for sale regardless of cause, but he usually demands control of the method. His propensity to use firearms and his marksmanship is well documented. It would appear that his natural inclination would make him an ideal assassin for our purpose," Toomas explained.

"Will we be able to keep them from finding out about each other?" Seymour asked.

"That is a very real concern, Seymour. At this point I'm not sure it would make any difference, because if you remember the details of the deal with Jacque, his pay is predicated on Sheik Omani's death. If he would die in a car accident today, we would still have to pay Jacque the money. Primarily because we can't be sure that the accident was not a result of Jacque's handiwork," Toomas explained. "The only way he wouldn't get paid is if the news media did not report the death as an assassination. In that event, our objective was not met, and Jacque forfeits the second half of his pay. If we negotiate the same deal with Manuel, the incentive is the assassination, not who commits the assassination. Therefore, I would suspect they would not concern themselves with each other's existence. But it is something we all should consider."

"I say we proceed as Toomas has outlined," Sergei interjected. "We need to protect our interests, namely that the Sheik is killed as planned. We can not be sure that whoever Jihad hires to protect Jacque will be up to the task. Even if Jacque survives, there is still the possibility he could fail. The probability for failure is magnified with having someone chasing him because his attention will be divided between killing the Sheik and staying alive. Having two men assigned to the same task doubles the chance for success. And most importantly, the CIA is aware of Jacque, but they won't be aware of Manuel, at least not right away. And they probably won't even consider a second assassin as a possibility. This should give Manuel an unhindered shot at the Sheik. The idea is a stroke of genius." Sergei leaned back in his chair with his hands behind his head and smiled as if he had just delivered a closing argument that could not be defensed. He smugly enjoyed his perceived victory.

"I agree," stated Howard simply. Seymour nodded in agreement as well.

The only one that stated any opposition was Jason, and it was more a discussion of the added difficulty controlling two assassins as opposed to the one. "Let's not congratulate ourselves before we've accomplished anything," Jason spoke up. "The idea certainly has merit, Sergei. But it also doubles the chances for something to go wrong, it doubles our chances of being uncovered and it doubles our chances of Jihad and the Zealots finding out we've been supplying both groups. There are very real problems with this idea, and if we are to proceed, we better set up regular meetings to keep abreast of events as they unfold. We can't afford risking things snowballing between meetings. Everything could come apart before we even knew it had started to unravel."

"Would you accept one of us taking responsibility for Manuel and reporting back to this group regularly?" Sergei directed his question to Jason but wanted everyone to consider it because it was a drastic change in how they usually handled business.

At first no one answered, they were all considering what this might mean to how the group was run. In the past, the group as a whole agreed upon almost all decisions. Or like earlier, when Toomas reported to the group his decision to hire someone to help protect Jacque. The group still had the opportunity to overrule his directive before it was actually carried out. Once they agree to this proposal, actions may be taken that would not be acceptable to the group as a whole, but they wouldn't be able to do anything about them because it would be too late. The implications of this decision were far reaching and everyone in the room was uncomfortably aware of that fact.

Seymour started the discussion. "I assume you have someone in mind, Sergei. Or are you playing one of your games again?"

"Of course, I have someone in mind, and no this is not a game," Sergei spoke in that indignant Russian manner the group had become accustomed to when Sergei wanted to appear insulted. "Toomas should be responsible and I suggest we meet at least once a week to review his actions and our progress. If at any time we feel we need control back in the group's hands, we simply do that. Let's be realistic," Sergei reasoned. "We are equal partners in this endeavor, and this is not child's play, if one fails, we all fail. If we can not trust each other at this point, it would be better if we quit now before we have reached what you Americans call the 'point of no return.'"

Toomas looked at the other three to see if he could interpret their feelings after Sergei's speech. But these were not men prone to give away their thoughts through their facial expressions or body movements. No, all three would have to state their opinion before Sergei or he would know what they were thinking, Toomas decided.

There was an interminably long silence before Jason started in. "I vote we give Toomas the authority, but we meet every fourth day instead of once per week. We can decide where the next meeting will be held before we leave today."

"I'll agree for now, and I agree with Jason about meeting more frequently," said Howard. "No offense Toomas, but I think the more frequent meetings are a necessity. We all have too much riding on this to become overly trusting."

"Since everyone is willing to trust Toomas for the first four days, I'll go along with it as well," Seymour said. Then he added, "I'm not convinced this is the best way, but like Sergei implied, we have already demonstrated we trust each other just by being here. So, there is little logic to suddenly not trust one of us in this. Since Toomas suggested the idea, he would be the best choice. What do you say Toomas?"

"I don't have any problems with it," Toomas said. "I can leave tonight for Lisbon, and with any luck have Manuel on the payroll by tomorrow."

Before anyone else could speak, Sergei jumped in. As he spoke, he turned to face Jason and said, "Jason since you seem to have the most reservations about this, would you be willing to choose the next meeting place? Or can you trust that to one of us?" Sergei added sarcastically, but with a slight grin on his face.

Toomas, recognizing the sarcasm in Sergei's voice and sure Jason did as well, intervened before Jason could respond. "Listen. It is important that we are as committed to each other as we are to our objective. Egos not withstanding, we should all treat each other with respect, and utilize the differences in opinion to find the weaknesses in our plan, then eliminate those weaknesses. The one thing we should not do is find fault with each other. It cannot benefit us as a group in any way. It is obvious we are all equally committed to the task at hand, and loyalties need not be questioned or opinions ignored." Toomas looked at Sergei throughout his own outburst to ensure it was understood. When he was satisfied that Sergei's sarcasm had been adequately addressed, he asked the group for suggestions on the next meeting location. No one answered, so Toomas asked if these accommodations might be acceptable.

Seymour's sensibilities would not allow him to return so quickly to a hotel like Le Seine, so he suggested the Grand Hotel in London. Jason seconded the suggestion, adding he had business in London to take care of before he returned to the States. Once everyone agreed to meet at the Grand in four days, the meeting came to a quick end. Jason, Seymour, and Howard, realizing there was nothing more to discuss, left. This left Sergei staring off into space, still very irritated at Toomas' reprimand and Toomas staring at Sergei in frustration at his apparent petulance.

The two men stayed like that for ten minutes before Toomas finally broke the silence. "Sergei, do you think it is wise to be so argumentative, particularly with Jason? You know as well as I do, that with his background, if he even suspects we're more interested in controlling the political environment than with making money, he and the other two will pull out. And we can't do this without them."

"He has Jewish blood, and I find it disgusting to be in the same room with him. Hitler was right; Stalin just didn't recognize the fact Hitler was doing us all a favor. If he had, Stalin would have helped Hitler annihilate them, and we wouldn't be faced with that problem today. Now I am forced to work with a half-breed Jew to finish the job Hitler started," Sergei spat back at Toomas.

"You miss my point Sergei. As a German, I know firsthand what the Jews have done. My country was split in two for forty years because of them; so, don't tell me what I already know. Remember, I found you; it wasn't the other way around. I put the wheels in motion, and I won't have you louse it up because you can't control your tongue. Jason is not the enemy right now. You will have your opportunity to deal with Jason anyway you chose after were done, but for the time being learn to get along with him."

"No!" Sergei interrupted, "Jason is the enemy along with every other Jew or half-breed. You can't tell me he's not the enemy. He's why we're here in the first place. Him and every other Jew... They are the cause for all our problems. And another thing, I do and say what I feel I have to, and just because you found me doesn't mean I have to follow you. You're not Allah. You're not God. You wouldn't even make a good prophet. You're just a German who hates Jews, like I'm a Russian who hates Jews. We have the same goal, and it benefits us both equally to work together, so don't act like I need you. You and your plan are just convenient."

Toomas walked over to the window and looked down at the street below. He thought for a moment, then turned back to face Sergei. "I realize you think you and I have the same objective, but mine includes the method as well as the goal," Toomas said angrily. "I know you're used to saying what you think without regard for what others may say or do. But Sergei," Toomas paused, then quietly added. "Your attacks on Jason must stop. They serve no purpose, and do not promote our cause. They will only serve to promote dissension among us, and we cannot afford to lose Jason's connections within the Israeli government. We will surely lose that if Jason gets fed up with your antics. Remember, he is in this only for the money, and we have to keep him believing that is all we're after."

"That is the one thing all Jew's want---Everyone else's money. You'll never see a Jew steal from a Jew, but he'll steal from anyone else and say, 'It's just business'," Sergei complained. Somewhat conciliatory he added, "I know you are right Toomas, but I think it is impossible to control myself around him. I'll try, but that's all I can promise."

"If we have that settled, I'll be heading to Lisbon," Toomas waited for Sergei. When he failed to get up from his chair, Toomas left without him.

Sergei got up and walked over to the window. When he noticed Toomas crossing the street, he realized he had been standing there for almost twenty minutes, dwelling on his anger. In the short time since Gorbachev's *perestroika*, the fall of the Soviet Union and Yeltsin's failed attempt at a market economy, the Jews have been able to take control of too many industries, he thought. Every time there have been violent demonstrations within an old Soviet state, a Jew was involved. They were either instigating the unrest, or the demonstrations were directed against them. In either case, they're a perpetual problem. Yeltsin should have given them all exit visas and sent them to Israel when he had the chance. Now too many of them don't want to leave because they are doing so well in the new Russian economy. Better than **real** Russians.

This is my opportunity to rid this planet of the Jews, and finish the job Hitler couldn't, Sergei thought. And Toomas will either accept it or he will have to be removed as well. Renewed, Sergei turned from the window and left the room.

- - - - -

Mr. Dent,

The man you are replacing has recently suffered a fatal accident. It would be in your best interest not to follow in his footsteps, or you might suffer the same consequences.

Eric crumpled the note and threw it in the wastebasket. It is obvious these people are well organized if they knew I was being recruited already, he thought. However, Jim's warning is even more ominous when you consider Steve and him were the only ones told where I was going to be staying. And, when I left Steve, he was in no condition to reveal anything to anyone either. In order for that note to have gotten here this quick, whoever sent it must have access to someone in the Agency, Eric reasoned. Tom may be more of a problem than originally thought. Eric continued to reevaluate who might be responsible for the note, but he always returned to the Agency as the most likely source of the leak. Eric continued thinking about this until his mind fogged over and he was deep asleep.

The next morning, Eric had just finished reading the last report when he heard the knock at the door. Upon waking up he had taken the key provided with the tickets for their flight to London and retrieved the files in the lockbox at the airport. He had spent the better part of the morning sitting in his hotel room wading through each report, and only left the room once to eat breakfast. As a precaution, he'd taken the envelope with all the reports inside with him.

Getting up from the chair, he walked over to the door and looked through the peephole to see who was there. Outside stood Steve. For the most part he looked as if he hadn't had much difficulty handling Eric's test. However, in one more hour it would have been too late.

Eric noticed Steve's clothes were new, which meant: first, that Steve had managed to get here with enough extra time to acquire his new clothes, and second, the trip was difficult enough on him to warrant him purchasing new clothes. A visual examination of the rest of Steve did not indicate he had received any substantial injuries other than those gained when Eric had originally knocked him out. He looked tired and a bit ragged from lack of sleep, but otherwise quite healthy. However, not being able to shave created a generally disheveled look that the new clothes could not mask. Unfortunately, Eric thought, Steve passed his test. Opening the door, Eric let him in.

Once in the room, Eric offered Steve a seat and proceeded to fill him in on select portions of the information he had just read. Eric did not let on to Steve that he had expected to be long gone before he would arrive. By beating the deadline, Steve managed to gain some semblance of respect from Eric, although Eric was not inclined to make Steve aware of that. Eric knew that Steve had to show genuine resourcefulness to have been able to travel that distance, in unknown territory, and with a headache compliment of himself and an outcropping of rocks. The lump on Steve's forehead was still the size of a silver dollar and it had turned a sickening blue. He seemed to ignore it as he sat down to listen to Eric's report. As Steve sat there waiting for Eric to begin, Eric decided to ease up on Steve just a bit.

"You look like you could use some aspirin. There's a bottle in the bathroom and if you want something to wash it down with besides water, there's four cans of a six-pack left soaking in ice in the bathroom sink." Steve just nodded, got up and walked into the bathroom. "While you're in there, you might as well clean up too," Eric added after the door had closed.

Steve stayed in the bathroom for nearly an hour. First Eric didn't hear any movement, then the shower was turned on and he could hear that for a while, then it was quiet again. Finally, Steve emerged from the bathroom refreshed, carrying two cans of beer and looking like he was ready to start over. He handed one can to Eric, then made himself comfortable in the only open chair left in the room.

Eric took the can, opened it and started in before Steve sat down. "Our flight is scheduled to take off at eight tonight, so if you have anything you need to do, you better do it now." Steve just shook his head no. "You'll be able to catch up on some of your sleep during the flight to London. In the meantime, I'd like to review the information in these reports. For the next hour, Steve sat mute while Eric explained what he wanted Steve to know about the contents of the reports.

3

- It is better you should not vow, than that you should vow and not pay.

"We'll be landing in Montreal at about 4:30 P.M., from there we catch SAS flight 101 for Heathrow airport. We'll arrive there around eight-tomorrow morning. I've made reservations to stay in a hotel across the street from the terminal, but don't plan on settling in. We'll be flying out that afternoon," Eric was explaining to Steve the travel arrangements for the next twenty-four hours. "I'll make reservations from the hotel for the next leg and tell you where we're going at that time. Were you supposed to check in at all in the near future?" Eric asked, then continued without waiting for Steve's response, "because once we leave London your opportunity to communicate with anyone will become severely limited for the next forty-eight hours."

"Tom figured you wouldn't just let me tag along without some sort of initiation," Steve responded. "So, he asked me to contact the Agency through one of the pre-established channels with the message, 'I'll be on vacation for awhile', if you allowed me to tag along. I was supposed to have that message in by midnight tonight. If he didn't hear from me by then he was going to assume you rejected the plan entirely, and he'd send out a search party to look for me starting at your cabin. He wasn't convinced you would accept Jim or me. By now Jim's told him you were going to test me, but he wouldn't know for sure whether or not I passed."

"Don't worry, if that's all Tom wanted to know, its been taken care of," Eric countered. "One thing you can say about Tom is, he's thorough enough not to rely on just one source for his information.

Someone saw you when we were at the hotel, and someone else is going to know whether we're on this flight, the next flight or in the hotel. I assure you; Tom's being kept up date on our progress. Once we get to London we'll disappear. In the meantime, we'll let Tom's paid sources do their job, so there's no need for you to check in."

The flight to Montreal was uneventful, but Eric was sure he saw the person hired to report their progress to Tom while they were still at the airport in Calgary. The man couldn't have been more obvious if he was trying to be noticed. He was waiting near the ticket counter when they arrived. He followed them to the restaurant and stayed there the whole time they ate. He sat at the counter and kept turning to look at them every couple minutes. Finally, he followed them to the gate and waited until they were on the plane. Eric noticed he was still standing at the window by the gate when the plane turned to taxi out to the runway. If Tom only knew how pathetic some of his hired help was, Eric thought.

Walking through the airport in Montreal, Eric kept panning the crowds to see if anyone had picked them up. When they arrived at the gate, Eric began looking over everyone in the immediate area but still didn't notice anyone paying them undo attention. And when they left the gate area, no one seemed to follow them. Both men slid into a large group of passengers as they made their way to the main terminal.

When the crowd started splitting apart at the terminal to go their various ways, Eric pulled Steve by the arm redirecting him to their next gate. Eric still had not noticed anyone following them. He decided that whoever was assigned to pick them up in Montreal was probably waiting at their departure gate. Not too bright, he thought, what if we changed flights. Sure enough, as they approached the next gate, a young man in his early twenty's, began watching them. This was the one, Eric decided. Turning to Steve he said, "We've got about an hour to waste. How would you like killing some time by playing with your boss's stooge?"

"What do you have in mind?"

"Let's go over by those lockboxes and I'll tell you." As they reached the wall of boxes, Eric reached into his pocket and removed some change. Finding some quarters, he instructed Steve to put his things into one of the boxes. "Now, if I know Tom this man has been instructed to follow me first and keep an eye on you second. We'll walk back to the bar, where you can go in and order something to drink. I'll continue back to the main terminal, I'm sure he'll follow me. Then I'll give the man an impromptu tour of the terminal and meet you back at the gate before we board."

"I'm supposed to trust you to come back," Steve replied more as a question than a statement.

"Don't be childish," Eric reprimanded him. Then added. "You sound like Tom. Think about it, I could have lost you on day one." Eric looked at Steve wondering if he was underestimating Tom's influence on him. Granted he had passed Eric's test, but he may think too much like Tom, and that would make him a detriment in the field. Tom's mental process was fine sitting at a desk in Langley, but not out here.

"OK, go"

Eric put the money into the slot of the lockbox, pulled out the key and handed it to Steve. "See you in an hour," he said, then turned and started walking back to the main terminal. As predicted, the young man at the gate quickly got up and began following. When he noticed Steve didn't follow Eric, but entered the bar, he paused momentarily, confused as to what to do. Making his decision to forget Steve, he picked up his pace to keep Eric in his sight.

Steve walked up to the bar, ordered a vodka gimlet, and asked the bartender the location of the nearest public telephone. At the phone he dialed, waited for the tone, and left the message, "I'll be on vacation for awhile." Pleased with himself, he hung up and returned to the bar. Finding a table in the corner of the room, he sat down to watch TV and wait for the plane or Eric whichever came first. Looking up at the TV screen, he noticed the Expos were playing the Mets. Never did like baseball on TV, he thought, too boring.

Once back at the main terminal, Eric looked for a ticket counter of one of the European airlines. Noticing there was no waiting in the line for Dutch KLM, he approached the counter. Nonchalantly he glanced around looking around for the young man following him. He noticed him leaning against the window watching the traffic outside. Confident the man could not be overheard; Eric asked the agent if he had any flights from London's Heathrow to Helsinki leaving anytime tomorrow. The agent gave Eric two choices, one at 12:15 and the other at 5:00. Eric decided the one at twelve was too early and purchased two tickets for the five o'clock flight.

Taking the tickets, he handed the agent a twenty and said, "That man over there by the window will probably ask you where I'm going. Eric pointed discreetly toward the window. "He's my wife's old boyfriend and has had problems accepting the fact that we are married. I was hoping you could help us get some privacy." Eric leaned over the counter and softly added, "We're supposed to be on our second honeymoon. You know what I mean." The agent nodded. "Would you be willing to tell him we went to Copenhagen or something like that?" he asked.

"I suppose I could tell him that if he asks," the agent said. "I just don't understand why some people can't let go. He's probably French, the French take love much too seriously," the agent added.

"Thank you so very much." Eric acted relieved, then hurried away.

As if on cue, the young man began to follow Eric. Instead of heading straight back to the gate, Eric went to the baggage claim area. The ticket purchase hadn't taken very long, so he had just under a half hour before the flight was scheduled to leave. As he entered the claim area, a crowd began to gather around a carousel. Eric immediately joined the crowd and began to float around as if positioning himself for his baggage. The young man tried to follow Eric, but as the crowd grew thicker it became more difficult. Eric continued to move through the crowd until he was confident the young man had lost his bearings. Then he broke out of the crowd and hurried to the exit. Eric looked back at the mass of bodies around the luggage carousel as he left the area but couldn't see the young man.

Returning to the gate, Eric arrived just as they announced, "We will begin boarding now. Anyone traveling with young children or needing extra assistance while boarding may enter through gate 12. Any First-Class passengers may also board at this time. For those of you remaining in the gate area, we will be boarding by row number this evening. So, if everyone will take a moment to look at their boarding pass, please take note of your seat assignment. We will be able to begin boarding in a few minutes. Thank you."

"I see you lost your young friend," Steve quipped as Eric sat down next to him.

"Only temporarily, he should be able to get here before we leave. Of course, that's assuming he figures out what happened," Eric replied.

"Those seated in rows 35 or higher may begin boarding now through gate 12. Any passengers in Business Class may also board at this time. Please have your tickets out and available for the agent at the door, thank you." The voice came over the loudspeaker.

"What happened?"

"I gave him a tour of the baggage claim area, and he must have gotten mixed up with the crowd."

"Are you ready to board?" Steve asked.

Eric nodded and said, "let's go." Getting in line, Eric continued to watch for the young man to see if he had made it back to the gate area before they boarded. As Steve handed the agent at the door his ticket, Eric saw the young man come running up. The man's eyes frantically searched the waiting area for any sign of Eric or Steve. Finally, he noticed Eric handing his ticket to the agent. Eric looked back one last time before he entered the gate and saw the young man. Relief was spreading across his face. Eric raised his hand to wave to him. Without thinking the man raised his hand to wave back. Realizing what he was doing, he sheepishly retracted his hand, turned, then walked away. Eric boarded the plane.

The plane was being pushed back from the gate before the young man left the gate area. Remembering Eric had purchased tickets from KLM, he headed back to the main terminal. When he arrived at the ticket counter, the original agent that had handled Eric's purchase was no longer at the counter. Approaching an unoccupied agent, the man gave a description of the agent and asked if he was still there. The new agent nodded yes, then disappeared through a door behind the counter. A few minutes passed before both agents came back out the door. The other agent pointed to the young man, said something, then disappeared again through the door.

The agent that had just been retrieved, obviously annoyed, walked up to the young man and asked tersely. "What can I do for you?"

"There was a man here, about a half hour, maybe forty-five minutes ago. He bought some tickets. I was wondering if you could tell me where he was going."

"First, we don't give that type of information out. And second, there were many men here during the past forty-five minutes. How the dickens am I supposed to know which one you're talking about?" The agent turned to walk away.

"Wait," the young man almost shouted. He looked around to see if anyone noticed. A few disinterested parties looked at him, then returned to what they were doing. For the most part no one seemed concerned that he had raised his voice. "He's about this tall," the man raised his hand to midway between his shoulders and the top of his head. "And his hair is kind of a dirty blonde. He was wearing blue jeans, a black and red plaid shirt, and a gray corduroy jacket. It's very important that I find out where he is going so, I can leave a message for him." As the young man was talking, he reached into his pocket and pulled out a twenty-dollar bill. Sliding his hand over the counter, he dropped the bill on the lower portion of the counter, where the agents worked, but people passing by would not see. He continued his explanation, "You see, I'm his brother, and our sister was seriously hurt in a car accident."

"You don't look like brothers," the agent replied, deciding to play with him a little.

"Look, what does it matter to you who I look like? I need to reach him. If you won't tell me where he is going, just say so and I'll speak to your supervisor," the young man added, deciding to change tactics and try a little coercion.

"Well," the agent paused, then continued. "I don't imagine there is any harm in telling you where he was going." Even if you aren't telling the truth what harm is there, the agent thought. Besides, you were both too willing to pay for help. "Copenhagen, then on to Helsinki," the agent said. Now I've done what they both wanted the agent decided, turning, he quickly disappeared through the door behind the counter.

The young man called after the agent, "What flights are they on?" But the agent ignored him, continuing through the door as if he hadn't heard. He decided he'd pushed the agent as far as he should, so he started looking for a pay phone. As soon as he located one, he headed over to it.

Now where had he put that phone number, he asked himself. His wife always complained about how disorganized he was, but he always put her off saying. "It may look like a mess to you, but I know where everything is." Now he was beginning to get a little worried, he had checked all of the pockets in his jeans, but no luck. His jacket pockets came up empty as well. Think, he said to himself, where would I have put that piece of paper? Without the report I won't get paid, he continued. Finally, with a sigh of relief, he remembered putting it in his wallet. Pulling out his wallet, he yanked everything in the one compartment out piece by piece. Rifling through each one in turn, he dropped them one by one on the bench. When he finally came across the paper, he unfolded it, looked at the number, then let out a long sigh of relief.

He pulled out a quarter, dialed the number and waited for someone to answer. After the third ring, he heard a voice. "Thank you for calling the St. Regis. There is no one available right now to take your call. After you hear the tone, please leave a message." The young man slammed the phone down. Grabbing the paper, he looked at the number again. Yes, he thought, I'm sure that's the number I dialed. He reached into his pocket for more change of course he had none.

After what seemed like an interminable amount of time waiting for the slowest clerk he could imagine, he was able to get change and was back at the phone to try again. This time when the recording finished, he left the message. "Both men got on the plane for London, and the blonde bought tickets to go on to Copenhagen then Helsinki." Then he added, "I expect to be paid by tomorrow." He hesitated then started to hang up when he heard the voice on the other end.

"Don't hang up!" There was a short pause then, "Was he alone?"

"When he bought the tickets?" The young man asked.

"No, you idiot. When he got on the plane for London. Was there anyone with him when he boarded the plane for London?" the voice repeated, exasperated with the young man's ignorance.

"Of course. Remember you told me there would be two men. One blonde, about..."

The voice on the other end interrupted shouting, "I know what you were told!" Then in a barely controlled voice added. "Both men boarded the plane for London. The blonde bought tickets to fly on to Copenhagen, then to Helsinki. Did you happen to find out if he purchased two sets of tickets?"

"No. The agent wouldn't give me that information." Feeling the anger in the voice on the other end, but not sure what he could do about it, the young man added. "He bought the tickets from KLM, if that helps."

"One more question, then you will get paid," the voice on the other end said. "Do you know the flight numbers?"

Without explanation, the young man simply replied "No." At almost the same instant he heard the familiar click of the receiver as the other party hung up, then he heard the dial tone. Now what am I supposed to do, he thought as he hung up the phone. He said I'd get paid after I answered his questions, but how and when? The young man continued to stare at the phone as if it could provide the answer or like a slot machine that would start paying him through the coin return slot. He never saw or heard the man walk up behind him; he was too engrossed in making sure he would get paid. He was totally unaware of the impending danger until he felt the stiletto in his back. For a brief moment he felt the knife's blade enter, then he felt a sharp pain as the knife was twisted viciously. He was about to scream, then everything went black. Briefly his shock was expressed in the contortions of his face, until it too went slack. No struggle, no noise, the blade had neatly penetrated his heart. The assassin caught the man before he fell and dragged him to the seat next to the phone.

Glancing around, the assassin checked to see if anyone had noticed, then pulled the knife from his back and laid it behind the now dead young man. He posed the young man in the seat as if he were sitting, removed his own hat and placed it on the young man's head. He tilted the hat forward to give the impression he was asleep, then quietly walked away.

- - - - -

Eric woke Steve up by shaking him lightly. "You might want to clean up a little bit before we land. The steward brought the amenity kit by while you were sleeping. We should be on the ground in about an hour."

"Thanks. I think I'll do that." Steve rubbed his eyes in an effort to wake up.

When he returned to his seat Eric immediately started to explain what was expected of him. "I had originally planned on checking into a hotel and letting you catch up on some lost sleep. However, you did all right sleeping on the plane and since Tom has had someone tail us at every stop so far, I think its time we make sure we've lost them. While we were in Montreal, I purchased tickets for the next leg. I had hoped it wouldn't be necessary, but I can't be sure at this point. If I assume the ticket agent spilled his guts, Tom will know where we're going, and by now he'll even know the flight number. Which means we'll...."

At the mention of Tom, a second time Steve couldn't contain himself and interrupted Eric in mid-sentence. "What's this obsession you have with Tom being at the bottom of everything? How do you know it's not one of Jacque's people keeping tabs on us? What makes you so confident they belong to Tom? Your arrogance makes me more than just a little nervous. I'm not so sure of who's going to be teaching who."

Eric couldn't help himself and started to chuckle. He wasn't trying to embarrass Steve, but it was obvious he didn't know how either of the two men, Tom, or Jacque, did business. "I'm sorry," he apologized. "I don't mean to belittle your concerns, but I've known Tom professionally for fifteen years and Jacque almost that long. Their styles, their skills, everything about these two men make it obvious who is responsible for these tails. And I assure you they have Tom written all over them. If Jacque knows about us, or me, because you won't concern him yet, he will rely on random sightings to keep tabs on me. He puts the word on the street that I'm back in business and anyone providing accurate information to him about my whereabouts will be rewarded. There really isn't a cleaner or more accurate method."

"Isn't that a little risky?" Steve questioned. "How can he be sure the information isn't tainted?"

"How experienced are you?" Eric asked. He was beginning to get a little worried that Steve may be more dangerous than helpful. This is information that anyone in the business should know. Surely Tom would not send someone out as inexperienced as these questions would indicate.

"The one thing that Jim left out in his explanation about me," Steve began, "was that I've never been involved with any international work. Up until this assignment, all my jobs have been domestic. You know as well as everyone else, you first have to prove yourself domestically before you can go international. Also, Tom felt it would give me an advantage when helping you because I'm an unknown entity."

Eric was not impressed, "If I'm supposed to be reassured because Tom thinks its a good idea, I'm not. But to answer your original question, 'How can Jacque be sure the information is accurate?' Jacque has established his "standards" so to speak. If anyone that supplies Jacque with information fails to meet those "standards". They do so only once. That makes the information very reliable."

"That is also why I'm so sure Tom's going to have someone at Heathrow to meet us. While giving our tail in Montreal a tour of the terminal I managed to pick up a couple airline schedules. We're going to have to change our flights, including the destination. As I said before, I can't be sure the ticket agent didn't tell him where we're going, and I'm not prepared to trust that he didn't. We can still get where I want to go, just not that way. We have a couple of choices, but we have to be back to the airport by 4:00 P.M. if we expect to have all of them. So, ... what we need to do is give our new tail, whoever that might be, a tour of London. This time I have to be sure no one knows where we're going."

"When we deplane, we'll put our things in a lockbox and head for the Tube. Once on the Tube, we'll split up again. We can meet at St. Paul's station at 2:00 P. M. That will give us plenty of time to get back to the airport before 4:00. Do you have any questions?"

Steve shook his head no. "Oh yeah, the station at the airport has maps so you'll be able to find St. Paul's," Eric added.

Steve deplaned first, positioning himself to view the rest of the passengers as they deplaned and to monitor the few people that were in the gate area waiting for arrivals on this flight or just curious, but bored, bystanders. Meanwhile, Eric waited until everyone had deplaned except the flight crew, then he got up, gathered his belongings and exited the plane. As he was leaving, he failed to notice the individual near the rear of the plane sit up. This new passenger grabbed his small carry-on bag and hurried to the jetway. As he approached the jetway, he slowed down to watch for Eric. But by this time, Eric already reached the end of the jetway and was entering the waiting area for the gate.

As Eric walked through the gate, he looked around as if expecting to be greeted by friends or relatives. With Eric's appearance at the gate door, Steve started panning the crowd looking for any clue that would give away the new tail. The attention of both men was directed at the crowd inside the terminal, allowing the last passenger to slip off unnoticed.

The man quickly mixed into the crowd at the gate, then headed off toward the main terminal. After walking past the next few gate areas, he came to one with passengers waiting to board a departing flight. Stepping out of the crowd, he walked into the new gate area confident he had eluded notice. He took a seat with a clear view of the crowd passing by. Reaching into his carry-on bag, he removed a book. Next, he placed the bag on the floor and pretended to read.

Eric and Steve continued the search for their new tail in the gate area until the area had emptied completely, including the flight crew. "Looks as if our tail has other ideas on where to pick us up." Eric motioned for Steve to follow him, then started for the main terminal.

"Do you think its possible Tom may have decided to wait 'til the next stop?" Steve asked.

"Not likely. He can't be sure we won't change plans. He has someone in place, we just have to figure out who and where."

As they passed the gate area, the man reading the book followed them with his eyes. After they had passed, he grabbed his bag and fell in behind the two men. Neither Eric nor Steve noticed since their attention was focused on the crowd in front of them as they tried to identify their new tail. All three men continued on to the main terminal with Eric and Steve completely unaware of their failure.

They exited the main terminal entrance, and Eric immediately began looking around for the nearest entrance to the Tube. Steve noticed the entrance first and pointed it out to Eric. By the time they reached the curb, the man following them had drawn up even with them a mere ten feet away on their right. Eric hesitated before crossing the street, continuing to evaluate his surroundings. He noticed both Steve and the still undetected tail look left, then right, then left again as if they were crossing a street in the States. This man, like Steve, was not cognizant of the different traffic pattern in England. This allowed their natural habit of looking first and last in the direction of oncoming traffic to give them away. Eric decided this man deserved watching, then looking right to ensure there was no oncoming traffic, stepped into the street to cross over to the Tube entrance.

As they entered the station, Eric noticed the foreigner crossed with them but seemed to lag their every move. Eric sent Steve over to the ticket counter to purchase a day ticket for both of them and a map for himself. Meanwhile, he continued to monitor this gentleman, who dawdled just enough to get in line behind Steve. Eric had to admit to himself that he hadn't seen this man before he saw him on the street. But he was becoming convinced he was to be their new tail.

When Steve returned with the tickets, Eric said under his breath, "We'll start off heading in opposite directions. Keep your eye on that one," he pointed discreetly. "If he follows you, take him to Harrods. When you get there, just window shop and stay in view of the Tube entrance. I'll get there as soon as possible. If he's following you, and it's not just a coincidence that he took the same train, it will become obvious while your there. If he doesn't follow you, don't forget to be at St. Paul's station by two."

The two men split after they entered the platform area. Steve to the near side, taking a train into London and Eric crossed over to the other side taking a train heading away from London. Eric's train came first, but the man had not even entered the platform area yet. Eric got on regardless. As the man entered the platform area, the train heading into London came into the station, and Steve quickly got on. He seated himself with a good view of the man to watch which car he entered. The man continued to dawdle and before long was left standing on the platform as the train pulled away from the station. Steve's immediate reaction was to get off at the next stop and return to this station to try and follow the man, but then he rationalized that he obviously was not following him, and it would be a foolish waste of time.

Four minutes later Eric arrived at the next stop, exited the train, and crossed over for the return trip. As soon as he sat down, he looked at the map of the Tube system on the wall of the car and started working out what was the quickest way to Harrods; he assumed the man had followed Steve. Before he realized what had happened, the Heathrow stop came and went without Eric noticing the man he thought was following Steve had entered the car immediately next to the one he was in.

Continuing to look at the map he decided the quickest route to Harrods was to take the red route to Trafalgar and then transfer to the blue route. Since Heathrow is placed a fair distance from London, Eric settled into his seat figuring he had almost a 45-minute ride to Trafalgar. Between stations he'd stare out at the countryside, which slowly became more urbanized as they approached London. The open fields were replaced by scattered houses, then to a mixture of stores, houses, and apartments and finally to stores, office buildings and apartments. With each stop more people got on the subway train than got off, and soon the car started to fill up.

Before long an older lady, who had given up any diet she may have tried years ago, sat down next to Eric forcing him closer to the window than he had ever intended to be. As with so many older women, her olfactory senses had waned over the years causing her to increase her dosage of perfume to the point that it overcame all other odors within five feet of her. A younger woman, probably her granddaughter, took the open seat across the aisle from her. They began talking, and as always, Eric was amazed that they, in theory, spoke the same language yet he could hardly understand a single word they were saying. Cockney was more a foreign language than a variation of English, Eric thought. As the two women continued to talk and the car slowly rocked back and forth on the tracks, the old woman would slide away from Eric giving him a little more breathing room. Just as Eric would begin to feel more comfortable the woman would punctuate something she was saying by repositioning herself in the seat, pinning Eric up against the window again and again.

As they left the last station before Trafalgar, Eric breathed a sigh of relief knowing that in five minutes he would be able to exit this prison and leave the large old woman to squash some other unsuspecting soul. Finally, the train pulled into the station at Trafalgar. Relieved and anxious to get some breathing room, Eric got up, and excused himself to the old woman as he tried to step past her. She, however, was too large to step past, and would have to move out of Eric's way in order for him to exit. At first the woman tried to turn in her seat, to let Eric past, but her bulk was even too large for this to work. She would have to stand up and move out of the way if Eric was to get past her, and it was obvious she had no intention of standing up until the car had come to a complete stop. This provided adequate time for the man tailing Eric to get to a door before the train stopped. When the door opened, he quickly got off and positioned himself unobtrusively at the far edge of the platform as if he were waiting for the next subway train.

Eric was becoming somewhat annoyed at the large woman because her interference was putting into doubt whether he would be able get off before the doors closed again. He if didn't get off at this stop, at this time, he might not be able to catch the next train in time to rendezvous with Steve by two. Exasperated, he grabbed the woman as best he could, forcing her out of his way. At the touch of his hands, she began spewing forth a string of obscenities, and then accused him of accosting her. At least that was what he thought she was saying. Odd, Eric thought, before I couldn't understand a word she said because of her dialect, but now everything she says seems perfectly clear. Ignoring the woman, as soon as he had enough room to maneuver past her, he did. Although not quickly enough, because the woman's oversized purse was able to find Eric's back with a loud whack before he was able to get far enough away.

Eric stepped out onto the platform just as the doors were closing, and the recorded voice was saying for the third time, "The doors are about to close, please keep all hands and feet away from the doors." Eric looked around the platform and noticed that most of the crowd had already left heading for the street above or transferring to another train. Eric began the walk through the station, to what the map on the wall of the car had coded, the blue route. At least with being one of the last people off, he thought, he wouldn't have to fight a crowd through the station tunnels.

The tunnels that provided access to the different subway routes always reminded Eric of an anthill. People were busy going back and forth with an almost orchestrated madness oblivious to each other. For the most part bumping and jostling was restricted to highly congested areas and was a result of too many people in too small an area. It was not because people were trying to cause problems for each other. Like the ants, everyone seemed to pursue their own interests with single-mindedness toward their own task, and it didn't allow for intrusion by others.

Eric continued through the labyrinth immersed in the task of locating the correct tunnel to get him to the proper subway train. He continuously monitored who may or may not be following him, more out of curiosity than intent, since he was convinced, the tail had chosen Steve to follow. Once he arrived at the correct platform, he entertained himself by watching the people as they entered the plat-form area. He watched as they took up residence to wait for the next subway train to arrive. Everyone positioned themselves, out of habit, in their favorite spot. This allowed each to enter the car that, for reasons understood only to them, had become their personal favorite. It was while watching everyone file onto the platform area that Eric noticed the man, he thought had followed Steve.

He walked in at the back of a group of three teenagers but was obviously not part of that group. Once on the platform, the man started looking around as if trying to find someone. Eric looked away as the man scanned the area where he was standing. Without looking at him, Eric walked to the farthest corner of the platform opposite where the tail had entered. Eric wanted him to believe he had found Eric, but not the other way around. The tail, in turn, moved closer to Eric always trying to keep him in view, but maintaining a minimum density of bodies between them. Eric turned toward the wall, located the map of the Tube system on it and began to study his route. The man moved to the center of the crowd, that was now becoming quite large, while waiting for the next subway train to arrive as he watched Eric.

A few more minutes passed before Eric heard the train coming, then moved off toward his right walking to the end of the crowd. The train came to a stop and the crowd parted like the proverbial Red Sea, to allow passengers getting off to pass through. Before all the exiting passengers were able to make it through, the crowd moved in mass toward the doors, carrying Eric with them. Without expending any personal energy, Eric ended up inside a car. Once there, he grabbed the pole nearest the door and forced the passengers still getting on to move past him. "The doors are about to close, please keep all hands and feet away from the doors," the recorded voice over the loudspeaker began.

Taking this as his cue, Eric moved to the doors and waited for them to begin closing. As they started to close, Eric stepped through then began looking for the man that had been following him. The subway train was pulling away from the platform before Eric could locate his face in the crowd, two cars behind the one he had just exited. Eric smiled when the would be tail noticed him standing on the platform---The shock evident in his expression. It'll be difficult for him to recover from this maneuver, Eric thought as he walked back to the map on the wall to determine the best route to St. Paul's station.

This was one of the main transfer points on the Tube, consequently, Eric expected to be able to catch a train that would take him directly to St. Paul's. Instead, he found the shortest route had him continuing from his present spot for three stops, then transferring to the brown route. It would take at least twenty minutes to get to St. Paul's according to the time estimates on the map. That would put him there thirty minutes early. Pleased at the thought of the extra time, he decided to be a tourist by taking in St. Paul's Cathedral while he waited for Steve.

The ride to St. Paul's was uneventful, a pleasant change of events after his ride with the old woman next to him. The route map time estimates were a little off. The ride had gotten Eric to St. Paul's with thirty-five minutes to kill. As he came up the steps from the subway, St. Paul's dome rose up in front of him like the morning sun, then was quickly replaced with a bustling street scene. The cathedral looked woefully out of place, crushed between city buildings that did not respect its auspicious history.

Old churches, like this one, always gave Eric a sense of serenity. He hoped the calm, peaceful atmosphere inside the church would replace the tension he felt over this whole ordeal he had been dragged into.

Eric stepped through the vestibule and was greeted by the beauty of the rotunda that drew his eyes immediately heavenward. Walking slowly, he stepped carefully through the sanctuary, his eyes still focused upward. He noticed a couple walking around a platform near the top.

Glancing around, he quickly located the stairway entrance. He paid the friar or whatever he is, thought Eric, the pound to gain access to the stairway. The church was not very busy, and the stairs were virtually empty as Eric climbed to the top of the rotunda. Once at the platform he started walking around it, admiring the work of the laborers centuries ago that had built this immense structure without any of the conveniences of modern construction equipment. No cranes, no power ladders, no forklifts, just brute force and primitive pulleys, levers, and such. To even get the construction materials up this high was a Herculean feat, much less being able to work with them once they were here. Eric looked around for the couple he had noticed from the floor of the church. They were still here, but oblivious to his existence, or anyone else's for that matter. They, too, were awed by the construction of the church, their facial expressions a testimonial to the fact.

Eric continued around the platform, drinking in every detail of the church as if he could somehow become one with it's history. While looking down at the sanctuary below, Steve walked into view, startling Eric back to reality. Eric looked at his watch and realized that 2:00 had come and gone. He had been so engrossed with his thoughts and the church; he had lost track of the time. When Steve looked up, Eric waved to him, motioning he would come down.

"If I remember right," Eric began after they had left the church. "There's a travel agency around here somewhere. I think it's just down the street here."

The street they exited on headed directly away from the front of St. Paul's church. So as one got further away from the church, an unobstructed view of the dome was possible. The dome was accented by the surrounding modern architecture of a more recent London. When Steve glanced back at the church, he was awestruck at the beauty of the mixing of the two eras in the single picture. The masters could not paint a more poignant statement of the times, he decided.

"You stay out here; I'll be right back." Steve watched as Eric entered the travel agency. Steve looked at the windows filled with pictures of warm, sunny beaches, snow covered slopes, planes, and cruise ships. All of them, beckoning the crowds that past by daily to reward themselves for their hard work with a vacation. As he peered through the posters, he could just see the back of Eric's head as he began talking to the travel agent.

"I've got two tickets to Helsinki, for a KLM flight from Heathrow at 5:00. Would it be possible to change these tickets for something going to Stockholm?" Eric asked the agent sitting at the desk. "Anytime tonight would be fine," Eric quickly added.

"Let me see the tickets," the agent responded. She reached across the desk and took the tickets from Eric. She started typing at the terminal in front of her without saying another word. A few minutes later she said, "I've got another KLM flight leaving at 4:45 and a SAS flight leaving at 7:00. Otherwise, you'll have to wait 'til the morning."

Eric looked at his watch; it was almost 3:00. "How long does it take to get to the airport?" he asked.

"This time of day, you can figure at least an hour on the Tube," then adding, "longer if you're driving."

"Better make it SAS at 7:00 then."

The agent reissued the tickets with the new flights, and Eric left. Without saying a word after coming out of the travel agency, Eric motioned for Steve to follow him, then headed back toward the subway station. The lunchtime crowds had trickled down to a few old men and women and the occasional teenager on the platform. I wonder if that agent knew what she was talking about, Eric thought, noticing the crowd was pretty sparse. Eric waited until the few people on the platform had gotten on the train, then chose a car that was empty except for a young couple at one end. They were too involved with each other to notice anyone else, Eric decided.

Once they were seated Eric started in, "I was able to lose the man that was following us."

"I wasn't aware he had followed anyone," Steve said. "When I left the station and he didn't follow me, I thought we were wrong about him."

"It seems he was a little smarter than the one in Montreal. He knew I wasn't going to head out to the country, so he waited 'til I came back, then got on the same train I was on." Eric decided not to tell Steve that he hadn't noticed the man was following him until he was well on his way to Harrods. "I was able to lose him along the way, but I expect he'll go back to the airport and wait for us to show up. If we assume he knows what flights we were scheduled on, and that he's smart enough to figure out we'll change those flights, we might as well expect him to be waiting for us near passport control. My contacts in London were never good enough to get me around passport control without help from the agency, so we'll have to lose him again."

As they talked on the ride back to the airport, the inside of the car began to get crowded. The young couple, interested only in each other, had been replaced by a potpourri of English men, women, and children. The two men fell silent, realizing that any further discussion could compromise their plans. One can never be sure who might be listening. Both men buried themselves in their own thoughts for the remainder of the trip.

Eric thought back to the old woman he had been stuck next to on the ride into London and shuddered to think she might return. As a rule, Eric was fairly tolerant of people, but that woman had left a lasting impression on him. Steve, on the other hand, was thinking about Eric.

Here was a man that had left this business, only to return to what might be the most difficult assignment he had ever been given. I can't imagine that revenge would be his motive, Steve thought. Eric just does not have the vindictive mindset that typifies a vengeful person. Maybe his time in the woods has mellowed him too much, maybe he won't be able to do what's expected of him when the time comes. Maybe Tom was right when he said, "Eric's left the business for the wrong reasons and may not be reliable, that's why we want you along. Regardless of whether he can handle this type of work anymore, you will learn from him. His contacts alone are invaluable. Just keep an eye on him and step in when or if he falters."

Time passed quickly, and soon the next stop was Heathrow. Both men got up and began making their way closer to the doors. As soon as they stood up, two people squeezed into their vacated seats. As the car slowed down and came to a stop, both men scanned the platform for the one who was following them earlier. As they expected, his face was not among the crowd.

Once inside the terminal they headed directly for passport control. As they waited in line, they constantly monitored the crowd inside the building. Steve saw him first. He was standing on the other side of passport control waiting for them. It was obvious he had already spotted them.

This time the man made no effort to conceal his intentions. Everyone knew what he was doing there, so there was no point in continuing a charade that no longer was fooling anybody. The man was going to watch both Eric and Steve get all the way through security. Steve nudged Eric, pointing at the man. Eric leaned over and spoke softly into Steve's ear, "When we get inside, we will both head for the gate. Along the way I'll stop to use the restroom, you continue on to the gate. I suspect he has been told to follow me first."

The two men continued through passport control without incident. After their passports were checked they had to go through security. There were four x-ray stations just inside a large holding room. It was built to handle a substantial number of passengers and their bags as they were being processed. The room may have been large to some design engineer at a desk, but during peak times, like now, it was grossly inadequate. Once Eric made it through security, he immediately began looking for the restroom. Spotting one down the concourse to the left, he turned to Steve and said loud enough to be heard be the man, "You go ahead. I've got to use the facilities." Then, without waiting for a reply, headed off toward the restroom.

Nearing the restroom door, Eric turned to see if he was being followed, but there was no one there. He searched the crowd to see if the man was just holding back but had no luck finding him. Continuing the charade just in case, Eric disappeared into the restroom, only to reappear a few minutes later. *I hope Steve's alert enough to realize he's still being followed,* Eric thought as he headed for the gate.

The crowd must have gotten worse because forward progress came to a stand still. Everyone was mulling around, going in circles, standing in circles or filing in and out of the duty-free shops. Regardless of what they were doing intentionally, or unintentionally they were keeping Eric from moving forward very quickly. Eric continued to fight his way through the crowd and eventually was rewarded for his effort. Once he was free of the crowd, he began running down the hall toward the gate.

Arriving at the gate, he saw a few people standing around in groups talking, but no Steve. Eric wasn't sure what to make of this turn of events. He had been so sure the man would follow him; he hadn't factored in the possibility he would choose Steve. *No one in their right mind should have risked following Steve instead,* he thought. *Doesn't this man know anything?* He asked himself. *If Steve and him were going to split up, he'd be following the wrong man. This is the perfect time to ditch both of them. Tom must be hiring some real no brainers.*

Eric was planning his next move when he noticed Steve exit a door down the hall and begin walking toward him. Eric began walking toward Steve, passing each other midway between the gate and the door. Eric continued on to the door Steve had come through and Steve continued exactly two steps past Eric before he turned around and said to him. "It seems he ate Mexican last night, and it didn't sit too well with him," Steve attempted a little humor. "He knew you wouldn't leave without me." He quickly added when he realized his joke was not very well received by Eric. Eric ignored Steve, motioned him to follow, and then continued to the restroom. Once inside the restroom, he looked under the doors of all the stalls to see where the man was. He saw feet in the last stall, so Eric walked up to it and pointed. Steve, not sure how to read Eric right now, just nodded his head yes. Eric tried the door. It was locked.

"Don't let anyone in," he said simply, then climbed under the door.

"I've already searched him," Steve said thinking he was helping. "But I didn't find anything. The only thing he said when he followed me in here was, 'Do we wait here for your friend.' Then I knocked him out. I don't know why, but he didn't seem to care that we knew he was following us. When I was walking down the hall, he was almost walking along side of me. I figured I had to take him out before I got to the gate or he'd know where were going, so I came in here."

The whole time Steve was talking, and even after he stopped, Eric didn't say a word; He just kept searching the man. It was obvious that if Steve had searched him, he had done a very poor job. His clothes were too neat, and his pockets were still organized. Keys and receipts in one, coins in another and the wallet was still in the left hip pocket. When Eric finished, everything was put in one front pocket and the wallet was put in Eric's coat. I'll have a better chance to go through that on the plane, he thought. Confident there was nothing of interest left in the pants, Eric began searching his coat. Inside one pocket he found a piece of paper with a phone number on it, prefix 01. Eric put that in his pocket and continued searching.

Once he was done, he pulled out a little capsule, put it under the man's nose and broke it open between his thumbs. He held it there for a few seconds until he was sure the man had breathed in enough. Then he pulled another capsule out, opened the man's mouth, leaned his head back, broke it open and poured the contents down the man's throat. The man was going to be here 'til long after the airport was shutdown tonight. He took one last look at the man as if he had forgotten something, then sure he hadn't, decided he could leave. He climbed back under the door. But before he pushed himself to his feet, he glanced at the man's feet, nothing suspicious there he thought.

Eric walked over to the sink and began washing his hands to rid them of the chemicals left from the capsule. While washing his hands he looked at Steve in the mirror and wondered why Steve hadn't searched him. Was he afraid of finding something he wasn't supposed to, or maybe Tom had warned him not to tamper with anyone he knew was assigned to us by him. Then there's always the possibility, albeit slim, that Steve was inexperienced enough to have made a mistake. Eric decided it was time to test Steve's knowledge.

Eric walked over to the towel dispenser, ignoring the air dryer on the wall next to the dispenser, and grabbed a towel to dry his hands. Then he retrieved the slip of paper with the phone number on it from his pocket and handed it to Steve. "What do you make of this?" he asked. "Does it look even remotely familiar?"

Steve looked at the number for some time trying to give the impression he was concentrating while he decided how to respond. It wasn't obvious by Eric's tone of voice what he was thinking. That worried him. He didn't recognize the number, and he wasn't sure Eric would believe him if he said so. He could feign recognition, but then he would have to convince Eric he couldn't remember any specifics about the number. Deciding he had taken about as much time as Eric would be willing to give him without increasing suspicion, Steve answered. "At first I thought I might have seen the number before, but I can't place it. I'd have to say I've never seen it before." Steve watched Eric for a reaction, but as one would expect from someone with Eric's experience, none was evident.

Hands dry and the question answered, Eric took the paper back. He tucked it in his pocket, motioned for Steve to follow him, and then left the restroom. At the gate area Eric watched for anyone that seemed to take too much interest in either Steve or him. He still wasn't convinced that they were home free. Tom was intent on keeping tabs on them, but to what extent he'd go, Eric wasn't sure. The girl in Calgary had nothing to do with Tom, which was obvious by the note. This meant Tom had gambled that they would use the tickets the Agency provided, unchanged. *Not the move of someone desperate to keep track of us,* he thought. However, he did have people follow him in Montreal and now London. Those people were not the highest caliber, he continued to analyze Tom's actions, but he was confident they were Tom's hired help. The one in Montreal was pathetic and this one was only slightly better. Deciding he never would fully understand Tom's methods, Eric went back to concentrating on the people in the gate area.

The group continued to grow, but it consisted of four distinct factions: those saying their good-byes to those leaving, businessmen, tourists on their way to Sweden and tourists returning to their homeland, Sweden. Actually, there were five groups; The last group included Eric, Steve and a few other passengers that didn't appear to fit in with any of the other four groups. Regardless of how many people entered the gate area, none gave Eric any reason to suspect they might be following them. He continued to watch but told Steve to board the plane while he waited 'til the very last moment to board.

Once Steve disappeared through the gate, Eric hurried to the nearest public telephone. Retrieving the slip of paper that he had taken from the man in the restroom, he began dialing the number to the States. After providing the operator with the Agency's AT&T calling card number, he was able to get through. On the third ring he heard the phone pick up a recording say, "Thank you for calling the St. Regis. There is no one available right now to take your call. After you here the tone, please leave a message." A smile broke across Eric's face, just as he thought. "Hello Tom," he began. "Just wanted to let you know you've got to start hiring a better class of help if you expect to be successful in this business. I certainly hope Steve is better trained than this exercise would indicate. Have a nice day." Eric hung up and returned to the gate area.

There were only five people left in the gate area when he decided he could board. One was a very good-looking young lady that was obviously distraught at her husband's leaving without her. She clung to him as if it would be the last time, she would ever see him, then finally released him to a barrage of tears. The other four were seeing an elderly couple off. Eric assumed they were all related, and the elderly couple was most likely the grandparents. With everyone aboard and the agent making the obligatory warning that anyone taking the flight to Stockholm should be on board now, Eric got up from his seat and headed to the gate. As the agent took Eric's boarding pass, she made no effort to hide her disgust with him for having waited so long to board.

Eric found his seat near Steve, and after stowing his belongings in the overhead compartment, sat down. Once in the air and after the announcement was made that they 'were free to walk about the cabin,' Eric went to the bathroom. Removing the wallet, Eric began to go through it. There were the usual collection of credit cards and twenty-five pounds in currency. Eric placed each item, including the pictures of family and friends, on the narrow counter around the washbasin.

He continued to look through the wallet searching for any hidden compartments, removing anything he found along the way, adding it to the growing collection on the washbasin. Confident he had found everything inside the wallet, he began to study the contents. Piece by piece he worked his way through the life of the man they had left unceremoniously asleep in the restroom back inside the airport. Eric studied each item as if it alone held the answer to all his questions.

Pictures will often provide unusual and unexpected connections to various people. He had hoped these pictures might do just that, but they didn't. Next, he started wading through the collection of paper slips, that all wallets contain---Those slips of paper that hold tidbits of information usually useful only to the owner. One slip did catch Eric's attention though. It contained a phone number with the familiar 01 prefix again. Eric decided that was the only thing worth keeping.

Before leaving the bathroom, he disposed of all the paper items in the wastebasket, then left the bathroom. As he worked his way back to his seat, he found an empty row, reached over to the center seat, grabbed the airline magazine from the pocket, and calmly deposited the wallet inside the same seat pocket. He had kept anything with the man's name on it and the paper with the U.S. phone number. With the wallet neatly disposed of, he continued back to his seat. Sitting down, he settled in for the remainder of the trip.

- - - - -

Inside the terminal, Eric deposited the items with the man's name on them in a wastebasket as they walked down the concourse toward passport control. After clearing customs, they headed to the front doors, and found a cab for the half hour ride to Stockholm. The taxi driver was given the address for the Hotel Ibis, a European version of a Motel 6.

It was late when they checked in, but as is common throughout the southern portion of Scandinavian countries, most of the population spoke English so check-in went smoothly. It was a common occurrence for the clerk to be approached by foreigners, without reservations and in need of rooms. They were able to get a single room with two beds. Eric declined when the clerk asked if he wanted the phone turned on.

He still wasn't ready to make phone calls within hearing distance of Steve. True, he could doublespeak with the best politician, but there is no reason to take the risk, he rationalized. Besides, there would be plenty of time to make phone calls when security was easier to maintain.

"We'll be heading back out to the airport first thing in the morning," Eric said to Steve. "What we both need is a good night sleep, because the next twenty-four hours are going to be long and miserable."

"I gather you're not going to let me in on where we're going," Steve said this out loud thinking Eric might volunteer the information if prodded. However, Eric just ignored his comment, and Steve decided not to press the issue. Sooner or later you're either going to let me into your circle, Eric Dent, or you'll regret it, Steve thought.

Morning came at 5:00 A.M. Eric rustled Steve out of bed and told him the cab would be there in fifteen minutes. He had already cleaned up, so the bathroom was all 'yours' he told Steve. Steve quickly got into the shower. Unsure of when he'd have the opportunity again, he wanted to take advantage of the facilities while he had the chance. While Steve got ready, Eric went to the front desk to make reservations on the first flight to Oulo. There were only two flights daily, the first would leave at 8:45 A.M., but the next one wasn't until 4:00 P.M. Eric booked reservations on the one at 8:45.

They arrived at the airport with enough time to get something to eat, so after checking in, they found a restaurant and had breakfast. Steve noticed during check-in that Oulo was in Finland and decided to try once again to get some information out of Eric. "I've never heard of Oulo. Where, in Finland, is it located?"

"Oulo is about halfway up the western shore of Finland, on the Bay of Bothnia. If the Bay of Bothnia sounds familiar, you'll remember it from the news. Russia plays submarine war games with Sweden in that bay, as well as other waterways around Sweden on a regular basis. Granted Sweden is an unwilling partner, but since it's Russia, they're compelled to play for security reasons."

"If I remember right, Oulo has maybe 75-80 thousand people. Like Sweden, most of the people in any of the larger cities of Finland can speak English fairly well. It's a required language in school and it's used often enough in business that the population as a whole is comfortable communicating in English. I don't get there too often, but I've been there enough to know my way around. Don't be too concerned with Oulo, because it's just one more leg, and is not the end of the road. Like I said last night, we've got a fair distance to go, and transportation becomes more difficult along the way."

"You mean we're going further north. What could possibly be of value up there?" Steve asked, his voice indicating genuine concern that Eric didn't have the vaguest idea what he was doing. "The problem we're dealing with is going to happen in the Middle East. Jerusalem, Tel Aviv, Beirut, or Damascus I could understand. Even Europe to do research on this situation because it's in Jacque's backyard. But Oulo, or worse yet, some remote village in the northernmost climes of Finland. Eric," Steve paused to think, then continued. "I know Jim told me to keep my mouth shut, but I have to tell you the truth; I'm not sure I understand what your doing, and I can't learn anything if I don't understand. I think it might be time for me to check in with the agency."

"First, you're not contacting the agency about anything," Eric stated matter-of-factly. "Second, Jim was right. You'll learn much more by keeping your mouth shut, watching, and listening. This concern you've shown for my approach is because you don't understand how it's done in the field, or who or what I know. You have one option and it's available to you at anytime--you can leave. I didn't ask to have you tag along, and I certainly won't accept you second-guessing any decisions I make. Now…is that clear?" Eric finished, staring at Steve while he waited for his response.

Then adding as an afterthought. "When it's appropriate I'll tell you what's going on, or if you can't wait, you can ask me. However, don't be surprised if you don't get an answer every time. Like I said, 'when it's appropriate.' Also, you should always remember one thing. Don't question my methods. I don't appreciate it. I don't expect it. And I certainly won't accept it, from you or anyone else."

Steve's shock was evident. He hadn't expected Eric's outburst. It was never his intention to piss him off, but he obviously had. "I'm sorry," he began. "I didn't mean to question your approach; I was just trying to get a better understanding of why we're headed north when the problem is south. I realize you can't be expected to trust me and I'm sure you know what you're doing. It was simply my way of trying to understand your approach. You haven't spent any time explaining what you're doing and to be blunt a few of the things you've done have left me wondering. I'm not sure how much I'll learn, when no explanations are forthcoming."

"Alright," Eric cut in, "what would you like explained?"

"Well, the first thing is why are we headed to northern Finland?

"You'll be happy to learn we aren't going to northern Finland. As I said before, we're on our way to Oulo, which is only an intermediate stop on our way to somewhere else. I can't tell you where until I'm sure it won't matter who finds out. I hope you can appreciate that, but regardless you'll have to accept it anyway. Right now, I have to verify the story Jim gave me, and that information is best gotten from only one person. And that's where we're headed. At this point in time, I have no intention of telling you who that is, or where he is."

"Alright, that's better than what I had a few seconds ago, so I can live with that."

"Not that you have a choice," Eric cut in.

"Why did you search the guy at Heathrow?" Steve changed the subject.

"That was something you should have done, unless you knew what you were going to find. For the sake of discussion, let's just say you were naive and made a mistake by not searching him. For all you knew that man could have been working for Jacque, not Tom like I suspected. Jacque has to neutralize or terminate us to be successful, and he will be trying to do that. We need to know what Jacque knows or thinks he knows about us in order to survive. Tails are our only source of that type of information at this time."

"You said you suspect that man was working for Tom, why?"

"Tom doesn't trust me. I'm sure you've been briefed to that effect, although I doubt you were given an explanation. Don't expect one from me either, but that is why your here. The training explanation was a weak excuse that I accepted for my own reasons. Because of his distrust, he was afraid I'd renege on the agreement and leave you along the way. You see Tom thinks everyone has his ethical standards, and that is exactly what he'd do, so he expected me to do the same thing. I didn't and I won't unless you give me reason to."

"I suspect you didn't search the man at Heathrow because you expected him to be working for Tom. A reasonable expectation, but in the future keep in mind it might be deadly. Jacque knows about us and most likely knows where we are, or that's what you should assume. His network of informants precludes his need to have us followed. Therefore, if we are being followed, and Jacque hired the person, his intention would be to terminate us. So, in the future, if you don't have the opportunity to question him, at least make sure you search him and learn as much about him as you can. In this case, you made a harmless mistake because he was hired by Tom."

Both men fell silent after their first real discussion about their assignment. Each, deep in their own thoughts, they barely heard the announcement to begin boarding their flight to Oulo. Since they were still sitting at the restaurant, they quickly paid for their meal, then hurried to the gate.

The plane to Oulo was a fifty-passenger prop that was returning after its initial morning flight to Stockholm from Helsinki. The plane made this trip twice a day. Helsinki to Stockholm to Oulo, then back to Helsinki. The second trip continued the same pattern. The plane did this five days a week and was nearly full for every flight. Eric and Steve must have purchased the last two tickets, because all the seats were occupied. Unlike flights in the States, smoking sections still existed, and Eric was quick enough to make sure he didn't end up there. Steve on the other hand wasn't so fortunate, and by the time they arrived at Oulo he smelt like he had smoked a whole pack of cigarettes all by himself.

The two men continued in silence as they left customs and began searching for a cab. Steve was pleased with himself. He felt he had managed to gain some level of trust with Eric based on his interpretation of their earlier conversation. Otherwise, he reasoned, Eric wouldn't have taken the time to teach him the 'tricks of the trade,' so to speak.

Eric, knowing that in reality he hadn't divulged anything of value, felt he managed to allay some of Steve's concerns at no real cost to his own security. Their silence continued through the cab ride. The only conversation was between Eric and the cab driver.

"Have you been here before?" The cab driver asked. "Because that address is kinda' off the beaten path. Ain't too often Americans come this far north to begin with, much less head out to the country like you two wants."

"I've got a relative out there," Eric lied. "We're just going out there to visit him for the day. I figured once we got to Stockholm that I'd never get a better chance to meet him. So, I called the other day and begged an invitation off him. We've never met, but he's my uncle, my father's older brother. When the family moved to the States, he was already grown and didn't want to leave Finland. Grandpa says he always was the independent type, so they left him here. I'll be the first one of the nieces and nephews to actually meet him." Eric added figuring the taxi driver might as well be convinced their just tourists visiting relatives. They'll be a little less memorable if they have a believable reason to be here.

"I've got relatives in the States too." The cab driver began, then he proceeded to tell them his complete family history, or least it seemed like he was. Neither man interrupted the driver---allowing him to monopolize the conversation would further reduce his ability to remember them. Eric would occasionally respond with "that's interesting" or "um hum" to assure the driver they were still listening.

Steve spent the ride watching the changing countryside. Oulo is a port city on the Gulf of Bothnia, and much of the agricultural and paper production of the northern half of Finland passes through the port on its way to various cities in Europe. As they left the city proper, the beauty of the country became apparent. Steve had always thought of Finland as a winter wasteland, figuring it was too far north to have any significant floral growth. However, he quickly realized how wrong his assumption was.

The landscape was covered with the deep green of lush grass covered fields and clumps of trees scattered throughout. Occasionally both were displaced by a large expanse of forest. Unlike the vast flat areas of the States, there were rolling hills everywhere with the occasional bluff jutting out. Many of the hills had houses at the top overlooking their farms. Wherever the land was flat enough to be planted, crops were flourishing in the Finnish climate. Steve marveled at how well the crops were doing in the stony soil so far north. Trees and grasses grew everywhere that crops weren't, giving the countryside a balance between civilization and nature that rarely exists elsewhere in the world. Engrossed in the countryside, he was caught off guard when the taxi came to an abrupt stop in front of one of the houses and Eric got out.

"Let me see," the driver put his hand on his chin as if steadying his head might make the calculation easier. "That should be about 85 Markka."

Eric handed him 100, told him to keep the change and thanked him for the ride. Turning to Steve he said, "Come on, let's see if Uncle Sven is ready for us."

As they neared the front door, Eric turned to Steve and said, "Sven is expecting us. I was able to get through to him while I waited for you in Calgary. He'll be taking us to a village on the east side of Finland called Suomossalmi. From there we make our way down to St. Petersburg or St. Petersburg as it's called today." Eric watched Steve's reaction to the news they were heading into the old Soviet Union, and then smiled. "Now you know why I didn't let you in on this sooner." Eric stopped talking as Sven, having seen them drive up, bounded out the door to greet Eric.

Sven was a big, strapping lumberjack type of a fellow, well over six feet tall and built like he could cut down trees the old-fashioned way, with an axe. Instead of greeting Eric with a handshake, he reached his arms around Eric's whole body and lifted him while giving him a hug. The taxi driver saw Sven pick up Eric as he drove away, reinforcing the story Eric had told him on the ride out.

"Eric, it's so good to see you. I'd heard you had quit, and I was afraid I'd never see you again," Sven almost shouted into Eric's ear. "And I see the man you told me about, completed your little game, so you let him join you," he continued as he looked over at Steve. Sven set Eric down and in a more conventional approach, extended his hand to shake hands with Steve.

"I have everything you asked for Eric. The bikes are in the Subaru, and we can leave whenever you give the word, but first we have some coffee, you tell me what's going on, then we can leave. Alright?"

"We have a little time, and you deserve an explanation. So, let's go inside where we can talk in private." It was apparent by Eric's demeanor that he had a great affection for this overgrown Fin, and Steve saw for the first time the more human side to Eric.

Eric took his time, explaining in great detail what he knew about Sheik Omani, the six-man consortium, and Jacque. With Steve in the room, he did not discuss Tom and the agency's involvement, except on the most superficial level. He was able to drop sufficient hints to Sven that direction from the Agency was less than desired without alarming Steve. Sven recognized that Eric was directing conversation around the topic of the agency and restricted his questions to the three approved topics. His questions were incisive and to the point. By the time they were finished he had a much better understanding of the task Eric had been assigned.

Sven pushed himself away from the table, stood up and said, "Let's go out to the shed so you can inspect the bicycles I was able to get for you. They are the mountain kind, so they should be rugged enough for your trip."

The three men left the house through the back door and walked through the backyard to a small shed that would typically be used for storage of garden and lawn tools. Steve couldn't help but notice the construction of this shed was considerably more substantial than one would expect for a building of this type or purpose. Once inside the shed, Sven turned the light on, and it soon became apparent to Steve why the building was constructed so well. The walls were lined with every imaginable piece of equipment one would need to construct explosives. At one end of the shed was a small bench, with a light overhead to provide adequate lighting for some of the more delicate work required when making a bomb. To the right, where the two bikes Sven had mentioned. "What do you think Eric? Are they what you wanted?" Sven asked.

"They're perfect, but you knew that already," Eric replied. "How long will it take to get there and exactly how far are we going to be from the border when you drop us off?"

"At the drop off, you will be less than fifty meters from the border." Sven was pleased to see Eric's face reflect satisfaction at the shorter than expected distance. "Sven can still surprise you at times, eh. After you called, I spent a day searching for this place. Once we get passed Suomossalmi there are some old logging trails that wind up to the border. They are left from days long past and have been forgotten by most people, even many of those living in the area. I had breakfast in one of the local restaurants and met an old fellow there who loved to show off what he knew. After a little while he volunteered to take me into the woods and show me the roads. I made a map," Sven paused and patted his left breast pocket then added, "it will take us right to border."

"Do you have any idea how often or what the timing might be for the border guards?" Eric asked.

"The guards do not schedule themselves with regularity," Sven answered. "They always travel in pairs, and the old man assured me they can come by anytime. Perestroika has not come to the border guards. They are still told to 'shoot to kill' anyone crossing the border in either direction. Soviet is open only in its propaganda, the people are still very much controlled by the government." Sven stopped in mid-thought, then said "I don't know why I try to tell you things you already know, but so many people are taken in by the Soviet story. I'm sorry. I digress. Suffice it to say, watch out for guards."

Eric and Steve each grabbed a mountain bike, then walked them over to put them in the Subaru. Sven picked up a couple things from the bench top and put them in a canvas backpack. As he left the shed, he carefully closed and padlocked the door, then followed them over to the pickup truck. The bikes were already in the back. They left the camper top open while they retrieved the rest of their things from Sven's house. All three men climbed into the cab: Steve in the center, Eric riding shotgun and Sven behind the wheel.

It was about 160 kilometers to Suomossalmi, but to Steve it felt like 300. By the time they reached the small city, although village might be a more accurate description, Steve's legs were beginning to cramp from keeping them balanced on the hump in the center of the truck's floor. When he saw the sign for the city, he breathed a sigh of relief and said, "It's a good thing we're almost there, because I don't know how much longer I could sit in this position."

"If Eric says it is alright, we can stop for some coffee and food," Sven offered.

"Since Heathrow things have gone fairly well, so I don't see any reason why not. Our trip will take the rest of the day and night, so we could use a little relaxation before we get started. Is there a place we might not be too obvious or where the clientele keeps to their own business pretty well?" Eric asked.

"Leave it to me. I don't make it over this way too often, but I know of a place where we should blend in alright."

They had taken nearly two hours eating and relaxing at the table before Eric decided it was time to leave. They left the restaurant heading almost due east directly toward the border between Finland and the old Soviet Union. About ten kilometers out from the restaurant they came to a logging trail that was almost completely obscured by the growth that had taken over since the trail had stopped being used regularly. As they pulled in, Eric could make out the path that Sven had made with the Subaru when he and the old man had come here two days ago.

The path wound into the woods quickly causing all three passengers to lose track of exactly which direction they were heading. If it weren't for the trail, they would have been lost shortly after they entered the woods. Although the trail was being overtaken by the new growth of grasses and saplings, it was still clear enough to follow, even for Eric and Steve. At irregular intervals, the trail would open up onto an area that had been clear-cut and the trail would all but disappear for a while. Then the trail would reappear, and they would head back into the woods, winding through thick trees again. This continued for what seemed like another hundred kilometers to Steve, who had returned to his center seat in the Subaru. But after less than thirty kilometers they came to another clearing and Sven pulled the truck to a stop just inside the trees.

"You follow the clearing to the right and in fifty meters you'll be in Soviet," Sven said somewhat smugly.

All three of them piled out of the truck to unload the two mountain bikes from the back. Sven pulled out the canvas bag he had tossed into the back of the truck and gave it to Eric. Eric looked at him, then opened the bag to see what was inside. Eric smiled, adding simply. "Thanks." Then went back to getting his things secured to the bike. After they had finished, he walked over to Sven, without saying a word he wrapped his arms around him and tried to pick him up like Sven had done to him earlier. He managed to get Sven a couple inches off the ground, but Sven was too big for Eric to lift him very high or hold him for very long. "When this is over, and I'm back in retirement, I'm going to come back here. Then you and I are going to spend the rest of the summer enjoying this country of yours," Eric told Sven. "One more thing before we leave. The money, that I knew you wouldn't accept, is under your pillow. I'm running out of places to hide that stuff on you, so next time maybe you'll just accept it like everyone else." Then Eric and Steve hopped on the bikes, shifting into low, they started riding through the tall grass toward the border.

"You forget Eric, there won't be a next time," Sven called after them.

They had been riding for an hour before they finally came to a road. Eric and Steve stopped at the edge just behind a clump of bushes and Eric untied the canvas bag Sven had given him. Opening it, he began to search through it until he found what he was looking for. He unfolded the paper and studied it for a few minutes, then handed it to Steve. "Sven drew a map. First, we follow this road south approximately seventy-five kilometers, then we head east on another road seven more klicks. At that point we'll be able to store the bikes and drive the rest of the way." Then changing the subject, Eric asked. "How well do you speak Russian?"

"I've only started taking lessons. I'm sure it sounds more American than Russian," Steve answered.

"In that case let me do the talking if we run into anyone." Eric stopped talking, then looked down the road. Maybe a half klick up there was a curve and Eric thought he heard a vehicle coming. "Get down," he said.

Both men laid their bikes in the grass, then Eric crawled to the edge of the road and looked in the direction of the curve. A few seconds later, an army jeep came around the curve and headed directly toward them. He could make out two men, one watching in the direction of the border while the other drove slowly down the road. As the jeep approached the area they had come from, it slowed down. Eric could see the lookout was saying something to the driver but couldn't make out what it was. The jeep continued to slow down until it finally came to a stop less than 100 meters from where the two men were hiding.

With the jeep turned off, Eric could now hear them talking but still couldn't make out what was being said. He was sure the lookout had noticed the trail the bikes had left in the grass, so he prepared himself for the confrontation. He knew the guards would have to be killed if they spotted them, because he couldn't risk them making a report. The lookout got out of the jeep and started walking into the grass, then stopped. First, he looked down the road in both directions, satisfied that no one was coming, he proceeded to unzip his slacks and relieve himself in the tall grass. When he was finished, he climbed back into the jeep, and they continued on their way. As they passed the clump of bushes Eric and Steve were hiding in, Eric could make out the driver reprimanding the lookout for his inability to hold it long enough to get back to their post.

They waited until they couldn't hear the sound of the jeep any longer before they climbed out. Eric asked Steve for the map and once he had it, pulled out a book of matches, lit one and burned the map. Turning to Steve he said, "I hope you memorized it, because if we get separated that will be your best chance to get out of this country alive." Then he mounted his bike and started down the road.

Eric established a quick pace for the ride to the next destination. So quick, that they covered the eighty-two kilometers in just under three hours. Without any warning, Eric turned off the road onto a narrow path. Eric rode his bike up to an old barn, opened the door then walked the bike inside. Steve couldn't help noticing the barn seemed to appear out of nowhere. Looking back down the path the way they had come; Steve couldn't see the road. The barn was situated just far enough off the road and behind a single towering blue spruce to be invisible from the road. The base of the spruce was as wide as the barn, completely blocking it from view. Steve followed Eric into the barn and was about to ask what it was doing out here in the middle of nowhere when he noticed the car.

Before Steve could say anything, Eric spoke up. "I usually enter and leave this country by the same route, so over the years I've tried to make the trip a little more comfortable. The first time I traveled the whole trip on foot, the next time I used a bike. After a while the bike was replaced with a motorbike and finally this old Russian car. It only had a range of 300 kilometers before I added the second gas tank. Now I can make it to St. Petersburg on the one tank. I do have to refuel before I come back, tho'."

"What do we do now?" Steve asked, realizing that St. Petersburg was probably 480 kilometers away and that meant there would only be enough gas to go maybe 120 kilometers. "You'll need more gas in order to get back."

"It's good to see you can handle simple arithmetic," Eric responded. Then he continued, "The man we are going to see should have taken care of that. If he did, we'll have a full tank and should be at his apartment late tonight." Eric walked over to a seemingly innocuous place in the barn and started to scrape the dirt floor with his foot. He then bent down, flipped open the lid to a metal container and removed a key. Walking back to the car he got in behind the wheel, inserted the key in the ignition and tried starting the car. The engine turned over slowly at first, then occasionally a plug would fire, and the engine would briefly crank faster then return to the slower speed. Every few seconds Eric would turn the ignition off, pump the gas pedal and then try to start the engine once again. Each repeat of the cycle would result in the plugs firing a little more until the finally the engine sputtered to life. It sputtered a few more times, then coughed like an old man trying to remove phlegm from his throat, hesitated as if to die once again, then stayed running. Slowly the engine went from a rough, halting idle, to just a rough idle.

Eric got out of the car and started unloading his bike, placing everything in the back of the car. Steve followed Eric's lead and soon the car was loaded with everything they had brought with them. Eric told Steve put the bikes in the corner of the barn while he opened the doors at the opposite end of the barn from where they had entered. After the doors were swung out of the way, he climbed back into the car and drove it out of the barn. Steve was already closing the doors when Eric returned from the car. After he finished closing the doors, Steve noticed the foundation of a house that used to accompany the barn. There didn't appear to be any other remnants of the exterior or the interior of the house. If it weren't for the foundation, one would not have had any idea that a house had once stood alongside the barn.

Eric returned to the driver's side of the car and waited for Steve to get in. He drove away from the barn using what was once the driveway going around the other side of the big pine tree. Looking back, Steve realized that the barn was clearly visible from the road when approaching from the opposite direction of the way they had arrived. Eric turned left, back in the direction of the main road. On the main road he headed south toward St. Petersburg.

It had been dark for hours before they came to the distant outskirts of St. Petersburg. The road they were on turned into Karl Marx Boulevard once inside the city, but Eric had no intention of taking this road too far into the city. As they approached the city, more and more lights appeared from the surrounding homes, peppering the darkness on both sides of the road. As the city began to surround them, the homes were replaced with darkened buildings that saw their occupant's leave at the end of each workday. Finally, these buildings were replaced with row after row of apartment buildings. This was as far in as Eric needed to go. Now all he had to do was locate the street.

That was no easy task since most of the apartment buildings had been built around the same time using the same drab architectural design and the same drab building materials. The streets were designed to be an efficient use of the land, so every two apartment buildings were followed by a cross street. The combination of apartment buildings and streets in this fashion yielded a very neat matrix. An efficient use of land it was, but it resulted in no easily recognizable landmarks for one to use when trying to establish location. Unless one traveled this route regularly, it was next to impossible to find the street you were looking for without slowing down at each corner to look at each passing street sign. Unfortunately, that is precisely what Eric found himself doing every time he returned to this city.

Eventually they located the street. Once on it, he was able to find the right apartment quickly because it was exactly the second apartment after the seventh block. Eric drove past the apartment, turned left, then continued for eight more blocks. He then pulled the car up to the curb, and as always, parked it in front of a different apartment building. He told Steve to leave the car unlocked, then got out and started walking back to the apartment he had intentionally passed. While walking he explained to Steve why the car needed to be left unlocked. All cars in a residential district warrant investigation. But an unlocked vehicle is assumed to be a government vehicle regardless of the tags. And since no one would be stupid enough to interfere with a government car. Hence, no need to lock it.

They were alone on the street, and the walk back to the apartment went by quickly. Each apartment building consisted of eight nondescripts, three room, government furnished apartments. Four apartments were on each of the two levels. They entered the first building on the left after they turned the corner. A hallway divided the apartments into quadrants, with an apartment in each quadrant. At the intersection of the hallways was a stairway that led up to the second level where the pattern was repeated in the typical innovative Russian style. The two men climbed the stairs, then turned down the hallway to their left.

Eric knocked on the lone door on this side of the hall. He could hear movement inside the apartment, but no one answered the door. Eric waited until the sound inside the apartment subsided, then knocked again. Again, he could hear movement inside the apartment, but again no one answered the door. Eric assumed that Jim was able to get the message to Josef about his arrival tonight, but if he hadn't, Josef wouldn't risk answering the door without knowing who was there. He looked at his watch. It was 2:00 A.M. Everyone should be asleep at this hour, so that was a good sign.

Eric walked over to the apartment door on the same wing. Placing his ear to the door, he listened for movement. Nothing. He repeated this at each of other two apartment doors. Then going back downstairs, he checked those on the first floor. During the whole ritual Steve, just watched Eric without uttering a sound. When Eric was satisfied that everyone was asleep, except Josef, he returned to the door. He knocked, then whispered coarsely, "Josef, it's Boris." They had chosen 'Boris' as his code name after Yeltsin took control from Gorbachev. Now they're staying with it no matter who gains control. Josef thought it was funny, and it gave Eric an acceptable Russian nickname---One that didn't raise too many eyebrows when used. Eric's ability to speak fluent Russian with the Slavic accent that was so prevalent around St. Petersburg, and a name like Boris, allowed him to blend into the St. Petersburg working community that Josef lived in.

Finally, they could hear Josef shuffle across the floor to the door. "Who's there?" he asked.

"Josef, it's Boris," Eric repeated, then waited. This time they could hear Josef as he disengaged the bolt, then opened the door.

"Quickly..." Josef stopped in mid-sentence. Eric had never brought anyone else with him and the sight of Steve struck fear into the older gentleman. Obviously, the KGB had gotten to Eric and everything he had worked for would end. He would soon find himself in some remote prison or worse---He would die during the KGB's interrogation. Not even getting the chance to be sentenced to that work camp in Siberia, he thought.

Josef was frozen in place, staring at Steve, oblivious to Eric's presence. Fear etched his face producing a grotesque expression. One that made Eric react instinctively. He pushed Steve inside the apartment, then grabbed Josef by the arm and dragged him back inside as well. He maneuvered Josef over to the small kitchen table and set him down in one of the chairs. Josef did exactly like Eric directed him, but his eyes never left Steve. This is getting ridiculous, Eric thought, he had never seen Josef lose control before, and he had to get him to snap out of it.

Eric started rummaging through the cupboards looking for the bottle of vodka that Josef always managed to have. There were times when Josef didn't have enough money for food, but he had his bottle of vodka. There were times when the stores would run out of food before he was able to get there, but he always got there in time to buy is vodka. Never had Eric been a visitor in Josef's house when he did not have a bottle of vodka.

Eric found the bottle, grabbed three glasses, and returned to the kitchen table. Josef continued to stare at Steve as if he were Stalin, himself. Eric grabbed him by the collar and began to gently slap his face, gradually increasing the force of the blows until he saw a flicker of pain in Josef's eyes. Then pinching his jaw near his neck, he forced the jaw open, and tilted his head back. "Pour the vodka directly into his mouth," Eric demanded. Soon, Josef started to cough, spraying the vodka over Eric's arm and the table.

"What's the matter Josef?" Eric asked.

For the first time since Josef laid eyes on Steve, he started to come out of his trancelike state. Slowly he took his eyes off Steve and turned to look at Eric. As recognition spread across his face, the fear slowly drained from his face. As the fear left, life returned to his eyes. Eric poured some vodka into a glass and handed it to Josef. Josef watched Eric, then haltingly reached his hand out to take the half-filled glass from Eric. With his eyes now riveted on Eric instead of Steve, Josef began sipping the vodka.

Steve grabbed a towel and cleaned up the vodka Josef had spewed over the table. He also replaced the two other glasses with clean ones. Eric took the bottle and poured some vodka in both glasses, handed one to Steve and motioned him to sit down. The three men sat at the table sipping vodka and silently watching each other. Josef continued staring at Eric until he regained his composure. Finally, Eric broke the silence. "Josef, we need to know what is going on. Why were you so frightened? Didn't Jim tell you I was coming?"

Slowly, haltingly Josef responded to each question. "I've seen a man who looks just like your friend," he began. "He works for the KGB. He's one of their assassins. I thought they had finally come for me. I saw you, but when I saw him, I no longer saw you. I thought I would handle death better than that." He paused then added. "But I guess I'm just an old man who's afraid to die."

Eric looked back and forth between Steve and Josef as he remembered the warning Jim had given him before he left. It's not possible, he thought, brushing Josef's accusation aside attributing it to an old man's fear of dying.

"Jim's message arrived early this morning. That is why I was still up at this hour. I was waiting for you. The message said you might have someone with you, so I was to expect two."

Eric wanted Josef to relax, so he began talking to him about old times. They spent the next hour rehashing the past. Telling stories, they had repeated hundreds of times before. Embellishing them just a little for Steve's benefit. With each story, each remembrance of days past, peace returned to Josef's eyes, until he interrupted Eric in mid-sentence. "Enough Eric, we must talk about why you are here. I have some very important information that you must know." Relieved, Eric stopped talking.

"That consortium that has been financing Sheik Omani has some very specific plans for the Middle East. First off, you should understand their motivation. As you may or may not be aware, the consortium is comprised of five men, each with considerable holdings in various oil companies throughout the world."

At the mention of five men, Eric interrupted Josef's explanation, "You mean six men, don't you?"

"You haven't heard then. Antonio was killed by a rival cartel. It seems a Colombian group had begun to expand into Antonio's territory. Antonio reacted quite violently to this event and had a few of his men kill a few of their men. Well, it turns out that the reason the Colombian group was expanding was to make room for one of the sons. Antonio's men, in their fervor to prove themselves to Antonio, killed the son by mistake. Antonio paid the price for that mistake. The loss of Antonio is not expected to affect the plans of the consortium in any way. At this point it is believed they will not even try to replace him."

"Anyway, getting back to the other five. The consortium has set for themselves the objective of replacing OPEC as the controlling force for the world's oil market. What they intend to do is throw the Middle East into such a state of turmoil, that the heads of state of all the various governments in OPEC will have to concentrate their efforts on solving the political issues rather than controlling the oil supply. In fact, their intention is to create enough confusion that their production quotas are all but ignored in favor of the needed revenue to finance their efforts to regain political stability."

This time Steve decided to interrupt, "On a temporary basis that might have some affect, but eventually those governments will regain control of their production and OPEC will regain its position of control. Besides, if they aren't controlling production, and production increases, anyone who tries to step in and control a glutted market is an idiot." Josef listened to Steve, then looked at Eric as if to ask if he should continue or if he should respond to Steve's comments. While he waited for Eric to respond, he refilled all the glasses with a healthy portion of the Russian vodka that was sitting on the table.

"Steve makes a good point," Eric started. "Won't increasing production exacerbate anyone's effort to gain control of the market? It seems to me they are approaching this from the wrong direction."

"You are both right and you are both wrong," Josef responded. "These men are very intelligent. What they want to do is force the circumstances in the Middle East to change. To them it is not immediately important whether peace or increased tensions result. What is important is that conditions change."

"Today the situation provides a precarious balance between all members of OPEC. It allows all of them to direct their resources to things other than defense. However, things are not so comfortable that either side can ignore defensive needs completely. A lesson learned well, I hope, by the Kuwaiti people. Regardless they all spend sufficient funds on defense to keep the public feeling safe, but not so much as to interfere with their developing economies. The peace that exists in the Middle East, albeit delicate, is the perfect balance to keep OPEC in power. They want to keep the price high enough to sustain their profits, yet low enough to control the supply. The absence of war, and the threat of war, keeps them in control. The consortium feels if they disrupt this delicate balance between peace and war, tipping it to one side or the other, they can supplant OPEC as the primary guiding force for the world's oil supply."

Eric thought for a moment, "The theory certainly sounds plausible, but if I were them, I wouldn't open any new Swiss bank accounts yet. If I understand your theory correctly, Sheik Omani's presentation as an unbiased intermediary to both sides is according to plan. If both sides accept him, he could be the force that tips the scales to an unexpected level of peace and trust. And based on news reports, the media is certainly convinced he can achieve that peace."

"I assure you Sheik Omani is not restricted to a media event though. The media plays an important role in this charade, but it is an unknowing participant," Josef informed them.

"Alright the media is accurate in this case," Eric conceded. "By elevating the Sheik to this level of prominence, and developing him as an international peacemaker, they have managed to achieve the peaceful side of their equation. Why then are they going to assassinate him? Haven't they positioned themselves to take control during this peaceful coexistence they've managed to orchestrate?"

Josef looked at Eric and a wide grin spread across his face. "This is why I've always admired you, Eric. While everyone else is charging around doing as they've been told, never questioning the rational behind the directives, you would stop and ask the tough questions. I must burrow and dig, gathering all manner of information. I talk to people, listen to their theories, and slowly piece together my own. Then you come along, I share what I know and in minutes you have either destroyed my theory, accepted it at face value or added some missing piece to the puzzle."

"You are right." Josef stared into Eric's eyes for a moment, almost willing him to find the flaw in what he was about to explain, then with the sigh of a tired old man, continued. "One would think the peace that exists in the Middle East because of Sheik Omani's negotiations with the various government's and his ability to include the more fanatical factions like the Zealots and Jihad Nadu's group in the negotiations would be adequate. But the consortium feels they can make the Sheik a permanent factor in all future talks between Arab and Israeli." Josef paused once again to fill the three empty glasses that were sitting on the table.

"The Sheik's death is going to be staged. I don't know how they're going to do it, but he will not die. Somehow, they plan on convincing the media and the world that he's been assassinated. A few days later they'll bring him back from the dead and present him as the only person destined to resolve the Middle East situation forever. By doing it this way, they envision catapulting the Sheik to the highest possible acceptance level among both Arab and Israeli."

"Can they do that?" Steve asked more of Eric than Josef, but Josef answered.

"Yes, I think they can. As I said before, these are some of the most intelligent men in the business world today. Almost all of them started from modest beginnings and have managed to rise to the top of one of the most competitive fields in the world. And keep in mind, they don't have to assassinate the Sheik, they only have to make the world think he's been assassinated."

"If they hadn't hired Jacque, I would have been inclined to believe this was going to be a charade," Eric interjected. "However, Jacque does not hire himself out with the intention of being made to look like a fool. In his eyes, he'll think he was made sport of if the person he is purported to have killed reappears a few days later alive. I can assure you, Jacque will be killing someone, and that person won't be coming back from the grave."

"In order for you to be successful, one of the things you are going to have to do is stop the assassination, regardless of whether it's real or not. You're right in thinking Jacque will kill someone, and that means you will have to stop him. But you knew that before you came here. You need to determine whom Jacque is supposed to kill first. You also need to find out how they plan on convincing the world that the person he kills is the Sheik. Finally, unless you want to make this assignment last your entire career, you'll have to dismantle the consortium, because as long as they exist, they remain a threat. I assume you are prepared for the fact that Jacque knows you've been hired to stop him."

"Yes, we've been expecting Jacque to show his hand by trying to track us, but it appears he's relying on word-of-mouth progress reports. Tom's the only one that has obviously tried to keep tabs on our whereabouts, but as is Tom's tendency, the class of people he hired made them relatively ineffective. That last one we dealt with was at Heathrow. I'm confident he has no idea where we are."

Eric and Josef continued talking while Steve played the roll of the proverbial child, 'seen but not heard.' Eric relied heavily on Josef's input through the years, so it was important for him to discuss strategies or theories Josef may have. While they talked, Josef would refill the glasses every time they were emptied. The conversation and the bottle ran out around the same time.

"I think this would be a good time to catch up on some sleep," Eric said directing his comment at Steve. After he said that, he realized Steve was no longer sitting at the table. He got up and walked into what would be referred to as the living room. This one was considerably smaller than the ones he was accustomed to at home; even the one in his cabin was bigger than this. Inside the living room he found Steve fast asleep on the sofa. "Musta' got tired of listening to you and I reminisce about the good old days Josef."

When no one answered, he walked back to the kitchen doorway and found Josef had put his head down on the table. He, too, had fallen asleep. Eric decided it was time for him to do the same, so he returned to the living room, picked a place on the floor, laid down and went to sleep.

4

- For the dream comes through much effort, and the voice of a fool through many words.

Toomas' plane touched down on runway 2-L, taxied and came to a stop at gate twelve. Before leaving for Lisbon, he had made a phone call to Doshe, his contact in the Zealots. Within half an hour of that call, he had gotten the Zealots to agree to hire Manuel. Someone in the Zealots will make the initial contact and set up a meeting between Manuel, Toomas and Doshe. Doshe will relay that information to Toomas as soon as it's available and accompany him to the meeting. Everything was taking place like clockwork, he thought.

Toomas gathered his things and headed for customs. Figuring the whole trip would not take more than a day; Toomas had only brought a carry-on for luggage. This allowed him to pass through customs with relative ease. As soon as he cleared customs he headed for the exit and the taxi stand. While on his way out, he noticed an Arab dressed in dirty blue jeans and green camouflage army shirt hurry past him headed for passport control and the concourse beyond. Curious, he stopped to watch as the man made his way against the flow of the crowd. At first, he thought he recognized the man from a fading memory of the past, but then decided it was probably just an overactive imagination. Toomas had never hired an assassin before, and maybe the stress that accompanies these types of activities was greater than he had anticipated. Toomas continued walking to the terminal exit trying to push the image of the Arab out of his mind.

When he checked into the hotel and was getting his room assignment, he checked with the desk clerk about Doshe's arrival. He discovered Doshe was already there and left a message for him to call room 225 as soon as it was convenient. Toomas took his time, not wanting Doshe to think he was too anxious. This was something Toomas had never done before, and it was very important for him to present the proper image to Doshe. Just as he would have done when he was working in the University, he waited for Doshe to contact him. It was important to Toomas to have people come to him, not the other way around. He felt it gave the impression he was the one in control.

Toomas settled into the lone chair in the small hotel room and reviewed his plan for what seemed like the hundredth time. Doshe was to have had one of his people make the initial contact with Manuel and set up a meeting between the three of them. If for any reason Manuel was not receptive to taking the job, Doshe would be informed as soon as possible, and they would decide of who would be the next possible choice. However, since Manuel was driven by money, Toomas was confident there would be no problem in convincing him to take the job. With the hiring of Manuel by the Zealots, the Zealots would be in the same position as Jihad Nadu's terrorist faction. And the consortium would have the option of accurately crediting either group as the one responsible for the assassination. Every time Toomas thought about the plan, he was even more impressed with the options that were available to the consortium as a result. The phone interrupted Toomas as he was thinking. Startled, he jumped unintentionally. Toomas got up from the chair and walked over to the nightstand next to the bed where the phone was sitting.

"Hello," he answered.

"Toomas? Is that you?" the voice on the other end asked. "This is room 225."

"Yes, Doshe it is me," Toomas said sarcastically, then added, "Whom did you expect, maybe Yassir."

"Enough with your pathetic German humor and just listen to me. We've been able to make contact and there is agreement to discuss the proposal tonight. We are to meet at a restaurant down by the wharf at seven tonight. We will take a taxi, so we need to leave by six. Meet me downstairs a few minutes before, alright?" Without waiting for Toomas to answer, he continued. "When we get there, we are to tell the bartender that we are guests of the owner and ask to use his private room for dining. Once inside the room, we are to wait for Manuel to make contact. If you don't have any questions, I'll see you tonight." Doshe hung up the phone without waiting for Toomas to respond.

The closer it came to six, the more nervous Toomas became. It was an unusual feeling for him, but then he had never knowingly searched out a killer before. Tonight, he was not only looking for one, but he was also going to hire one. Toomas kept telling himself that what he was doing was the best thing for all concerned. The consortium could not and need not understand all the reasons behind his plan. They saw it only as a method for controlling the world's oil market, and that was fine with him. They could be content in the knowledge that what they were doing was for their own economic benefit. But sooner or later, everyone would know and agree that what he was doing was the only way to resolve the problems in the Middle East permanently.

At precisely 5:45 Toomas left his hotel room and went downstairs to wait for Doshe in the lobby. Toomas always liked to be the first to arrive when dealing with Doshe. It somehow gave him the feeling he was a better businessman, had a better business acumen than a Jew. Never let it be said that a Jew could outwit a German he thought as he waited for Doshe arrive.

Doshe walked in with one minute to spare. He noticed Toomas look down at his watch, then with a disparaging look, watched him as he walked over. He wasn't sure, but he suspected, Toomas, like so many other Germans today and in the recent past, held a certain contempt for his Jewish lineage. Toomas could never be accused of treating Doshe with any obvious disrespect, but there was this perpetual feeling of distrust that seemed to pervade their conversations. This ensured Doshe maintained a healthy skepticism when dealing with Toomas. He walked up to Toomas and said, "Guten Tag." Since Doshe was born and raised in Germany, he spoke fluent German.

He had emigrated to the U.S. immediately after the war and was one of the first to move on to Israel after it became an independent state. It had taken two decades after reaching Israel before he could speak to a German without being repulsed. As time passed, the memory faded, and the wounds healed. He was able to separate his hatred toward Hitler and the military regime from his hatred toward the cowardice demonstrated by the German people for not coming to their rescue. Now, Doshe just felt sorry for a people that had been incapable of accepting responsibility for their own inaction, a people that needed a scapegoat to blame for their economic woes. He understood, although he did not believe it was an acceptable excuse, why the German people might blame a race that had had some measure of economic success where they had failed. He could also understand and forgive those that did nothing because they feared their own meager existence might be destroyed as well. And those that feared they might be the next victims of Hitler because of some remote genetic characteristic or predisposition.

Now the circumstances had changed. Instead of being the recipients of hatred within a country, they were the recipients of hatred between countries, and for many of the same reasons. Neither circumstance was an uncommon occurrence, for throughout Jewish history they were often despised by their neighbors. As far back as the time of Moses, when Jews were kept as slaves to the Egyptians and then escaped to freedom their neighbors had sought their destruction.

Whether those neighbors were located physically near them or separated by the borders of a country did not seem to matter. Doshe had resigned himself to accepting the fact that because of his religious beliefs, he would always be a pariah to the rest of the world. It was this fact that made it imperative to any and all Jewish people that a strong Israel must be maintained. For without Israel, they would forever be the scapegoat of society, taking the blame for everything negative that happened in the world. A strong Israel simply provided a buffer between the rest of the world and the hatred that world had for them.

"Well, are we ready to go?" Doshe asked. Then without saying another word, walked out the front door hailing a taxi as he went. A taxi pulled up to the curb, and both men got in. Doshe give the name of the restaurant to the driver, and the driver nodded his understanding as he pulled the well-worn cab into traffic.

They arrived at the restaurant with twenty minutes to spare, so they sat down at the bar to have a drink. "Couldn't we just give the bartender the message and wait in the room? Is it really necessary to wait until exactly seven?" Toomas asked.

Doshe was surprised to hear anxiety in Toomas voice. He had always considered Toomas to be a man of control, and this was out of character for him. "I was told to request the room at seven. I'm not sure that we can or can not enter before, but it is not important. We are not in danger here and I have been assured that many people use this room for various activities. Therefore, it would be foolish to concern ourselves with details that may only make us look suspicious. It is best if we just wait patiently for our turn and simply act like two men out for a drink after work."

Toomas reluctantly accepted Doshe's reasoning and began concentrating on controlling his fears. This was not like him. Granted he had never hired an assassin before, but then he had never shown fear before either. Doshe was right, they must not draw attention to themselves by showing their fear. As time passed, Toomas slowly regained his composure. His confidence returned as the fear was melting away.

"Sir," Doshe called out to the bartender in Spanish, figuring it was similar enough to Portuguese for him to understand. The bartender, an average looking man in his thirties, walked over to him to see what he wanted. "I was told to request the owner's room at seven. Would that be available now?" The bartender looked at Doshe as if he was expecting him to keep talking. When Doshe didn't continue, the bartender folded his arms and bent down to lean on the bar. As he stood there leaning on the bar, he unfolded his left hand from his arm and opened it palm up. Doshe interpreted the actions correctly, and taking a bill from his pocket, placed it in the bartender's open palm. The bartender looked at it but didn't move.

Doshe repeated the process until the bartender was satisfied and said. "Follow me." The three of them walked single file to the end of the bar at the rear of the room. Rounding the bar, a short narrow hallway came into view. There were two doors in the hall, one halfway down on the left and one at the far end directly opposite from where they stood. The bartender pointed to the door at the end of the hall, then returned to an obviously impatient customer at the bar. Doshe and Toomas silently walked down the hall to the room.

Doshe expected to find the room empty. He expected Manuel would make them wait for some indeterminable amount of time until he or one of his cohorts decided to join them. Instead, he found three men sitting at the table in the room. The room was obviously set up for the purpose of meetings, formal or otherwise. It was furnished with an oval oak table with eight leather chairs placed around it. At one end of the room was a chalkboard with oak doors that swung closed to give the impression it was a cabinet. The room was typical of what one would expect to find in a large corporate conference room, certainly not the back room of a bar on a wharf in Lisbon.

Doshe had never met or seen any of the three men before. Manuel, whom he had seen a picture of in the newspaper years ago, was one of the three. At the time of the picture, Manuel had been picked up for questioning by the police and was considered the prime suspect in a murder. As it turned out, the police could not compile enough evidence to convict or even take it to trial, so he was ultimately released. The man in the middle looked like to be the same man he'd seen in the newspaper article---Manuel. But Doshe wasn't sure he could trust his memory. The two men, flanking Manuel on each side, certainly looked like bodyguards. Even sitting, it was apparent the one on the left was very tall. He was a full head taller than Manuel. The one on the right, appeared to be more Manuel's size, but had the build of a professional wrestler. Manuel had taken the seat on the same end of the table as the chalkboard. Doshe decided to take the seat directly opposite of Manuel at the other end of the table. The opposite power position, he thought.

It was clear to Doshe that negotiating with Manuel directly would require a high degree of confidence. Presenting an image of equality would be essential. This concerned him because Toomas' anxiety, which was apparent even to the most casual observer, would make that a difficult task. No one said anything as they entered the room, and the resulting tension provided the energy for Toomas to regain his confidence. This was his element, the actual confrontation. His fear was always least controlled when anticipating a situation, but once he was confronted, the in-control Toomas would take over. And that is precisely what was happening.

Doshe sat down and looked directly at Manuel. Toomas followed him to the same side of the table but did not seat himself right away. After Doshe was settled, Toomas walked around the table to the other side. With each step he gained a little more of the self-confidence he expected of himself. The fear he was fighting earlier, and was so unaccustomed to, was dissipating. Slowly, as he approached the other side of the table, he gave each person from the other side a thorough examination. Reaching for the back of the chair, he pulled the plush leather chair away from the table and stepped in front of it. Prior to seating himself, he looked directly at Manuel and speaking with authority said.

"Your two bodyguards will have to leave before we begin negotiations." He paused for effect, then continued. "That's not part of the negotiation either."

Manuel looked at Toomas as if to give him a warning to be careful but remained silent. After what seemed like minutes, but was really only a short pause, Manuel spoke. "After we talk for a few minutes, I will decide if my men can stay, or should leave."

"Doshe, I believe it is time to go." Then turning back to Manuel Toomas added, "I'm sorry if this meeting has caused you any inconvenience. Maybe sometime in the future we will require your services and we can try again." With that said, he motioned for Doshe to follow him as he started for the door. It wasn't until he reached the door that Doshe realized he was serious and quickly caught up to him. Toomas opened the door and they left.

Once the door was closed, Doshe started in on Toomas. "What in Hades are you trying to prove? Not only have you made it impossible to ever work with Manuel again, but also, he is probably angry enough to blackball you with everybody in the business. You'll be lucky to find anyone to replace him, and if you do, they certainly won't be of his caliber."

"Manuel will either learn he is an employee, or he won't be hired," Toomas responded simply. Both men walked down the hall and around the corner to the bar. Toomas asked Doshe to request the bartender call a taxi. The bartender responded by pointing to a pay phone on the wall in the corner of the room. While Toomas was looking up the phone number to make the call, Doshe ordered a drink. He couldn't imagine what was going through this crazy German's head. Why would anyone want to piss off a man whose sole expertise in life is killing people?

Doshe downed the first drink without stopping for air and ordered a second. Neither of them noticed the two bodyguards as they passed the end of the bar heading directly toward Toomas at the phone.

The next thing Doshe was aware of was someone tapping him on the shoulder. His first thought was of Manuel. Manuel was angry and had decided to teach these gringos a lesson. Doshe turned on the bar stool to face his attackers and found just what he expected, Toomas, bracketed between Manuel's bodyguards. "Manuel decided to hear us out on our terms," Toomas told him. "The bodyguards will remain out here."

When they returned to the conference room Manuel had moved to the center of the table and spoke first. "It is a pleasant change to deal with people who are not intelligent enough to show fear when they are in danger. When I was younger, I would have accepted that type of behavior because I was trying to make a name for myself. Now that I am older, I accept it because it happens so seldom. Suffice it to say, it is a good thing that you didn't try this during those middle years. Now what is so important that you feel it is necessary to insult my friends by keeping them out of the room?"

Toomas and Doshe remained standing while Manuel was speaking. They waited, as if questioning whether the bodyguards were really gone, or simply out of sight. Convinced they had won this consideration, Toomas sat down and now Doshe followed suit.

"The reason we've come to you is your one of the two most feared and respected assassins in the world," Toomas began. Before continuing he paused allowing Manuel a chance to respond. When he didn't, Toomas continued, "I represent a small group of... let's say... businessmen, that have determined it would be in their best interest if you would remove a certain individual from their lives. I must caution you; this person has become relatively famous in the past year and is reasonably well protected. I also suspect that if and or when you complete the task, there will be a rather large contingent of people throughout the world that will begin the task of hunting you down. We might be able to provide you some protection at the time, but you will not be able to count on us. Before I go any further, I need to know if this job would be something you would consider and what type of price range to expect." Toomas stopped talking to wait for Manuel's response. As he waited, the eyes of the two men locked on each other. Throughout the introduction, Toomas had tried to get a measure of the man, not just the assassin. Now, his thoughts returned to that as he waited. Manuel had listened attentively but had done nothing that could be used as insight into his inner being.

"Let me correct some erroneous assumptions on your side of the table," Manuel started in. "You used the term assassin; I think of myself as a mercenary. I'm paid to fight someone else's battles. In this case, you and your merry band of fellow businessmen have decided to do battle with someone, but don't want to get your hands dirty. So, you are looking to hire me. Just remember, it's not only the person that pulls the trigger, or whatever else it takes, whose hands are dirty. It's anybody and everybody who's involved. So, you're the assassins, I'm just the weapon."

"The price is determined by the difficulty of the task, and the importance of the target... And by the way, Jacque is the second best." Now it was Manuel's turn to sit back and wait for a reaction. However, neither Toomas nor Doshe reacted to his accusation. This would make an interesting group at a poker table, Manuel thought.

Up to this point Doshe had remained quiet, listening and watching the two men as they jockeyed for position at the negotiation table. Now it was time for him to step forward and become the bargaining agent for Toomas. "We'll concede your point about who's the assassin because it's really just an exercise in semantics. As far as you or Jacque being superior, we are of the opinion there isn't any difference between the two of you. The only reason we're here tonight, and not with him, is this meeting was set up first. We were told Jacque would not be available to meet with us for at least three days. Unless we come to an agreement with you tonight, we have every intention of negotiating with him at that time. Tonight, might seem a little hurried to you, but if we agree to meet with him before you accept the deal, we will feel obligated to give Jacque a chance."

"You're an intelligent man Manuel, or so I've been told. Why do you think we were so willing to walk away earlier? Because we don't have to rely on you," Doshe answered his own question before Manuel had the chance to. "Right now, we don't feel obligated to go with either one of you. We believe either of you would be acceptable." Doshe leaned back in his chair and let this message sink into Manuel. He couldn't help noticing there appeared to be just the least bit of jealousy apparent in Manuel's reaction every time Jacque's name was mentioned. It was obvious he didn't appreciate the reference to their skills being equal.

"Let's say, for the time being, that I'm interested. Who is the person you want killed?" Manuel liked using words that vividly defined what his job was like: killed, murdered, and wasted. Most people that hired him didn't like to use those words, so it gave Manuel a feeling of superiority. He also felt it enhanced his bargaining position by intimidating his potential employer's conscience.

"We won't be giving you that information until we have an agreement."

"And I told you, the price is affected by the target. Famous or politically important people will cost more than the average clown walking down the street."

"For the purposes of pricing, assume an important person will be the target, and set your price. If I remember right, the only other criteria you used was difficulty, and this one will qualify in that category as well." Toomas sated. Manuel moved his head up and down as a slight smirk crossed his face. He was enjoying these two characters. They weren't his typical clientele. Normally he did all the talking and the buyers all the listening. With these two it was a contest. "If we feel the price is fair and you can meet our timing, the deal is done. Otherwise, we wait to talk to Jacque." Toomas had also noticed that using Jacque's name seemed to stir something in Manuel, so he used it in an attempt to set the hook so to speak.

"All expenses, regardless of size, will be paid back to me. I don't provide receipts, and you don't question the bills."

"You'll receive twenty-five thousand a day for expenses, and you pay for everything," Toomas countered.

"Buying people today is expensive, make it fifty a day and an even one million for the hit and we'll call it square." Manuel sat back in his chair for the first time and relaxed. They could name the President of the United States for that kind of money he thought. He looked to Toomas, then back to Doshe, unsure of which one had the final say in the negotiations.

"You'll report to Doshe everyday and notify him of the target date as soon as you make that determination. You will also complete the task within ten days."

"I can call Doshe everyday, and he can relay any information to me you like. But … I will not report to him about anything. This business does not respect people that talk too much, and I don't have any desire to risk my neck by providing you with a corporate report on a time interval. He will find out about the killing when the news media reports it like everyone else. As far as the timing, I shouldn't have any problems with meeting your ten-day limit. One last thing, I'll take the ten-day expense money as a retainer, but the clock doesn't actually start ticking until I receive the money. Anything left over from the expense money can be deducted from the one million."

"We have a deal then?" Toomas asked.

"Yea. Now who's the target?"

Before answering Toomas glanced over at Doshe. Doshe had been quiet during the financial negotiations, just listening and watching. When he saw Toomas look his way, he nodded. "I'm sure you heard of a man called Sheik Omani." Manuel showed absolutely no reaction when

Toomas said the name. At first, he was a little concerned by the lack of reaction, but he continued anyway. "We will provide you with a detailed itinerary of his planned activities for the next ten days. We should be able to have that to you by morning, along with the balance of your expense money."

Doshe took over at this point and filled Manuel in on details of the Sheik's tendencies and his security forces. Throughout the briefing Manuel would at most nod to show he was listening. Occasionally he would close his eyes, lean his head back and rotate it in small circles as if he were so bored as to be falling asleep. Eventually Doshe finished and asked Manuel if there was any other information he might want Doshe to get for him. Manuel shook his head then said; "you said you were going to provide the balance of the expense money tomorrow. That means you're going to have to have paid some of it tonight."

"You're right." Both men were impressed that Manuel had caught Toomas' earlier statement and remembered. Based on the way he listened to Doshe's briefing, they were beginning to question whether Manuel was the right choice. This helped ease their fears a little, because he obviously listened better than they had thought he had.

Toomas pulled out the tails of his shirt to reveal a money belt. He untied it and removed it from around his waist. After that one was removed, the strings of a second belt were revealed with the carrying pouch against Toomas' back. He untied that one and set it on the table next to the first belt. Then he removed three neatly bundled, crisp packets of German marks and handed them to Manuel. "There should be fifty, one-hundred-mark bills, in each bundle," he said. Emptying the second belt he handed Manuel three more bundles of crisp one-hundred-mark bills. Toomas then rolled up the pant legs of his trousers revealing eight more bundles like the first six. "You'll have to excuse me for a moment." He unbuttoned his shirt, and another money belt was revealed wrapped around his chest. Finally, he stood up, lowered his trousers to around his knees and removed the last eight bundles of money. "That should be 125 thousand marks. I wasn't sure how much you would need to get started, so I brought as much as I could comfortably carry without it showing."

Doshe looked, first at the money, then at Toomas. He couldn't believe what he just witnessed. That idiot, he thought, had just carried 125 thousand marks into a meeting with a hired killer. They were lucky to be alive, there's no telling what might have happened if Manuel had suspected the money was there at the start of the meeting. I'm sure we wouldn't be sitting here right now, he continued.

"The marks are alright tonight. They tell me you're serious, which is good. However, the rest of the money should be in American dollars. Dollars spend better everywhere. We'll call this first installment an even 70 thousand dollars. You'll still owe another 800 thousand dollars or so before it's even."

Toomas quickly realized that what Manuel was saying meant he understood the deal to be 1.5 million German marks. Toomas had always assumed they were talking American dollars, because like the man says, 'dollars spend better everywhere.' This meant the total cost to the consortium had just been reduced a little over 600 thousand dollars. Toomas looked Manuel straight in the eye and said, "It's your money. I'll pay it in Aussie dollars if it makes you happy." Toomas paused then added, "if that's all, we'll be leaving." With that, Toomas and Doshe stood up to leave.

Toomas reached his hand out to Manuel to seal the deal with a handshake. Manuel looked at the outstretched hand, looked at Toomas, then went back to counting the money. "If you're waiting for a handshake to ratify this deal you'll be here long after the Sheik's dead," Manuel said. Holding a bundle of money up in both hands he added. "This is the only handshake I trust, and my reputation is going to have to be what you trust because you're not getting anything else. Handshakes don't guarantee anything and maybe this is the day you'll learn that."

As soon as they appeared in the bar, Manuel's bodyguards headed for the conference room. Toomas and Doshe stopped only long enough for Toomas to make the phone call for a taxi. With the call completed, they stepped outside to wait, thinking it may be the safest option. Neither man spoke. Both were thinking this was neither the time nor place to discuss what had just transpired. Doshe was pleased because they, the Zealots, would finally be rid of this interfering Sheik that was making a compromised Israel more Arab than Jew. And Toomas was pleased because his plan was coming together unusually well.

When they arrived back at the hotel Toomas immediately made plans to leave. Only one day had passed since the consortium's last meeting, and he wanted to take advantage of the remaining time before the next one to clear up some details. After a few phone calls, he was booked on the first flight out in the morning to Paris. From Paris he would connect with Lufthansa and be in Frankfurt by early afternoon.

Doshe returned to his room, gathered his things together and headed back down to the front desk to check out. He'd made arrangements before Toomas arrived to stay with an old friend of his, and he wanted to put distance between Toomas and himself. He wasn't sure why, but for some reason he was beginning to suspect that what happened tonight might backfire on him. He couldn't quite put his finger on it, but he had this uneasy feeling, almost a premonition that what originally sounded too good to be true, was just that---Too good to be true.

The feeling continued to hold his thoughts captive while riding back in the taxi. The more effort he put into ridding himself of the idea, the more convinced he was that Toomas had another agenda. When Toomas asked him to help set up the meeting with Manuel and explained the reason for the meeting, Doshe was ecstatic at the opportunity to get rid of the Sheik. But now, as he thought about the whole thing, he couldn't come up with any good reasons why Toomas should want to do this. And that was the part that concerned him most. In the past, Toomas or one of his men would always offer a plausible explanation for any requests they made. But this time, there wasn't any, just the objective---Hire Manuel to assassinate Sheik Omani. Doshe was beginning to suspect Toomas was setting him up for something.

When he arrived at Ariel's house, he would make plans to have Toomas followed.

- - - - -

"Doshe, it is so good to see you again. When my wife told me you would be stopping by today, I said to her. 'No, you lie to me. You make a joke out of our friendship. You should be ashamed of yourself, woman.' But my wife refused to listen to me, reassuring me that it was not a joke, and that you had just called asking if or when you could visit. Doshe," Ariel wrapped his arms around Doshe and gave him a bear hug, then kissed him on both cheeks. "Why does so much time pass between visits? Why are everyday tasks more important than maintaining friendships? I do not understand the world today. Yesterday you were in Israel and I'm sorry to say, I did not even think of you once. Now, twenty-four hours later, you are a guest in my home. Doshe, I missed you. Enough of that, I talk like an old woman. Maybe you are here because the meeting I set up for you did not go well. Maybe your uncle has failed you. Please, tell me what I can do to make amends?"

Ariel was the classic, storybook, elder in a Jewish home. He was as entertaining as he was efficient, and he talked too much. At least the young people thought so. However, as each generation passed from youthful knowledge to middle aged ignorance, Ariel's 'talked too much' label would evaporate. It was still true that Ariel talked profusely, almost to the point of monopolizing conversation. But if one listened closely, peppered throughout his diatribe would be insightful editorial comments that improved one's understanding of each situation. Ariel had become a sort of elder statesman in the Jewish community. And with the advent of Israel, the Jewish community needed people with these skills.

Ariel was a small man, almost to the point of petite. He was small boned, thin but not gaunt, and was barely five feet tall with his shoes on. The hair that was left was mostly gray, and so was the beard that he kept neatly trimmed. He was an Orthodox Rabbi and seldom was the top of his head uncovered, which if it were, would reveal no more hair then when covered. He took pride in his knowledge of the Torah and would not allow for liberal or fanatical interpretations of it or any other part of the Scriptures. It was his consistency in thinking that caused his opinion to be sought regardless of religious differences or fanaticism. Since thoughts were not binding on either party, Ariel was perceived as the perfect neutral party.

He had also developed a reputation for his rational approach to resolving many of the more esoteric problems facing Israel. Disputes over land or the final boundaries of an Israel were not as important to Ariel as disputes that were based on different interpretations of the Torah. Boundaries were a constantly changing fact of life, but God's Word was the never changing voice of God. Ariel would not accept that God's Word had to be interpreted differently as the world evolved. Nor would he accept the argument that Israel's boundaries today, had to reflect the boundaries of Israel during the time of David either.

His arguments were often cited during debates, and he was credited with one of Israel's most well-known quotes. "Throughout our history, including the time immediately after being led out of Egypt, our people saw the size and shape of the Holy land change, often on a yearly basis. Many times, our forefathers became captives of others and could not claim possession of any land. Boundaries are dictated by God, and we are merely the recipients of His will. Therefore, God is better served by understanding His Word and leaving border disputes to Him. Did He not make it possible for Israel to exist again? Did He not provide us with a portion of Jerusalem? If it is His will, will He not provide us the opportunity to regain control of the Holy land and city as He sees fit?"

Since Ariel was convinced that God's will affect everything, many assumed he would quietly accept whatever life delivered up to him as God's` will. However, Ariel was just the opposite. He believed adamantly that God's will was best expressed through the active participation of His people in every facet of life. Seldom could man circumvent God's will; therefore, everyone should do everything in their power to promote their own objectives because God would use them and mold their effort into His plans. It was this belief that brought Ariel into the position of supporting the work of men like Doshe. Hiring an assassin was just another example of how God could use men for Holy retribution, that message was proclaimed loud and clear throughout the Historical books of the Scriptures.

"Ariel, you did not fail me. Why I even answer that question I don't know. Because when have you ever asked me a question you didn't already know the answer to?" Doshe replied and returned the greeting by kissing Ariel on both cheeks. "You have not changed one iota Ariel."

"You are right. My people tell me that Manuel has already made reservations on a morning flight to Paris. I would assume he has plans to either follow the Sheik for a little while and learn his ways, or maybe he will go ahead and take care of the business in Paris, I do not know. In either event, you heard the news, didn't you?"

"I don't know. What news?"

"The Sheik will be meeting with Abraham and Jihad in Jerusalem, followed by a news conference the day after tomorrow. There is purported to be a breakthrough of sorts on a negotiated control of the entire city of Jerusalem. The Sheik was expected to arrive some time tomorrow, Abraham and Jihad as well. After they have had a chance to review the proposal a final time, each will be given the chance to back out prior to the news conference."

"What is King Hussein's reaction to this arrangement? To the casual observer, it would appear that he has been ignored in the negotiations once again."

"Supposedly, the Sheik met with the King prior to discussions with the others. The results of that discussion should be fairly obvious at this point if you believe the rumors. Why he is not included in the news conference, I don't know. If I were to hazard a guess, I suspect he was invited, but declined in an effort to continue straddling the fence. This way he can wait to see the outcome before he is required to commit."

Doshe changed the subject. "Do we have anyone that has the ability to delay Manuel?"

"No. Not if we ever wanted to see them alive again. Why do you ask?"

"I can't be certain. But if I had just hired someone to assassinate the Sheik, I think I would want the news conference to happen first. The assassination could cause problems if it occurs before. Namely any agreement they had reached would become null and void. Do you have any details about the agreement?"

"No. I was simply told it would revolutionize the way everyone views the Middle East."

"Well, I had hoped to be able to spend tomorrow here, but based on this new information, I better head back first thing in the morning."

"My wife told me you had some unfinished business and that is why you were stopping by. I am wondering what that was."

"Yes. Yes, I had forgotten. This news leaves me very uneasy about the next twenty-four hours and for a moment there I had forgotten why I wanted to see you in the first place. But this news makes my request even more important. I need someone to follow the German, Toomas. This whole idea of him wanting to assassinate the Sheik has me a bit confused and I was hoping a tail might enlighten me a little."

"Certainly. If you would like I could make the call immediately."

"That would be great. You will do it now?"

"Come into the kitchen with me." Both men had barely managed to creep into the living room during this entire conversation. They had been so engrossed in what each other was saying; they would take a step, then talk. Take another step, then talk. The net effect left them standing near the middle of the room. Ariel walked out of the front room and into the kitchen where the only phone in the house was located. While he dialed the number, he asked Doshe who was now seated at the table, "Do you mind if the tail is a woman? I know this French woman, whose reputation is less than honorable, but whose work is impeccable. One of the best in the business. I think she lives in Paris but happens to be in Lisbon at the moment and could pick up Toomas at the airport. I assume he will be leaving tomorrow morning, since it's too late to catch anything heading that way tonight."

"You surprise me, Ariel. When did you become liberal enough to hire a woman to do a man's job?"

"That is the problem with most Jews today. They don't understand the Biblical relationship God has set forth between a man and a woman. They misinterpret subjugation to mean women cannot do anything a man desires to do. God used women for all manner of things, either because man was unable or unwilling to do His work. God's primary directive, as it pertains to the subjugation of women to men, was in the realm of spiritual leadership---The priesthood. In every other aspect of life, women were used by God with equal success and failure. They may not have been our choice, but they were His choice. God didn't exclude them from doing His work, even when men were available. So, what are you saying? You don't want me to call her? I did not realize you were such a chauvinist."

"No, no, no." Doshe blurted. "I'm sorry Ariel. I didn't mean to imply she could not or should not be used. I... just thought or I didn't expect... ah... never mind. I trust your judgment and have no problem hiring a woman for this. I guess I just didn't expect you to." Slowly Doshe's face returned to its normal color after the berating he had just taken from Ariel. Of course, he didn't mind a woman doing this. He had never been one to think women should be relegated to the home. He was much more enlightened than Ariel, he thought. Yet somehow, Ariel had made him feel like just that, a chauvinist,

"Hello. Marie?" Ariel started speaking to the person on the other end of the phone in Portuguese, then switched to French. Another thing Doshe learned about Ariel tonight. He had never known Ariel to speak in any languages other than Portuguese and Hebrew. He continued to listen as Ariel talked, managing to pick out the occasional word he thought he understood. After a couple minutes of talking, he heard Ariel say, "Au revoir," and watched him hang up the phone.

"It is set. She'll pick him up at the airport tomorrow, and if he's made his reservations, she may be seated next to him. Or at the very least she'll be on the same flight."

- - - - -

Jihad was sitting in the small room alone. He had given each man a task and they had all left to attend to them. He was tired. He had been up all night with the representative from their benefactors, arguing. They were becoming more demanding with each donation, he thought, and Jihad was concluding that they should be replaced. Their demands were becoming unreasonable and were starting to interfere with his own objectives. He would have to go back on the road searching for a new source of income. Or maybe an old one, he thought. He knew he could always go back to Qhadaffi as a last resort, but that would not be an improvement. He didn't like dealing with a mad man, and Qhadaffi was as mad as they get. Jihad decided to put the thought out of his mind. He had taken the money, so until these new requests are fulfilled, they would continue to be bound to this group.

He had resigned himself to the continuing relationship and was beginning to formulate his plans to meet their latest requests when Jamaal entered the room. Jamaal was Jihad's second in command. Any task that Jihad felt required his own personal attention, could be assigned to Jamaal. In fact, it was this dual leadership that allowed this group to accomplish so much, with so few. The leadership question had been addressed early in the group's evolution from the "gang of five" as children, to the terrorist group they are today.

Throughout their childhood and the gang's early existence, the rest of the members would treat both boys as the leader. Once they graduated to tasks that required a singular leader, the tasks were evenly divided between the two young men. As negotiations with other groups increased, circumstances dictated all activities be funneled through one person to minimize confusion. Both men came to the realization that they could no longer function in the informal dual leadership role that had evolved naturally.

Late one night, when both had been hired separately to do the same task, Jihad had figured it out just in time to divert a disaster. Soon after, he approached Jamaal about the need to centralize leadership in one man. Jamaal had been coming to the same conclusion for some time and argued convincingly that Jihad should be that leader. The result was not unlike the coalition formed by the Israelis, Yitzhak Shamir, and Shimon Peres. When the Israeli people could not make a clear-cut choice between the two political factions in the eighties, those two formed a coalition government that proved unusually strong. The only differences in this case were both men had the same objective. Also, the sharing of power would take place out of the public eye. The visual leadership would not alternate between the two men, but they both knew the actual leadership was still very much a mutual effort.

"I was not able to hire Manuel as a decoy," Jamaal started to explain. "His pride would not allow him to be used as a decoy for Jacque. It was his position that he would be more useful if he were hired to deal with Eric, himself. We talked at length, and I finally agreed to his position, contingent on your approval."

"You obviously feel it was the right decision, so of course you have my approval. Does he require anything from me?"

"No. I told him I would have an answer for him today. He seemed satisfied with that."

"Jamaal," Jihad started very slowly, pausing with each sentence as if he were having difficulty breathing when in reality, he was having difficulty saying the words. "You are aware our financial supporters sent a messenger today." He waited for Jamaal to acknowledge he knew, and then continued. "They have requested the most blatant show of affection for our Jewish enemy than ever before." Jamaal nodded again, misinterpreting Jihad's slow speech as a need for confirmation with each statement. "I am to meet publicly with Sheik Omani, Abraham and Doshe in Jerusalem tomorrow." Jihad paused a very long time before he revealed the last part of the request. "We are to sign an agreement of truce. The Zealots, the Israeli government and us are to demonstrate to the world our desire for peace by agreeing to a thirty-day truce, negotiated by the Sheik." This last statement bothered Jamaal as much as it did Jihad.

As a group, they had sworn to eliminate the Jewish element from their land. Those that did not die would be driven into the Mediterranean Sea. Their existence had been predicated on the singular objective: Repossession of all Palestinian land, regardless of cost. Now with this turn of events, there objective was being subjugated to that of a third party. They had been coerced into this position, but could not, while maintaining their own integrity, disregard the agreement.

"If we stopped accepting their assistance, when would we be released from any further obligations?" Jamaal asked. This was what Jihad, and he must do, sever the relationship as soon as possible, and they both knew it. But unlike their counterparts the PLO and other such organizations, it was understood that they must first fulfill their obligation. This was one of the most highly regarded differences between them and other factions that claimed to protect the Palestinian interests. If their word weren't any good, they would be no better than Jews.

"This is all they asked for; the meeting and honoring the truce. In thirty days, we will be debt free, Allah be praised. However, we have not found a new source of income, so those thirty days will pass quickly. If you could begin the search while I go to Jerusalem, we can get a head start."

- - - - -

He walked up to the ticket agent and asked for a ticket to Paris. The transaction went smoothly. He handed the agent his credit card, then the agent returned the card with his purchased tickets when he was finished. After he looked at the tickets to confirm the departure time, he signed the receipt. Picking up his tickets, he headed off to his favorite coffee shop near his departure gate.

Like a chain smoker smoking cigarette, he waited for his flight's boarding announcement while drinking one cup of coffee after another. This would be his last chance to enjoy this particular pleasure until he had completed this assignment. Coffee did an excellent job of providing just the tiniest flutter in one's hands. And his hands, or more accurately his job, required the same steady hands expected of a surgeon. But in his case, if his hands slipped the person didn't die. In other words, he failed. So, today he'll indulge in this simple pleasure, for tomorrow Eric may die. He smiled at the thought.

The announcement came and after an additional twenty-five minutes went by, he was on his way to Paris. It was going to be necessary for him to uncover Eric's trail, and there was no telling how cold it would be. All the German and Doshe were able to tell him was that Eric had made it to Heathrow. Also, that Eric had at one point bought tickets to Helsinki. But the man assigned to follow him at Heathrow, was found unconscious, not dead, so it was unlikely he used those tickets. It was just a matter of talking to the right people. And he had the connections to all the right people. Manuel looked up just as a man walked by his seat on the way to the restroom. It was the German.

Toomas saw Manuel just as Manuel looked up to see him walk by. Neither man acknowledged the other. Toomas continued on to the restroom while Manuel pretended to return to the magazine on his lap. He had opened it when he sat down twenty minutes earlier, but he had yet to turn a page, until now.

Inside the bathroom Toomas was able to allow his fear to bubble to the surface. He looked at his face in the mirror and noticed beads of perspiration covering his forehead. He went about his business: Cleaned up, then splashed cold water on his face to cool down. He thought about the man sitting a few rows behind his seat. Of course, Manuel would head to mainstream Europe, Toomas thought. It was unlikely he could set up all the necessary details for the assassination from Lisbon. Toomas continued to reassure himself that there was nothing unusual about Manuel being on this flight. Then, when he felt, he could comfortably return to his seat while maintaining a controlled appearance, he did so.

As he walked by Manuel this time, he passed by without looking. He took his seat, removed the airline magazine, and began reading to pass the time for the remainder of the flight. When they deplaned, both men continued their charade of not knowing each other. Once inside the terminal at De Gaulle airport, Manuel disappeared into the crowd. Toomas didn't see him again until he was leaving passport control, heading on to one of the moving sidewalks that would transport him to the main terminal. The moving sidewalks were encased in a transparent Plexiglas bubble like structure that gave the airport a futuristic appearance. Through the glass the sidewalks looked like spokes of a wheel, carrying passengers to different levels between the concourse and the terminal. Through the Plexiglas walls he could see

Manuel's back as he stepped off the sidewalk at the lower level of the main terminal. He watched as Manuel disappeared into the crowd. I hope that's the last time I see him, Toomas thought.

Toomas had carried on all his baggage, so he bypassed baggage claim, stopped to exchange some money, then headed directly to the main terminal doors to catch a taxi into Paris. The airport was situated well outside the city proper and the ride, to the hotel near the Louvre, would take more than an hour. Once there, he was to meet Sergei in the hotel restaurant to get an update on the planned meeting in Jerusalem. The last time they had talked, Jihad had yet to be informed of the truce agreement he would have to support, and Toomas was curious how he had received the idea.

Doshe was not pleased when Toomas requested, he attend the press conference, or more accurately demanded that Doshe be there. But he calmed down considerably when he learned Toomas would be hiring Manuel to assassinate the Sheik. It was obvious that Doshe was agreeing to participate in the meeting because the man given credit for the truce would be dead in the near future. And if the man were dead, the truce probably would be too. Therefore, the meeting would cause no real problems as far as the Israeli government and the Zealots were concerned.

By the time Toomas had gone over all these things in his mind, the taxi was pulling up to the front door of the hotel. Toomas climbed out of the cab, peeled off one hundred thirty francs from a roll of bills he retrieved from his pocket, and handed them to the driver. Toomas checked into the hotel, took his bags to the room, then went back down to the restaurant to wait for Sergei.

Toomas was seated at a table and decided to have something to eat while he waited for Sergei to arrive. He gave the waitress his order, then settled back to watch the people in the restaurant. Since the hotel was located across the street from the Louvre, it was frequented mainly by well to do tourists and businessmen trying to mix business with a little sightseeing. However, as would be expected, it also had its contingent of local shopkeepers and salesclerks that would eat there on special occasions. The resulting mix of customers gave the restaurant a truly international flavor. Before Sergei arrived, Toomas recognized five different languages spoken; English, really American, Swedish, German, Arabic, Japanese and of course French. He also heard one language that he did not recognize but assumed it to be an African dialect based on the dress of the speakers. Everyone was engrossed in their own world. And that, he thought, is precisely why I like having meetings in public places.

There was an enhanced level of security discussing sensitive topics in a public arena that wasn't possible in the private, but rented, meeting rooms used by the consortium. It was, for the most part impossible to bug a public meeting place. Conversations could be overheard, but if people were monitored continuously, anyone paying too much attention to their conversation was easily noticed. Identification of the party was more likely, making elimination of potential security problems easier.

On the other hand, all the places the consortium typically met were ideally suited for bugging. Quite often they were remote hotels with nonexistent security for its guests. If the hotel did provide security, it was more of a token effort and was easily compromised.

Sergei spotted Toomas, waved off the Maitre' d and confidently walked over to the table Toomas was seated at and sat down. "You are looking particularly pleased with yourself," Toomas said to the Russian. Sergei was indeed pleased with himself, and in the traditional Russian fashion he looked like a cat that had eaten his fill at your expense. Sergei didn't answer; he just sat there looking back at Toomas with a wide grin on his face.

"Based on the way you look; it is apparent you were successful in convincing Jihad to participate in our little public show of unity." Toomas' tone of voice made the statement sound as if he'd asked a question. Sergei simply nodded his confirmation. "Well, you will be pleased to find out that I have been able to negotiate a mutually satisfactory deal with Manuel." One always had to omit certain details when speaking in a public place, but as long as both parties understood the topic well enough, that was seldom a real problem. Anyone listening would simply think they were two businessmen discussing a deal they had been working on together.

"When will he go on the payroll?"

"He accompanied me here, so as of this morning he is drawing pay for his expenses. As a result, I've had to cancel my flight to Frankfurt. And at this point, I may decide to go to Jerusalem and get a front row seat for the news conference."

"I think it would be better if you were not present. It minimizes the chance that anyone can figure out what is happening. Besides you will not learn anything there that you can't get from the news reports."

"I suppose you are right."

"Did he offer any time schedule for accomplishing his assignment?" Sergei asked, redirecting the conversation back to the topic of Manuel.

"No. Manuel is very much an independent worker. It was my impression that he would begin immediately to deal with our friend, Eric. Then he would move on to the more important task. However, he did not explicitly say what his plans were."

"Where should we go from here?"

"Since everything seems to be under control, I think I'll reschedule my flight to Frankfurt and be on my way. Unless of course you have something else that you feel needs my attention." Sergei shook his head no.

The remainder of their meal was eaten in silence. When they had finished, Toomas picked up the tab for both of them as he stood up, "I will see you at our next meeting," he stated matter-of-factly, then left Sergei sitting at the table. Sergei remained seated for a little while reviewing the recent events in his mind. Not completely satisfied with his thoughts, he left the restaurant barely aware of his surroundings, immersed in his mind's world.

When Toomas stepped onto the sidewalk, he looked right first, then left. A quick assessment of the tourist activity on the street convinced him a cab might be impossible to get so he looked around for the entrance to the Metro, now he would have to take the Metro to the train station, then transfer to a train for the interminably long ride out to the airport. Unknown to him, one of the women sitting at a table near Sergei and himself had left the restaurant at the same time Toomas had. The two women had come into the restaurant after Toomas and had sat drinking coffee during their entire time. One of the women now followed him down into the Metro station and joined him on his trip to the airport.

5

-For it comes in futility and it goes into obscurity, and it's name is covered in obscurity.

"Joan I'll take some of the luggage down and have the front desk call for a taxi if you can finish the rest of the luggage and get the kids ready. Alright?" Peter picked up two of the oversized, overstuffed, hard shell suitcases that were stacked near the door, then he tried to grab a third cosmetic case with his left hand. The other suitcase in that hand dropped back to the floor; so, Peter reached down to try again. This time he tried sliding the larger case under his armpit before grabbing the smaller cosmetics case. It worked, briefly, then the larger case started sliding down his side. No matter how much pressure he applied to the case, it continued its slide back down to the floor. Peter's right arm had gotten tired holding the one case while he was struggling with these two, so he set everything down and sat on the edge of the bed to rest for a moment. He stared at the pile of luggage on the floor. Deciding there was no way to avoid a second trip back to the room, he grabs one large suitcase and the cosmetic case and started for the door.

"Joan" he yelled, then waited for her response. "You going to answer me or not!" His voice had a hint of frustration in it. As he listened for his wife to answer, he heard the water from the shower and realized it was drowning out his voice. He set both suitcases down once again and walked over to the bathroom door. He opened the door and stuck his head in to look inside. Both boys were in the shower. At seven and nine years old, he was surprised his wife was still able to get them in together. She must have threatened them, he thought. At the moment,

Joan was trying to wipe the steam off the mirror long enough to use it but was not having much luck. "Honey," he called.

Joan turned to look at him then asked incredulously, "You're done with the suitcases already?"

"No. I haven't even taken them downstairs yet. I figured you couldn't hear me when you didn't answer."

"I'm sorry dear. I didn't realize you were talking to me. What did you want anyway?"

"Never mind. How much longer will you be, so I can tell them when we need the taxi?"

"Everything is packed except the cosmetic case. I have the boys' clothes already and they should be done with their shower any minute. Boys," she called. "How much longer are you going to be in there?"

"I'm not coming out 'til you get outta here mom," Jimmy, the nine-year-old answered.

Peter was getting impatient waiting for all of this but managed to keep it hidden inside. He closed the door, decided to take one load of luggage down, not call for the taxi just yet and see where everyone was when he returned. As he walked away from the bathroom door, he heard his wife say, "Don't be so prudish Jimmy. I've seen you more times than I care to remember and besides I'm your mother, so don't be ridiculous." Peter picked up the cosmetic case and placed it on the bed so he wouldn't take it by mistake. He moved the two largest suitcases near the door. He opened the door to the hallway, stuck his foot out to hold the door open, grabbed the two suitcases and left the room. Just as the door clicked shut, he realized he had forgotten the room key. "Shit!"

- - - - -

John walked into the Metro station with everything he owned on his back, inside his backpack. When he left home this morning his father didn't even say good-bye. He had become accustomed to his son wandering off, gallivanting around Europe with nary a care in the world. At first his father didn't mind the thought of his son taking a few months off before going on to the University, but the few months had grown to a year, and now he was starting his second year with no end in sight. When John had finished touring all of Europe and then extended the boundaries to include the Middle East and North Africa, his father had suggested he might delay that portion of the trip. John wouldn't listen, saying he was learning more on the road meeting people of different cultures and hearing new perspectives on everything from raising children to nuclear holocaust to cooking. He would never be able to learn these things in school, and once he started back in school, he'd never have the chance to do this again. Life and living would become too complicated, too dependent on others and others too dependent on him. He'd be just like his father, too tied down. So, the last time he had left home they had argued, not a hateful argument where feelings and relationships were permanently damaged, because his father would never allow things to go that far. But it was enough that both understood the uncompromising positions they had each taken. Now their conversations avoided his trips as much as possible.

His mom made a big fuss about him leaving. He'd be lonely going to Israel by himself, she explained. She raised the same concerns every time he left to tour another country. She had accepted, albeit somewhat hesitantly, his desire or need, as he called it, to do this. She had made it perfectly clear that she expected to be kept well informed of his whereabouts, at least weekly. To this end she had supplied him with enough paper, pens, envelopes, and stamps to write twice a week. She never figures out the stamps don't work where he's going, but John had stopped telling her long ago. She figured this way he would write to either her or his latest girlfriend. In either event she would know what was happening on his trip. The girlfriend would receive the brunt of the mail the first month, but then she would tire of him being gone so long and find someone new. At this point, John would start writing more regularly to his mother.

John got off the Metro when he reached the train station to make the switch to the train that would take him to the airport. He had decided that he was getting too far from home to hitchhike or take trains the whole way, so he would fly to Jerusalem and start the touring from there. He briefly toyed with the idea of flying into Beirut and starting from there but decided it might be better to get near the area first and assess the risk more accurately. If it proved to be safer than the media portrayed on the nightly news, he could always get there by ground transportation. However, if the news was accurate in their descriptions of the constant violence in the city, Beirut could be avoided completely on this trip.

John removed the backpack from his back and set it on the ground. Reaching into his pocket, he pulled out a handful of change and started plugging one of the ticket machines on the wall. It was early in the morning, consequently the station was full of commuters on their way to work and a line quickly began to form behind him before he was able to select his ticket from the machine. By the time he had his ticket in hand and was able to get out of the way, there were two angry Frenchmen and three, even more angry, Frenchwomen in what was supposed to pass for a line behind him. Before he could pick up his backpack, he was jostled aside so one of the women could get in and buy a ticket. This was just one of the reasons why John was not in a hurry to finish his formal education only to join the rat race. Unlike them, his only concern was to get to the airport before his flight left at 11.15. Plenty of time, he thought. John put his arms through the straps, hitched the backpack up on his back and left the growing line at the ticket machine. He walked to the appropriate line of turnstiles leading to the train he would need to take to the airport. He put his ticket in the slot on the side of the turnstile and walked through.

- - - - -

"Did I get a copy of your itinerary yet?" she asked.

"No, but the itinerary's in my briefcase with the tickets. Would you mind getting them out for me, and check to see what time the flight leaves? I thought it was around noon, but I can't be sure."

His wife walked out of the bedroom and started looking for his briefcase. The last time she had seen it, it was in the kitchen, so she went there first. She found the briefcase exactly where she thought it was, sitting in the corner. Grabbing the briefcase, she tossed it on the kitchen table and opened it. Inside it was his typical mess, she thought. She started rifling through the pile of folders but couldn't find the itinerary. Next, she started looking behind the pockets: The ones designed to hold the files she had just gone through, but he never used. They weren't there either, which meant she had to look inside each folder.

"Do you know where inside your briefcase they are?" she yelled back to him.

"If they're not right on top, I'm not sure what I did with them," he replied.

"Before I go through everything, is it possible you might have put them somewhere else?"

"Did you look in the front room?"

She didn't say anything knowing it wouldn't do any good. She just thought, of course I didn't look in the front room, you told me they were in your briefcase. How in the world does he manage everything when he's gone and doesn't have me to rely on? Somehow, he manages to get home all right, which means he CAN take care of himself. But when he's home, he's like the proverbial absent-minded professor. Still, his boss must think highly of him. He's had three promotions in the last four years, and the next one will make him a vice president. At thirty years old, that's quite an accomplishment.

She looked around the small room, not quite sure what she expected to see. As her eyes scanned the room, she saw the corner of something on the floor next to the coffee table. She walked over to get a more complete view of it and saw the familiar shape of an envelope with airline tickets. The same one she had become so familiar with due to his many short trips. He had obviously tossed it on the table, or actually tossed it at the table last night when he got home. However, instead of landing on the table, it found it's way to the floor. Once she had it, she removed one of the three copies of the itinerary and began reading it.

"I found it. It was on the floor in the front room. It says your flight's at 11:15. That doesn't give you much time, it's almost nine now and it takes an hour to get there." She stopped speaking long enough to finish reading the itinerary, then added. "You're getting in pretty late tomorrow night; I hope you weren't planning on me meeting you at the airport."

"As a matter of fact, I was." Walking into the front room Desmond continued talking. "Since I've been working so many long hours and it's our anniversary the following day, the boss man said I could take the day off. I figured maybe you and I could get out to the country for a day. Spend the whole day eating, drinking, and making love. What do you think?"

"It had better not rain." Then she smiled and added, "Sounds great. I'll make the reservations so we can leave right from the airport as soon as you arrive." She walked over to him and began to adjust his tie.

"Don't even think about it, we don't have time." He said this because every time she helped him get dressed, she had other things on her mind. "You should have thought of that this morning when you said no, now it's too late." Leaving his wife standing there looking disappointed, Desmond headed for the front door. "I'll get the car and meet you in front in five minutes."

- - - - -

"Excuse me Ma'am. Your ride should be here in a minute. If you would like to take a seat over there, I'll let you know as soon as it arrives." The airline agent was speaking to a very old woman. Taking her arm, he led her to a seat just inside the gate door. After she had been seated, she reached out with her hand to take the tickets and see where the old woman was going. "Would it be alright if I looked at those? That way when your ride arrives, I can have all the gate information available and make sure you get to your gate on time."

Slowly the old woman started to release her grip on the tickets, the whole time keeping a watchful eye on the agent, unconvinced yet that the agent was acting in her best interest. Once she had the woman's tickets in her hands, the old woman just stared at her. It wasn't an angry look, but rather one dominated by fear of the unknown. She had only flown once before in her life, and that was forty years ago. The memory was well faded, but her fear, both then and now, was very real.

The agent opened the packet containing the tickets. She took great care to control her movements and ensure the old woman could see exactly what she was doing. She removed the tickets and looked for information about the next flight. Once she found the flight information, rather than taking the tickets with her to the ticket counter, she handed them back to the old woman and said. "While we wait for your ride, I'll go ahead and check your seat assignment. If you don't have one, I'll go ahead and make one for you, if that's all right? This way when you get to the next gate, everything will already be in the computer." The old woman nodded her head ever so slightly showing she understood.

The agent returned to the counter and started looking for the gate information. She checked to see if the flight was on time and confirmed the old woman's seat assignment. After a reasonably short time, she returned to the old woman and asked, "The agent in Lyon did not give you a seat assignment, would you like a window seat on your trip?" The old woman nodded once again, and the agent continued. "If you would like, I can issue you a boarding pass right now, but I would need your tickets." This time the old woman shook her head not vigorously. "Alright, it's not necessary. Just check-in when you get to the gate." The agent returned to the computer terminal at the counter but kept a watchful eye on the old woman just in case she needed something else.

As the agent finished at the counter, a young man, pushing what amounted to a wheelchair, came up to the counter. The young man was really just a boy, barely eighteen and not much bigger than the old lady he was going to have to transport. "Is that the old geezer?" He asked pointing at the old woman sitting near the gate door, then continued. "Where does she have to go?"

The agent proceeded to provide him with all the necessary information, and then added at the end. "Please be nice to her. She's confused and just a little bit frightened."

"No problem." The young man wheeled over to the old lady and started talking to her. Soon she was smiling and even chuckled out loud once or twice. The agent watched as the young man gained the old woman's confidence. Soon after he arrived, the boy was able to convince the woman to allow him to assist her out of her seat and into the wheelchair. The agent was amazed at the gentleness the boy showed while assisting the old woman. As he wheeled his cargo past the agent, she heard him say to the old lady. "Don't you worry. Jean Paul will have you to your gate in time to have a beer, read the newspaper and pick up some young Rabbi on his way back to Jerusalem." The old lady just sat in the wheelchair with a huge grin across her face and no trace of the fear that was so prominent just a few minutes earlier.

- - - - -

Manuel was in the Pigalle section of Paris putting together the last details before he headed to the airport. The flight to Jerusalem was scheduled to leave at 11:15, and he wanted to get there between 10:45 and 11:00. This way there would be little time for security to do a formal check on the baggage he was checking. He knew that checked baggage seldom received the scrutiny that carry on items did, but he didn't want to give some over conscientious baggage handling security person the opportunity either. He also did not want to take the chance that the baggage did not make the flight, ending up on some later flight, or becoming another lost baggage statistic. In either case, timing was the key issue.

He had managed to bribe one of the baggage handlers to make sure his luggage made that particular flight. The handler had agreed that in the event it somehow missed the flight, he would immediately call a special phone number. One of Manuel's people would answer the public telephone, at the airport, then retrieve the luggage as quickly as possible. As long as this maneuver could be completed by noon, no one would be hurt. Of course, the man who would retrieve the suitcase was experienced in disarmament and would disarm the bomb within minutes after it was in his possession.

The last detail left was to pick up the luggage. Manuel approached the ladies lingerie shop acting like a curious tourist shopping for his wife or girlfriend. He looked at each item in the display window, taking his time as if he were picturing that wife or girlfriend in each item of clothing. The sexier the outfit, the longer he dwelled on it. Finally, after giving the impression he might move on, he stepped up to the door and quickly entered the shop.

As he stepped inside the lingerie shop, he was momentarily startled by the ringing of a bell that was bumped when the door opened. The bell rang a second time as the door closed, but Manuel no longer heard it. Once inside, he glanced around to see if there were other shoppers and was pleased to see it was empty. He made his way to the counter at the back of the store. By that time, the owner, who had heard the bell, appeared at a curtain covering the doorway to the back room. Manuel walked straight through the curtained doorway. The owner held back the curtain as Manuel walked through.

Manuel waited for the owner to take the lead, then followed him down a narrow aisle. On either side of the aisle were boxes stacked to the ceiling containing women's lingerie. At the end of the aisle was a break in the wall of boxes that revealed another doorway opening to a stairway leading down to the basement. Silently, they both went downstairs. At the bottom Manuel saw piles of arms, legs, torsos, heads and various other body parts: a collection of mannequin pieces strewn throughout the basement. He also noticed a long workbench stretching the entire length of one wall. Half of the bench was cluttered with more body parts, with a naked, headless woman sitting near the center. The bench was divided, not by a partition, but rather by the disparity in appearance between the two sides.

The other half of the bench had a very neatly, organized wall of tools directly behind the bench. A lone metal suitcase sat atop the bench, looking drastically out of place among the basement graveyard of mannequin parts. The owner walked over to the suitcase, clicked open the clasps, then opened the lid. Inside was filled with various pieces of clothing, toiletries, hair dryer and a small tape player. He removed the hair dryer and grabbed a screwdriver from off the wall. After he removed the three screws that held the two halves of the hairdryer's outer casing together, he popped the body of the hair dryer apart.

He set both halves on the bench top and proceeded to explain to Manuel the protection he had built into the hairdryer so that it would pass x-ray examination. Each half of the hairdryer was fit over an exactly matched, quarter inch thick lead casing. Between the casing and the plastic outer shell of the hairdryer, he had fashioned an imitation coil and fan. Neither looked like their counterparts until viewed under x-ray; at the moment, the coil looked like a jumbled piece of wire and the fan looked more like pieces of broken fan blades. Manuel listened but felt the man's claims were too farfetched to be relied on and was glad he had made the arrangements to circumvent the x-ray examination altogether.

Next, the creator went on to describe the workings of the bomb itself. A pressure-sensing device, very similar to those used in home barometric pressure gauges, but considerably more accurate and slightly reduced in size, was used as the timing device. This was connected to a nine-volt transistor size battery that was connected to a capacitor. The capacitor was used to collect the charge until it could detonate the plastic explosive. Flipping a switch, he completed the connection that would allow this process to begin when the desired elevation was achieved. The remaining portion of the hollowed-out chamber inside the hairdryer was filled to capacity with the plastic explosive. The totality of the explosive force was equal to approximately ten sticks of dynamite. This was enough to blow a reasonable size hole in the baggage compartment from anywhere inside that compartment; decompression would take care of the rest.

The pressure-sensing device was set to complete the circuit with the nine-volt battery when the plane reached an elevation of twenty thousand feet. The plane would continue to climb to its cruising altitude somewhere over thirty thousand feet but would never make it. The resulting explosion in the cargo hold would cause sufficient weakening in the main body of the airplane that decompressurization would occur and the plane would simply come apart in flight. Between the explosion caused by decompressurization and the shearing force of the wind at that elevation and speed, within seconds the plane would fall from the sky in thousands of pieces, and everyone aboard would become a statistic.

Manuel was impressed. Other than the one detail where he tried to be more sophisticated than was realistic by camouflaging the bomb as a hairdryer, the device was perfect. Manuel handed the man the small leather pouch he had been carrying. It contained the agreed upon price of 100,000 francs. The bomb maker opened the pouch and looked inside. He did not remove any of the bills or try to count them. These two men had worked together before, and he knew that the total would be correct. Satisfied, he rebuilt the hairdryer, placed it in the suitcase, closed and locked the case, then handed it to Manuel. Throughout the demonstration Manuel had remained silent, and he continued to do so now as he took the suitcase and left without so much as a thank you. The bomb maker walked over to a stack of mannequin heads, selected one, then returned to the headless, naked mannequin on the bench and began to reassemble it.

Out of the store, Manuel walked to the corner, turned right, walked three more blocks, and then climbed into a waiting taxi. "Charles De Gaulle airport," was all Manuel said. The car pulled away from the curb headed for its new destination.

Manuel paid the driver and gave him a normal tip, not wanting to draw any more attention to himself than he might already have done. He climbed out of the taxi and went directly to the terminal check-in counter for the flight to Jerusalem. As he waited in line, he noticed the time was exactly 10:45. The line only had three people in front of him, but there was only one agent handling purchases and check-in. Someone must have taken an early lunch, he thought. Fortunately, everyone in front of him was simply checking in with little or no luggage. After a short five-minute wait, it was Manuel's turn. He checked his lone suitcase, received his seat assignment, then started for the gate. Before he reached passport control, he had disappeared into the milling crowd and was able to exit the terminal unnoticed.

- - - - -

All international luggage would automatically pass through an x-ray machine on its way through the luggage transfer station. Luggage was allowed to collect until a flight was getting ready to be boarded, then all the bags, regardless of destination, would be sent through the machine as quick as possible. Those going on to that flight would be loaded immediately onto a wagon and transported out to the plane. The rest of the luggage would be sorted by flight and set aside. The metal suitcase had arrived barely in time to be included with a group waiting for its turn through the machine.

The baggage handler started tossing bags onto the conveyor, without regard to how they were positioned, and as fast as he could. His supervisor had told him too many times, "The regulations say all international luggage must be x-rayed before it can be placed on a plane. It doesn't say we have to study the damn things. Just get this job done as fast as possible."

Each x-ray machine had to be monitored by a trained technician; someone who had been formally trained to recognize all manner of contraband. However, since this person was also employed by the airline, he had been assigned other duties as well. Consequently, he too would try to speed the process along as best he could. If the contents of the luggage looked suspicious, it was taken off the conveyor as it exited the machine and would be rerun after the rest had passed through. Since the conveyor was seldom stopped, most luggage was viewed on the monitor for no more than a few seconds as it passed under the x-ray machine.

The metal suitcase was tossed on the end of the conveyor and slowly made its way to the machine. As the suitcase passed through the x-ray machine, the technician reached down his leg to swat at a mosquito and momentarily took his eyes off the screen. His eyes returned in time to see the hairdryer in the center of the screen, then the next piece started appearing on the monitor and he turned his attention to the new piece. At the end of the conveyor, the metal suitcase was picked up and tossed on the wagon being loaded for the next departing flight at 11:15.

- - - - -

"When will the police escort arrive? And have they said how many men they will be sending?" The Sheik's personal secretary was asking one of the many people hired to help move the Sheik from destination to destination.

"They are sending just two." The little man responsible for making sure all of the creature comforts the Sheik demanded were available, answered. He was not the one the question was directed toward, but he seldom was. Few people wanted to talk to him because he had the reputation of monopolizing, controlling and never knowing when to end a conversation. The natural result was few people talked directly to him, at or about work, and even fewer spent time with him socially. "It seems the French police decided the Sheik was only worthy of a motorcycle cop at each end of the motorcade," he continued volunteering his own opinion.

"Considering the motorcade, as you call it, consists of only a limousine and a second car, two policemen should be more than adequate."

"Someone of the Sheik's stature should command at least four policemen," the little man whined.

The secretary suddenly realized what he was doing, so he didn't respond to this last remark. The only way to end this pointless conversation was to stop talking. Once the little man realized he was being ignored, he left the room in search of someone who would listen. He stopped just long enough in the next room to review the checklist and verify the Sheik's itinerary, then headed off to check on the Sheik's progress and possibly engage him in a little discussion. The door to the Sheik's room was open, but the secretary stopped just outside and knocked on the wall. The Sheik came to the door, saw his secretary, and invited him into the room.

"I'm here to remind you the flight is scheduled to take off at 11:15 so we will have to be leaving in no more than fifteen minutes. Is there anything I can do for you before we leave?"

The Sheik walked over to the door and closed it. He returned to a seat at the writing table in his room and invited his secretary to sit as well. Before he spoke, he stared into his secretary's eyes for a few minutes. Then, as if he were very tired, he let out a prolonged sigh and began. "Sylvan, we have known each other for many years, not in time, but in spirit. You know my sole purpose in life is to resolve this never-ending dispute between Arab and Jew for all time."

Sylvan opened his mouth to speak, but the Sheik held up his hand, indicating he was to be silent. Sylvan and the Sheik had been brought together by their mutual desire for peace in the Middle East. Both men viewed that portion of the globe as the single most important political arena in the world. Many individual countries were more powerful, but none were more important.

"I received a call this morning that I can not ignore. And I would like you to reschedule my flight for later this afternoon." Sylvan's face gave away his concern for how this might affect the meeting, so the Sheik tried to address that right away. "We will continue with our same plans for the meeting tomorrow. The only change will be we, you, and I, will arrive in Jerusalem this evening rather than this afternoon. I don't see any reason why everyone else should wait for me, so they may go ahead on this morning's flight. Also, since the media continues to follow my every move, do not inform them of my change in plans. The police have already been informed that I will not be inside the limousine they are escorting. Of course, this is a request, but if you agree, I would like you to stay behind and accompany me later this afternoon."

The Sheik paused a moment to allow Sylvan to absorb what he had just been told, then asked him if he had any questions. Sylvan had just one. 'What was so damned important that the Sheik had to cancel his flight?' But he realized that since the Sheik hadn't volunteered that information, it was not the type of question he wanted to hear, so he shook his head no. "If not, I assume you will be going to the airport with everyone else to make sure they all get off on time." Sylvan just shook his head again. "Then I will meet you back here this afternoon." Sylvan knew he had just been dismissed. He got up from his seat and left the room, closing the door on his way out.

Sylvan immediately started gathering everyone to the hotel lobby. The conversation with the Sheik had put him behind schedule and if everyone was going to make the flight they would have to hurry. No one in the party looked even remotely like the Sheik. So, the news media should be able to figure out the Sheik wasn't in the party heading to the airport, he reasoned. Then again, the media is not exactly made up of the intellectual elite so maybe they won't figure it out, he mused. In any event, he would stick someone in the limousine in a feeble attempt to hide the obvious.

The media had previously decided that the real news event would take place tomorrow in Jerusalem. So, there was only a smattering of local reporters to witness the Sheik's departure. None of them noticed that it wasn't the Sheik climbing into the limousine. They knew their audience didn't care, so neither did they. Their departure from the hotel was as normal as any activity could be.

- - - - -

After his secretary left the room the Sheik removed the flowing robes, a mixture in style of Arab desert whites and Levitical priestly robes. The combination left his audiences wondering if his heritage was Arab or Jewish. The result, as calculated, allowed both sides to claim him as their own. And if the truth were known, he truly wanted to be able to fit into either camp.

His father had been a pure-blooded Arab as far back as he could trace his own history. His mother didn't claim the purity of race that his father did. Not because she couldn't, because as far back as she could trace, her own Jewish purity was maintained. However, she had been taught the history of the Jews too well. And she knew the probability that she was truly a pure-blooded Jew was very remote. It never occurred to her to make that claim, because to her it was an abomination to claim purity in race if it were not so. She knew that as far back as Biblical times; her race was often characterized by its inter-marriage tendencies. That was one of the great issues of the time, often sighted by God as one of the reasons for His wrath to be poured out against them. No, his mother couldn't claim purity in race, but her Jewish lineage was the most important thing in her life. Because for her as with any devoted Jew, her lineage was also her religion.

It was odd that parents, raised decidedly Arab and Jewish, could meet, fall in love, marry, and have a child. The result was Sheik Omani, a man that fit the criteria for both races. The most important lesson he learned from his parents had been taught to him through example. They showed him how two, diametrically opposed, religious and geopolitical views could coexist peacefully. They taught him the homeland for one, was the homeland for the other. And if they couldn't learn to compromise, couldn't learn to share the land, the result would be the destruction of both---a lose proposition.

Israel, Syria, Jordan, Lebanon and portions of Saudi Arabia, Egypt, Iraq, Iran, as well as other modern-day countries were only the reflection of modern-day borders. They had little to do with the heritage of the people from a historical perspective. Those lands, regardless of borders were the same homeland for both races. There was not any rational explanation why the two groups could not exist in harmony in the same land. To this end, Sheik Omani was dedicated. His parents raised him with this belief, and he in turn was trying to pass this understanding on to the people of those countries.

The public knew very little about the Sheik's past. What they did know, or thought they knew, was more rumor than fact. It was a carefully constructed and a well-orchestrated image that was projected to the public. Those behind the Sheik wanted all parties to believe he was one of their own. It was believed this could best be accomplished by creating an image that would appeal to both races at their most basic level. To the Arabs the Sheik became a well-educated, wealthy, even powerful Arab of almost royal lineage. His ideas demanded consideration because they were founded in success.

To the Jews throughout the world, he represented a Joseph-like existence in the camp of the enemy. A man of God, who is capable of understanding and living within a heathen environment, and even being successful in that environment. He could exist in the world of the Arabs, without becoming a part of the Arab world. And more importantly, he could live in the world as a Jew without being tainted with the hate of anti-Semitism.

For both, he represented a potential solution to the never-ending war. And except for a few radical groups on both sides, a peaceful, but fair, coexistence was the desire of most working-class Arabs and Jews. He knew the solution had to be founded on mutual ground, literally. Since both factions viewed large areas of the Middle East as their birthright, territorial rights to the land must be negotiated. But those rights had to encompass a wide range of uses, both secular and religious, both Arab and Jew. No man or country had been able to come close to accomplishing that. Jimmy Carter is credited with some measure of success based on the camp David Accords, but that success was more ethereal than real. It would take someone with a unique mix of understanding for both views, and that understanding was at least perceived to exist in the Sheik.

With the robes removed, the Sheik was able to dress more comfortably in sport coat and slacks. The robes served a purpose in maintaining a public image, but they were simply too obvious to allow him to traipse around the city without drawing attention to himself. After changing he left the hotel for the meeting with his parents. His mother had called early that morning requesting that his father and her be able to talk with him privately before the news conference in Jerusalem.

- - - - -

The gate area was getting crowded by the time Sylvan was able to get his small entourage there. A Frenchman had created quite a stir in his pursuit of a young lady that resulted in a delay at passport control. No one had been able to get through until a security guard removed the man from the area. He had managed to occupy the attention of everyone there, effectively stopping all passengers from getting to their gates. Getting everyone through passport control had taken a little longer than the time he allotted. Still, the boarding had just begun when they arrived at the gate. Sylvan stayed at the gate area until everyone in his party was on board the plane, then left.

Peter, Joan and the two boys had managed to get all six seats in the row to themselves, and the two boys spread out to take advantage of the extra room. Each had laid claim to a window and was giving a description to the other of what was happening on his side of the plane. Since both were talking at the same time, neither heard what the other was saying. Peter and Joan were just happy the two boys weren't fighting with each other anymore and were just sitting there enjoying the tranquil noise.

John had been assigned a seat next to the old lady and was spending his time reassuring her that air travel was indeed safe. He repeated the oft quoted 'flying is the safest mode of travel' statement, but that didn't seem to impress her very much. As far as she was concerned, it wasn't natural to get something this heavy to defy gravity and fly. John decided on a new approach: If he couldn't convince her, it was safe, he would take her mind off of it by talking about anything and everything else he could think of. It seemed to work. After a few minutes she was busy telling him her life story. As she spoke, she was smiling, laughing at her own jokes and describing everything with her hands. She didn't even notice when the plane was pushed back from the gate and began taxiing to the runway.

Desmond, being an avid smoker who sometimes survived on Gaulliet cigarettes instead of food, had requested an aisle seat in smoking and found himself alone with the three seats on his side of the aisle and one row separating him from the lavatories. Shortly after he sat down a very attractive middle-aged woman took the window seat across the aisle from him. While she settled herself into the seat, first putting a piece of luggage in the overhead bin, then sliding another under the middle seat in front of her, she would periodically glance at Desmond to see if he was watching. After the flow of passengers coming into the plane slowed to a trickle, the woman got up. As she was getting out of the row she looked directly at Desmond as if to invite him to speak, then disappeared into one of the lavatories. This did not go unnoticed by Desmond. He decided he might take the opportunity during the flight to spend some time trying to get to know this woman. Whenever Desmond found himself in the position to flirt with a woman, other than his wife, he did.

The plane taxied out to the runway and joined the small line of planes waiting for their turn to take off. Each plane, in its turn, was given clearance for take off and did so. There were no prevailing winds to dictate which runways to use, but there was sufficient air traffic to justify using one runway for take offs and another for landings. Consequently, the line disappeared rapidly and soon the plane was accelerating down the runway for take off. The take off went without a hitch and shortly thereafter the no smoking light was turned off.

Desmond, and his newfound companion in the row across the aisle, immediately reached for a cigarette to smoke. Desmond jumped at the opportunity to strike up a conversation by hurrying over to offer her a light.

Once the angle of ascent lessened enough to allow for movement in the cabin, the stewardesses began getting ready to serve drinks and a small snack. The plane had now been in the air for almost twenty minutes and was approaching the border between France and Switzerland. They were fast approaching a range of the south-central Alps that would force them to climb to their cruising altitude quickly. They had just passed the French border when the pressure device completed the circuit and the capacitor began collecting the charge. Within sixty seconds it had reached capacity and ignited the plastic explosive.

The explosion did just what it was designed to do; it ripped a one-foot diameter hole in the fuselage. Everyone on board heard the explosion, but due to the muffling effect of the wind and the added sound of the engines, they did not realize what had happened. Inside the cockpit the pilot and copilot heard the sound and noticed panel alarms starting to light across their control panels. The plane started to decelerate then lurched violently to one side. The pilot increased the throttle and started to push forward on the wheel to stabilize the aircraft. He was hoping he could buy a little time to give himself a chance to figure out what was happening.

"What the hell is going on?" the pilot asked no one in particular. "Notify the control tower at Geneva we've got problems"

Everything inside the cargo hold was being sucked out while the fuselage wall around the hole continued to rip apart. The hole was increasing in size with each passing second, and the sound of wind was beginning to be heard inside the cabin. It grew steadily louder, and slowly some of the passengers were becoming aware there was a problem. But they still weren't able to analyze if their fears were well founded or not.

Soon, the plane began to shudder uncontrollably, and the pilot realized he had lost control of the aircraft. Whatever happened, he thought, neutralized his ability to fly the plane. He couldn't bank right or left, increase, or decrease altitude. His last bastion of control was limited to the throttle when he realized the plane was coming apart around him.

The sound of the fuselage shredding apart underneath and around them was the last sound anyone heard as the plane came apart. No one knew what happened and within a few short minutes after the initial explosion, they disappeared from radar.

- - - - -

"An Air France flight, on its way to Jerusalem, disappeared today in the south-central portion of the Alps over Switzerland. We have an unconfirmed report that the plane suffered a rapid decompressurization and came apart in flight. Terrorist activities are suspected but have not been confirmed. No group has come forward to claim responsibility for the disaster."

"Swiss officials are searching for the area by plane looking for any sign of the wreckage. One Swiss official made the remark 'It looks like we might have another Lockerbie here.' Air France was quick to deny they had been warned of a possible bombing on the flight and said drawing parallels to the Lockerbie incident were premature."

"We will continue to keep you informed of the developments as they occur."

-For the living know they will die, but the dead do not know anything.

"We have an update on the Air France plane that crashed in a sparsely populated area of the Swiss Alps. Swiss officials have been able to determine the general line of the debris and are slowly making progress throughout the area to search for any survivors. The debris is scattered in an oval shaped area, approximately fifty miles long and thirty miles wide, thirty miles east of Lausanne, and north of Lake Geneva. Swiss officials have located a large portion of the mid-section of the fuselage, and are locating many smaller portions of the plane, as well as luggage and portions of bodies. A temporary morgue has been set up in a school building in the closest city, Chatel-Denis."

"Air France officials continue to deny any knowledge of a bomb threat prior to the flight. However, Swiss officials have issued a statement saying, in effect, that a bomb is believed to be the cause of the crash. The in-flight recorder has been recovered, and it is speculated that Swiss officials have found some indication, based on the recording, that an explosion did occur during the flight."

"No group has come forward to claim responsibility for the crash of the Air France plane. However, it has just been learned, Sheik Omani was originally scheduled to be on this flight, but a last-minute change in his personal itinerary resulted in only his staff making the flight. The Sheik and his personal secretary had been rescheduled on a later flight. The Sheik was supposed to travel to Jerusalem to take part in a joint news conference with representatives from the terrorist group led by Jihad Nadu, the Zealots, as well as a representative of the Israeli government. That news conference has been indefinitely postponed, at the Sheik's request. The Sheik is presently enroute to the crash site headquarters in Chatel-Denis. And has sent personal messages to families of those in his party that were on the downed plane."

Manuel walked over to the television in his hotel room and switched it off.

－ － － － －

"Where the hell was Dent?" Tom had summoned Jim into his office at Langley the minute he heard the news of the plane crash. He had been aware that the Sheik was booked on the flight, and also, that the Sheik had not been on it. "This was exactly the thing we hired Eric to prevent. Have you been able to locate him yet?" He yelled at Jim the second he had walked through the door.

This was the angriest Jim had seen Tom in quite some time. Jim knew the first question was rhetorical, but the second question was not, and Tom wasn't going to like the answer to that question either. "We have every agent in Europe looking for him. Any sign of him or Steve, and you'll be the first to know. But you know as well as I do, If Eric decides to go underground, the only way we will find him is if we get very lucky."

"I don't believe in luck, and you know that."

"We lost him two days ago. He's also made it clear that Steve will not be allowed to contact us until Eric decides it's time. We are just going to have to wait until he decides to resurface. Regardless of what happened, we should be thankful the Sheik wasn't on the plane. This buys all of us another chance."

"I don't care how you do it Jim, but I want to speak to Eric."

Jim would usually try to appease Tom any way he could, but there was no way he could honor this request. So, for one of the few times in his career, he stood up to Tom. "Tom, you can be as unreasonable as you want. But I can assure you that even if we find Eric; he won't talk to you. Anything you want to say to him will have to go through me... or possibly Steve," He added, then continued. "Assuming Eric hasn't dumped him yet. Eric took this assignment against his better judgment, and for his own reasons. You can choose to believe otherwise, but I assure you of one thing: You hold no power over him."

"It was Eric's responsibility to neutralize Jacque, and it's obvious he hasn't done that yet. When do you suppose he'll get around to it? Before or after the Sheik's dead?" The disgust in Tom's voice was directed at Jim as much as it was Eric.

Jim decided to tell Tom something he had just heard an hour ago but had not been able to confirm. "Tom," Jim's voice took on an eerie quality that caught Tom's attention. Up until now, Tom had nervously been pacing back and forth behind his desk. But now he stopped and stood facing Jim.

"Yes?"

"You need to know that we can't prove what I'm about to tell you, but we are reasonably sure it will be proven true shortly. One of our agents in London was able to confirm Jacque was in the city for the last two days. In fact, he was in London the same day Eric was there. The agent has been able to tail him the whole time, and he feels positive there was no way Jacque could be responsible for the bombing. One more thing, we checked his file for confirmation, but found out something we already knew. Jacque has never used a bomb during any assassination."

"You're implying someone else is trying to assassinate the Sheik?"

"Precisely."

"That doesn't make sense. Jacque's been hired to kill the Sheik, but he doesn't even try. Meanwhile, some third party, with no apparent motive, and who we weren't even aware existed, tries. He or she, plants a bomb on a commercial flight, kills maybe one hundred innocent people, but misses the target. Not because the target survived, but because he wasn't even there in the first place. Jim..." Tom paused, completing one lap of his pacing sequence before he continued. "I'm not inclined to believe Jacque wasn't behind this. Our agents are good, but if Jacque wanted to, he could make the arrangements without our agents finding out. And Jacque's an assassin. Since when do assassins get particular on the modus operandi?" Tom asked rhetorically. "Simply put, don't waste time looking for a third party. Concentrate your efforts on how Jacque was able to pull this off and make sure it doesn't happen again. And somehow you need to get hold of Eric and get an update. We can't have him floating around Europe uncontrolled. Or at least not without knowing where he is or what the hell he's up to."

Tom stopped pacing long enough to seat himself at his desk. Jim recognized this as the telltale sign that the meeting was over, so he left Tom's office. Tom waited for fifteen minutes, and then he too left the office, signing out as he exited the building. He didn't head home, because working where he did, at the level he was, gave him access to information that was not readily available to others at Langley. He knew exactly where the monitored phones in the surrounding area were, and he needed some privacy. He drove due west just over forty miles until he came to a Laundromat.

The Laundromat served a small, unincorporated village that looked like a page out of a 1940's issue of Look magazine. The newest building there couldn't have been less than forty years old, and the building that housed the Laundromat must have been built around the turn of the century. It was an old, one-story brick building, and the mortar between many of the bricks was almost completely weathered away. The clay tiles around the parapet wall had been replaced with a metal cap through the years in a piecemeal fashion that created a perforated look to the roofline. The decorative masonry work that bordered the walls was still relatively intact. Except for a few bricks that had fallen out, and the resulting gaps that had been filled with a lighter shade of mortar as prevention against further decay, the building had maintained its turn-of-the-century charm.

Inside the Laundromat a row of washers lined one wall opposite a row of dryers. The washers were the old front load style with a window in the front door so one could be mesmerized by the continually changing pattern of the churning clothes and suds. The dryers, just as old as the washers, were commercial grade dryers that almost burned the water out of the wet clothes. On the wall above the washers, was a sign that outlined the rules of the Laundromat for the patrons. The sign was faded so badly that one could barely make them out. They were legible only if the light hit the board just right and there was enough time to meticulously study them. Of course, the average patron had plenty of time for that, but not Tom. A sign over the folding table gave the prices for washing, 25 cents, and for drying, 10 cents. At the far back corner of the Laundromat above the door to what was really just the janitor's closet filled with cleaning supplies was a sign that read 'Manager's Office.' On the wall next to the door was a pay phone.

Tom took a quick look around to make sure no one was in the Laundromat then headed straight back to the pay phone. He gave the operator the AT&T calling card number, then waited for someone to answer. As the phone at the other end started ringing, he played with the peeling paint on the wall in an effort to paint in reverse. After the eighth ring, just as Tom was getting ready to hang up, he heard.

"Guten Tag."

"What the hell's going on? He was supposed to wait until the news conference." Tom was livid, almost yelling into the phone. Then he heard someone come into the Laundromat through the front door at the other end of the room. He struggled to gain control of his anger as he waited for a response.

"No need to get excited. We have everything under control."

"Are you saying you knew he would try this early?" Tom tried to whisper, but his anger caused his voice to steadily rise throughout the question. The woman, who had come into the Laundromat and was filling a washing machine with a load of clothes, turned, and looked at him as he finished speaking.

"No. We didn't expect this to happen quite so soon. But we have sent word to him to wait, at least until the news conference is well under way. You should remember, we do not know for sure that he was responsible."

Tom was visibly upset but managed to control his voice this time. "What do you mean, you're not sure who's responsible? We can't afford mistakes at this point."

"I am simply saying that it could have been a real terrorist activity. There are other groups that would like to see the Sheik dead too, and this method certainly isn't original. Don't be so paranoid."

By this time the woman had started the washing machine. Giving Tom a final look, she left the Laundromat. Tom started in again. "This doesn't have anything to do with paranoia, and you know it. If anything would have happened to the Sheik before the conference, we would have lost the effect. Our entire effort would have been wasted. You and your merry band of oilmen would have nothing to show for your investment. And the rest of the world would be without..." Tom allowed his silence to finish the thought.

"What else would you like me to say, Tom? We are taking precautions to make sure this doesn't happen again. And that is assuming it was Jacque in the first place. If it was someone else, there is nothing we can do."

Maybe he was right. Maybe it wasn't Jacque, but rather some fanatical terrorist group who's timing was just poor. Tom stopped talking long enough to consider what the voice on the other end was saying. He had been one of the best analysts the agency ever had, and even though he was an administrator now, Tom knew he should approach the situation analytically. If he relied on his innate abilities, he would draw the right conclusion.

While Tom was thinking, the voice at the other end remained quiet. Silently waiting for Tom to respond. Finally, Tom broke the silence. "When is your next meeting?"

"In two days at the Grand hotel in London. Why do you ask?"

"Is everyone expected to be there?"

"Everyone except Antonio. In fact, that brings up a question I've been meaning to ask you. Is there any reason to replace him?" Tom started to interrupt but was unsuccessful and was forced to wait until the voice finished talking. "We don't feel a presence in that part of the world is that advantageous to the group at this point in time. Our inclination is to let the group function with the five remaining members and only consider a replacement if, after a trial period, we feel it is warranted."

"You're ahead of me. What happened to Antonio?"

"American intelligence, a contradiction in terms if you ask me." Before Tom, could respond the voice continued, "Antonio was killed by a rival drug cartel a few days ago. Everyone else knew, I'm surprised you didn't."

Tom ignored the cut, then answered the original question about replacing Antonio. "We may have to replace him. I'll reevaluate our position and let you know before the next meeting. If there's nothing else, I'll be going."

"It was your nickel." Click!

- - - - -

Sheik Omani watched the news in horror. He couldn't believe his entire entourage had been killed in the sabotage of the flight to Jerusalem. The local police had notified him immediately upon his arrival at the airport in Jerusalem about the tragedy. He had managed to catch an early afternoon flight and had not heard of the crash before he left Paris. What would cause anyone to be so fanatical about anything that killing innocent bystanders could even be considered, he thought? He knew the response that 'Allah had willed it' would be mouthed throughout most terrorist camps in the Middle East. However, if they were after him, they failed. So, his brothers would appropriately chastise whoever was responsible.

Sylvan had watched the news report with Sheik Omani in silence. Finally, he broke his own silence by asking the Sheik how they should handle the logistics of the news conference and the funerals without appearing crass. "Since we are already in Jerusalem, and the news conference is set for tomorrow, do you want to postpone it or go ahead as scheduled?"

Sheik Omani stared straight ahead at the television, mesmerized by the broadcaster's account about the alleged bombing and subsequent plane crash. The news crews televising the crash sight were providing gruesomely graphic pictures of the crash scene. Pieces of clothing, luggage and metal were strewn about as if a wind had littered the countryside with the remnants of a picnic that had been left to the elements to recycle. Except these things were not paper plates and cups and bits of spoiled food, but rather the remains of human lives destroyed by an act of terrorism. The Sheik's hatred for the situation in Israel and the surrounding countries fed upon this scene of destruction until he rededicated his life to resolving this issue forever.

He answered Sylvan's question with a renewed commitment to the task. "I will reschedule the news conference as soon as possible, while showing appropriate respect for the lives lost in this disaster. In the meantime, you travel to Chatel-Denis and act as my official representative at the site of this destruction caused by Satan himself. Your first priority will be to gather whatever remains you can of those from our group. Second, you will locate as much of their personal effects as you can and gather them together for shipment to the next of kin. I will prepare your way with a communiqué to the Swiss police and give you a letter to carry with you. The letter will identify you as my personal representative to anyone that questions your right to be there. Finally, gather as much information about the plane crash that you can. We must determine the who's, and the whys of this for ourselves and respond accordingly. Do you have any questions?" Sheik Omani stopped as abruptly as he had started. He had not looked up at Sylvan the entire time he was speaking. Even now he continued to watch the carnage that was being played across the television screen for the world to see.

"No.... I believe I understand what you want me to do." Sylvan waited a moment for the Sheik to respond, but when none was forthcoming, he quietly left the room. He had never seen the Sheik so completely enthralled before, but then he had never known the Sheik to have experienced death so intimately either. Before this, violence and death had always been removed by distance and the nameless faces of lives unknown. This time the faces were those of friends and coworkers. Names that were familiar. And the Sheik's reaction was obviously one of great pain.

After Sylvan left Sheik Omani continued to stare at the television, waiting for any new reports on the incident. It was early morning before the Sheik fell asleep. The television was still on, and he was still sitting in the same chair he had been in when Sylvan left that afternoon.

─ ─ ─ ─ ─

Jacque had received word that Eric had left his friend Josef and was on his way to Frankfurt. He had not been able to gather any information on Eric's traveling companion, Steve, other than he was with the Agency. He had been following Eric's travels into and out of the Soviet Union but had no intention of confronting Eric yet. The last agent he had disposed of was typical of the Agency; well trained, but not particularly inventive. Eric, on the other hand, was best left alone until Jacque had the time to devote his complete attention to him. It was better to wait for Eric to get within range on his own, without interference. Regardless, when the opportunity to deal with Eric presented itself, or was forced upon him, he would be ready. He had always respected Eric as his equal and saw no reason for questioning that judgment now. Sooner or later, he would have to deal with Eric, but for the time being he would simply keep track of him.

It was time for Jacque to set into motion his plans for Sheik Omani.

─ ─ ─ ─ ─

"Do you think the plane crash had anything to do with Jacque and the Sheik? Or was it like the news media is alluding to? Just some fanatical terrorist group that has no respect for lives, even innocent ones." Steve was asking for Eric's opinion as he watched the German news coverage of the day's events. Steve understood maybe ten words in German, but he was sitting on the edge of his bed watching the broadcast as if he understood every word. He had been glued to the TV since they had checked-in earlier, and felt he was actually understanding a large portion of the broadcast.

Eric had not filled him in on any of the details of his private talk with Josef, keeping the wedge clearly visible between the two of them. When they left Josef, Eric had not told Steve where they were going. Once they arrived in Frankfurt, Steve wasn't informed where they would be staying either. Not knowing why, they had come to Frankfurt, or Eric's immediate plans for the future, gave Steve sufficient reason to bury himself in the news coverage of the plane crash. Steve was irritated but had come to the realization that Eric was only going to tell him what Eric wanted him to know, and it was best not to press the issue. Every time he started to press Eric for more detailed information, Eric would simply clam up. Steve was slowly concluding that he would get more information from Eric if he simply left him alone.

"I can assure you that Jacque had nothing to do with that attempt on the Sheik's life." Eric finally answered.

"What makes you think it was an attempt on the Sheik's life?" Steve thought he recognized a crack in Eric's defense mechanism and decided, against his better judgment, to pry as much information as he could out of him while he was willing to talk. This was the first time today that Eric actually responded to something Steve had asked. Usually, any comments or questions by Steve were ignored. Eric initiated conversations. It was not the other way around.

"Well," Eric paused and Steve started to worry he had decided to end the conversation even though it hadn't really started. But before he could think of something to say, Eric continued. "If you look at the history of these types of incidents, they are always directed at some organization or country. Take the Lockerbie incident for instance, it was directed specifically at the U. S. government, trying to make the point that no one was afraid of the U. S. The hostage taking, throughout the 80's crossed national lines, directed at specific countries. The embassy takeover in Iran, and even the killing of athletes at the 1972 Olympics in Munich are all examples of the same thing. Planes are blown up to make a point. In this case, I think it's apparent they don't want the Sheik to continue his efforts toward peace in the Middle East. Actually, killing the Sheik may have been a secondary benefit, the primary motive was probably to get him to stop his efforts. There's no doubt it was an attempt on the Sheik's life, possibly to scare him, but Jacque wasn't responsible."

"You seem awfully sure it wasn't Jacque." Steve interjected the statement, hoping to keep Eric talking.

"Jacque and I go back quite a few years. In fact, in the early days, before Jacque decided there was more money to be made killing for hire rather than killing for principle, we actually worked together on a few assignments. What one has to understand about Jacque is: He has some very strict standards. The first one is innocent bystanders are part of the equation."

Steve took a chance and interrupted Eric, "What do you mean by 'part of the equation'?"

"We, Jacque and I, treated every assignment as having a distinct and unique best solution, not unlike mathematics. We felt innocent bystanders should remain innocent bystanders and that required very selective methods. Whatever method was chosen had to be able to affect only the target. In other words, we couldn't use a shotgun in a crowd so to speak. It forced us to be very accurate."

"That seems like an awfully civilized approach to a barbaric task. How far did you carry that rule?"

"As far as we could. It was paramount that we neutralized the target, not someone near the target. As agents for a government, it wasn't done as a noble act, but because killing the wrong person or worse, innocent bystanders, would have serious ramifications if the public became aware of the incident. As a result, we both settled on methods that required proximity to the target or extreme accuracy. We became proficient in Tai Kwon Do, the use of most hand combat weapons and firearms. We were the best in the business, Jacque for the French government, and me for the U. S. government. When Jacque decided to make a little money doing this kind of work, a mercenary for spies you might say, these techniques had become habits. For the most part his work was still under the umbrella of covert activities, even though he was no longer employed solely by the French government."

"I had been briefed about his start as an agent, but no mention was made about this interim step."

"I never quite understood why they portray Jacque as defecting from 'good to evil', unless they're trying to project some false image intentionally. The fact is Jacque evolved very slowly from a highly regarded agent, one of the best in the world, to a hired assassin. He became disenchanted and confused about why some people would be identified as targets for neutralization, and others, by a very arbitrary method in his mind, were not. This apparent contradiction in categorizing people affected Jacque deeply. My personal opinion is that in order for Jacque to remain in this line of work, it was necessary for him to remove himself from what he considered part of the process of identifying the target. By becoming a contract killer he could ensure innocents were not lost due to carelessness. And he could rationalize that he had nothing to do with the decision-making process of determining who would die. He could wash his hands of the ethics of the business. He was simply paid to do a job,"

"The killing was alright? It was the method of identifying the person that was morally wrong?" Steve asked incredulously.

"It's not as strange as it sounds. As long as anyone of us can rationalize an acceptable reason for what we do, we can continue performing. The minute we start to question the ethics of our actions in broader terms, it will very quickly become an albatross around our own neck. In simple terms, if we have to justify every act, based on its inherent morality, we would either go crazy or refuse every assignment. Remember, Jacque understood the need, he just couldn't come to grips with the who."

"This same morality is one of the reasons he has become one of the best, if not the best, assassin in the world. He is hired knowing that the target will be neutralized with the least possible loss of human life. Most people that hire assassins are not looking for the Rambo style of killer. You know, the one that takes everyone within a mile of the target out with the target. Most of the time they don't want unnecessary attention drawn to the act and taking half a dozen innocent people along with the hit will get you just that. They want a very neat removal of their problem, and with Jacque that's what they get."

"It wasn't always that way, was it?" Steve had been briefed on the reason why the Agency felt confident they could lure Eric back into the fold for this one last job. He decided that since Eric had been talking at length with little encouragement it might be the time to bring up that tender subject.

"No, ...it wasn't." Eric stopped talking and seemed to withdraw into himself. Steve quickly realized his intrusion into Eric's private domain had probably concluded the conversation prematurely. What Steve had been told, and he had hoped to confirm both for himself and the Agency, was how Jacque had become responsible for the death of Eric's wife. Since Eric quit the Agency after her death and refused to offer any explanation as to how or why it happened, the Agency had to rely on itself to piece together the story.

It was common knowledge that Jacque had been hired to neutralize an American Colonel who had been given credit with subverting an Iranian military action during the Iran/Iraq conflict in 1986. The Iranians believed his intervention had prevented Iran from establishing a decided advantage over the Iraqis that could have led to an outright Iranian victory. The Ayatollah Khomeini then issued a directive to have the American Colonel put to death for interference with the divine will of God.

Most Iranians make very poor assassins due to their flare for suicidal methods. Consequently, a call for volunteers went out over the airwaves of Iran. However, the Prime Minister directed his people to hire Jacque and ensure the Ayatollah's directive was successfully carried out. By the time the negotiations with Jacque had been completed and he accepted the assignment, the Colonel, a John Stevens, had been reassigned state side.

As luck would have it, Colonel John Stevens was Eric's wife's uncle. She had spent a number of summer vacations with her uncle at different bases throughout the world, and a very close relationship developed. Her parents decided the opportunity to expose her to different cultures by visiting her uncle during the summer was too good to pass up. So, every summer, from the time she was twelve until her second year in college, she would spend at least one month of her summer vacation with her uncle and his family. She was an only child, except when she became a part of her uncle's family. While visiting her Uncle she became child number four in a family with three other children. She grew to cherish the time with her adopted family. The Colonel and his wife became a second set of parents to her. And that relationship continued after college, then during her marriage to Eric.

Jacque had no way of knowing how close the relationship between Colonel Stevens and Eric's wife had become, or even the fact they were related. If he had, he probably would have turned down the assignment. When he was hired for this particular job, he was simply told the target's name, given a picture and some cursory background information. That was the only information the Iranians could supply at the time. It was standard operating procedure, and Jacque had little reason to investigate further on his own, other than what was necessary to complete the assignment. With the deal settled Jacque headed to the U. S. to fulfill his objective.

At the time of the assassination Eric was still working for the Agency. He was traveling in Eastern Europe where his latest assignment had taken him. Meanwhile, Jacque caught up with the Colonel in Washington D. C. When the Colonel had returned to the States, he was reassigned to the Pentagon. His wife and family had temporarily settled in Omaha, a location they were comfortable with because of a previous base assignment. Since the school year was almost over, the Colonel had gone ahead to the Pentagon without his family. His family would join him after the school year was completed.

Eric and his wife set up house outside of Laurel, Maryland. This allowed his wife relatively easy access to her job as a journalist for the Washington Post and provided him very easy access to the facilities of NSA, at Ft. Meade. Eric had an office inside NSA's main building, which was used on an infrequent basis. The office gave him instant access to the secure community at NSA and Langley, while providing reasonable proximity to his wife's job. Everyone was satisfied with the arrangement.

With news that the Colonel had been transferred to the Pentagon, Eric's wife immediately insisted he stay with her, at least until he was able to find appropriate living quarters for him and his family. She reasoned that with both of them working in D. C., and Eric out on assignment; she had the room, could use the company, and would love the chance to repay for the many great summer vacations she had as a child in his many homes. Even if the Colonel wanted to refuse, he knew better and agreed to stay with his niece.

For the next few weeks, it became a routine for them to drive into D. C. together. The Colonel would drop his niece off at work and continue on to the Pentagon. When the day was over, he would return to pick her up, and they would ride home together. What they didn't realize during the last week was Jacque was monitoring their every move; establishing patterns and schedules, so he could assassinate the Colonel without hurting the girl. Jacque claims he had no idea who the girl was, and some theorize that if he had, he would have refused the assignment.

For some unknown reason Jacque, whose tendency was to use fire-arms or other handheld weapons that required accurate target selection, chose an explosive device that was triggered by pressure. He assumed it offered ample protection because whenever the girl was in the car, she drove. The mechanism was placed under the driver's seat and set so that the pressure needed to detonate the bomb would require the driver to weigh at least 200 pounds. Eric's wife was a mere 115 pounds, so the theory would appear safe in practice. Jacque expected the explosion to take place outside the office doors of the Washington Post after the girl had left the car and the Colonel had walked around to the driver's side and taken his place behind the wheel. Throughout his surveillance, this had been the most reliable pattern. To further protect the girl from unnecessary harm, Jacque had built into the trigger mechanism a two-minute time delay. This was based on the average time it took the girl to say good-bye and get far enough away from the vehicle to be completely safe.

This particular day, the Colonel had to be to work earlier than usual and instead of dropping off his niece at the newspaper, she dropped him off at the Pentagon and took the car to work. That shouldn't have been a problem, but Jacque knew when routines were disrupted, for any reason, plans based on those routines often went awry.

Jacque had originally planned to observe the explosion from a booth in the all-night diner across the street from the usual drop-off location. The booths were lined along the front of the diner with large windows that started at table height and reached to the ceiling. The crowds on the sidewalk were not large enough at that hour of the morning to block his view. This would allow him a relatively unobstructed view of his work while he ate breakfast. However with the Colonel's change in plans, Jacque had to modify his own as well. He decided to spend his day baby-sitting the vehicle in the parking ramp. He knew he wouldn't have the chance to remove the bomb, so all he could do was monitor the situation as it unfolded. About five in the afternoon, an hour after he had expected to see the girl, he noticed the Colonel and the girl come walking into the parking ramp together. Obviously, the Colonel had decided to meet her at the newspaper and either caught the bus or a ride from someone else. She walked to the passenger's side, unlocked the door, then headed around to the driver's side door. Jacque was relieved. It always bothered him when his target could not be taken out cleanly, and he had just come way too close to be taking the girl's life with the Colonel's. He immediately decided he would remove the bomb that night, then develop a new plan that wouldn't endanger the girl.

The two arrived home at six-thirty and disappeared into the house. Based on their usual schedule, Jacque knew he wouldn't be able to go after the bomb until eleven or twelve that night. He decided to head over to a local drive-in, get something to eat and wait for the two of them to go to bed.

Shortly after Jacque had left, the Colonel and Eric's wife came out the side door and headed for the car parked in the driveway. As they walked, a few feet apart, they were talking back and forth, when she tossed the keys up into the air for the Colonel to catch. He grabbed the keys, walked to the driver's side door, and got behind the wheel. They both strapped their seatbelt, then he backed the car out of the driveway. They were just pulling away from the house when the explosion occurred

The previously tranquil setting of the neighborhood was shattered. What was left of the car after the explosion was engulfed in a bright orange flame licking at the air. There was absolutely no way anyone could survive. Neighbors came rushing to front windows and a few gathered up enough courage to step outside to get a closer look at what was happening. A few even called 911, although it was too late for that to do any good.

A small crowd quickly gathered on both sides of the street talking furiously while watching the car burn. They weren't quite sure who was in it or how it happened. What remained of the car was no longer recognizable. The paint was completely burned off by the time the fire had burned down enough for people to get close to it. The misshapen body, a result of the explosion and subsequent fire made the body style indistinguishable. Still, no one realized it belonged to one of their neighbors.

Within a few minutes of the first 911 call the police arrived. They immediately cordoned off both ends of the street. Intuitively they knew they arrived too late and there wouldn't be any survivors. Now it was just a matter of containing the crowd and ensuring no one else would get hurt. As soon as the fire was put out, they could begin the gruesome task of removing the bodies and trying to determine exactly what happened.

Seconds after the police arrived, both a fire truck and an ambulance drove up. The firemen managed to contain the fire quickly, even though it had spread to the blacktop street when the gas tank had exploded spewing gas in an arc fifteen feet from the rear of the car. Eventually the fire got hot enough to ignite the asphalt in the road, a rare but not unheard-of occurrence. Once the road fire was put out, they were able to douse the remaining fire that continued to consume the car and its occupants. Jacque, returning from the drive-in, saw the commotion as he prepared to turn down the street. Instead of turning, he continued straight for a block, then parked his car and walked back to the police barricade.

He watched as the fire was finally put out completely. A police-man and a fireman approached the burned wreckage from opposite sides. Both men carefully approached the car. Their eyes scanned the burned-out vehicle looking for any sign the fire might flare up again, ready to get back quickly if it did. The policeman got to car first, but immediately turned away and started to retch. The fireman, having seen this type of disfiguring death on too many occasions before was able to control himself. He looked inside the car to assess who or what had been inside. He waved his colleagues back from the car as he peered inside, fearing they would approach before he was able to determine if it was safe. What he saw came close causing him to react the same way the policeman had. This was worse than he had expected.

He hadn't felt this way since the first time he had seen someone die in a fire when he wasn't much more than a rookie. The passenger, whoever or whatever it was, had been burned beyond recognition even to point of not being able to determine if it was a man or woman. The driver, from the waist down, didn't exist. The fireman walked around the car to assist the policeman back to the curb, and to give himself time to regain his own composure. Back at the curb, policemen, firemen and the ambulance attendants formed a big circle. Their discussion centered on how to go about the cleanup without disrupting any evidence.

Jacque continued to watch the investigation and cleanup until the crowd started to thin. At that point he decided to leave. He had become accustomed to death: In his line of work, it was a requisite. However, he still had problems dealing with his emotions when a bystander was taken with the target, an unusual trait for an assassin. Right now, Jacque was emotionally drained. In his eyes, he had failed miserably. Whoever the girl was didn't matter: She should have been protected. The Colonel, on the other hand, was a job deserving of every dollar he was being paid.

Jacque returned to his motel room, which was little more than a bed with a roof overhead. He had located the motel when he first arrived in the States. It was situated just north of the beltway around Washington D. C. on a side road grossly undersized for the traffic it was expected to carry. It afforded him reasonable proximity to D. C., where they worked, and Laurel, Md., where they were living. The motel offered absolutely no perks. The room had nothing more than the bed and a color TV for furniture, but without the benefit of a mint on the bed before retiring. The only positive thing going for the room was its cleanliness, a rarity in this price range.

Early the next morning Jacque left his hotel room and went across the street to the all-night diner to purchase the morning newspaper. While he plugged the box with the proper change, he scanned the morning headlines looking for some mention of the bombing. The top half of the front page didn't mention anything, so as soon as he had the paper in his hands, he unfolded it. He scanned the remaining headlines on the front page. Near the bottom, on the left side of the paper, he saw the half-inch headline, which read:

COLONEL STEVENS AND NIECE
KILLED IN TERRORIST ATTACK

This is what he was looking for. Confident he was acting suspicious, he folded the newspaper, placed it under his arm, and walked back to the motel.

Once inside the room, Jacque started reading the article. The headline provided the official confirmation that he was looking for. His first objective had been met---he'd killed the right man. He was always just a little apprehensive until the news media confirmed the proper kill had taken place. The next detail was to establish what clues, if any, the police had regarding the bombing.

He read the article carefully, paying particular attention to any comments made by the police and any editorializing done by the writer. Quite often the reporter is provided information that he is asked not to repeat in his write-up, but which affects how he actually writes the article. In this case there wasn't anything that wasn't explicitly stated. The headline provided the most obvious detail by relating the death as a terrorist attack. Although terrorists weren't directly responsible for the attack, the State Department was right in its assessment that the act was a result of the Colonel's involvement in the Middle East. The article briefly described how the Colonel had intervened in the Iran/Iraq war, and the subsequent call for his assassination by the Ayatollah. It did not directly blame any known terrorist group or the Iranian government, but it stated unequivocally the State Department's belief that ultimate blame would be placed there.

Toward the end of the article, it started to describe the history of the Colonel's career and his relationship to the girl. Jacque continued to read, more out of curiosity than any need for more information. However, the last paragraph of the article caught Jacque's attention, jolting him back to reality.

> Cathy Dent, the wife of Eric Dent and a news reporter for this newspaper, was the woman killed with Colonel Stevens last evening. Cathy was the Colonel's niece, and he was staying at her home prior to moving his family east this summer. Cathy had been an employee of the newspaper for four years and covered local D. C. government news. She had been married to Eric Dent, a federal government employee, for five years.

Jacque became painfully aware that he had just killed the wife of an old nemesis and friend. His investigation of the Colonel did not include the Colonel's extended family; consequently, Jacque had not been aware of Cathy's last name. Even if he had known the name, he doubted he would have considered the possibility she would be related to Eric. The last thing he expected was that there would be any connection between her and anyone he might know. Certainly not someone he still considered a friend.

"You should know," Eric began, "I need to talk to Jacque before I take him out. And I'll kill you if you get in my way."

Eric hadn't said anything for the last fifteen minutes. He had stood at the window, just staring out at the street. Now he makes a simple but clear demand. Steve was caught off guard by Eric's directive, and at first didn't offer any opposition to it. After he had a chance to consider what Eric was feeling, he replied. "I can't imagine what you went through or are going through now. But I'm here not just to learn, but to help stop Jacque and I intend to do just that. I hope you get the chance to talk to him, but I can't let your needs come before the assignment. You know that." Steve added that last statement with just a little sound of desperation in his voice. This was the first time he had stood up to Eric and he wasn't sure how Eric would react. As he finished this bolder than normal statement on their assignment, he looked at Eric and could feel Eric telling him he'd never get the chance.

Steve decided it might be in his best interest if he could redirect the conversation to a less emotional discussion about the plane crash. He felt that if he allowed Eric to dwell too long on the memory of Jacque and his wife it might cause permanent damage to the tenuous relationship they were developing. In order for him to complete his assignment, he had to remain close to Eric. This much he had learned while with him. On his own he wouldn't stand a chance trying to follow Eric as Eric chased Jacque. He was too efficient, too knowledgeable, too unpredictable. Eric was a professional, and no matter what Steve thought about his own abilities, or Eric's sabbatical from the business, he recognized that he couldn't consider himself Eric's equal, yet.

"If Jacque wasn't responsible for the bombing, do you have any ideas who might be?"

"At this point, no. There is probably a half dozen or more organizations with connections to the right people. People with the technical expertise to pull this off. You have to remember, that what they accomplished was not really very difficult. There were only two critical aspects of the operation. First, they had to hire someone or have the experience themselves, to construct a bomb and camouflage it well enough to get it past baggage security. Do you have any idea how easy that is? Or don't they teach you things like that anymore?" Eric asked the question matter-of-factly, but it came across thick with the intended sarcasm.

Steve, at first offended by Eric's remark, prepared to say something equally sarcastic when he realized that wouldn't help his cause. Instead, he responded softly that he had indeed been taught those things. Eric continued. "Let's assume the appropriately constructed bomb is available, which is the second critical aspect of the bombing. And the one that limits the number of people capable of doing this job. The next step is to get the bomb and bag on the right plane. Here you have a choice; you can take your chances by timing your arrival at the airport to maximize the probability that your bag will in fact be transported on the same flight your booked on. Or you can plant someone inside to help ensure your bag makes the flight. If you're a trained assassin, you'll do both. If you're a terrorist, you'll take your chances because the target isn't anywhere near as important as the message."

"So which one do you think it is?"

"I leave for Paris in two hours, and I intend on finding that out once I get there. It's up to you, but I would like you to go to Chatel-Denis to dig around the crash site and see if you can learn anything there. We can meet in Paris in say . . . thirty-six hours. On the other hand, if you don't trust me, you can tag along. We can cover twice the ground if you're willing to take a risk. But, like I said before, it's up to you."

This twist caught Steve off guard. Tom had instructed him that Eric would probably try to lose him whenever he could, but so far, he hadn't. Now he was being asked to trust Eric for a short period of separation, but with the promise of reuniting. He really shouldn't, but the question of trust was a two-way street. Steve decided it was time he tried the other way on this street. "When's the next flight to Chatel-Denis?" He asked.

Eric walked over to the desk in their hotel room and pulled open the center drawer. Inside were two sets of airline tickets, one for each of them. He handed Steve his tickets. "Your flight leaves fifteen minutes before mine. I'll be staying at the Hotel Ibis on Rue St. Catherine's."

- - - - -

When Eric deplaned, he went straight to the airline ticket counter for the carrier of the ill-fated flight that had crashed in Switzerland. As he mulled around the area, he watched the two ticket agents service passengers, checking baggage and giving them their seat assignments. After what seemed like an unreasonably long wait, everyone in the line was taken care of and the agents disappeared through the door behind the counter. A short while later, both agents came back through the door. Stepping on the baggage scale, they slipped through the opening in the counter, and headed off for what Eric assumed was their break.

While Eric had been waiting, he monitored the agents actions to determine where they kept the baggage tags behind the ledge on the counter. As he continued to mull around the area, he worked his way along the counter so he could reach the baggage tags quickly without drawing attention to himself. Eventually he found just the right location and nonchalantly reached across the counter. He grabbed both a pen and a couple baggage tag, then calmly pulled his arm back. He quickly deposited the tags inside his coat pocket, and at the same time retrieved a piece of paper from the pocket.

At that moment, one of the two agents returned from their break. She walked up to Eric and asked if he needed any help. Eric acted as if he couldn't understand what the agent was saying, then replied in English he was just borrowing the pen. He handed her the pen to reassure her that the pen was indeed all he had taken. Although she was not proficient in English, she was able to convey to Eric that it was all right for him to use the pen, but she would appreciate it if he would return it when he was finished. There is a tendency for most people to think these are perks from the airline, and we are always running out of pens when we can least afford to. Eric assured her he would return the pen as soon as he was finished. Satisfied, the agent left, disappearing through the door behind the counter once again.

Eric took an address label for baggage from the dispenser on the counter. He wrote a short 'Thank You, Eric D.' for the pen, slid it into the clip and tossed them together over the ledge of the counter and left the ticket area. He walked back around to an area with public seating. While walking he tore off the baggage routing portion of the claim tickets and tossed those in a waste can as he passed by one. Now he started looking for the signs indicating the direction to baggage claim. When he found one, he moved off in that direction.

He approached the baggage carousel and watched as the luggage went around and around, pretending to look for his own luggage. While waiting, another flight had come in, and soon new luggage was appearing on the carousel. He continued to watch as their owners picked up the luggage from this flight until there were only two pieces remaining. At this point, the charade had lasted long enough so he headed over to an office just outside the baggage claim area.

Inside the office, he told the gentleman at the counter they had lost his luggage. Then he asked if they would please check in the back to see if it was overlooked or misplaced or possibly even arrived on another carrier or earlier flight. After some discussion back and forth, Eric provided a generic description of the missing luggage. Finally, the man traipsed off to look for the bags. Five minutes later he was back telling Eric there was no luggage like that back there. If he could provide the address where he would be staying while in Paris, as soon as it arrived, he would see to it that it was delivered to him.

Eric refused to accept the man's suggestion, so the conversation between the two men continued. Slowly Eric became more forceful in his demands that they find his luggage, and he couldn't wait for it to be delivered. 'Who knows when?' The airline employee continued trying to reason with Eric, but to no avail. Finally, as tempers were beginning to flair, but before anyone had dug in their heels, Eric proposed a compromise. If he were allowed to go in the back, look around for himself and talk to the baggage handlers, he would be satisfied. Then, with or without the luggage, he would leave peaceably and wait for his luggage to arrive at the hotel. The airline employee, uncomfortable with the small crowd forming while they had been debating, conceded to Eric's suggestion. Feeling defeated, he escorted Eric back to the baggage area.

Incoming and outgoing luggage were handled in the same area, which Eric had suspected and was relieved to find out. On one side of the room was the tractor and wagons of the most recent flight's luggage being unloaded. The tractor was parked alongside a conveyor that carried the baggage to the baggage claim area. On the other side of the large warehouse like room, against the wall, was another conveyor that led back to the ticket area and transported the luggage of departing passengers. Toward the center of that side of the room, was a short conveyor, interrupted by an x-ray machine. There were three men working the outgoing luggage: one loaded the conveyor, the second watched as the luggage passed under the x-ray and the third unloaded the conveyor then loaded the luggage on to a wagon.

The clerk introduced one of the baggage handlers on his side of the room to Eric with a brief explanation of why Eric was there. Then he left Eric to talk to the people on his own. Eric quickly explained what he was trying to do to the first man, and then walked away from the handler as if he were going to inspect some luggage against one of the walls. After he completed his inspection of that luggage, he walked over to the outgoing baggage area and started asking the x-ray technician a question. The technician didn't respond to Eric's inquiry until the last piece of luggage had made it through the x-ray, then he turned to Eric and asked him to repeat the question. Eric took note of what he perceived was probably increased scrutiny of the outgoing luggage due to the plane crash.

Eric described one of the pieces of luggage to him and asked if he had seen anything like it. The technician couldn't believe the description, "That could match half the luggage that passes through here each day," he replied.

Eric worked the conversation around from his lost luggage to a general discussion of airline security in light of the recent terrorist activity. He asked the technician what his opinion of the whole situation was. By now, all three of the baggage handlers had joined in the conversation with Eric, and Eric was trying to read their reactions to his questions. Each question became more pointed than the previous one until one technician calmly informed him that he had been instructed not to discuss the incident with anyone. Then added, the day of the crash all baggage had been x-rayed as per standard operating procedures. Eric noticed that one handler in particular had become more nervous than the others and would go back to work periodically to avoid the conversation. Eric decided this was the one he wanted to talk to. He ended the discussion by thanking them, then left the baggage handling area.

Back in the office, he informed the clerk that he hadn't found anything, but he appreciated the help and would look for the luggage to be delivered to his hotel as soon as it arrived.

Eric left the baggage office, heading back up to the ticket counter. He noticed the same ticket agent was at the counter. The one who interrupted him while he was stealing the baggage claim and routing tags, and she was still alone.

Remembering he had feigned the inability to speak French, he began in English. "Excuse me miss." She looked up from whatever she had been writing, and with her eyes she answered him. Eric continued, "I've just come from the baggage claim area, and was extremely pleased with the way my problem was handled by the personnel there." He stopped speaking long enough to judge whether she understood him, then continued again. "I would like to send a letter to your management, commending them. Could you provide me their names and who and where I should write the letter? I would have asked them, but I don't want them to know."

The agent listened intently to Eric's request, and as he finished, a big smile broke across her face. She replied in a heavily French accented English, "Oui. One moment. I must call for that information." She picked up the phone, dialed a four-digit extension, then waited for someone to answer. As she began talking, Eric monitored her conversation with whoever was on the other end, looking for any clues that she might not have believed him. However, she did exactly as she promised.

"Could you ask which one does what job so I can include that in my letter as well?" Eric interrupted her as she was talking. She nodded her understanding, then repeated Eric's request to the voice on the other end.

She was off the phone in a couple minutes with his information and handed him a piece of paper with the four names on it. Behind each name was the French job title. She reached across the counter, and as she pointed to each title, she translated it to an English equivalent for Eric. The man he was looking to identify was either the baggage handler I or II. Since he was the younger of the two men by quite a few years, Eric decided he must be Guy LaManeix, the baggage handler I. Eric asked the ticket agent for her name as well, so he could include it in the letter. She was appropriately embarrassed but provided it anyway. Eric thanked her and left.

He took the train to Paris, checked into the Hotel Ibis, and then called one of his ageless contacts to start the search for Guy LaManiex's home. After the phone call, he went down to the restaurant to get something to eat while he waited for his friend to do the research and come up with the address.

The Hotel Ibis is part of a chain of hotels with the same name that have targeted the middle-class traveler market. They are considerably more expensive than the hostel type accommodations that students use to save money while touring Europe. However, they are considerably less expensive than the typical tourist or businessman's hotel.

Their locations are usually a little less convenient to tourist attractions, but not far enough out of the way to be impractical. This one was located at the Place De la Republique on the Boulevard Magenta. The building was eight stories high, and its original design was as an office building. It had been renovated when converted to a hotel, but the floor plan made the original design obvious. The front desk and restaurant were on the first floor. All the rooms were on the second floor or higher. The exterior of the building had not been modified in any way with the conversion, keeping its office building appearance. Except for the small Hotel Ibis sign above the entrance, one would have no way of knowing it was a hotel, because it blended in quite well with its surroundings.

The rooms were the typically cramped style of European hotels. Eric's room barely had enough space for the single bed, the nightstand, and a desk with a top so small an opened newspaper hung over on all four sides. The renovator's had somehow managed to squeeze a shower, commode and sink into the bathroom. However, there was only two feet between the commode and sink, so if one backed away from the sink to quickly, they could find themselves sitting down. And there was only three feet between the door and shower, providing the total of six square feet for moving around the bathroom. If the bathroom door was open, the closet door couldn't be, and visa versa. And if either door was open, one had to climb over the bed to get to the other side of the room. The motif was decidedly modern, and the furniture was built for price, not comfort.

Eric stopped at the front desk to see if his friend had called back and was pleased to find out he had. Back in the room he didn't waste anytime before returning the call. A few minutes later Eric left his room, heading over to Guy LaManiex's apartment.

Guy was a relatively young man and had chosen to live in an apartment building that provided convenient access to the nightlife on the Champs de Elysses. After paying the rent and other living essentials, he had enough money left over to spend at least one or two nights a week in the bars, chasing women and being generally rowdy. If he was frugal, he could sometimes stretch three nights out of his income.

Like his father, at an early age he decided the University was not for him. His grades through high school confirmed that fact. So even if he had a change of heart, and wanted to pursue a higher education, it was too late. No University would have accepted him. Knowing this, he had gotten a job as a janitor for the airline right after graduation. He went from janitor to a dock man, and recently to a baggage handler. He figured he was climbing the corporate ladder quite well. It had only taken him eight years and he had almost doubled his original starting salary. Guy was pleased with what had transpired in his life so far, and his disposition was a reflection of that contentment.

Growing up in the city he had never caused his parents any undo concern. He would get in the occasional scuffle with friends, but as he grew, those became less frequent. Guy never quite made the connection between the number of times people chose to fight with him was shrinking as he was growing. At twenty he stopped growing. But at six foot three, he didn't think of himself as small. At that same age he began to fill out and started his job unloading trucks, cargo planes and any other load that passed through the airline's cargo business. The result was a formidable six-foot three man weighing two hundred thirty pounds of solid muscle.

Guy's first reaction when he had been approached about ensuring the suitcase made the flight, whether it was x-rayed or not, was to ask why. But, without asking his supervisor for an explanation, he was assured that this was common practice for the airline to offer specialized services to some of its better customers. After thinking about what his supervisor had told him, Guy decided it wasn't his place to question his supervisor's directives even though they were outside company policy. He had been told too often in the past: 'We don't expect you to understand, because you can't see the big picture.' Guy knew that to be true. As it turned out, he didn't have to break company policy because the suitcase made the flight and was x-rayed.

Guy had forgotten about the incident until the police questioned him. They asked about the baggage handling practices for the flight that blew up over Switzerland the next morning. The police didn't actually ask him if he had been instructed to do anything out of the ordinary, and he didn't volunteer the information. All their questions addressed whether or not the baggage was in fact x-rayed and handled according to regulations. Since all of it had been, Guy saw no reason to tell them about his special instructions for the one suitcase. Guy's story had agreed with the other baggage handler and the x-ray technician, so the police had been satisfied.

Eric wasn't able to get to the apartment before Guy got home from work. Regardless, his contact had not been able to tell him whether or not Guy lived alone, so the chance of finding an empty apartment was probably limited anyway. Guy lived on the fourth floor of the building, which housed a tavern on the first floor and apartments on the five remaining floors. While Eric was climbing the stairs to the fourth floor, he decided to take his chances and talk to Guy inside his apartment rather than wait for him to come out by himself. On the second flight of stairs, he passed a woman who looked to be at least forty and was obviously dressed to sell. As they passed on the stairway she took hold of his arm and offered her services for a small remuneration. Eric declined her offer, but thanked her anyway, and added he was just here visiting a friend. Disappointed at the loss of a sale, she frowned at him then continued down the stairs. On the street she quickly forgot about the man on the stairs and concentrated on locating potential buyers.

Eric came to the fourth floor and walked halfway down the narrow hall before he came to Guy's apartment. He knocked on the door, then waited for an answer. After a few seconds he heard footsteps on the hardwood floor, and Guy yelled, "I'll be there in a minute Marie." Eric didn't answer; he just stood at the door waiting. Finally, he heard footsteps approach the door, the handle turned, and before Guy could open the door on his own, Eric slammed his shoulder into it as hard as he could. The corner of the door caught Guy on the side of his face, and he fell back from the door, as much from the shock and pain, as he did from the force of the door.

Eric stepped inside and closed the door before Guy realized what had happened. Then Eric grabbed his arm, twisted it behind his back, and at the same time turned him around and tripped him. Guy fell to the floor on his stomach with Eric on his back. Then Eric rolled him to one side and put a knife to his throat. "Twitch and your dead."

"All my money's in my wallet. Just don't kill me." Guy had not seen Eric well enough to recognize him when he came in, and now with the knife to his neck, he was afraid to turn his head and look at his assailant. He figured correctly he would have a better chance of living if he did exactly as he was told.

"I don't want your money and if you answer all my questions, you'll be home free, and no one will get hurt." Guy nodded his head in the affirmative, assuring his attacker he would answer everything as best he could. Guy knew he had heard this voice before, but he could not place when or where.

"There was some special baggage that required special handling the other day. I've been informed you were responsible for the special handling. Is that true?" Guy was considering whether to tell the truth when Eric pulled his arm up tighter sending a sharp pain through his shoulder.

Quickly Guy changed his mind and spit out an answer. "Yes, but I was only doing what the boss told me to do."

"Exactly what were your instructions?"

"I was told there would be a piece of luggage coming in late that had to make the flight to Jerusalem. It was supposed to be a metal suitcase in excellent condition. Small enough to be carried on. In fact, more tourist types probably would carry it on the plane. Anyway, all I was supposed to do was keep a look out for it on the outgoing baggage conveyer, and make sure it was transferred to the x-ray conveyer in time to make the flight."

Eric listened to Guy's voice to determine his state of mind as well as hear the actual details. Guy's manner and voice indicated he was probably scared enough to be telling the truth. He also wasn't hesitating to think about his responses. He was just blurting out the answers, totally unaware of their significance. This helped convince Eric he was telling the truth.

"You sure you weren't told to make certain the suitcase made the flight but wasn't x-rayed?"

"No!" Guy answered emphatically. He was surprised by the question and scared by it at the same time. This is exactly what he was afraid the authorities would think once he heard the announcement, they suspected a bomb was responsible for the plane crash over Chatel-Denis: They think I was somehow involved, he thought. "I had no idea there was a bomb in it. My boss told me to keep an eye out for it and make sure it made the flight. That's all I know. I had nothing to do with it. You've got to believe me." He pleaded.

Eric recognized the panic creeping into Guy's voice and knew it was time to leave. Guy was big enough that if he panicked, Eric might have to use more force than he wanted to, and some one could get hurt. Eric took the knife away from Guy's throat and tossed it on a chair next to him. Next, he grabbed Guy's hair at the back of his head and pulled the head up as far as it would go. Guy started to yell out in pain just before Eric slammed his head back down against the hardwood floor. Guy's voice went eerily silent. Eric rolled him over ready to hit him if necessary to make sure he was out, but a quick look at Guy's eyes confirmed it wouldn't be necessary.

Eric removed a roll of white medical adhesive tape and a small piece of rope from his coat. First, he tied Guy's hands behind his back, and then taped his mouth shut. He removed Guy's wallet and took the seventy-two francs he found inside it to make it look like a robbery. Eric tossed the wallet on the chair next to the knife, then grabbed his knife and left. Before he closed the door, he made sure it was unlocked. Even if Marie didn't have a key, he still wanted her to be able to get in to help Guy when he woke up.

As Eric walked down the stairs, he pulled a piece of paper from his pocket and started looking at the names and addresses he had been given from his contact. All four names with their respective addresses and job titles were listed. When the information had first been supplied, Eric almost didn't bother recording it figuring he would only need Guy's. Then he thought better of it and wrote them all down. Now he was glad he had. He could take the Metro and be at the supervisor's apartment within the hour, continuing the interrogation with him.

— — — — —

Steve knocked on the door to the hotel room prepared to wait for an answer. Before he had finished knocking the voice on the other side yelled, "Who is it?" Steve really hadn't expected Eric to be in the room when he arrived and was somewhat disappointed to find out he was there. He had checked into a room himself and hoped Eric would be out. That way he could go back to his room, leave a message for Eric, and get some sleep while he waited for him to return.

"It's me," Steve answered.

"I'll be right there." A few seconds later Eric was opening the door for Steve. "Come on in." He motioned for Steve to come in, then closed the door as soon as he stepped inside. "I didn't expect you quite so soon, but I'm glad you're here. I think I know where our bomber came from. I don't have a motive, or a name yet, but I'm convinced it wasn't Jacque. Were you able to find anything out?"

"No. At this point the only confirmed bombing of that flight is with the news media. None of the Swiss or French officials investigating at the crash site are confident enough in what they've seen to conclude there was a bomb. There are a lot of theorizing and hypothetical projections, but very few hard facts. That's why no official word has come out backing the bombing story. They continue to sift through the rubble but are determined to eliminate all other possible explanations for the crash before crediting some group or some person with a successful terrorist act."

Steve stopped speaking, giving Eric the opportunity to ask questions but Eric was preoccupied in what he had learned and didn't seize the opportunity. He had only half listened to what Steve said, more or less shutting him out after he said neither group of officials was ready to give credence to the bomb theory. Finally, Steve got tired of waiting for Eric to say something, "I know you were convinced before we left Frankfurt that Jacque had nothing to do with the bombing..." Exasperated that Eric continued to ignore him, he added sarcastically. "I'm supposed to be impressed."

7

-All a man's labor is for his mouth, and yet the appetite is not satisfied

Sergei entered the pub with the Russian flair that was as much a part of him as dry British humor was a part of most Englishmen. He walked toward the bar as he looked the place over trying to locate an open seat. Spotting one near the far end of the bar, he headed over to take what he presumed was his spot. Sergei's personality made him assume that once he determined what he wanted, everyone else would simply step aside to let him have it--therefore, it was his seat. However, this particular seat belonged to an older gentleman that frequented this pub four nights a week and had been doing so for longer than the present proprietor had even owned the place. The seat Sergei had chosen was not available tonight. Consequently, when the older gentleman was returning from the restroom and noticed Sergei was on a collision course with this special seat, he yelled across the room loud enough that everyone in the pub heard him. As one, the pub full of patrons turned to look at Sergei. "Don't even think 'bout it, ya bloody pup!"

Sergei was the only person in the pub not to hear the old man, much less realize he was the one being spoken to. As he approached the seat, he reached to pull it away from the bar and sit down. By this time the old gentleman had gotten close enough that he raised his arm and, with the added extension of his walking stick, was able to slap it across Sergei's knuckles as they rested on the back of the stool. Sergei cried out in surprise and pain at the crack of wood on his hand. Releasing the stool, his arm recoiled for protection. As he rubbed his wounded hand, he traced the stick back to its owner. Finally, he noticed the old man who was now standing next to him. Without a word of explanation to Sergei, the older gentleman slid past him and climbed onto the stool.

"What in the hell do you think you're doing old man?" Sergei exploded at him. Again, everyone in the room turned to look at Sergei, but this time with a little less propensity to forgive his indiscretion. It was their belief that Sergei was showing the natural barbaric response they had come to expect from foreigners... Didn't he realize that he was a guest in their establishment and consequently should act as such, they collectively thought?

"Look lad," started the older gentleman. "You probably weren't aware that this is my seat, and I can forgive you for that. However, you would be wise to accept that fact and move on. The people in this pub don't particularly fawn over foreigners in the first place. But you're startin' to create a scene, which ain't goin' ta help you a bit. I may be a cranky old bean and might even have some enemies here tonight, but you--You're standing alone.

Sergei looked around and quickly confirmed what the older gentleman was saying. Almost everyone in the room was staring at him, and none of them seemed interested in joining his side of the fray. He turned back to the old man and said. "Seems I've mishandled the situation, and hope you'll accept my apology. To demonstrate there are no hard feelings, could I buy you a pint?"

A broad smile broke across the old gentleman's face as he turned to the bartender. "Joan, I'll be taking a pint of bitters, on this young man. And why don't you pour him one as well, so he can taste what a real British beer tastes like. I'm sure all he's ever had is that tourist crap they pass off on ya when you're at the airport."

Joan looked Sergei in the eye, smiled, and then gave him a wink. She handed the old gentleman his pint of beer then motioned for Sergei to follow her. She picked up his beer, walked around the bar and led him to a table in the corner of the pub. The pub was really one big room, separated near the midpoint with two half walls that jutted out into the room. Decorative spindles were placed at one-foot intervals along the walls, spanning the space between the top of the half walls and the ceiling. Sergei had been directed to the corner around the half wall on the opposite side of the entrance. The resulting view of the entrance was blocked; first by the spindles, then by the milling crowd that seemed to have a never-ending trail of people walking between the tables scattered about the room and the bar.

Setting the pint of bitters down on the table, she said in a soft, barely audible voice. "Simon likes to make a scene when anyone tries to take his stool. But all he's really after is a free pint. You were smart to give it to him, 'cuz it keeps everyone happy. Not that they'd a done anything to you if ya hadn't. It just keeps everyone happy."

"I appreciate the explanation. It helps to understand what makes people tick. Besides, a pint of bitters is a cheap price to pay for peace among strangers." Joan started to turn away when Sergei added. "There will be another man coming shortly, and from this location it will be hard to watch for him. If you notice him, a blond German, could you send him my way?

"A blond German won't necessarily stick out in this crowd. Could you be a little more descriptive?

"Trust me. This man will stick absent, as you say."

Joan gave Sergei a quizzical look but accepted his assertion that she would be able to recognize the man. She returned to the bar, and along the way collected three additional drink orders from various tables. Each time a voice would yell out, "Joanie dear, could you bring us..." without stopping or turning to see who or where the voice came from, Joan simply yelled back. "Got it." Then added the appropriate order to the list. Or at least Sergei assumed the order was right because no one ever bothered to correct her.

Sergei settled into his seat to watch the crowd while he waited for Toomas to arrive. This was the second face-to-face meeting these two had since the entire group met on the outskirts of Paris three days ago. Events were beginning to accelerate, something they all expected to happen as the plan came together. Still, even to Sergei who usually complained about what he called 'a snail's pace,' events were starting to happen in rapid succession. First, the group gave Toomas singular control over hiring a second assassin. Then, Toomas had successfully identified and hired Manuel. He, in turn, would appear to have already made an attempt on the Sheik's life, a tad bit ahead of schedule, and fortunately unsuccessful.

A loud raucous cheer going up from the crowd on the other side of the half wall interrupted Sergei's thoughts. He looked around and discovered he was the only one left on his side of the divided room. Everyone else was crowded around the center of the half room, yelling and cheering. The crowd was successfully, although unintentionally, blocking any view Sergei might have had. This continued until Sergei could no longer contain his curiosity and stood up to see what all the fuss was about. Sergei walked around the crowd trying to find someplace to see through but didn't have any luck.

By now the crowd noise had settled down to a constant hum with only the occasional outburst when something, unseen by Sergei, happened in the center of the crowd to set it off. Sergei walked back to his table, pulled out a chair and stepped up on to the seat. Now he could see above the crowd, but still couldn't look down into the center to make out what was grabbing everybody's attention. Stepping from the chair to the table he was able to gain a little more height. Now when he looked around the room his view was completely unobstruct-ed. He could clearly make out Joan, behind the bar, laughing at the various comments being shouted toward the center of the crowd. And as he scanned the crowd, he saw Toomas walk into the pub.

Toomas stood just inside the door as he scanned the room looking for Sergei. Before Sergei was able to climb down from his perch on the tabletop, Toomas spotted him. Sergei could tell by the expression on Toomas' face, he was not amused. In Sergei's hurry to get down from the table to the chair and finally to the floor, he unwittingly put his weight on his right foot which was too near the edge of the table. Immediately he knew he made a mistake. He also knew he wouldn't recover in time. Sergei tried to maintain an upright position with his body, as the table slid out from under him. With his arms flailing in an effort to keep his balance, the table and Sergei cashed to the floor.

Sergei ended up with his legs spread out in front of him and his back resting against the tabletop that was now at a forty-five-degree angle to the floor. His beer mug had slid off the table and was lying on its side next to him in a puddle of beer. As he fell, he kicked the chair he had been trying to step on across the room into a corner of the half wall. The hum of the crowd stopped as everyone turned to see what had happened. When they realized it was only the newcomer and not one of their friends, they turned their attention back to the center of the crowd, ignoring Sergei.

Toomas walked over to the bar and asked for a towel to clean up the mess he was sure to find by Sergei. With towel in hand, he walked around the crowded table and over to Sergei. He tossed Sergei the towel, told him to clean up the mess, and then walked back to the bar to get both of them a pint of beer. With the attention of the crowd still centered on the table, Toomas was quickly able to get his beer and return to where Sergei was now standing. Sergei had also managed to set the table and chair right and was in the midst of wiping up the spilled beer. Toomas set both beers down, selected a chair that offered him the best view of the room, and settled in to watch Sergei play the part of a janitor. When Sergei was finished, he took the towel back to Joan, then returned to face Toomas.

Toomas motioned for Sergei to take a seat but continued to watch the crowd for a short moment before he spoke. Without turning to Sergei, he began. "This would appear to be one of your better selections for a meeting place. The patrons obviously entertain themselves quite well. While you were perched high a top the table, did you manage to see what was captivating the audience so completely?" The sarcasm in Toomas voice was matched in intensity only by the still red-faced Sergei's embarrassment.

"As a matter of fact, just as you walked in, I thought I could make out an arm-wrestling match. But I'm not positive. It's hard to believe that something so barbaric could be so captivating. I really expected the English were too civilized for that sort of simplistic entertainment."

"Aren't you a tad bit judgmental for someone who just bounced his rear-end off the floor after falling off a table, not a chair, and in a pub, not in the privacy of their own apartment?" Toomas asked incredulously.

Sergei didn't bother to respond to his question but asked his own instead. "What was Tom's reaction to the failed attempt on the Sheik's life?" Before Toomas could answer, he added. "I assume he recognized this was an attempt."

"He certainly did. He's not aware that we hired Manuel, so naturally he concluded that Jacque was responsible. Since he believed it was Jacque, and we had agreed that Jacque would not try anything before the news conference tomorrow, he was pissed. He was convinced that Jacque was either acting on our orders or was ignoring us altogether and has established his own agenda. In either event, he wants us to reestablish control over Jacque and assure him it wouldn't happen again."

"What did you tell him?"

"I explained to him that Jacque wasn't involved, and that it was pure coincidence that the plane the Sheik was supposed to be on was the target of a terrorist attack. These things happen in the world today, and just like everyone else, it's beyond our control."

"Do you think he bought that explanation?"

"I can't be sure one way or the other, but he really doesn't have any choice. Sooner or later both the Swiss and French investigative teams will confirm the bombing. At that point, the accepted explanation will be the terrorist theory. The only remaining unknown would-be which terrorist group is responsible."

"A convenient scape goat group will be identified I suppose."

"Exactly. Unless they are somehow able to trace the bomb back to an individual, which I think is highly unlikely, that would be the easiest conclusion to reach. Let's face it, the media has already established the belief in everyone's mind that it was an act of terrorism, so all the investigative efforts will be directed toward that end. Regardless of whether the evidence points that way or not, they'll manage to bias their interpretation of the data that way."

That is one of the things I like about you Toomas: Your cynical belief that everyone is led around like cattle to the slaughter. I could not help noticing in your earlier description of your conversation with Tom that you didn't tell him we hired Manuel?" The inflection in Sergei's voice made the statement sound like a question.

"That is one of the items I thought we could discuss later, but since you brought it up... My initial thought was, no is, not to tell him anything at this time. If need be, we can always inform him later. But right now, having a few secrets from Tom is probably a good thing."

"What should be our approach in the meeting tomorrow?" Sergei changed the subject. Is there anything I should be aware of?"

Toomas thought about the questions Sergei was posing for a few minutes. "Let me answer your second question first, no. You know everything there is to know about what transpired since our last full group meeting. As to the other question, I am not planning on springing anything on the group like I did last time so there should not be any reason to change our approach. Unless of course, you know something I don't but should."

Sergei shook his head no in response to Toomas' last statement, then Toomas continued. "There is one more thing you should know since it pertains to Tom but won't affect tomorrow's meeting. Also, because I plan on discussing it with the rest of the group one on one to get a measure of how receptive everyone might be, and you might as well be first. I don't want it to take the form of a formal request, because I haven't convinced myself it has sufficient merit. However, I would like everyone to begin thinking about it, because there may come a point when we have to act."

Sergei interrupted, "Toomas, you're rambling. I don't need all the analysis you're going through to broach the subject. Save it for when you're trying to convince me of something."

Toomas ignored Sergei's comments because he had come to expect a certain level of rudeness from the Russian. He had to continually remind himself that the two of them had the only pure motive in this endeavor, and there were certain things he would need from him. If he allowed Sergei to irritate him to the point he reacted, or did something to alienate him, Sergei might not be available when he was needed the most. They were not here strictly to achieve a monetary benefit like the rest of the group, consequently, his relationship with Sergei, although shaky at times, was very important. The only problem with that was as time progressed, they both were becoming even more dependent on each other.

"Tom was unusually nervous when I spoke to him. He's always been more or less an administrator, which can justify a certain level of unwarranted concern on his part. But with his experience in covert activities, he should be able to cover up his emotions better than he did. At some point in the near future we, as a group, may need to sever our ties with him. I am not sure he is needed any longer based on what he brings to the game." Toomas held up his hand to keep Sergei from interrupting again. "Don't answer now, just think about it. Like I said, I will be canvassing the rest of the group individually, so just be prepared for the proposal at some later date."

During the conversation, unnoticed by either of the two men, a woman with jet black hair had separated from the crowded center table group. She had taken a seat at the table on the other side of the half wall across from Toomas and Sergei. Now that the arm-wrestling contest had ended, an Englishman made his way over to her table and sat down. He was desperately trying to pick her up, which helped them blend into the scene at the pub. Without much effort, she was able to keep him hoping, while she listened to the conversation on the other side of the wall.

Toomas and Sergei had one more beer, then left. Once they were outside, she excused herself to the gentleman seated at her table and went over to the public telephone. It was mounted on the wall near the entrance, and although she had to fight the flow of the crowd in the pub, she still managed to beat another woman to it. She gave the operator the number she was trying to reach in Lisbon, then added her credit card number to pay for the call. In a few more seconds Ariel was on the other end. Then she gave him a detailed report on the conversation she had just overheard.

- - - - -

"I have confirmation that the bomb was put together by a specialist in Paris at the request of a Spaniard or Portuguese."

"Isn't there a man from Lisbon by the name of Manuel or Manrique, or something that begins with man who has a fairly good reputation as an assassin?" Steve asked Eric.

They had spent the day going in opposite directions pursuing the same lead. Steve had been using Agency contacts, while Eric relied on old friends and contacts from his past. Steve had drawn a blank, but Eric had managed to unearth the bomb's creator and even managed to speak to him. The man couldn't or wouldn't tell Eric whom he made the bomb for. He wouldn't even confirm it was his handiwork that was responsible for the explosion, which was unusual for a man with his ego problem. However, Eric was able to locate someone that claimed a bomb left the dress shop in a suitcase the same day of the ill-fated flight. The person also described the carrier as someone obviously of Spanish descent. Eric immediately thought of Manuel, because he was the most famous Hispanic assassin in that part of Europe. Also, he was the only one sophisticated enough and who had the kind of connections necessary to pull this off. Most Spanish or Portuguese assassins that Eric knew were capable of killing a target that walked up to them and identified himself, but if any more effort than that was required, you might as well forget it.

"You were right the first time; his name is Manuel. He's considerably more ruthless than Jacque. And as you can see, he doesn't care how many? Or who else is killed in the process. Manuel is recognized as one of the premier assassins in the world, albeit less sophisticated, but still only second to Jacque. He got started in the business because he was a sharpshooter, literally deadly with a rifle from almost any range. As time progressed, he naturally experimented with other methods for those circumstances when a rifle wasn't appropriate. Word is: He has recently become enamored with the destructive capability of bombs and now uses them almost exclusively. If whoever hired him wasn't aware of that, they might not have expected him to use explosives. The only thing I couldn't find out was who was/is this customer. That's what I want you to find out. It's too much of a coincidence that two people want the same man dead at the same time, And I've got this sick feeling that somehow Manuel and Jacque are connected."

"You mean they might be working together." Steve made the statement sound more like a question.

"It's possible. My contacts tell me Jacque isn't the same man he was before Washington. But none of them could say whether he would actually take on a partner. With the possibility of two assassins, we can no longer be working on the same one. It seems Tom might have been right for once. Anyway, I would like you to determine if Manuel is our other problem, then get back to me as soon as possible."

"You want me to take him out of the picture?" Steve asked incredulously, unsure if he understood Eric's intent correctly.

"No. I don't believe that would be wise at his point. If Manuel is our man, we may need to ask him a few questions first. And we can't do that if he's dead. What I want you to do is go to Lisbon. There's a little tavern down by the wharf that he uses as his home base. Most of his jobs are negotiated there. You need to find out who may have hired him. Get descriptions of everyone that he's met with at the tavern during the last week or so. Or if he traveled, find out where he went. I'll put you in contact with a man who lives on the wharf. He'll help you get around down there without getting yourself killed. Once you have that information, get back here. I'll keep this room rented for the next week. If I have to leave Paris, which I suspect will happen long before you get back, I'll leave an explanation of how and where to catch up with me. Do you have any questions?"

"What will you be doing while I'm in Lisbon?"

"I'm going after Jacque. At least to the point that I can figure out where he is going. Up 'til now we've been filling in background information, sort of recording history. But now it's time to figure out where everything stands, then begin looking ahead to what's going to happen tomorrow. I can't do that until I find out where Jacque is."

Steve mulled this over for a few minutes. He had looked at the Chatel-Denis trip as a chance to prove to Eric he could be trusted. Now it appears he had done just that. While separated he had refrained from checking in with Tom because he didn't want to take the chance Eric would find out and have it destroyed the budding relationship that he had worked so hard building. However, this trip would take considerably longer, and he was more than a little concerned he was giving Eric far too much latitude. He knew Tom would not approve, but he couldn't think of a way to avoid it without casting doubt on his motives. He decided to do as Eric asked and told him he'd leave right away. He also decided it was time to check in with Tom.

With Steve out of his way, Eric could head to London to get a firsthand view of the consortium. According to his sources, they were meeting at the Grand Hotel in London tomorrow. Five of them had met just three days ago in the outskirts of Paris, but that was all the information his informant was able to provide. Other than Josef's explanation of their motive, his other sources had not been able to add anything knew to Eddie's Prophetic Report. Eric was beginning to appreciate that although the consortium was supposedly inexperienced, they were both efficient and effective. Additionally, they were doing an excellent job keeping themselves well hidden.

- - - - -

On arrival to London's Heathrow airport, Eric hailed a taxi for the ride to the Grand. He was dressed in a business suit and identified himself as a Mr. D. Roberts when he checked in. He went out of his way to explain to the front desk clerk that he was here on business for a U. S. import/export company specializing in soft goods and would be here at most two days. It was important that his messages be delivered promptly, and naturally he would show his appreciation for good service. To reinforce the image, he was trying to present, he tipped the bellman 5£s when he delivered the single bag to his room. Eric knew the best way to guarantee good service was to demonstrate a willingness to pay for it. Word would spread quickly from the bellman that the American in room 2112 tipped handsomely.

Eric inspected the room, then opened the suitcase and removed an old English tweed suit and a bowler hat. He went into the bathroom with the suit and when he emerged about an hour later, he had been transformed into an old English gentleman with graying black hair and a snow-white beard. He used a walking stick to steady himself and hunched his back over ever so slightly to give the impression he was even older than he looked at first glance. He went over to the door and looked through the peephole to make sure the hall was clear before he stepped out. Satisfied, he left the room. Slowly he made his way down the hall to the elevator. Returning to the front desk in the lobby, he was pleased to see clerk that checked him in was still working. He walked up to the counter and without waiting for the clerk to acknowledge his presence asked where he could purchase a copy of the London Times. The clerk gave no indication he recognized Eric while he gave him directions to the gift shop. Confident his disguise provided adequate cover; Eric began his search of the hotel.

He walked around the lobby getting a feel for the layout, including the conference rooms that fronted on the lobby. He doubted the consortium would be found meeting in one of these, but he wanted to consider all the options. In plain view of the front desk were four conference rooms, each capable of holding forty or fifty people. These were directly to the left of the front desk and lined that wall of the lobby.

Eric walked past the entrance of each room and saw the names of the organizations that had rented them and the times they would be occupied. As he came to the first door, he opened it and peered inside. He was surprised by the size, thinking fifty people could fit very comfortably while working in there all day. With each conference room, he would open the door and peer inside. When he opened the last door, he found himself looking at a room full of faces staring back at him and the speaker's back who was standing just inside the door. The speaker turned to him and asked if he wanted to join them. Eric violently shook his head no, then said to the speaker in a gruff voice.

"This isn't the restroom?" Then let the door close by itself. As the door was closing, he could hear laughter erupt inside the room.

A fifth door was now visible. This last door could not quite be seen from the front desk. The door opened to a hall that led to the right. Eric hadn't been aware of this part of the hotel and started down the hall to investigate. A sign was attached to the wall that read, **CONFERENCE ROOMS E - S.** Below the sign was an arrow pointing down the hall. The hall made another right turn about thirty feet down. It looked as though it could be a hall anywhere else in the hotel, with doors alternating from side to side for the whole length. There were fifteen doors in all, but instead of being numbered, they continued the alphabet that began with the four conference rooms in the lobby. At the end of this hallway were double steel doors labeled, **FIRE EXIT.**

Eric continued his charade opening each conference room door and looking inside. Each room was set up almost identically; the only thing that changed from room to room was the number of chairs around the table. There was a table in the center and usually ten chairs placed around it, although some had as few as six and one as many as thirteen. At the far end of the room was a clean white markerboard, and in the corner an easel with a blank flip chart. The first three rooms had been used earlier in the day and still had the empty coffee cups, glasses and plates strewn across the table. The rest of the rooms were empty. Eric couldn't find any signs indicating what organization or group was meeting in which room, so he headed back to the front desk to ask the clerk.

"Where's the list for what's group in which conference room tomorrow?" Eric demanded of the clerk. The clerk that was at the desk earlier had been relieved by a young girl that looked like she was barely out of high school. Caught off guard by Eric's gruff manner, she reached under the counter, removed the conference room schedule for the next day and handed it to Eric. Eric quickly stepped back from the desk, twisting the sheet of paper in his hands as if he were trying to improve the lighting to make it easier to read. It was too late by the time the clerk realized he was out of her reach.

While Eric was reading the schedule, it dawned on the young clerk what she had done. "Sir. Sir. I'm sorry but you're not supposed to have that. If you'd give it back to me and tell me who you're with, I can tell you which conference room your group is scheduled to be in tomorrow."

Eric ignored the clerk and continued to read the schedule. All but five of the rooms were rented for tomorrow and reading the names of the groups gave no indication which one might be rented by the consortium. Eric did notice that the first nine rooms were scheduled, then the next five were empty, but the last conference room was also scheduled. He read the name of the group purported to be renting conference room S; The **EAST/WEST REVIVALISTS.** The name offered no clue as to the real occupants, but the number expected in the group was five. Sufficient evidence for Eric to conclude this was probably the consortium. There was only one other group of five, but they were in conference room E. Too close to the front for their kind of work, he thought.

Eric handed the sheet back to the girl at the desk and said, "I'm not so old as to need some young pup to read to me. Thank you very much." He didn't wait for the girl to respond but turned and shuffled away. The girl mumbled something intelligible under her breath about old people being rude, overbearing and an argument for euthanasia, but Eric ignored her and kept walking. Soon he was back down the hall with the conference rooms. He went to the last door on the right, opened the door and stepped inside.

The conference room was set up exactly as expected; table in the center, ten chairs around it, a flip chart on an easel and a markerboard. Eric set his walking stick on the table, then walked around the room inspecting every nook and cranny. When he was finished familiarizing himself with the room, he left and returned to his own room. He was there for a very short time, then left again still dressed as an old man. While in his room, Eric had used the phone book to locate a store nearby that sold electronic equipment.

He found one within walking distance and soon was on the street looking for the store's name on each building. Finding it, he entered through the single door entry. Once inside the store, he started looking for a small Dictaphone style tape recorder among the stacks of electronic merchandise. The store he found himself in obviously relied on volume, not service or merchandising. There were only two salesclerks for the twenty customers presently in the store. At each stack of merchandise, there was a sample of the component set up for demonstrations. It was intended to allow the customer to take the equipment through its paces. The store was filled with mostly young people, and it appeared to Eric that every one of them was testing a different piece of equipment at the loudest possible volume. It also sounded like each one had decided to listen to a different piece of music. The resulting din was almost unbearable and caused the wood floor of the store to pulsate.

As he passes each person, he'd comment on how clear the sound was, then he'd turn it down. Most would reach over after he passed by and turn the sound right back up. But a few just left it where he set it. Regardless, Eric's efforts were drowned out by the remaining systems, and he soon realized his efforts were falling on deaf ears. Eric must have squeezed between a dozen people and their respective test equipment on his search through the store before he came to a section dedicated to tape recorders. The type of recorder he was looking for wasn't found with the rest of the recorders; consequently, he started working his way toward one of the salesclerks.

The salesclerk was attending to a young man dressed in one of the more unusual clothing combinations Eric had seen. His hair was even more bizarre than his clothes. It was cut short along the sides, but the top, which was obviously heavily greased, was about two inches long and stood straight up. The right half of his hair was dyed purple with a black lightning bolt in it, and the left half was dyed black with a purple lightning bolt in it. Eric tried to make out what the man was saying, but it sounded like a foreign language with a British accent.

Without waiting for an opportunity to break into the conversation, Eric interrupted. "Missy... I said Missy." Eric took hold of the girl's arm and shook it gently to get her attention. When she looked at him, like a bothersome bug, he burst out. "Do you have any miniature tape recorders, missy?" She looked at him for a few seconds as if she were trying to determine exactly what type of bug he was. Then just as Eric was getting ready to ask her again, she answered.

"Yes… they're in the back room. I'll have to get one for you." There was another long pause before she turned to the young man with the strange hairdo and said. "Excuse me, Terry. It'll only be a min." Then turning away from both of them, she started walking toward the back of the store. At the same time, she motioned for Eric to follow her. As she walked, she asked Eric. "How small are you looking for?"

"The smallest one you have."

At the back of the store, they came to a curtain-covered doorway. She shoved the curtain to one side and walked into the back room. At first Eric was tempted to follow her, but then thought better of it and waited just outside the curtain for her to return. He took his walking stick and slid the curtain back 'til he could watch her. But she soon disappeared behind more stacks of electronic equipment. While waiting for the girl to return, Eric decided the only difference between the showroom and the back room was the lack of demos available to play in the back room.

Eric got tired of watching for the girl to come back and turned his attention to the customers in the showroom. Terry's 'min' had turned into five minutes before she came back out carrying a small box in one hand and the miniature recorder in the other. She explained to Eric how it worked, told him the price, then started to leave. Before she managed to get very far, Eric stopped her to tell her he'd take it. She looked at the recorder now in Eric's hands, let out a loud sigh as if she'd just been asked to do the impossible, then glanced over at the odd looking fellow named Terry. She yelled to him, "Terry… give me another min, will ya?" Terry was busy dancing to the music he was playing, oblivious to what she had yelled.

She motioned for Eric to follow her once again, but this time to the front of the store. At the counter Eric noticed she had overlooked a minor detail: She hadn't included any tapes with the purchase, so he brought that to her attention. It was apparent by her reaction she was not thrilled with Eric's latest request, but silently she headed off toward the back room again, presumably to get one. Five more minutes passed before she returned with a package of three miniature cassette tapes. After collecting the money for everything, the girl headed back to her friend without uttering another word to Eric. Terry, who was still dancing and still very much unaware of his surroundings, didn't bother to acknowledge the girl when she returned. Eric was just happy to be leaving the store.

He returned to his hotel room to begin his reconstruction project. He opened the box, removed the tape recorder, and started to inspect it. He needed to determine how best to rig it to start taping. After close inspection, he decided the power switch could be left on, and without taping, shouldn't drain the batteries since the unit didn't actually use any power unless taping. To start recording, he needed to depress a button. That meant he needed to rig something to depress the button at approximately the right time, on some cue or action that was reliable, or he would have to start it himself. The last method was preferred, but not possible. He thought about the alternatives for a while before settling on one, then left the hotel in search of a store that still carried mechanical alarm clocks.

He returned a half-hour later with the alarm clock in hand. He removed the back and stared at the workings for a few minutes. He was studying the mechanism that released the spring, drove the hammer, and rang the bell. Soon he was satisfied he could make it start the tape recorder reliably. The first thing he would have to do was remove the bells. He couldn't risk them being jostled in any way, notifying everyone within hearing distance of its existence. Next, he carefully removed the cam that allowed the hammer to retract each time it struck the bell in preparation of striking the bell again and again. Finally, he removed the hammer. This would be the critical part of his crude, remote, ON switch.

Using the hammer as a basic model for the design, he fashioned a new one. This one was twice as long and had two right angle bends in the opposite direction. It allowed the hammer to clear the back of the alarm clock casing but maintain the same stroke direction. It also doubled the stroke of the hammer, giving it a greater range to depress the button. He installed the new hammer in the clock, set the clock on a piece of paper and set the alarm. Marking the hammer location on the paper, he waited for the alarm to go off. After the alarm moved the hammer, he measured the stroke---eight millimeters. The stroke was just a tad short and may not reliably press the button far enough in to start the tape recorder.

Eric removed the hammer. He fashioned a new hammer that was three times the length of the original and reinstalled it in the clock. After the alarm went off, he measured the stroke distance---13 millimeters. Eric reset the alarm on the clock, then held the tape recorder against the hammer. A few minutes later the hammer moved, the button was depressed, and the tape recorder started recording. Only one problem remained: Using the original cam to create the hammer stroke also allowed it to retract with each revolution of the cam. The hammer would repeatedly strike the button with each subsequent revolution of the cam, until the spring driving the cam unwound. Although the sound was not loud, in a quiet room, over a prolonged period of time, it could take on the dimension of a small explosion.

Once again, Eric dismantled his contraption and removed the cam from its tiny shaft. This time he attached a metal protrusion onto the cam that was long enough to catch on the hammer. He secured it to the cam a quarter revolution past the elongated portion of the cam. If it worked, the piece of metal would catch on the hammer and stop the cam from revolving, not allowing the spring to wind down.

Eric rebuilt the clock one more time to test his latest modification. He held the tape recorder against the hammer and waited for the alarm to set off the sequence. Click---the sound of the hammer depressing the button, then it started to retract. Click---the hammer hit the button a second time. Before the hammer had retracted completely again, it stopped moving. I can live with that, thought Eric. Finally, he set the alarm to go off five minutes before the scheduled start of tomorrow's meeting. If it starts the tape before they arrive, they won't hear a thing.

By the time Eric finished fashioning his new, remote, timer con-trolled, 'on' switch, activity in the lobby was back down to a normal level. Eric had wrapped the components in his tweed jacket; still dressed as an old man, he made his way back to the conference room. When he arrived at conference room S, he found the door locked. After a few seconds of manipulating the lock mechanism, he heard the familiar sound of the bolt sliding. He opened the door, and stepped inside to a very dark, windowless room.

He removed the alarm clock and tape recorder from his jacket, setting them down on the table. Digging into his pocket, he found his penlight flashlight and started looking around the room for a location to hide the recorder. He looked up at the ceiling, then pulled a chair out from the table. Using the chair as a step, he climbed up on the table. He reached both hands over his head and pushed against the ceiling tile. The tile went up into the space between the ceiling and the floor above, and then he slid it to one side. Using the flashlight, he studied this new space. Ideally, he wanted the tape recorder at the center of the ceiling to maximize its range, but if someone looked up here during the sweep for bugs, it would be seen. There were four light fixtures equidistant from the center of the room, that offered the only visual protection for the tape recorder should someone actually look up here. He decided to hide it behind one of them.

Eric slid the ceiling tile back into its place and moved to the edge of the table at the front of the room. He slid back another ceiling tile next to one of the recessed light fixtures and pointed the flashlight into the new opening. The fixture held four fluorescent light bulbs in a two-foot square box entirely recessed into the ceiling creating a five-inch-high visual obstacle. Eric climbed back down off the table and moved the tape recorder and clock below the light, then climbed back onto the table. He picked up one item at a time and placed it on a ceiling tile. Next, he moved the tape recorder, so it was situated between the light fixture and the wall. Finally, he attached his makeshift timer. Before climbing down, he set the alarm on the clock, then slid the ceiling tile back into place. With that done, he climbed down from the table and moved a chair, so it sat directly below the recorder. Now he sat down to wait.

After three or four minutes he thought he heard the double click of the hammer striking the tape recorder button. He climbed back up, slid the tile back out of his way and checked the tape recorder. Sure enough, it was taping. He slid the tile back into place one more time, climbed down off the table again and went over to the door. He opened it to make sure no one was in the hall, then in a normal speaking voice said. "This is a test. This is just a test. If this were a real emergency, you would have been advised to tune to a local radio station." Corny, but effective, he thought. He reopened the door to confirm the hall was still empty. It was. Satisfied, he climbed back on the table for what he hoped would be the last time.

He slid the tile back and reached inside to turn the tape recorder off. He rewound the tape and played it back to himself. At first, he could barely hear what was recorded, but then he realized the volume was set too low. As the tape played, he slowly turned the volume up until he was satisfied with what he was hearing. "... a local radio station." Eric rewound the tape, turned it on record, and recorded the silence over his testing message. He repeated these two more times to further erase his voice, and making it difficult at best to reconstitute his voice. Although something of his voice would linger, any computer-generated effort would hardly work well enough to make his voice recognizable. He wasn't sure how well the consortium would search for bugs, but he assumed some effort would be made to make sure this room was sterile, unless of course, they were idiots. By taping over his voice repeatedly, and having handled the equipment with latex gloves, he limited the possibility they could trace it back to him. Assuming they even find the recorder, he thought.

He set the alarm for five minutes before eight o'clock in the morning, then slid the tile back into place. The tape was good for two hours per side, and while reading the instructions, he found out the recorder was equipped with auto reverse. So, he would be able to get a full four hours of the meeting. If the meeting went longer or started before eight, there was no telling what he would miss. But without the tape recorder he would have missed everything, so he was satisfied with the plan regardless. As he prepared to leave, he looked around one last time to make sure he didn't leave any evidence of his work behind. Satisfied the room was the way he found it, he left.

When he stepped into the hall it was empty. The lobby was crowded, but he was able to quickly work his through and return to his room.

Toomas and Sergei arrived at the room at the same time, seven thirty. Neither man said a word until they had finished their sweep of the room for bugs. They both looked for the traditional, or what they perceived as traditional bug, a small, easily hidden, microphone. They looked under all the furniture; behind every picture hanging on the wall and even removed the cover to all the outlets but didn't find anything. Toomas started to speak, but Sergei held up his finger indicating he should remain silent for a moment. Then he climbed on the chair near the door and stepped up onto the table. He reached up and removed one of the ceiling tiles and started looking around between the ceiling and the floor above. He didn't have a flashlight, and very little light from the room entered the space, so he couldn't see very well. Not satisfied with the results, he reached his arm into the space and felt around. A short time later he removed his hand. The only thing he learned by that exercise was how much dust can collect between the ceiling and the floor above.

"Well Toomas," Sergei began. "It would appear that we have a secure meeting place. Sometimes I wonder if we are not just a little paranoid, but then I realize the precautions are for our own good. Because we are just a little paranoid," he added. A wry smile broke across Sergei's face as he paused to think about what he had just said. "That always reminds me of my father, because he was particularly fond of saying the same thing just prior to doling out some form of punishment. However, since we have never found anything, I wonder if it really is necessary."

"You know it is." Toomas said with obvious disgust in his voice. The search had taken almost the entire half hour and Jason arrived just in time to hear Toomas' response. "Do I detect a touch of anger in your voice, Toomas?" He asked as he walked around the table trying to decide where he should sit.

"Who's angry?" Howard asked as he entered the room. "Not that silly Russian again?" He looked at Sergei and gave him his version of a wry smile. Howard took the seat at the end of the table, opposite the chalkboard.

What is the matter with Sergei this morning?" Seymour asked no one in particular as he entered the room. "I suppose you're upset that the coffee and rolls have not arrived yet. Well, you can relax. I checked with the front desk on way here, and he assured me they would arrive momentarily. So, if you can just remain patient for a little while longer, breakfast will be served."

As if on cue, there was a knock on the door. Through the open doorway everyone could see that the cart with their morning refreshments had arrived. "Now, isn't that quaint. Come in. Come in." Seymour spoke to the waitress pushing the cart. Then looking at his watch, he said to everyone in his room. "Precisely eight o'clock. When will you all learn? The English do not believe in being, as you Americans are so fond of saying, fashionably late."

The waitress proceeded to roll the cart with various pastries and morning beverages into the room. No one spoke as she transferred the contents from the cart to the table. When she was done, she asked Seymour if he would need anything else. He told her everything was exactly as he had requested, and if they needed anything else he would be sure to contact her. Then he thanked her and closed the door behind her as she left. Then turning back to the group, he said, "Toomas. I'm to assume you have taken care of the arrangements we discussed at our last meeting."

"That is correct. We were able to employ him at a slightly reduced fee, compared to his counterpart. It seems he assumed the deal was priced in the currency of the employer. Since he equated me with the employer's role, he expected the price was in Deutsche Marks, not dollars as we had budgeted. The net result is a substantial savings over what I thought I was negotiating."

"Can we expect the same quality of work from him as we can from Jacque?" Howard asked, showing concern. "I must say, it bothers me the man didn't try to negotiate a better price. It makes me feel a little uncomfortable relying on someone who isn't quick enough to negotiate, and as a result settles for substantially less money than we were willing to pay."

"Don't worry too much over that. He did not ask for more money as part of his fee. But his expenses, at fifty thousand a day, put the total cost at close to the million-dollar mark. So, if you figure the total cost for Jacque was just over one million, Manuel is a little cheaper, but certainly no bargain. The savings come in because I thought we were negotiating in dollars not marks. If it had been dollars, the deal as negotiated would have cost 1.5 million. So, Howard, you do not have to feel as if the man is less than you bargained for, because as you can see, he did alright for himself."

"Believe it or not, that does make me feel better." Howard responded to Toomas' remarks.

"The next order of business, and if we weren't all so greedy it probably should have been our first order of business, is: Whom do we credit with the bombing? Or are we to assume it was pure coincidence that the flight the Sheik was scheduled to be on was blown out of the air?" These were the first words Jason had spoken since his little jab at Sergei when he came in. He had been quietly listening to the conversation so far and was not impressed with everyone's concern over the details pertaining to the costs when the group had not yet been briefed on the obvious attempt to assassinate the Sheik.

"Based on our research into Jacque, it is safe to conclude he was not responsible. However, with our limited knowledge about our new employee, I don't feel qualified to draw the same conclusion about him." Up to this point he had been scanning the room while speaking, directing his words toward everyone. Now he turned and looked directly at Toomas.

"Was the bombing an act of terrorism as the news media has implied? Or was it really Manuel just using a modus operandi we did not expect from him?"

"I do not know. It is not within my ability to confirm that one of the two men we hired was responsible should the Sheik die. It is entirely possible that the bombing was as the media is speculating, an act of terrorism. Must I remind everyone that the deal calls for payment to both parties regardless of how the man dies?"

"I think you are avoiding the reason for the question. The way the man dies or the fact that we would have to pay for it is of no concern to any of us, but the timing is another matter. Jacque was told not to start until tomorrow. Was Manuel given the same time constraint?"

"Are you accusing me of something? If so, come right out and say it. I ask you, why would I do that? No purpose would be served by not telling Manuel of our timing requirements."

Jason did not immediately respond to Toomas, but he noticed Toomas never really answered his questions. At this point, Howard interjected, "Is the decoy ready Sergei?"

Sergei was startled out of his daze by Howard's question, then relieved that the conversation was being redirected. "Like any good Russian, I am true to my word. I told you he would be ready for tomorrow's news conference, and he is."

"Will we have a chance to see him in action before he gets the acid test in front of the media and the rest of the world?"

Seymour, I spoke with you last night about getting a television and VCR for today's meeting. If you were successful, I think now would be an excellent time to do so." Seymour excused himself, got up from his seat, and left the room." Meanwhile, Sergei continued, "If I could not present him in person, I thought it would be appropriate to provide a tape as an alternative. It was my contention that if he was deemed acceptable by this auspicious group, he might be used at the news conference tomorrow in Jerusalem."

"You really think he is ready," Jason said incredulously. The news seemed to placate Jason, who only a minute ago was ready to tear into Toomas."

"Not only do I think he is ready, but I am also so sure of it that I have taken the liberty of sending him to Jerusalem for tomorrow's news conference. The Sheik has already been informed how we want the situation handled, should everyone agree with my assessment of the decoy's readiness. He will be waiting for my phone call today to inform him of our decision. I might add that this man has exceeded my greatest expectations. He is so convincing, that I dare anyone to tell the difference."

Sergei continued, describing the mechanics of how he was able to transform this relatively obscure man into a public figure. Seymour was just returning as Sergei finished describing the methods used to reinforce the physical gestures and idiosyncrasies common to, yet unique in every man. "These subtle gestures are the differences between an accepted decoy and a professional impersonator. An impersonator is only trying to give the impression he is someone else, and he uses gestures to help create that image. But he doesn't concern himself with the accuracy of those gestures in his version of the person he is impersonating. Everyone knows he is not the person he is impersonating, yet they are still awed at his ability to convince them he sounds, and to some small degree, even looks like that person. Our decoy not only has the natural appearance of the Sheik, but also sounds like him, walks like him, and uses the same arm, hand, and body motions. His facial expressions for joy, anger, love, contentment, every emotion you can imagine have been replicated in him."

Turning to Seymour, "If you have that machine ready, we can show everyone what I mean. I have brought two tapes. One that we used for training the decoy: A tape depicting the Sheik himself as he confers with an unseen aid. The second is our man's rendition of the same scene. I will not be telling you which one is which until after you have viewed both. I assure you; you will be impressed."

Sergei walked over to the cart containing the television and VCR. Seymour had everything set so all he had to do was insert a tape and press PLAY. Immediately the Sheik's familiar face was seen across the screen. His face almost covered the entire screen, and he was rambling on about his philosophy on why Arab and Jew hate each other. He described what he interpreted were the primary reasons for their hostility toward each other. But more importantly, he outlined his solution to their problem.

Slowly the camera moved back and his whole body was visible. He was standing, talking to someone just out of view of the camera. He was dressed in the traditional white Arab robes that had come to be synonymous with his image. With his full body in view, he began to walk around, actually pacing back and forth as he continued speaking. He would use his hands and arm movements to emphasize what he was saying during different parts of his speech. Occasionally he would pause from speaking, then he would stop walking as well. It would appear as if he was in deep thought over some troubling item that had just come to him. A concept he hadn't had the chance to absorb into his overall worldview. Then without warning he would start speaking again, usually on a new train of thought, but not always. And, as if his own voice were the cue, he would begin pacing again.

The person he was speaking to was never seen or heard, but it was obvious by the Sheik's actions he was speaking to someone he had great respect for. During the course of the tape, which lasted a full fifteen minutes, the Sheik's voice ranged from sad and contemplative to ecstatic and on fire, from passionate to carefree. His physical motions matched his voice in fervor and commitment.

Sergei surveyed the other members of the consortium as they watched the Sheik on tape. It was clear by their facial expressions the Sheik was having the same effect on them that he had on so many other people in the world. It was certainly understandable how the Sheik was able to gain support from both sides, when his charisma could affect even the men who used and controlled him. Without hesitating, the first tape was replaced, and the second tape was started.

It was clear the locations were not identical, nor even the clothes. This Sheik had a baby blue trim around the collar of his robe. The camera moved back from the close-up as it did in the first tape, to reveal what could certainly pass as an identical twin to the man in the first tape. Sergei had been able to achieve the similarity in physical features that had been lacking just six months ago.

As this man spoke, the charisma that was so strong in the first tape almost seemed stronger the second time around. Although the words were not identical, the message was the same. And although the motions and movements had not been choreographed, the same feelings and emotions were telegraphed to the audience. Sergei had indeed managed to create a second Sheik Omani. A clone so accurate, that he could probably convince the real Sheik that he could not possibly be himself. Assuming the first Sheik was in fact the real Sheik.

At the end of the tape, Sergei took his time walking back to the television ignoring the hum of the gray and white snow that covered the screen. No one spoke, creating a deafening silence. Each member of the consortium was engulfed in his own thoughts as each considered the ramifications of what they had seen. A second Sheik, who they controlled, first would help establish their power base in the Middle East, then throughout the world. Their plan was coming together better than expected: Their power would be equal to none.

Toomas was the first to speak, and he spoke to the group as a whole. "It would appear that our Russian friend was not exaggerating in his description of the decoy. I certainly could not tell which one was the Sheik. I think if we all guessed, we might find both men receiving two votes, Sergei notwithstanding." Then turning to Sergei, he said, "You have exceeded our expectations, Sergei. I thank you for your tireless effort. An effort that has proven fruitful before its time."

Each man in his turn rose from his seat, and echoed Toomas' message, but in their own words. Each acknowledged Sergei's enormous accomplishment and stated their appreciation. When they finished congratulating Sergei, Toomas spoke to the group once again. "Something that I'm sure did not go unnoticed but is the most revealing and warrants specific attention is that both men presented identical philosophies but used different words in their speech. You could say different approaches; still, they came across as if they were identical people. I, for one, had expected a carbon copy of the two men: a stage presence, a man playing the part of the Sheik. But it appears Sergei has developed much more." Turning to Sergei he asked. "Who wrote the script for the decoy to follow? For the words could not possibly have been his own."

Sergei's smile slowly stretched across his entire face until his mouth seemed to swallow the rest of his face. When he was sure everyone was growing impatient waiting for his response, he finally spoke. "Toomas, you have identified the truly magnificent accomplishment in this task. The decoy was provided the theme, the central premise he was expected to present. Then he was shown the tape of the real Sheik Omani. He was allowed to see it as many times as was necessary, but he could not memorize it. He was told this would be his final exam. **He... himself.**" Sergei emphasized the man again. "**He** had to develop the speech, the presence, the image of the Sheik. **He** had to be able to think like the Sheik, act like the Sheik and look like the Sheik. **He** had to become the Sheik. That is what we tried to accomplish. And, I believe we have."

"Unless someone has an objection, I would suggest that the decoy is ready, and we give him the opportunity to demonstrate his skills in the field. We can inform the real Sheik Omani today that he is to let the decoy handle the press conference in Jerusalem tomorrow. Toomas turned to each to get their vote. First, he looked to Seymour. He nodded his head yes. Next to Howard, seated at the opposite end of the table. He also nodded in the affirmative. Finally, he turned to Jason, who without hesitation and in anticipation of Toomas' question, was already shaking his head yes. "It is unanimous. Sergei, it would be appropriate for you to relay the message to both the decoy and the Sheik."

Jason, sensing the meeting was nearing its natural conclusion decided it was time to speak. "Before we bring the meeting to a close, I would like to discuss two more items. To continue the discussion on our decoy, I would suggest we refer to him as something other than 'the decoy.' Possibly we could call him Oman 2, or something along that line. At least everyone would know which one was being referred to without giving away his questionable origin." Continuing, but directing his next statement directly to Sergei he added, "With that as my prelude, I was wondering Sergei. Oman 2 is so convincing; how will we be able to tell him apart from the real Sheik. Especially since both will play extremely important roles for us, albeit certainly with very different endings."

"You raise a very important issue. But that is a problem we had anticipated. I decided to give Oman 2, as you call him, a tattoo in a location hidden from the general public's view. This way if the problem of identities ever occurs, we can resolve it easily without compromising him to the public. Does that meet with your approval, Jason?"

"An excellent idea Sergei. I commend you once again for anticipating a difficult issue. The only other item I was hoping to be updated on was do we have any additional information on Eric Dent? Has he been taken care of? Is he still a threat? Is Jacque or Manuel expected to take care of him now that we have two on the payroll?" Jason stopped, looking around hoping for someone to provide the update.

When it was obvious none was forthcoming, Toomas interjected. "Jihad informed us last time that he hired Manuel. I did not want Manuel to know we were also behind his hiring by Jihad; consequently, I did not discuss that issue with him at all. It would be my contention that Jacque, not both, is the only one making plans to deal with him. I would assume he would deal with him before he tried anything on the Sheik, but the bombing may prove that theory false. In either case, taking care of Eric in a timely fashion could be the difference between success and failure."

"Would it be appropriate to get word to Manuel, through Jihad, about why Eric needs to be taken care of? He may not have any idea that Dent is looking to make his job impossible."

"It's doubtful he would be able to get word to him in time, but we can take that precaution just in case."

The conversation ended abruptly leaving a feeling not unlike that of a first date. That period in time at the end of the evening when conversation has haltingly come to an end, and both stand at the door unsure what to do or say next. There was little else to discuss, until one or both of the assassins reported back that they had neutralized Eric. Or the news media reports the tragic death of one Sheik Omani.

"The next meeting," Howard began. When no one interrupted, he continued. "I think it might be worthwhile to schedule the next meeting in Jerusalem. It would give us the chance to view firsthand, the area and people that are the center of our focus right now and into the indefinite future."

"I do not like the idea!" Sergei exploded at Howard. "It is not necessary for me to experience the Jewish idiots up front and per-sonal. I know what they are like. Remember, thousands came from my homeland and the native countries of the rest of you as well. You may go there and meet if you'd like, but you will do so without me."

"Sergei, I didn't realize Jews could cause you so much consternation. I always thought Russians, being superior to Jews, would find them an insignificant nuisance. But if you feel that strongly about it, do you have any other suggestions?"

Toomas had stared at Sergei throughout Howard's comments. Now he spoke before Sergei could respond to Howard. "I think it would be most appropriate to do as you say, meet in Jerusalem. It would be good for Sergei to get over his psychological problems. And what better way for him to do that, then to meet them head on. If no one else objects, I will make arrangements at the Star of David Hotel."

Sergei was so taken back by Toomas' comments he was unable to respond. Instead, he just stood there, staring at Toomas, his anger apparent to everyone in the room.

8

-Even when the fool walks along the road his sense is lacking, and he demonstrates to everyone he is a fool.

Eric retrieved the tape recorder and was heading back to his room to evaluate the worth of its contents. He knew, by the length of the meeting, he had not been able to capture the entire meeting on the single tape. But he had managed to tape the bulk of it. With almost four hours of the meeting on the tape, he was confident he would learn more than a few new things about the consortium and its plans. He spent most of the day keeping an eye on the room and its occupants and had little time for anything else. Consequently, he was famished and ordered a meal from the hotel restaurant to be delivered to his room

As he approached the door to his room an uneasy feeling came over him, as if he were being warned of some impending danger by an unseen but sentient being. The feeling grew with each step he took, bringing him closer to his room. When he reached the door, he began to look for the small thread he had placed between the door and the jamb. It was still securely in place, but so was the feeling that he was walking into a trap. Rather than ignoring his senses and walking into his room, he stood outside the door. First, he listened at the door, while considering his next move. If someone were inside, they were clearly finished with their work, because the silence in the room was absolute, except for the whir of the air conditioner. If they were still there, they would have the element of surprise on their side.

He considered the only other alternative to gain entry to his room, the window. From what he could remember, there was the imitation balcony outside the window of each room. It wasn't a functional balcony by any means. It was there for the sole purpose of giving the person looking at the hotel, from the neighborhood, the visual impression that each room had a balcony. But in reality, what they had was a balcony railing. Each railing was a black wrought iron railing that extended a foot past each window on either side, and six inches out from the wall of the building. From a distance, in a postcard or a travel brochure, it would give the visual appearance of a balcony. What concerned Eric was that the distance between balcony railings was probably no more than three feet. Someone could use them to maneuver along the wall to his room, and then enter through the window.

Eric put the tape recorder inside a coat pocket and prepared to meet the unseen danger he thought was waiting for him inside the room. He unlocked the door, stood to one side of the doorway in case it was booby trapped, then slowly opened it. Nothing happened. He paused for a moment, quickly surveyed the perimeter of the doorway looking for any clues, then stepped inside. It was late in the afternoon, but with the drapes drawn, the hotel room was barely light enough for him to see through the shadows.

Once inside the room he closed the door. Then he stood perfectly still as his eyes became accustomed to the low light, and he was able to study every object inside. Again, he was looking for any indication that someone had been there or might still be there. Not convinced that he was overreacting, he cautiously approached the window to examine the handle and lock. As he approached the window, his apprehension heightened, but he still couldn't see anything. Just as he realized why the window was still open, a shadowy figure burst through the closed window.

Eric reacted, without thought, reflexes taking over. His right arm came up to counter the blow, then he felt the sting of the knife as it sliced through his heavy tweed coat and reached the flesh of his forearm below. The wound was deep enough to force Eric to retract his arm, but not before he had brought his hand, fingers rigid and fully extended, up into the solar plexus of his attacker, just below the end of the sternum.

His hand penetrated the soft flesh, and his attacker felt immense pain. He felt as if Eric's hand was able to pierce his body, reaching into his chest, grabbed his heart and squeezed the life out of him. That was the last thing his attacker would experience before he passed out. Eric released his grip, and his would be assailant fell to the floor.

Eric let the man lie on the floor while he rushed into the bathroom and removed the tweed coat to examine his own wound. His attacker had not been able to utilize the proper force of his flying attack. Too much effort had been spent maintaining his own balance prior to the flying attack, while he was hunched over hanging onto the windowsill. The knife had cut into the muscle three inches below the elbow, but fortunately only penetrated a quarter inch. It was painful but was not bleeding very much. He cleaned the cut carefully, then grabbed a shirt, cut off a sleeve, and wrapped it around his arm. Finally, he folded one end under and pulled the other tight to secure it in place.

He returned to the dead man lying on the floor in the bedroom. The man had fallen forward onto his stomach beyond the end of the bed. While Eric was rifling through his back pockets, there was a knock at the door followed by, "Room service."

"Just a minute," he yelled. He looked around to see if there was anything he could do with the body quickly. But he realized he was stuck: if he opened the door, the body would be in clear view of the waiter. But if that weren't bad enough, the odor of the man's release of his bodily fluids in death had already filled the room. Eric called back to the waiter outside, "Could you just leave the tray outside?" Then as he took out a five-pound note and slid it under the door, he continued, "This is for you." The waiter took the five pounds and slid the bill under the door to Eric, asking him to sign it next to the room number at the bottom. Satisfied, the waiter left.

Eric let out a heavy sigh of relief as the waiter's footsteps could be heard as he walked away. He looked through the peephole to make sure the hall was empty, then retrieved the tray with his supper. He set the food down on the bed and returned his attention to the dead man lying on the floor. As expected, there was nothing in his pockets that would identify him or explain who sent him. Eric knew there were plenty of reasons for someone to want him out of the picture, but fortunately this man wasn't going to be the one to master that task.

Eric dragged the body closer to the bed, then slid him under. The odor alone would preclude the ability to hide the body in the room, but there were few alternatives at the moment. He decided that the body would have to wait until after dark, when he could dispose of it anonymously.

Eric sat down on the bed and readied the tape recorder to help pass the time. There was little else to do while he waited for dark to come. He would have liked to eat, but the smell in the room made him nauseous, and the thought of eating would only heighten that feeling. So, Eric turned on the tape instead.

He had missed the first few minutes of Sergei and Toomas' conversation while they were checking the room for bugs, and the tape had ended almost exactly at the end of the second videotape. The body of the discussion, that had been the prelude to the videotape, was recorded. None of the discussion after the videotape had ended was recorded. This left Eric convinced that the intent of the consortium was not to assassinate the Sheik, but rather the decoy. It was apparent they would not be through with the Sheik upon his staged demise. But…Why? It just didn't make sense.

First, they created the Sheik. Then they mold him into a superhero of sorts, capable of achieving peace in the Middle East. Or at least that is the impression they are trying to present to the rest of the world. Then their plan, as I am given to believe, is to assassinate him, catapulting the Middle East into chaos. This will allow the oil consortium to take control of the world oil situation because most, if not all of the OPEC countries, are thrown into the turmoil as well. While the Middle East is engulfed in war, and the surviving OPEC resources that aren't destroyed in the first major battles are diverted to that war effort, the door to controlling the rest of the world's oil supply is opened to the new consortium. However, this plan does not require a false Sheik. In fact, the only reason that Eric could think of is that the Sheik is actually a part of the inner circle of the conspiracy, not a fabrication, and his life, not the person Sheik Omani, is to be spared. Uneasily Eric settles on this explanation for the decoy. Because that would mean the decoy was to be killed, and the man who plays the part of Sheik Omani today would live, although not as the Sheik.

The sun had set hours before, and the activity on the street outside his window had dwindled to almost nothing. He checked the time: it was one in the morning, time to dispose of the body and prepare for his trip to Jerusalem. He left the room and went downstairs to the front desk to see if he could find out if there were any empty rooms on his floor. There wasn't anyone at the desk, so he climbed over the counter and looked at the computer monitor for a few seconds, then started typing. The person on the night shift was probably in back trying to stay awake. If he was quiet enough, he should be able to get the information he needed and be gone without disturbing him or her. The software used a familiar operating system, and Eric's understanding of computers was sufficient for him to locate which rooms were devoid of occupants.

Armed with this information, Eric headed to the room he had chosen, and broke into it. He looked around to make sure it was in fact empty, and judging by the dust on everything, it had been unoccupied for some time. He retrieved the body of his attacker from his room and placed him in the bed of the empty room. Rigor mortis had already begun to set in, compounding the already difficult task of moving a dead body between rooms. That finished, Eric returned to his room to get what little sleep he could before leaving in the morning.

- - - - -

Doshe's wife was awakened in the middle of the night by the obnoxious ringing of the telephone. It must be past midnight, she thought as she reached for the phone on the nightstand. What idiot would be calling Doshe at this hour? She knew it wasn't for her, and it was hardly unusual for Doshe. But as often as it happened, she was still irritated anew at it happening again. She picked up the phone, but before she could say hello, the voice on the other end started in.

"Doshe, it's Ariel. I have gotten my first report from Marie. You will be shocked at what she was able to find out."

"Ariel, what in the name of Abraham, Isaac and Jacob are you doing? Don't you realize we are trying to sleep? All day long the phone sits, quiet, waiting to be used. Then nightfall comes and it rings forever. Doshe is sleeping, can it wait until morning, or must I wake him?"

"I am so sorry to disturb you at this hour. But you know I would not call unless it was extremely important, and Doshe did give me explicit instructions to call him at any time. Whenever I heard something."

Without warning, Doshe's wife set the phone down and Ariel could hear her trying to roust Doshe out of his sleep. Doshe was able to sleep through a bomb raid, and often had in the early days of settling in Israel. However, his wife was a much lighter sleeper, and suffered from lack of sleep because everything woke her up. Now the ringing phone, seemingly an every night occurrence, had taken the place of the bombs and made it very difficult for her to get adequate sleep. Meanwhile, her husband slept easily and often, and no matter the number of times he was awakened during the night to take a phone call, upon hanging up, he would immediately fall back to sleep. So, she was forever tired, and he was always well rested.

"Ariel, I'm so glad you called," he answered the phone as if he had been up all night just waiting for his call.

"I have gotten my first report from Marie. You will be shocked at what she was able to find out." Ariel repeated the opening line he had used when speaking to Doshe's wife. "She managed to follow the German to Paris where she overheard bits of a conversation he had with the Russian, Sergei, in a restaurant near the Louvre. Then he flew back to Germany and took care of business for a day or so. But then he met the same man, Sergei, in a pub outside London. She is sure these two men are not quite what they seem to be. Based on her report, they are indeed involved in something that does not include the rest of the group." Ariel stopped his explanation to ask Doshe a question. "How well do you know this group that is supporting you outside official channels?"

"We know who they are, by name, occupation, that sort of thing. We're also aware that they support other groups in the Middle East, but we have not been able to confirm the names of any of the other groups. We know that their common denominator is oil, but since we are not an oil power, that doesn't concern us. Based on oil being their motivation, we've made the assumption that they are targeting OPEC. That is about the extent of our knowledge. I should add we were not concerned with their motivation until recently, and that is why I asked for your assistance. We have begun a full investigation into the backgrounds of each of them, from birth to the present. We are sufficiently concerned with their recent activities that we fear they may actually be a threat, not benefactors. Unfortunately, we probably should have done this sooner. Now, why do you ask?"

Ariel cleared his throat as if what he was about to say would require a long diatribe, and then started in. Of course, Ariel always tried to give the impression that what he would have to say would be long, in depth, and insightful. However, that rarely happened. "Then you were aware of this Sergei?"

"Yes"

"Did you know they, the German and Russian, were in bed with an American named Tom? And that this Manuel was not supposed to even try anything until after the news conference. This Tom, whoever he is, was very upset about the bombing, or more accurately, the timing of the bombing. However, one interesting thing about this was he thought someone named Jacque was responsible, and no one tried to convince him otherwise." Ariel paused to take a breath, then said, "He wouldn't be thinking the assassin Jacque, would he? Because that would mean they have hired two men for the same job."

"I don't know." Doshe considered for a moment the implications of hiring two assassins. Then decided he didn't have enough information because there was not any rational explanation to justify two killers. "My guess would be they had discussed hiring Jacque, but then for some unknown reason chose Manuel and did not want to tell this Tom what they had done. At least not yet."

"Well, your guess would be wrong, because Marie was able to confirm they hired both Manuel and Jacque."

"Are you certain of that?" This was an unexpected twist.

"Absolutely. When she was in the pub, she was able to overhear their entire conversation, and she was adamant on this point. She recognized the importance of it and wanted to make sure I did as well. Neither of them was supposed to try anything until after the news conference, and that was why Tom was upset. She did say, the German did not seem to care that Tom was upset though."

"Fair enough. Do you have any other information on this Tom?"

"No. Marie was able to bribe the receptionist because his office was in an office complex. The receptionist works for almost everyone in the building, so she has no loyalty to any of them. The receptionist is a bit nosey, so when an overseas call comes in, she has the tendency to listen in, hoping to hear the voice of someone important. Well, she also leans to the greedy side. So, when the call came in and Marie was there, the receptionist, for a small fee, allowed her to listen instead. However, all Marie could report was the name, and a few incidental details of the conversation. So, what I've given you is all there is."

"Just to make sure I have all of this right, let me feed some of this back. Sergei, a member of the group, is meeting secretly with Toomas, also a member of the group. That implies they probably have an agenda, similar, but different from the rest of the group. The group also has a connection with an American named Tom. However, they are not keeping him entirely informed. We do not know who Tom is or whom he works for. Is that correct?"

"Yes"

"The group has hired two men to assassinate the Sheik. Tom is not aware of this, and they have no plans to tell him. Also, neither ass-assin has been informed of the other one, although it is safe to assume they will become aware of each other sooner or later. They may have a timetable, but the attempt on the Sheik's life, if that is what the bombing was, and I believe it was based on what you just told me; was outside of that timetable."

Ariel had relayed everything Marie had told him, and he knew some of the information would be troubling. Doshe was pleased with the fruits of Marie's labor, but it was taking time for him to understand the implications of what she had found out, particularly the ramifications of two assassins. And he wasn't sure if time was an ally or a foe at this point. But he feared it was working against him. Slowly, a theory developed that fit this new data. Unconventional as it was, this idea offered some unique opportunities. "Did Marie offer her own opinion about anything, or was she simply reporting the information?" Doshe finally broke the silence.

"She was not asked for her opinion. Lacking understanding as to the specifics of why she was following this individual, she would not be inclined to formulate any. Or if she did, she certainly would not offer them without being asked. And I did not ask."

"Is she Jewish?"

"No."

"Can she be trusted? Or should she be replaced with someone who is more devoted to protecting the Jewish existence? What I am driving at is this: I am beginning to suspect this consortium is not looking out for the best interests of our people or Israel. Not a particularly brilliant assessment, I realize, but there are many people in Israel that desperately want the Sheik to be successful in bringing peace to this part of the world. As she continues to follow Toomas, she will begin to understand their plans and the impact those plans have on us, as Jews, and Israel. If she truly is neutral, she will probably report the details as accurately as she can. However, if she is like most of the world, her natural inclination would be to withhold critical information." Doshe's own explanation had convinced himself; Marie had to be replaced with a Jew. Realizing this, he didn't wait for Ariel to respond to his questions, but added, "She will have to be replaced."

The two men understood each other. Without question, Ariel recognized and agreed with Doshe's conclusion. They could not risk trusting someone to be neutral and yet committed to the degree that may be necessary, particularly if that person did not have the same things at stake. No Gentile could possibly understand the importance of this issue, but then no group of Gentiles had ever been persecuted throughout history, the way the Jewish people had. Both men understood that it would take the dedication of a Jew, whose very existence may be held in the balance, to provide the security required for this task.

"Ariel, I know of a woman in Tel Aviv that could take over for Marie. Her name is Maruch, and her dedication to the Jewish people is easily documented. Do you know where she could pick up Toomas?"

"Not before he reaches Jerusalem for the news conference. Marie had no idea where he was headed after the meeting. However, she does check in on a regular basis and may know next time she calls. If she does, I can let you know the German's itinerary. In the meantime, you might want to get Maruch to Jerusalem." He paused for a moment, then added, "Because that is where I would suspect the German will end up."

"An excellent suggestion. I'll have Maruch in Jerusalem by tonight. I will notify you as soon as she establishes herself with Toomas. Then you can relieve Marie of her obligation."

- - - - -

The news conference was set for one in the afternoon, and Sergei was barely able to get the decoy and himself to Jerusalem in time to work out the details with the real Sheik Omani on the substitution. He had explained in painful detail exactly how the decoy for the news conference would replace him. Now, his immediate concern was how to execute the replacement of the Sheik with the decoy, while maintaining the cover-up. He couldn't just march his man out because the hotel was crawling with news media personnel. And even though every effort had been made to downplay the Sheik's presence, the perceived attempt on the Sheik's life had only served to exacerbate the situation. The Sheik had become too important a personality, and the resulting entourage of reporters was growing steadily, making the switch more difficult by the minute.

Sergei called the Sheik from his room, but Sylvan answered. "Hello."

"I need to speak to Sheik Omani," Sergei spoke directly into the phone, exaggerating his already pronounced Russian accent. His intent was to speak directly with the Sheik because Sylvan was neither a part of the plan nor aware of it. However, it was Sylvan's responsibility to screen all inquiries for the Sheik, and whenever possible, he was to handle them himself. Sergei thought by making it obvious who he was, he would be able to circumvent Sylvan's standard delay tactics, allowing him to get through to the Sheik sooner.

Sylvan would have none of it. "The Sheik is not taking calls at the moment. He is preparing for his news conference at one this afternoon. My name is Sylvan. I am Sheik Omani's personal secretary and speaking with me is like speaking with the Sheik, himself. May I inquire as to the nature of your call?" Sylvan had recognized the voice on the other end of the phone as the obnoxious Russian that the Sheik has granted, against Sylvan's recommendation, a number of private interviews.

Disgusted, Sergei swore at Sylvan, then added. "No, you may not inquire. Sylvan, you know who this is. Now it is very important that you allow me to speak to the Sheik immediately." Sergei's voice steadily rose in intensity as well as decibels.

"Your voice does sound the least little bit familiar, but I can not recall the name. As I stated earlier: Speaking with me is like having an audience with the Sheik, himself. If you could state your business, maybe I could be of assistance. You will never know unless you give me a chance."

Sergei stood in his room holding the phone in front of him, as if the phone had taken on a life of its own. As if it could be reasoned with, which was not the case with Sylvan, Sergei thought. He was flabbergasted at the gall of this two-bit secretary, thinking he was somehow qualified to answer for the Sheik. Keeping him, Sergei, from speaking to the Sheik directly was unconscionable. Without bringing the phone back up to his mouth, he yelled at it. "Sylvan, I will have your job for this!" Then he slammed the phone down in Sylvan's ear.

Sergei began to explain to the decoy about what had just happened, but Oman 2 had not only heard the entire conversation but was able to explain to Sergei why Sylvan was doing what he was doing. He suggested Sergei try the direct approach. Go to the door and making sure your voice was loud enough that the Sheik could hear, repeat the conversation with Sylvan. Somewhat assuaged, Sergei left the room to confront Sylvan at the door to the Sheik's room.

Sergei knocked on the door and waited for Sylvan to respond. But instead of hearing Sylvan's voice, he heard the familiar click and jangling of a security chain, as whoever was on the other side unsecured the door prior to opening it. When the door opened, he was greeted by the Sheik, "Hello, Sergei. When I awoke this morning, my message light was on. It seems Toomas wanted to prepare your way, so he sent a FAX briefly telling me of your impending visit. When I overheard Sylvan's responses on the phone a few minutes ago, I surmised he was talking with you. You see, he reserves that voice for complete strangers, and you. For some unknown reason he finds you overbearing, or so he says. I hope you can find it in your heart to forgive him."

From the moment he opened the door he began speaking, not allowing Sergei to respond. While talking, he reached for Sergei's hand and directed him into the room. A number of reporters, who had noticed Sergei approaching the door to the Sheik's room, were already descending on them like vultures, and the Sheik wanted him inside before he would have to make a statement. One reporter placed his foot just inside the threshold of the door to stop the door from closing. But the reporter was not prepared for the Sheik's response. The Sheik looked at the foot, swiftly brought his own foot down sharply on the toes inside the offending shoe. The reporter quickly withdrew his foot, and the Sheik nonchalantly closed the door. The reporter turned to a number of his colleagues to see their reaction to what the Sheik had done. But with the door closed, they quickly lost interest and returned to their spots at the end of the hall to sit and wait until the next opportunity came along.

The Sheik continued to talk after the door closed, "After hearing the way Sylvan treated you, I explained to him that in the future, you are to be given free access to me at anytime. He assures me that he can do that, although not before warning me about how dangerous you are. He has returned to his room to complete the final details before the news conference, so we can speak freely. Did the rest of the group concur with your opinion pertaining to our mutual friend?" Although the Sheik had said they could speak freely, neither man felt secure enough to divulge the information outright.

"That is why I am here," Sergei replied. "If you think it would be appropriate for someone of your stature to visit my room, we can review his progress report. In my haste to get here, due to your personal secretary, I forgot them in my room. Would you like to accompany me?"

"I would indeed."

Getting out of this room and back to Sergei's would present a more difficult task. The Sheik made a phone call to Sylvan and asked him to engage the reporters in the hall with some conversation. While he was keeping the reporters occupied, Sergei could go out and wait for the elevator to arrive. When the Sheik heard the doors to the elevator open, he could slip out of his room, and hopefully get in the elevator before anyone could corner him.

Sergei watched for Sylvan to pass his view as he peered out the peephole. Upon seeing Sylvan, he waited another thirty seconds to give Sylvan time to engage the reporters in conversation, then headed for the elevator. As he walked toward the elevator, he glanced back at the group of reporters to see how well Sylvan was doing. To his credit, Sylvan had taken a spot against the window, and the five reporters had created a semi circle around him, all facing the window. One reporter quickly glanced at Sergei when he heard the door open, but when Sergei closed the door, and the Sheik wasn't with him; he turned his attention back to Sylvan.

There was only one other room, Sylvan's, separating the Sheik's room from the elevator. He would have to listen closely, but he should be able to hear the elevator doors open when it arrived at the floor. Hearing them, Sheik Omani quietly opened the door, glanced at the reporters, and then moved toward the elevator. He listened as he walked to the elevator hearing Sylvan describe the circumstances that led up to the Sheik and himself missing the ill-fated flight over Chatel-Denis. He noticed Sylvan was taking certain liberties in his description, not unlike the methods he used when screening people from the Sheik. The Sheik would have liked to stay and watch Sylvan work his spell on the reporters, but he knew he couldn't. He slipped out and quietly, but quickly, strode unmolested to the elevator where Sergei was waiting, holding the door open.

With the Sheik safely inside, Sergei allowed the door to close. None of the reporters noticed the Sheik leave his room. They rode the elevator in silence. Neither man spoke until they were inside Sergei's room, then the Sheik's trained replacement walked into the room from the adjoining doorway. Both men stood there staring at each other. This was the first time they had actually seen each other in the flesh. Previously they had only seen videotapes of the other.

Sheik Omani was the first one to speak, "So this is how the rest of the world sees me. I do not know whether to be impressed or depressed. May I ask you your real name?"

"Greg Herms. In case you are interested, I am of mixed German and Arab descent. That is probably why the physical features were not so different from your own to start with. The mixture, although not Arab and Jew, yielded a similar result. You should be aware, that portions of my appearance are the handiwork of two Russian specialists, and one American. Judging from you, they did an adequate job."

"Yes, they did." Both men continued to evaluate each other, at least the physical appearance. Finally, Sheik Omani turned to Sergei and asked, "Am I to assume you would like to test Mr. Herms out at the news conference, or did you have some other plans?"

"It is the group's unanimous decision to give Greg the opportunity at this afternoon's press conference. I thought before we committed to that, it would be a good idea for the two of you to meet and get your opinion. Also, if you agree, we might have time to test him with Sylvan."

"The conference is less than two hours away, so I do not believe there would be adequate time for the test with Sylvan. We need to decide now--if we should risk using Mr. Herms at the news conference."

Greg's gaze had been fixed on Sheik Omani ever since he entered the room. He was continuing his training by comparing himself to the real Sheik, making mental notes of slight nuances in the real Sheik's movements. "First, call me Greg. And I agree with you entirely. Time is limited. By using the news conference, if Sylvan detects something is amiss, he will be forced to wait until after the news conference to confront me. Before that time, we can switch back, causing him to question whatever it was he noticed. In essence we truly get an acid test in front of the public, the news media and the most important person of all, Sylvan. And we get his feedback, without risking exposure"

Sheik Omani was impressed. Although he had not said it that was exactly what he was thinking. He considered for a moment the possibility they had successfully trained him to think the same way, and what it would mean to the person who controlled him. This whole ordeal was a getting bit unnerving. It was difficult to accept a carbon copy of oneself sitting across the room. But that was exactly what he was seeing. He was trying to find anything in the man that would give him away as an imposter, but he couldn't. Finally, he concluded: This man was not an impersonator; he was the Sheik!

"You could not have memorized my talk since I have the tendency to speak extemporaneously at these news conferences. A fact I am sure you are aware of. Could you give me an example of what you plan to say?" Sheik Omani figured if there were going to be a fault in the plan, it would show up very quickly in the verbal presentation.

Greg looked at Sergei, who remained relatively quiet up to this point, for approval. Sergei simply nodded his head, so Greg began speaking.

"I have chosen this location, between the western wall of Solomon's Temple and the Mosque, to remind everyone here of our religious roots. Albeit that heritage is different for both Arab and Jew, the Holy Land is the same for both. We," he paused and spread his arms out to encompass the entire audience, "you and I, Arab and Jew, Islam, Christian and Jew, recognize this land as the Holiest of Lands. No other place on this Earth can lay claim to the cataclysmic events in mankind's history that unfolded right here. No other place on Earth experienced the footsteps of greater men," he paused again for emphasis, "or of God. It is here that the birth of our religious beginnings took place. It is here that our faith in God, like a seed, first germinated, then sprouted, and finally, in full bloom, burst upon the rest of the world."

"When I look out over the remnants of Solomon's Temple or turn and see the great dome of the Islamic Mosque, or turn again in the direction of Golgotha, I see the greatness of God coming together in one place. I do not see what the rest of the world sees. I do not see the unrest, the fighting, and the killing that the world sees. I do not see the fanatical religious war that the world sees. I do not see the beginning of the end, as the world fears."

"But I see a Jewish people who have demonstrated God's commitment to them by shear survival. A people that should have ceased to exist centuries ago, yet they have returned to their homeland to worship the God of their fathers. I see the followers of Mohammed as far as the eye can see; Worshipping, serving the God of the Prophet Mohammed. Returning to the precepts outlined in the Koran while the rest of the world purposely moves away from their own religious upbringing. Moslems, serving their God with a fervor the world has never seen before and may never see again. And I see thousands of Christians making their pilgrimage to the birthplace of their beliefs. Men, women, and children who have heard the Gospel of Christ and have come to Him for salvation. Gentiles and Jews from every walk of life, from every country in the world. People with nothing more in common than their singular belief in the Jew, Jesus Christ."

"No! This is not where the world will end. This is where man began and will continue forever."

"To prove to the rest of the world that what has been said here today, has never been truer than it is right now: I have brought with me representatives of three purported terrorist groups. Each will represent the fanatical factions of their religion; Moslem, Jew and Christian. First, I present to you, the leader of the Christian Liberation Front, stationed in Lebanon, Jerome Bechard." A tall, slender man of obviously mixed heritage walked out onto the center of the platform and stood next to the Sheik. The Sheik turned toward the man, and wrapping his arms around him, gave him a hug, then kissed him on both cheeks. A smattering of cheers went up from the audience, but it was readily apparent that few followers of the Christian Liberation Front had made the trip from war-torn Lebanon to Jerusalem.

"Next, I would like to present to you Doshe Shimon, the leader of the Zealots." The sound that erupted from the audience was deafening. Even the Sheik paused for a moment, taken back by the reception for the man that was often credited with restarting Jewish nationalistic fires that had been long dead. A man, whom the crowd should despise for his lack of concern for human life, was receiving a hero's welcome. Sheik Omani walked up to Doshe, and as with Jerome Bechard, gave him a hug and kissed him on both cheeks.

"Finally, a man who needs no introduction to the Arab or Jewish community, but a man who has never been captured on film, and thus remained unrecognizable to the world, the leader of the Arab's for Religious Freedom group, Jihad Nadu." As Sheik Omani spoke, and the audience became aware of whom he was going to introduce, all sound emanating from the audience stopped. The voice of the Sheik alone was heard. Only a few seconds passed from the time Sheik Omani announced Jihad to the time he stepped out onto the platform, but for that brief moment, time stood still. Then as the audience, many for the first time seeing the man they had only heard about but had come to idolize, exploded into a frenzy. Sheik Omani, as with the two men before Jihad, walked up to him, gave him the hug, and kissed him on both cheeks, then turned to the audience to speak. But the crowd was still in an uproar, and despite the Sheik's feeble efforts, they continued heaping praise on Jihad.

It was a full five minutes before the sound of the crowd died down enough for the Sheik to speak, but finally he was able to continue. "It would appear as if I might have made the right choices." Again, the crowd erupted, and the Sheik stood helplessly on the platform waiting for the noise to subside again. This time the Sheik waited for the silence to come from a crowd that had exhausted its enthusiasm, rather than try to continue before the audience was ready. When at last it was, he held up his arms, turned in every direction to emphasize the need for silence, then started in again. "These three men have agreed, in principle, to work together for the common good of all mankind to end the fighting. Between the four of us, I merely as the mediator, we will strive for a corporate goal that meets the needs of everyone, yet compromises no one."

"I have been told by various leaders of the world today, that what I seek to accomplish with these men is an impossible task. To those men I say: He who is afraid of defeat, has been defeated already. We," and he grabbed the hands of Doshe and Jihad and motioned for Doshe to take Jerome's hand. Then the four men raised their hands in unison above their heads. "We are the new leaders of the world, because we are not afraid of defeat. We will establish a new hierarchy in the world, where peace emanates from the Middle East. We will teach by example, and the world will covet that example and that example will be peace."

He lowered his hands, and they were again four men, individual in body and spirit, but with a singular objective. He looked out over the crowd, not speaking, just studying the sea of faces. Then he bowed his head in silent prayer. The people, not understanding why he had stopped speaking, began to talk among themselves and the sound from the crowd slowly increased. As their attention returned to the stage, they noticed the Sheik had bowed his head and remained silent. Then they became self-conscious, and began to quiet down, until everyone was quiet again. While the Sheik's head remained bowed, it seemed as if the whole city of Jerusalem had come to a halt and was silently praying with the Sheik. This continued for a few more minutes, and then slowly the Sheik raised his head to speak again.

- - - - -

Manuel had stationed himself on the roof of a building that housed an open market at street level. The second floor contained the living quarters for the owner. He managed to get himself past the owner's wife who had been tending customers up until the time the Sheik appeared on the platform and began speaking. At that point, all of her customers left the store, making their way to the rear of the crowd. At the same time, Manuel slipped by her unnoticed making his way to the stairs at the back of the building that led up to their three-room apartment.

As he approached a platform on the steps, he heard the woman's husband moving around the apartment. The stairs were against the back wall and made a ninety-degree turn at the corner of the building back toward the front of the store, then continued up a few more steps. There was a window at the platform that looked out over the alley behind the store. It was this window Manuel was trying to get to. From the window ledge he could pull himself and his rifle up to the roof.

He waited, and in a few seconds, he heard the footsteps of the man on the floor above, going away from the stairs. Manuel seized the opportunity by quickly climbing out the window and pulling himself up onto the roof. A one-foot-high parapet wall providing him with the barest of protection surrounded the roof. On either side of him, was another building that continued up, one more story. Typically, either one would have been preferred by Manuel over the building he was using, but they both housed relatively quiet businesses. Consequently, they would not have provided sufficient natural diversions to allow him access to their roofs.

Manuel crouched down, and slowly made his way to the front of the building. As he neared the front, he laid down on the roof surface and crawled the last few feet. The surface of the roof was searing hot, requiring him to constantly change positions to keep from burning himself. He had planned ahead for this by wearing heavy clothing underneath the Arab robes, but the latent heat in the surface of the roof was still too much for even that to be effective very long. After changing positions, Manuel would try to ready himself and his equipment for the task at hand. Complicating the situation, and subsequently slowing him down even further, were those same extra layers of clothes. They caused him to perspire more than he normally would have under similar circumstances, making it difficult to see as he assembled his rifle. However, he continued to work diligently and was finally able to get it assembled. Finally, Sheik Omani appeared in the rifle's sight.

The Sheik had his head bowed. He had been that way for some time now, and Manuel centered the crosshairs of the scope at the Sheik's forehead. Figuring the distance and the angle, the bullet should hit somewhere above the mouth, taking the Sheik out relatively painlessly. Before he could squeeze the trigger, the heat below his body became unbearable again, causing the crosshairs to begin wavering. Manuel pulled the rifle back and repositioned himself to allow that part his body to cool.

He returned to the prone position that offered him the same target and was pleased to see the Sheik was still standing with his head bowed. Knowing the timing requirement was limited; Manuel quickly took aim and managed to get the cross hairs centered on the Sheik's forehead again. However, just before he began to squeeze the trigger, he sensed someone was watching him, and he stopped. Turning his eyes to the right and upward, without moving the rifle, he was able to see the head of a man come over the top of the parapet wall on the building next door. With the head, was a familiar steel cylinder being positioned toward him. Realizing he had little time to squander, Manuel turned his own rifle away from the Sheik, and ignoring the burning flesh underneath the robes and extra clothing, he aimed at the head, now fully visible over the parapet wall and pulled the trigger. His new quarry had no warning before the bullet penetrated his skull. It entered through the eye socket and exited through the top of his head, taking with it a large portion of the back of his skull. The force of the bullet had caused the body to lift up, then fall back, leaving the man's left arm dangling over the parapet wall. The arm was the only visible evidence to those on the ground that anything had happened.

Manuel knew he might have lost the opportunity to kill Sheik Omani, because the sound of the gunshot, although muffled between the buildings, undoubtedly caught someone's attention. And although the recipient of the bullet was out of view, the roof where he was laying offered minimal protection from curiosity. He was sure, someone would investigate the noise sooner, not later. So, if he were to finish what he had come here to do, he had to move quickly. He returned his attention to the Sheik, who no longer was standing with his head bowed, but was walking around the platform waving his arms and speaking. Manuel decided his window of opportunity was lost, and he would have to get out of there. He couldn't afford the time to see if the Sheik gave him another target like the one, he just lost. Disappointed, he dismantled his rifle and returned it to it's canvas carrying case, then made his way to the rear of the roof. For a moment he considered leaving the body without searching it, but then decided it was too important a task to be left undone.

Standing on the parapet wall, he jumped straight up and managed to barely get a finger hold on the parapet wall above. Pulling himself up, he brought his left leg up over the wall, then rolled over and dropped down to the roof. He made his way over to the body, which was laying face down on the roof. Under the heat of the mid-day sun, the fresh blood had already begun to coagulate. He checked the back pockets looking for anything to give him a clue to the identity of his assailant. He removed a wallet and began searching through it until he found a driver's license that had the man's picture on it. He took note of the name, but it did not strike a familiar chord, so he set it aside in his mind as an item to be addressed later.

Manuel grabbed hold of the man's right shoulder and arm, then as he stepped backward, pulled the body over on its back. The left eye, where the bullet had entered, was missing, but other than that he looked like he might be sleeping. He compared the face to that on the driver's license and was satisfied with the match. Whoever he was, he was at least consistent, Manuel thought. He still assumed the driver's license contained a false identity, but the name may be traceable, so he slid the license into his pocket. He continued his search by checking the front pockets and found a handwritten note on stationary from a hotel in Lisbon. The name of the hotel was not familiar, but it stated he was to meet an E. D. at a place called The Last Supper at 8:00 P.M. Manuel considered it might be worth his time to see if the E. D. was Eric, and decided he'd be at this restaurant when whoever E. D. was showed up.

Satisfied that the corpse had provided as much information as it was capable of, Manuel decided it was time to leave. He rolled the man back over into the position he had found him, but this time kept the arm back from hanging over the parapet wall, then left. On the roof below, he retrieved his own rifle, then waited for the storekeeper and her husband upstairs to be preoccupied. Quickly, he climbed back through the open window and exited through the store's front entrance.

"So, in conclusion, I would like to leave this audience with this one request. Give us, these three men and myself, but mainly these three men, the opportunity, through time, to resolve the disputes of all the peoples native to this part of the world. Provide us the most important resource available: A time of uninterrupted peace during the discussion phase of these negotiations. For without peace, our attentions will be diverted to the conflict at hand, and away from the final resolution of these problems. Thank you for your attention, and may God bless our discussions with fruitful results, in all of our lives."

The Sheik gave the signal that the news conference was over, and that he would not be entertaining any questions from the news media. Most of the television stations that had covered the event continued with live coverage. They brought their panels of experts on, one by one, to begin dissecting what they thought the Sheik meant. Meanwhile, the Sheik and his three companions walked to the edge of the platform and engaged in conversation with the audience below.

The stage had been hastily constructed this morning near the front of some shops that overlooked the largest open area between the Mosque and the Wailing Wall. The curtain had been installed so that once the four men decided to exit; they would be behind the curtain. No one would be able to see them. Even from the side, because the curtain wrapped around, extending to the front of the building. Finally, the four men left the stage. Immediately backstage, an escort accompanied them to the front door of one of the stores behind the curtain then directed them to the rear of that store. There, two limousines were waiting to take them to the Sheik's room at the Star of David Hotel. The Sheik directed Doshe to climb into the one he would be riding in and directed Jerome and Jihad into the other one. With the four gentlemen safely settled into their respective limousines, the drivers began the short journey back to the hotel.

"Now I can see why Sheik Omani would not tell me who I would have to negotiate with. If I had known Doshe were to be there, he would be dead right now." Jihad was speaking more to himself, than to the fiery Jerome Bechard, but with the remark, Jerome looked at him as if he wasn't making any sense. Then turning to look directly at Jerome, he added, "And what the hell are you doing here? Doshe should be the epitome of the people you hate. Responsibility for every bomb they drop on Beirut or anywhere else in Lebanon, rests squarely on his shoulders. Or have you suddenly become oblivious to the plight of your people?" Jihad didn't really expect responses to anything he was saying from Jerome. He was speaking more out of anger for having been duped by Sheik Omani into being here than anything else. It just so happened that Jerome was available and by necessity had become the audience.

Up to this point Jerome had remained quiet, allowing Jihad to vent his frustration, but now he turned to Jihad. First, he looked into the eyes of his companion in the limousine to ensure he had Jihad's attention, when he was satisfied, he did, he spoke. "You are here for the same reason Doshe and I are here. To not be here, would be a disservice to your cause. Sheik Omani has somehow managed to build a global reputation for negotiating mutually acceptable peace plans. But if you look at his record, he hasn't really accomplished anything. One year ago, he was nothing. Today he is a hero. The news media has created a myth, and we must live with him for a short while, then he will be gone. That is why we are all here and if you don't know that, I am truly disappointed in the man I have heard so much about." Jerome extended his hand to Jihad, "It is good to meet a man whose work I have often admired."

Jihad felt a little ashamed of what he had said, then extended his hand to accept Jerome's. "You are right of course. If I had the time to consider the invitation, even knowing Doshe was to be included, I would have come. And if it had not been Doshe, it would have been some equally repulsive Jew. At times I let my passion speak for me, it is a curse I have come to accept."

"Passion speaks for each of us, or we would not be who we are today."

"Yes. I suppose it is as much a blessing as a curse...you have taught me many things over the years, Jerome. I have watched you successfully resist the Jewish attacks on your land and your people. Attacks the Jews excuse by blaming a false Syrian threat. Although my people do not have land to call their own, I know that when we do, we will have to continue to endure the Jewish attacks much the same as you do today. You have established the standard by which we will be measured."

"That is not true, but I thank you for your kind words anyway. Before we arrive at the hotel, I have one thing to ask you. As a prelude to my question, I think you should know that my inner circle and I have agreed to accept any reasonable peace proposal Sheik Omani offers, as long as it does not include any border changes that reduce the existing land area. We have agreed that this requisite would have to be met for any existing Arab lands, not just Lebanon. My question for you is: How seriously are you approaching these negotiations? In other words, are you prepared to do your part to achieve a workable peace agreement?"

"If you mean, are we going to be as liberal in our approach to the peace process as you have chosen to be: The answer is no. If you mean, are we going to seriously negotiate all issues, except, as you also identified, no changes to any borders that result in a reduction of Arab lands: The answer is yes. Our state must come from Israeli occupied land. I would not be here today; if I felt the Sheik was not receptive to all ideas. My only fear, and it should be obvious, is that Doshe and all Israelis are going to try to use these negotiations to enhance their image of being the martyr to the rest of the world."

"We can not allow them to turn this process into another opportunity to demonstrate to the world how reasonable they are, and how unreasonable we are. The Qhadaffis and Husseins of the world have tarnished the image of all Arabs enough by being irrational, we must not do the same. Doshe, I am sure, recognizes this peace conference as an opportunity to push for an Arab/Jewish accord that portrays the Israelis as the rational party. I don't intend on letting him succeed at our expense. It is time we establish the same image for the Arab world as well."

"Excellent. Then we are in an agreement. We should have no problem demonstrating to the rest of the world the Arab people are ready for peace. Let the talks begin." Jerome smiled as he made this last statement. This was the first time Lebanon had been included in the equation for peace. a primary reason for past failures. And now, he thought, the Arab circle, like a noose, had finally been closed around Israel by a united Arab world.

The limousines pulled up to the Star of David Hotel. All four men exited quickly, hurrying into the relative safety of the lobby. Prior to their arrival, all unregistered guests had been escorted out of the building and ushered to an area away from the entrance of the hotel. The police had cordoned off the area immediately in front of the hotel allowing the four men to traverse the distance from the limousine to the hotel's front door unmolested by the crowd. Near the end of the news conference, many of the spectators had made their way to the hotel. The crowd at the hotel had swelled significantly from the few people that were typically on the premises.

- - - - -

Eric watched the entire news conference while standing among the mixed audience that had gathered in Jerusalem to hear what Sheik Omani had to say. He continually surveyed the rooftops and windows of the surrounding buildings, in search of either Manuel or Jacque or Steve. Steve was supposed to have met him at the hotel last night but had never arrived. Eric had briefly considered going out and looking for him but decided that would have to wait until after the news conference. At the moment his attention was best spent trying to locate Jacque.

When Steve was still unaccounted for in the morning, he set his network into motion, trying to locate him. He felt certain that Steve was not betraying him. He would not be the least bit surprised to find out Steve was still busy tracking Manuel, but he needed to be sure. He had been able to establish some small level of loyalty in Steve, consequently Steve's tardiness was perceived as an item to be concerned about for his own safety, rather than anything else. Using his sources to find Steve was probably the best approach, he thought. Since they were already looking for Jacque, it would be easy to include Steve in their search. Eric went back to scanning the rooftops again thinking the news conference offered the perfect opportunity for Jacque to assassinate the Sheik.

The Sheik had just bowed his head as if he was about to pray, when Eric's eyes were stabbed with a bright reflection coming from the roof of a building two blocks east. He stopped panning the surrounding crowds and buildings to focus his attention on the reflection. Just as quick as it had appeared, it disappeared. Eric continued staring at the location just above the top of the front wall. He thought it was probably just the bright sunlight reflecting off a particularly reflective stone in the wall, but he wanted to be sure. Just as he convinced himself that it was precisely that, it reappeared.

Eric froze, becoming a statue among the throng of spectators. It was imperative that he maintain a stable focal point. The reflection should not be intermittent, unless it was the result of something moving on the building or something attached to the building moving. Eric squinted, trying to reduce the reflection as much as possible to see if there was a logical explanation for this phenomenon. When the reflection disappeared again, he thought he saw something being pulled behind the wall.

The next time he saw the reflection, he was sure it was the result of something being moved into the sunlight rather than something attached to the building. Finally, he decided it was worth investigating and started for the building. As he moved toward the building, he kept his eyes on the reflection, but with his first step, the angle changed enough that the reflection disappeared. What Eric saw made him want to start running as fast as he could toward the building. But he knew that would be the worst thing he could do. Fortunately, the crowd was too thick for that anyway. All he could do was walk, as quick as possible, squeezing through the crowd as he worked his way to the building.

Eric was positive he had seen the unmistakable sheen of a rifle barrel. If he was correct, he knew he had little chance of reaching whoever was controlling the rifle in time to stop him. As he made his way, much quicker than he should have been able to in this crowd, he kept monitoring the top of the store front for any more signs of the rifle or rifleman. He managed to reduce the distance to one block, when he saw the rifle barrel extend just past the edge of the wall again. This time there was no reflection, and he could see clearly it was the barrel of a rifle.

Any lingering thought Eric might have had about chasing a mirage had been totally eliminated. Confirmation of the weapon convinced Eric he needed to work harder to get through the crowd. He was down to the last one hundred yards and could now make out the front entrance. He stopped to get his bearings before continuing. As he looked through the crowd, the heads of the people appeared to sway like wheat in a field on a breezy summer day. Catching short glimpses, Eric could only hope that the roof contained Manuel, and that Steve was somewhere, unseen, but ready to intercede.

As he increased his effort to get through the crowd, the mass of humanity began to shift. Instead of moving closer to the building, the crowd carried him further away. It was as if the crowd had sensed an impending danger somewhere behind them, and they were moving away from it to a place of safety. And in the process, Eric became an unwilling participant. The distance that just a moment before had been decreasing was now almost doubled.

Eric looked up at the top of the building and saw the end of the rifle barrel being steadied in preparation for a shot. A total sense of helplessness came over him, and mentally, he began preparing himself for what was about to happen.

The rifle shot was barely audible over the naturally occurring noise of the crowd, but Eric recognized it for what it was and increased his effort to fight the movement of the crowd even more. To the rest of the crowd, the sound was no different than the pop of a cork being removed from a champagne bottle. They continued their thrust forward, unaware that anything out of the ordinary actually happened, but still moving in anticipation of that yet undefined disaster.

Eric had been staring at the rifle barrel. But a fraction of a second prior to hearing the shot, the barrel disappeared from view. He assumed the marksman, whether it was Manuel or Jacque he still didn't know, had for some unknown reason pulled back prior to firing. Regardless, the outcome would be the same. Expecting the reaction of the crowd to be violent, Eric prepared himself for the ensuing rush forward once the crowd realized what had happened. When no reaction from the crowd was forthcoming, Eric turned to look at The Sheik, expecting to see him crumple to the stage as a bloodstain grew on his clothes. But instead, the Sheik lifted his head as he completed his silent prayer and began speaking to the audience once again.

The push of the crowd played itself out, and once again Eric was able to make progress toward the building. He continued to monitor the rooftop as he worked his way to the building, but whoever was up there was staying out of view. Eric began to question whether he had actually seen or heard anything. It was possible, he presumed, that an overactive imagination, due to stress or the heat, could have produced a mirage. Regardless, Eric continued working his way until he finally reached the front entrance of the store.

The store was a Hebrew version of a novelty shop. Selling bowls, jugs, pictures, scarves and just about any other hand made trinket one could imagine. An older woman of obvious Arab descent was watching the store. She had dark olive skin, and her face had the leathery look of someone that had spent too many days under the harsh Middle East sun. She was dressed in a beige, single piece dress that if the arms and neck opening were sealed up, could have passed for a large cotton sack. Around her neck was a wide, multicolored silk scarf, that hung down passed her waist.

Eric approached the woman and asked if anyone had come through the store during the last half hour. At first the woman stared at Eric as if he were some grotesque alien, then finally she shook her head no, but still didn't speak. Eric continued by asking if there was any way to the roof from inside the store, and again the woman just shook her head no. Finally, Eric asked if he could look around the back of the store for a way to the roof, and if she would mind if he went up there. Again, the woman didn't say anything, instead she pointed to a door at the back of the room.

Eric took her response as an invitation to try outside, and proceeded to move toward the door she had pointed to. The door opened to the alley behind the store, which was barely wide enough to drive a compact car through. But even that would be impossible, because every store used the alley as interim storage for their garbage. The resulting mess barely left room for a person to wade through while still maintaining contact with the ground.

Stepping out to the middle of the alley, Eric looked at the uninterrupted store wall. Each store had been built using the previous store as the starting point. Since the same type of construction was used for all the stores in this section, the only way to tell where a store began and ended was by the varying height of the rooflines. The rear walls produced a continuous, but irregular border between the sky and earth. As he panned the rear walls, he noticed the store next to the one he had just exited had a precariously stacked pile of bags and boxes that appeared to be a crude set of steps leading up to a window ledge. From there it was relatively simple to pull oneself onto the roof above.

Eric started climbing the primitive stairway, grasping desperately for any handhold he could find on the building to maintain his balance. When he reached the window, he looked inside and saw an apartment. It was in use, but at the moment unoccupied. He assumed the boarder was probably somewhere in the crowd listening to the Sheik's speech. He climbed onto the windowsill, which allowed him to reach the top of the wall with his hands. As he pressed each foot against the window frame, he pulled with his arms and walked up the window frame until his forearms were above the wall. Then, as he hung there, he swung his left leg up and over the wall. Then he pulled his body up until he was lying on the parapet wall.

Without thinking, he rolled off the wall onto the roof. As soon as his hands hit the surface, he realized his mistake and scrambled to his feet. He looked at his burnt hands and was thankful they hadn't been burnt severe enough to blister. Now he knew why the rifle barrel had been retracted so many times, he thought. Eric had originally assumed it was simply a precautionary measure. Now he knew the person was probably trying to reposition himself periodically to keep from getting burnt.

Eric turned toward the wall that separated him from the roof that had contained the marksman. He was unsure of who or what he was looking for, but he was convinced he had to at least investigate the roof. He didn't really expect to find anyone still up there, but in this business one could never be sure. Oftentimes, the most valuable clues were found in the most unexpected places.

However, as experienced as he was, Eric was not prepared for what he saw. Laying face down on the roof was a man who had lost the back half of his head to a bullet. That was the shot, he realized. Spread out in a grotesque pattern from the body were bits of bone and flesh, and splotches of blood. Eric approached the body tentatively. As he looked down, he was thankful that whoever he was had little time to feel the pain of his own death. Eric reached down and grabbing the man's shoulder and waist, turned him over.

The combination of the heat and shock forced Eric to reach out for the parapet wall to steady himself. Then slowly, he lowered himself down until he was sitting on the wall. He returned the blank stare of Steve's face: the bullet had entered through the eye, killing him instantly. It certainly made it easy to determine who the marksman was. Whatever Steve had been able to find out in Lisbon was lost forever, and Eric's task had just become that much more difficult.

The circumstances left no alternative but to search Steve's body. Eric didn't really expect to find anything, but his professional instinct made this a requisite. He ripped open the shirt, not wanting to take the added time to unbutton it and inspected the upper torso for anything that Steve might have attached to himself. Then, before removing the jeans, he searched the front pockets. Finding nothing, he continued his search by removing Steve' shoes, socks, and jeans. Rolling Steve over on his belly, Eric inspected his back. Seeing nothing, he turned his attention to Steve's clothes, rifling through every pocket, then the shoes and finally turning the socks inside out. Inside the left shoe he found a folded piece of paper with a phone number on it. It contained the familiar 011 prefix of the States, and momentarily Eric considered what this might mean. He made a mental note to check the number out before he called the Agency and reported Steve's death. Satisfied that he had searched everywhere, he stuffed Steve's wallet and a set of keys into his own slacks and prepared to leave.

He wasn't pleased with the thought of leaving Steve lay here to decompose on a hot, bug infested rooftop of a nondescript store in Jerusalem. But he knew that was exactly what he had to do. First opportunity I have, Eric thought, I'll give the authorities a call. It wasn't that long ago when he wouldn't have given it a second thought. Now that he has removed himself from the Agency's influence, he has begun to develop a sense of responsibility to people in general. Some said he'd developed a conscience. And even though Steve started out on less than positive terms with Eric, in their short time together, Eric had begun to respect him. Within reason, Eric would try to do what he could for him.

Back at the hotel Eric went through Steve's wallet. It contained the traditional items; money, credit cards, pictures of friends or family. Of course, the pictures would be fake, but they still gave the impression he had a family. This thought made Eric pause. He hadn't considered that Steve had a family, but he had to. Everyone does. Then he remembered something Jim had told him while they were standing near the horses outside his cabin. Jim had told him Steve was very special to Tom, and to be particularly careful because their relationship contributed to his loyalty.

Eric pulled everything he could find out of the wallet and laid it out on the bed. Money, credit cards, pictures, a receipt, and scraps of paper with one-word messages, but nothing of obvious value. Next, Eric removed the piece of paper with the phone number on it and placed it alongside the other things. He stared at the agglomeration of items he had retrieved from Steve, desperately trying to visualize something that wasn't there. He spent the next hour arranging and rearranging the one-word messages trying to make sense out of them. He didn't have any luck. The words laundry, Paris, Josef, and key eluded every attempt at understanding. They appeared to have been written at different times, on separate and distinctly different paper. Eric wanted them to be connected. Paris and Josef were obvious references to places they had been together, but key and laundry appeared to be nonsensical. Finally, Eric decided to set them aside for consideration at another time. Stacking the four slips together, he folded them and put them in his own wallet.

Next, he turned his attention to the phone number. After considering it for a moment, he decided to make the call. But before he did that, he wanted to call Jim and inform him of what happened to Steve. Eric looked at his watch and made a quick calculation, it was four in the morning on the East coast. He'd be waking Jim up. Perfect, he thought. This would be the best time to catch him near a phone. After the fifth ring, Jim's familiar voice could be heard as he answered.

"Hello, I'm not here right now. But if you would leave your name and number, I'll get back to you as soon as I can. Beeeeep"

Eric paused for a moment disgusted that these damn things had managed to infiltrate the Agency. "I'll call you back in exactly thirty minutes. Its four A. M." Then he hung up.

Eric waited the obligatory thirty minutes, then started the process of direct dialing Jim's phone again. This time the phone had just started the second ring when Jim came on the line. "Hello."

"Awfully big of you to answer this time. I suppose you were listening in last time while you decided if you should answer it?" The disgust in Eric's voice was obvious, but Jim ignored him.

"These things are great." Jim stated matter-of-factly. "I've been able to increase the amount of sleep I get by answering only the important calls. It rings long enough to get me coherent before it answers, and if the party stays on the line long enough, and, I think I should speak to them, I pick up. Otherwise, if I don't want to talk to them, I go back to sleep. People like you, who hurry through their messages, then hang up. Well...for people like you...it doesn't work. Now, what bad news have you got for me?"

"Steve's been killed."

There was a momentary pause as Jim absorbed this information. Then, in his unique way, he moved on as if Steve was strictly a strategic instrument. Eric knew Jim was feeling the pain of Steve's death, but it would not be allowed to interfere with the business at hand. "What happened? You didn't kill him, did you?"

"No. I had actually begun to trust him. In fact, it was because I trusted him that he got himself killed. He was tailing Manuel when all he was supposed to do was a little investigating. But he got too close."

"Manuel." Jim was clearly shocked. "What the hell was he doing tailing Manuel? Jacque hasn't been removed from the picture or I would have known. What's going on Eric?"

Eric gave Jim a brief run down of what he considered to be the most important items. He didn't want to relay too much information over the phone, because there was no way to ensure the security of the line. Jim still worked for the Agency, so it was almost a foregone conclusion another party, most likely Tom, would hear that everything they said.

"They've hired two assassins." Jim repeated the last thing Eric had said. "That doesn't make sense," Jim paused then continued. "Unless they are positioning themselves to place the blame at the feet of either Jew or Arab. I suppose, it gives them the flexibility to place blame on whichever group they think will generate the most violent reaction. I'll see what I can do about replacing Steve," Jim said changing direction.

"That won't be necessary. I took Steve along because it was expedient. I don't have the time nor the patience to start over with someone else."

"You won't have to. We have our own expertise when it comes to dealing with Manuel, so we won't require your assistance. What it will do is allow you to give your undivided attention to neutralizing Jacque. Our people on the other hand can neutralize Manuel."

"And probably get in my way in the process," Eric cut him off. "No! Let me handle it. From what I can tell, this consortium has an excellent chance of pulling this off. We don't need to increase their chances by dividing control. I can take care of Manuel myself."

"And if you don't?" The question hung in the air, unanswered. Eric was beginning to appreciate the full ramifications of what would happen if the consortium were successful, and secondly, the risk he was asking Jim to take. He knew the chances of being able to neutralize both Jacque and Manuel in time, were limited at best. Particularly since Manuel had already started his onslaught on the Sheik with a vengeance. Just stopping Manuel may give Jacque the opening he needs, and Eric knew he couldn't risk that. But then again, he wasn't sure who he could trust either. Steve was the product of a man and organization that Jim didn't even trust, and now Jim was asking him to trust that same organization again. Eric made his decision, hoping he wouldn't regret it. He would accept Jim's offer of help, although he wasn't convinced it was the best decision.

"When can I meet this person?" Eric finally conceded.

"Where are you staying?"

"I was at a place called Le Heim, but I'll be moving. Have the person check-in at Le Heim, and I'll make contact with him or her. Who are you thinking of sending, anyway?"

"John Calding. He's in Tel Aviv right now. He should be able to be there by this evening. Eric, I want you to call me after you meet John. I know your going to think I'm being overly cautious. But its clear things are not what they seem to be, and I think you and I need to communicate more frequently."

"I'll call you." Eric hung up without waiting for Jim to respond. Something in the way Jim sounded at the end of the conversation bothered Eric. It was obvious by his doublespeak he was trying to relay a message, and if Eric was right: It contained a warning about this new man. Well, Eric thought, I'll know in about five hours. When he gets here.

- - - - -

"You did alright Jim. The warning at the end did not go unnoticed, but then I'm sure you warned him about Steve as well. I've always said you worry too much. Eric and I do not get along because he has the tendency to be too much of a maverick for my tastes. But I'm not out to get him. Have you forgotten? I was the one who recommended we bring Eric back out of retirement for this assignment. I suggested Steve accompany him only to allay the fears of the others, not because I have some hidden agenda. Believe it or not Jim; **we** are on the same side. I want--no this country needs--Eric to be successful."

"Whether we agree with Sheik Omani or not, is irrelevant. He has become the focal point of all Middle East peace negotiations, and we have to accept that. Even President Harris has acknowledged the man's position. He's here to stay, unless of course, the consortium is successful and takes him out. But that is precisely what we are trying to circumvent. The consortium has raised the stakes with the hiring of a second assassin, and Eric needs our assistance. Trust me. That is what he is getting. Remember, John was your choice, not mine."

Tom was right, and that is partially what bothered Jim. He had been able to confirm his suspicions that Tom was indeed connected to the consortium. Tom had been tailed from the moment Jim had been informed about the plane crash, because Jim was certain the crash was an attempt on the Sheik's life. He figured if Tom were connected, he would make contact. So, following his hunch, he had Tom followed. The trip to the Laundromat for a phone call provided Jim the first hard evidence of a connection. Tom's phone call to Toomas had been traced, after the fact, so they were not able to record the actual conversation. However, based on the phone number he called; Jim considered the alliance with the consortium confirmed.

Jim hadn't known Steve that well, but Jim knew John personally. And it was impossible for John to be a part of this, or so he thought. Now Tom had him wondering whom he could trust beside himself and Eric. Jim looked at Tom, then said. "Don't be so paranoid Tom. I didn't mean to imply that I didn't trust you. With today's electronic intelligence, one can never be sure a device is secure. I was simply trying to relay my concern for Eric's well being to him. Admit it Tom, you're worried too. That's why you wanted Steve sent along in the first place, or so you said. Now that Steve is dead, our task has gotten that much more difficult. Eric is probably the only man we have who is capable of neutralizing Jacque. But now we have to deal with Manuel too. Let's face it, we're in a world of shit."

- - - - -

While Eric talked to Jim, he unconsciously removed the slip of paper with the phone number on it. The number had started to stir within him some unknown feeling of recognition, so he decided it was time to see who answered. He stared at the number, trying to remember if he had ever dialed it before. As he studied the number, he remembered why it looked familiar. It was on another slip of paper that he had taken from the man at Heathrow. Taking out his wallet, he removed that piece of paper from the compartment he had stuffed it into.

011-1-703-225-2225

The numbers were identical. He had no idea where Steve might have gotten this phone number. It's possible Steve had always had it and Eric was just not aware of it. The area code was familiar and indicated it was for somewhere in Virginia. Which could mean this was the number he was supposed to call on his periodic checks with Tom. But then why would the man in Heathrow have that number as well? Unless they, meaning Steve and the tail in Heathrow, were somehow connected, he reasoned. That would certainly explain why Steve hadn't bothered to interrogate him. They were working together, and he knew it.

This wasn't making any sense. The other possibility was that Steve had come across this number in his investigation of Manuel while in Lisbon. But that would imply a connection between Manuel, the tail, and this unknown person in the States. But Eric knew that Toomas hired Manuel: The tape recording of the consortium's meeting in London verified that fact. So, what possible connection would he have with someone in the U. S.? Eric began to feel the person at the other end of this phone number would be the only way to answer that question, but first he needed to find out who that was.

Eric decided it would be wise to use a public telephone for the call rather than create the paper trail to his room. He left his room and fortunately found a phone booth in the lobby that offered enough privacy to make the call. He began dialing direct using the international access code then the phone number, but midway through; an operator interrupted him.

"I'm sorry, but you can not dial international calls directly from this phone. You'll have to dial the operator first and get assistance from them. Thank you." Click. Bzzzzz. The message was in Hebrew, and Eric was barely able to understand what he was supposed to do. He had been exposed, theoretically to enough Hebrew to be fluent, but realistically he was at best, merely competent on a subsistence level. Considering how seldom he had used it in the past, he was surprised he understood enough to figure out what the voice wanted him to do.

Eric started to re-dial, this time prefacing the number with the obligatory 0, to notify the operator of his need for assistance. With the help of the operator, he was connected in a relatively short time. The phone just finished its tenth ring when a voice on the other end said, "Hello." Eric didn't answer because he immediately recognized the voice. Unfortunately, he couldn't put a name to it.

"Hello? Hello?" Click. Bzzzzz.

Whoever answered had gotten tired of this game quickly and hung up. Eric knew he had heard the voice before, but still couldn't recall where or who it was. He half expected Tom to answer and was more than a little disappointed when he didn't. However, the voice was familiar, and it may still lead back to Tom, he thought. Eric returned to his room to pack and check out. He was running out of time before this new Agency lackey, John Calding, arrived. And he wanted to be at his new location before that happened.

He hadn't wanted to accept any assistance, but he knew Jim was right. There was no way he could guarantee that both Manuel and Jacque would be neutralized in time. The fact was, he wasn't sure he could even neutralize Jacque in time. He'd had no luck locating Jacque so far, seemingly always one step behind. And his network of sources had only been capable of providing him with the most rudimentary information about where Jacque had been, not where he was at the moment or much less where he was going. Eric figured he would have this John Calding pick up where Steve met his untimely demise, chasing Manuel. Meanwhile, he would concentrate his efforts on actually locating Jacque. He was finally convinced that what he was hired to do was necessary. But along the way, he also became convinced that his job would not be complete until he was able to identify all those who were behind it and stop them permanently. Josef was right again, he thought.

9

-Consider the work of God, for who is able to straighten what He has bent?

John Calding was a tall, well built, ex-football player that had been exposed to the workings of the intelligence community through his military term. He had ridden the ROTC wagon through college and received his degree in military science from an off breed design your own degree program available at the state University.

The reason he had chosen ROTC was because no colleges offered him any type of football scholarship, although he had been scouted regularly throughout his senior year. Without exception, everyone told him that he had all the necessary tools to be a great tight end, except he was just too thin; he didn't have enough bulk. None of them wanted to risk a scholarship on someone they felt wouldn't be able to survive the season. Over the summer between high school and college he bulked up considerably, gaining substantial strength with the added bulk. Regardless, when he arrived at college and decided to try out as a walk-on, the first day of practice the football coach converted him from tight end to defensive end. The coach told him the greatest need was on defense, and John could help immediately in that capacity.

John Calding was the type of person that when told he wasn't good enough would promptly go out and prove his detractors wrong. So that is exactly what he did. He became a member of the local health club, and began an intensive program to bulk up, with the instruction of the trainer at the club. The trainer, an ex-pro football player, was well versed in the art of bodybuilding with chemicals. He designed the program, monitored and tracked John's progress and administered the steroids. Mid-way through the fall semester, the results really began to show, although he was still considered a bit too fragile for a tight end.

Truthfully, the coach had converted him to defensive end because he was overloaded at that position and felt confident, he wouldn't have to use John, except in practice. Unnoticed by the coach, John continued to "fill out," as his dad was fond of saying, and near the end of the season, John was noticeably bigger than he had been at the start. In practice he was beginning to compete favorably with the starting defensive end, a senior. With two games left in John's freshman year, the starting end went down with a knee injury, and without thinking, the coach gave John his chance. From that point on, John became the starting defensive end and never relinquished it throughout his college career.

John never did get a scholarship and had joined the ROTC to supplement himself financially. As he attended their version of boot camp and the mandatory sessions, he began to enjoy it. When he graduated from college and was drafted in the seventh round by the Tampa Bay Buccaneers, he didn't even bother to hire an agent. He told the Bucs coach he had no intention of trying to get out of his military obligation, and if they wanted to wait for him, fine, but he might not be worth a damn by the time he got out. That was the last time he talked to any pro football team about playing for them.

John received his commission as a First Lieutenant in the Army, was sent to school for electronic intelligence training, and was sent to West Germany for his first tour of duty. After eighteen months there, he was reassigned to a unit in the National Security Agency at Ft. Meade, Maryland. It was here that he was exposed to the various workings of the different intelligence branches of the military and the government. It didn't take long for John to realize that if he left the military and came back into one of the civilian branches of the intelligence community, he would be able to continue working in an area he thoroughly enjoyed and be paid much better than he was as an Army officer.

As he neared the end of his commitment to the Army, he began developing his contacts to come back as a civilian. His immediate supervisor assured him he would be reemployed the day after his commission expired. However, while visiting his parents during his last leave, he received a recruitment letter from the CIA. His first inclination was to discard it without reading it because he had already made plans to go back to NSA as a civilian at a G-17 level. But the letter generated interest in the CIA and piqued his curiosity, so he read the letter. It didn't really offer him an irresistible sales pitch, but it did provide a toll-free phone number he could call to get more information, and to speak to a recruiter at the Agency.

The recruiter didn't sell him on the CIA either, but he did convince him he had nothing to lose if he stopped in and interviewed with a few people at Langley when he got back from leave. He decided there was no harm taking a look and keeping his options open, so he agreed. That's when the real sales pitch began, and although he knew he wasn't seeing the real CIA, his own sense of adventure took control, and he signed up on the spot. That was just over fifteen years ago, and he has never regretted his decision once. This was exactly the type of life he had always envisioned for himself, and the intrigue of the covert community provided him with the energy needed to excel. John Calding loved his work, and he had every intention of doing this work until the Agency deemed him too old to function in the field. Then he would take the mandatory desk job back at Langley, doing much the same thing he would have done at NSA, interpreting field reports.

When John landed at the airport, he wasted little time in gathering his belongings from the overhead compartment and getting through the crowd to the front doors. He was the first passenger from that flight to exit the building and was sitting in a taxicab, riding to Le Heim, no less than fifteen minutes after the wheels of the jet had touched down on the runway. He leaned back into the seat and thought about what Jim said when he called to give him this new assignment.

"John, we need your assistance stopping an assassination. We've confirmed that there is a plot to assassinate Sheik Omani. We have had one casualty so far, and the only other person assigned in the field has been able to verify there are two assassins."

"Who was killed? Do I know him?" This was the single issue that bothered John about this work: The killing never stopped, and it was usually a friend. Field agents, although they numbered in the hundreds, were a close-knit group, and in time, everyone seemed to meet everyone else. So, it was seldom that one didn't know the victim.

"Actually, you don't. He went through special training and was new to the Agency. He was finishing his training on this assignment with Eric Dent."

"Eric's back?" John asked, obviously surprised.

"We were able to lure him back for this one assignment. And I talked him into taking Steve, the agent who was killed, along for training. We were looking for Steve to become Eric's replacement. He'd shown the same propensity for this work that Eric had during his training. He was a natural. Unfortunately, he ran into someone else just a little better at this job before he was ready. Manuel."

"Manuel." John let the name roll off his tongue as if it deserved some level of reverence. "That man is probably the most ruthless assassin in the business," he stated matter-of-factly. "He never concerns himself with who else dies in the process, or how they die," he added thoughtfully. John was thinking about a reported kill, credited to Manuel, where the assassin killed four children and two women in the process of eliminating one man. What was particularly heartless was the fact that none of the innocent victims were dead after the attack. One child managed to hang on for two days, before the loss of blood, lack of nourishment and finally the loss of all hope, combined to kill him. He was only nine.

Manuel had been hired to eliminate a middleman in a drug cartel, out of Colombia. The man was an American who'd been handling the financial transactions inside the States for a pipeline of cocaine. The cartel mistakenly thought he stiffed them, when in fact he had been stiffed himself. Manuel was hired, came in with a small band of men mainly for his own protection and automatic weapons blazing. The strafing didn't kill anyone at the time, but the target was flushed out and caught trying to escape through a patio door. There he received twenty-one bullets in his upper torso by the time they were finished. The initial surge into the building left the two women and four children wounded. Manuel just left, leaving the screaming women and children behind to die. It was three days before anyone discovered the bodies at the remote ranch, outside of Tucson. Autopsies revealed the first one died approximately four hours after the attack, and the last one, the nine-year-old boy, lingered for almost two days later before succumbing to his injuries.

"Exactly. Near as Eric can tell, Steve managed to surprise him as he prepared for his second attempt on the Sheik's life. He was given a bullet to the head for his troubles."

The thought of what Jim just described sent shivers up John's spine. This was a common hope among agents that death would come quickly if it were to come at all. Agents that survived any length of time didn't dwell on the thought of death. But being human, John often found himself wondering what it would be like to die.

"Am I to take up where Steve left off? And, if Manuel is the second assassin, that only leaves Jacque for the other one. That's how you lured Eric back, isn't it?" John was developing his reasoning as he spoke, but knew he was right before Jim could respond.

"Yes."

"It'll be good to see Eric again. It's been close to twelve years, but I always liked him. Did he remember me?"

"He didn't say. To tell you the truth, I had forgotten that you two had worked together on a few assignments in the early days. He wants you to check in at a place called Le Heim, in Jerusalem. Do you know where it is?"

"Ya, it's kind of a second-class hotel. Clean though, and off the beaten path. Away from the tourist areas," he added.

"Can you get there tonight?"

"That shouldn't be any problem. There are regular flights between Tel Aviv and Jerusalem. I assume Eric will be contacting me after I get there."

They continued to talk for a few more minutes, but the conversation turned away from business and on to more pleasant things; friends, relatives, and the latest Washington Redskin game.

- - - - -

Between the flight and the taxi ride to Le Heim, John had ample opportunity to consider his assignment. He hadn't had the pleasure of going up against Manuel, because he was typically not assigned neutralization objectives.

He was used mainly as a negotiator or interrogator. That's where his physical prowess was utilized to its fullest. He needed to be able to overpower his adversary, but keep them alive, because dead men don't tell you very much. His exposure to killing someone was typically restricted to self-defense. Special agents, like Eric, were reserved for neutralization assignments. He wasn't sure why he was chosen for this assignment and regretted not having asked Jim. He could only assume it had something to do with timing or his own knowledge about the Middle East. He was probably the foremost knowledgeable field agent on Middle East operations in the Agency. And it could very well be that his knowledge was needed in this situation. Then there is the other possibility; he was simply the closest agent and would be able to replace Steve the quickest. In either event, he was heading into a situation he was not as well prepared for, as he would like to be.

John arrived at the hotel a little before seven in the evening. There was still plenty of light, but the sun was low enough in the sky to cast elaborate oblong shadows everywhere. It was still visible over the smaller buildings surrounding the hotel but would disappear behind the taller ones. John climbed out of the taxi, paid the driver and grabbing his two carry on bags strolled into the hotel. Le Heim was at best a tourist class hotel for the regional population. But realistically, it more accurately fit the description one would expect of a second-class youth hostel.

There were a total of two bathrooms; one for every four rooms. In theory, each room was capable of handling four occupants. Two could fit in one bed, although the mattress was not much larger than a typical double mattress. Two more could set up temporary sleeping arrangements on portable army cots which look like they had been purchased directly from an army surplus store in the States. During the peak season, such as Passover, Le Heim would be full. This meant sixteen people shared each bathroom. To John's good fortune tonight, one room was empty, and the remaining three had single occupants.

The hotel was actually a converted store. The lobby and manager's office were in the front of the building, and the guest rooms were in back, two per side, separated by a narrow hallway. The building had a second floor that mimicked the first-floor layout, except for the front of the building. Above the lobby and office in front, was a two-room apartment where the owner, and manager, lived.

The owner was a middle-aged man with black hair and a black beard speckled with strands of gray, beginning to add character to his appearance. He had the perfect personality for this type of work; consequently, he enjoyed the varied people he would meet while they spent time at his establishment. When John walked into the somewhat dimly lit lobby and paused to allow his eyes to acclimate to the lower level of light, the owner quickly came out from behind the small counter and offered to take John's bags, then led him to the counter. Through a constant stream of chatter, he checked John in, then came back out from behind the counter to carry John's bags to his room when they were finished.

John declined the man's offer and picking up his own bags strode past the counter to the hallway that would lead him to his room. John was given room number four. It was supposed to be the last or second door on the right. At the door he set his bags down while he unlocked the door. Then kicking the door open with his foot, he grabbed the bags and quickly entered the room before the door had a chance to swing shut again. He set both bags on the single bed, then noticed the door was still open. He had been staying in commercial hotels too often, he thought. In those, the doors wouldn't stay open unless they were blocked open.

As John walked over to close the door, he surveyed the room. It consisted of the single bed, and a nightstand with a telephone on it. He guessed the nightstand was supposed to double for a desk since they had managed to slide a chair under it on one end. Other than those items, the room was empty. John removed his bags from the bed and lay down to wait for Eric's call. He hadn't realized how tired he really was, but within minutes he had fallen sound asleep.

When he woke the room was pitch black. Immediately he sensed he was not alone. His first inclination was to bolt from the bed, but whoever was in the room already had the advantage and that would only add to it. He continued to lie still in an attempt to convince the intruder he was still asleep, hoping for at least a small element of surprise. As he lay there, he slowly moved his eyes to one end of the room, then began panning across the room without moving his head. He started on the outside wall that contained the lone window to the room and worked his way to the door side.

When he had retired for the evening, he had closed the window. But since it did not have a latch, he was unable to lock it shut. Now, looking at the window it was obvious that this was the method of entry used by the intruder. The top of the aged and cracked double hung window was down a good six inches from the top, allowing the soft night breeze to blow the curtains occasionally. Next, he brought his eyes down the interior wall to the left of the bed, and then scanned the wall the whole length of the room. Nothing. Returning his eyes to the window, he started scanning the wall on his right. Again nothing.

Whoever was in the room had to be crouched down next to his bed on the left side since the right side was against the wall. Adrenaline started to race through his veins as he prepared to use this information to give him the advantage, to transfer the element of surprise to him from his adversary. When he had lain down on the bed, he had been expecting a call from Eric at any moment. Consequently, he was still fully dressed and lying on top of the covers when he woke up, leaving him uniquely prepared to deal with an intruder. Slowly, John took a deep breath. Then as he began to exhale, he pushed off the wall with his right hand, and pounced on his unsuspecting guest.

The first thing John felt was a sharp burst of pain as his arm was punctured. He yanked his right arm away from what he thought was the weapon. When the pain persisted, it became obvious what had happened. He grabbed the animal with his left hand and started to tug at it. Immediately the head of the animal released its grip, turned, and tried to bite his hand. He grabbed the telephone receiver with his good hand and brought the receiver crashing down onto the animal's head that had reattached itself to John's arm. Immediately, he felt the warm liquid start to run down his arm, but he wasn't sure if it was from him or the animal.

With the force of the blow, the animal was dislodged from his arm, and fell to the floor, stunned. John reached over to the nightstand to turn on the light. He wanted to see what he had so foolishly attacked. By now the animal had regained its composure and jumped up on the windowsill. It jumped again to the top of the window, then out it went. John was able to make out the silhouette of a big black alley cat just as it disappeared out the window. He got up and walked over to the window to make sure of what he had seen, but by that time it had vanished into the darkness of the alley.

John slammed the window up and shoved his shoe underneath the top of the double hung window to hold it up and keep it closed. Then he headed down the hall to the bathroom to clean up. As he gingerly dabbed at the open wounds from the cat's claws and teeth, he began to relax. He decided the cat, although painful, was a much safer adversary than who he had envisioned upon first waking up. His first thoughts were of Manuel. But then he reasoned that there was no way Manuel could know he had been sent as Steve's replacement. He reached for the soap again, and this time began to scrub with a little more force. The initial sting of the water from dabbing the wounds had acted like a mild anesthesia, numbing the claw marks enough to allow him to clean up more vigorously a second time.

He knew that the potential diseases that a stray cat carried, if left unattended, could be just as deadly as Manuel. And he had no intention of being the victim of an alley cat. He continued to work the lather into the wounds, until the stinging began to numb his arm further and the pain receded some more, then he bent over the sink to rinse the soap off. As he was rinsing the soap off, the air to his lungs was suddenly cut off. He lost precious seconds before he realized the source of the pain: Something had been placed around his neck and was slowly, painfully, cutting into his throat. He reached up with both hands and began grasping at the wire trying to get a finger hold and pull it off to allow his burning lungs to fill with the air they so desperately needed. But the wire was now cutting into his throat, and he was beginning to feel the warmth of his own blood as it began to coat his neck.

Suddenly the realization of what was happening exploded in his mind and he began to panic. In seconds he was going to be unconscious, then dead if he didn't do something now! He looked at the mirror in front him hoping to at least get a glimpse of his attacker. All he saw was his own face staring blankly back at him with blood streaming down his neck. With every bit of energy that he could muster, he brought his right arm forward, then slammed his elbow back into his attackers side as hard as he could. Momentarily the tension on the wire was relaxed. John took in a burst of air, without stop- ping to enjoy it. Quickly he recoiled his arm and repeated the blow. The wire loosened some more, and John began what he hoped would be the final blow. Again, he slammed his elbow into his attacker's side. This time he carried the blow through, forcing the man to release the wire completely and fall back against the door.

Hope returned to John as he prepared to turn and fight his attacker face to face. As he turned, he felt a burning sensation in his side, and he reached for it. His hand caught hold of the knife blade as it was being removed from his side. His fingers curled around the blade, and he could feel the metal warmed from his own blood as it cut through the flesh of his fingers. The quick loss of blood was causing him to lose consciousness, but before he passed out, he managed to turn and face his attacker. Much to his horror, he saw it was Manuel.

"How did you know?" He managed to ask, then collapsed as he crumpled to the floor.

Manuel stared at him for a second, then calmly stepped over his prone body and began cleaning up in the bathroom sink. He carefully scrubbed all the blood off his hands, then cleaned the knife. When he was finished, he stepped back over John's motionless body without looking down. As he exited the bathroom, he closed the door behind him.

He went to John's room to search through his belongings. He was looking for any clue that might tell him where he could find Eric but came away empty. His network of informants had failed miserably in keeping tabs of Eric, and he wasn't doing any better himself. It seemed all the reports told him where Eric had been, never where Eric was now much less where he might be tomorrow. He was hired to kill both Eric and the Sheik, and he was beginning to think that he might not get the opportunity with Eric.

- - - - -

Shortly after Eric finished talking to Jim about replacing Steve, he received information pertaining to the whereabouts of Jacque. It seemed Jacque had found his way to Jerusalem and was causing a stir with many of Eric's contacts. Jacque was contacting them in his efforts to find Eric. This surprised Eric because Jacque should have been concentrating his efforts on making plans for assassinating the Sheik, not wasting time looking for him. It also bothered him because it meant Jacque knew Eric was looking for him. He'd hoped Jacque wouldn't learn of his return to the game until it was too late. Their knowledge of each other neutralizes any advantage Eric might have gained because Jacque thought he was out of the picture. Or more accurately, should never have been in the picture at all, Eric thought.

Eric had to delay his initial contact with John and follow up on the lead he had been given concerning Jacque. He briefly considered leaving a message for him at the desk of Le Heim but decided there wasn't any need since John had been instructed to wait for Eric to contact him. Eric was thankful he had done just that, because for the first time since he began this assignment he knew where Jacque was. Now he was able to put his network of moles in motion, and he should be able to keep tabs on Jacque's every move. As soon as he finished briefing John, and was sure Manuel could be dealt with effectively, he would be able to deal with Jacque.

The morning sun was already having its effect even though it had not quite cracked the horizon. The varied shades of darkness in the night were giving way to distorted shadows as the morning light slowly increased. Eric was making his way to Le Heim, and for the first time since this episode began, he was truly feeling in control. He had managed to locate Jacque, and he had a trained, trustworthy agent in John, to deal with Manuel. He was even beginning to feel confident he understood the consortium's basic motive. Granted he still had questions, like what motive separates Toomas and Sergei from the other three in the group? How does Tom fit into this whole picture? Why did the consortium hire two assassins, although Eric thought he had a good understanding on this one? But the most puzzling of all: Why go to such great lengths in creating a second Sheik? This one bothered Eric the most.

As he approached the front door of Le Heim, he decided he would know the answers soon enough. The lobby door was unlocked, not because Jerusalem was a particularly safe city to be in, but because this owner never had a problem. So, when the lock was broken years ago, he just never got around to replacing it. Eric, who stayed at Le Heim on a number of occasions through the years, was well aware of this, so he walked right in. He stopped at the front desk to look at the register and see what room John was in. He took note of the number and headed down the hall. When he knocked on John's door, it swung open.

The room was empty, but it was apparent from the disarray that John had not been the last person in here. John's two bags were thrown against the wall and their contents were strewn about the room. It was obvious that whoever had gone through them had simply thrown each piece as it was removed from the bags, then reached for the next one. Eric walked around the room, not touching anything. He was looking for any clue to where John might be. The fact that he wasn't here led Eric to presume nothing bad had happened to him yet.

Satisfied that the room was not going to provide him any insight into John's whereabouts, Eric left. As he stepped out of the room, he paused to look both ways down the hall as he considered which exit to use. The front door or the rear exit near the bathroom? He decided to use the rear exit and wait for John's return in the alley. He should be able to stay out of sight in the back, he thought. As he walked toward the bathroom, he saw a dark stain on the floor near the door. He also noticed a sliver of light coming through the gap between the door and the threshold. When he was close enough to inspect the stain, he glanced down at it assuming it would be the result of some innocuous puddle of water or some such thing. He was surprised to see it was caked on to the floor and had a brownish color. Curious, Eric reached down and scrapped it with his fingernail. The top layer scrapped off revealing the still wet blood below. Without opening the bathroom door, Eric knew what he would find.

Eric glanced around. He knew he had to verify it was John who lay dead in the bathroom, but at the same time people would be getting up at any moment and begin making there way to the bathroom. He could not risk being found with a dead man. Everyone would assume he did it, and his task was difficult enough without having the police chasing after him for a murder he didn't commit. Regardless, he knew he had to confirm what had happened, so he opened the door. At death, John had collapsed and fallen between the toilet and the sink. The opening between the two was not wide enough to allow his body to complete the fall to the floor. Consequently, he was stuck in the most precarious position. His head was lying against the sink, almost perched there as if it were some grotesque ornament placed there by an interior decorator with a morbid sense of humor.

Eric reached for John's arm and tried to move it. It was his way of determining the time of death. If rigor mortis had completely set in, he would have had to been killed almost immediately after he arrived. Since there was a reasonable amount of free movement left in his arm, Eric surmised he could not have been killed too many hours ago. There was little Eric could do for John now, so he laid the arm back down and prepared to leave the hotel. He used the rear exit because up to this point no one had seen him and there was no need risking exposure to a guest now.

Once in the alley, Eric considered his next move. He knew he would have to contact Jim again to inform him what happened to John and try to convince him not to send another replacement. Time was already a precious commodity and losing more to this type of activity was expensive. What he really needed was someone to take the burden of Manuel off his shoulders permanently, not create additional problems. And wishing wasn't going to do him any good, he thought.

Maruch knew that she would be expected to do more than just keep tabs on the German, Toomas. When Ariel contacted her, he went into great detail about what the circumstances were. Or, at least how the Zealots, of which she was a member, perceived them to be. It was their fear, including Ariel and now Maruch's, that it was possible and probable that the Zealots were being set up to take the fall for the assassination of Sheik Omani.

This would be a travesty. Because even if it didn't start a war immediately, all support from the rest of the world, particularly U. S. support, would be lost and the end result would ultimately be a war anyway. If no one supported them, nothing would stop the Arabs from attacking Israel from all sides. It would only be a matter of time until they were wiped off the face of the earth. Hitler's vision would finally be realized.

That might make a lot of people happy, thought Maruch, but I have no intention of giving up my life just to make some Gentile jump for joy. As far as she was concerned, she had given far too much of her life to appease overbearing, obnoxious, heathen Gentiles already. She had reached a point in her life where she would rather fight to her death for her beliefs and or her people, than be led like a calf to slaughter. It was unconscionable that anyone would think they could use Jews this way.

Maruch was a mere twenty-five years old, but she had already run the gamut from liberal peacemaker when she entered college, to hard-line conservative hawk today. Her belief that the Arab and Jew could live together had been destroyed. When she entered the University of California-Berkeley, she was cut from the same liberal cloth as George McGovern, Edmund Muskie, Walter Mondale, the Reverend Jesse Jackson, and Bill Clinton. She was so enthralled and convinced at the liberal rhetoric, she had established herself as off limits to any young man that did not hold to the same political ideologies that she did. It didn't take long for everyone to know where she stood with respect to any human rights issue.

Consequently, when she applied those same principles to Israel, a country she despised at this point in her life, she was incensed by their actions. She couldn't understand how they could lay claim to a block of land that had not been theirs for the last two thousand years, then through an expansionist war, extend those boundaries at the expense of innocent Palestinians. She could not understand how they could refuse the right of the Palestinians to the exact same thing they had: An independent state. It was her desire to see Israel become a melting pot for the two races. Arab and Jew coexisting peacefully. Commingling racially would serve to eliminate their inherent hostility for each other, since both would become one. She saw Israel as the perfect place to demonstrate to the rest of the world that Arab and Jew can unite under one flag, one country. They would become a people who stood together for the common good. If it could happen in Israel, it would be the catalyst to the rest of the world. It would happen everywhere.

But what happens so often during the transition years between adolescence and adulthood, circumstances and events would change the way Maruch viewed the world. Her parents were very well off financially, and Maruch had reaped the benefits of their wealth. She never attended a public school, always having the distinct disadvantage of attending predominantly Jewish private schools. And as is so often the result, she became enamored with a utopian existence that could not stand up to the rigors of the real world.

She seldom experienced the prejudice that is so common to the Jewish child receiving an education in the public school system. She was buffered from the day-to-day experiences that would normally toughen her personality and allow her to develop a sense of pride in her heritage. Instead, she became disenchanted with the views of her parents and their friends. She saw them as being unreasonable, and unforgiving. She would ask them over and over again: Why can't you forgive and forget the events of the past? Why are all adults hell bent on tormenting themselves and future generations because of past Hitlers in the world? Those events happened decades, sometimes centuries ago. The world's conscience could never allow something like that to happen again.

It is that rose-colored world that she envisioned herself entering when she walked around the campus of Berkeley that first fall. It was a world that simply needed to be told of the benefits that working together would yield before it would do just that. She was completely unprepared for that first encounter with a group of young Arab men that were sent to the United States from Iraq to pursue their own education. She couldn't understand why they would pick on her simply because she was a Jew. One of the men had even accepted help from her, while doing homework in the student cafeteria. He couldn't solve a particularly difficult calculus problem, and readily accepted her explanation of how the equation was solved.

But when he was with his own kind, his enmity toward her was painfully evident. All Arabs knew that Jews were the scum of the earth. They were placed here, at best, to be servants of God's chosen people. It was expected of her to offer him help in the cafeteria, and she should have known that the thank you he gave her at the time would repay any debt he owed for her kindness. So, she shouldn't have been surprised when he treated her poorly when he was with his friends. Besides, they didn't physically hurt her. They just played with her and maybe embarrassed her.

That was Maruch's first real exposure to people that, although they had no reason to hate her personally, despised her simply because of what she was. If that had been the only such experience, Maruch, who was predisposed to forgiving the sins of others, would have quickly forgotten about the incident. But these young men, another group from Iran, and even a few Americans with no connection to the Arab world would confront her any chance they could, on or off campus. The trait Maruch discovered disturbed her most was each of them would leave her alone when they were alone. But if they were in a group, they were brutal. Occasionally one might even say "Hi" to her as he passed in the hall or on the street. But if there were two or more together, they had the courage to attack her verbally. And on occasion, it would escalate to something physical, like shoving and slapping her.

As each semester passed, Maruch would become less enthralled with her idealistic approach to solving the Middle East crisis. She began to understand that it was more than just a religious difference that separated the two races. There was a true hatred of the one race for the other. Granted it was not innate. It was a learned hatred. But it was hate, nevertheless. And Maruch was beginning to feel the birth pangs of that hatred growing inside herself. She fought it as best she could, but the group of Iranians and Iraqis were becoming bolder with each encounter. So bold in fact, that the same young man that she helped in the cafeteria as a freshman, produced a pear sized bruise on her arm when he hit her with a closed fist during one particularly physical encounter.

That happened the first week of her junior year. The same group of students had returned from Iraq, minus one whose grades were just too poor. They ran into her on her way to a lab, literally. The altercation quickly elevated from verbal abuse to jostling her back and forth among the five of them. They gathered around her in a circle. The ringleader started it by pushing her across the center of the circle. A second one caught her and pushed her back. This continued until she lost control of the books she was carrying, and they tumbled to the ground. Maruch decided she had taken enough abuse at the hands of these idiots, so she struck out blindly at the nearest one. Being accustomed to fighting, he reacted without thinking, deflected her blow and punched her in the arm. It was the first and last time she would allow one of them to make her cry but cry she did.

She hadn't cried like that since she was a child. She had fallen off her bike, skinning her shin on the curb in front of the house. At the time it was severe enough that her mother took her to the emergency room to have it dressed. Then, she was crying mainly from the pain of the injury, and only a small amount due to her embarrassment. Today, although the pain was severe enough to warrant her tears, she cried because she knew they had won. She was beginning to hate Arabs.

This school year seemed even longer than the previous two, but Maruch stayed in school. She put up with the harassment by withdrawing inside herself. Maruch also decided she needed to be able to take care of herself and began a course in self-defense. She settled on a course in karate. She practiced her moves, but purely from a mechanical viewpoint, ignoring the philosophy behind the martial art. She was taking the course to learn how to protect herself, not how to live her life, she reasoned. The instructor insisted one could not become proficient at the ancient art without mastering the mindset. However,

Maruch's anger served as a replacement to the Japanese philosophical approach that was supposed to control her movements.

Maruch was at best an average student when she started the class. But as the year unwound and the incidents between various Arab groups became more frequent and more physical, her dedication to the course grew. The instructor saw her skills blossom and began to use her as an example to the rest of the class of how understanding the philosophy of karate was the soul difference between Maruch's skills and theirs. Maruch allowed the teacher to ignorantly credit the Eastern mindset for her improved abilities. Because, she reasoned, it was impossible for him to understand what she was going through. He could never understand the hurt of anti-Semitism, nor could the rest of the Gentile world.

Her senior year came and brought with it her test for a first level black belt. Her teacher was pleased when she passed, and he was able to make the presentation to her in front of a new class of beginning students. He used the opportunity to preach to the class about the Eastern way of life, and Maruch stood by silently, oblivious to his words. It was so typical of the world to take credit for something they had nothing to do with, thought Maruch. But Maruch was becoming accustomed to this, so even now as the instructor was tying the black belt around her waist; she silently accepted his explanation to the rest of the class for her success. He could not possibly understand that her hate for Arabs was the sole driving force behind her success. He had never experienced the blind hatred of anti-Semitism, and never would.

Maruch continued with her karate lessons, honing her skills, and concentrating on her speed. For the most part she was able to avoid confrontations this year, and to date, none had escalated past the verbal abuse she was now accustomed to. This suited her fine because she was still inclined to avoid physical confrontations whenever possible. Even though she hated Arabs, she still felt that violence solved nothing. She was intent on trying to deal with all problems through rational discussions. She had been raised to work problems out, not beat them up.

During the Thanksgiving holiday many of the students left the campus. They either went home to visit relatives, or simply to put distance between themselves and the school. Some students, like Maruch, viewed the long weekend as a rare opportunity to use the schools facilities unhampered by the typical crowds of a normal weekend. Maruch had become a loner of sorts, spending all of her time in class, at the library, at the karate studio or in her dorm room. This weekend she spent much of her time at the library and a lab.

As she returned to her room, around ten-thirty Friday night, she noticed the group of Iranians that had caused the hermit in her to take control of her life. It was obvious by their rowdy behavior they had been drinking. In an effort to avoid them, she looked for an alternate route trying to skirt walking past them. Even though she felt capable of handling herself around them, she still preferred avoidance to confrontation. Glancing around, she saw she was near the lecture halls and decided to go in there. She knew if they didn't see her, they wouldn't bother her. She could wait inside for them to pass, then be safely on her way.

As she watched out the glass doors for the five of them to pass, clearing the way to her dorm room, she heard the unmistakable sound of a door opening, then closing. Immediately the sound of footsteps followed, as they came toward her from the other entrance. She saw three of the five men as they cleared the corner of the building and came to a halt in front of the sidewalk that led up to the door, she was standing behind. She stepped back to get out of their view, then realized she was being cornered. The footsteps she heard behind her belonged to the other two men. Opening the door to a lecture room, she slipped inside and hurried as quietly as possible down the steps to the door used by the professors to enter and exit the lecture room.

She opened the door at the front of the auditorium and stepped into the arms of one of the men. "I got her," he yelled to his companion. He had entered the lecture room and was coming down the steps to the front of the room. By the time he caught up to them, Maruch and her captor were at the front podium, waiting for him. The other man had already notified the three remaining men outside. And to Maruch's dismay, now all four of them were coming down the steps.

Maruch realized she didn't have any other alternative but to use force. She had been training for over a year for just this circumstance, but still felt inadequate to handle the situation. She had hoped she would never be required to use her training, but she realized now she had no choice. The man holding her released her with a push and she stumbled toward the podium. As he reached out to grab her again, she reacted. She caught her balance, took a half step back, and then spun around. As she spun, her right foot swung out in a long arching motion, striking the left side of his face. He crumpled to the floor. The blow was not meant to take him out, but it had been unexpected, and the force was sufficient to knock him to the ground. As he landed on the floor, his head snapped back hitting the concrete floor with a thud, knocking him unconscious.

Maruch didn't have time for remorse because the remaining four men were already to the bottom of the steps and had seen everything. As she started for the door, one of the men anticipated her intentions and cut off her path. She looked around for another escape route, but the other three were covering the two aisles back up the steps. There was no escape. She slowly stepped back toward the podium as she furiously tried to devise a plan of action. The four men began walking toward her, closing off any escape routes while encircling her at the same time. It was obvious by their expressions that this encounter would be considerably more violent than any of the previous ones. She was unsure if it was on account of their buddy lying on the floor, or some other perverse reason. But she sensed their intentions had been determined long before she had hurt their friend.

At this point she had no alternative but to fight. She prepared to take on the first one, deciding on a move similar to the one she used successfully the first time. She picked out the closest one and began her spin. She brought her right foot up to face level and kicked her assailant. Like the one before him, he crumpled to the floor although he remained conscious. The other three men hesitated when she began her attack. Maruch took advantage of this miniscule opportunity to go on the offensive again.

The spinning kick had left her positioned in almost the exact same place as when she started. Picking out her next target, she brought her arm up and began a blow destined for the soft flesh at the base of the neck near his shoulder. The blow, if delivered properly and with enough force, can temporarily paralyze one side of a man's body. And that was Maruch's intent. She knew her only chance of escape at this point was to neutralize each one of them, and her plan to do that was taking shape only as time unfolded.

By this time the slight advantage she had achieved by going on the offensive had dissipated. She was striking the one man, but the other two were free to attack her, each from a different side. Their timing was excellent: one diving at her legs, the other at her waist while she was bringing her rigid hand down unto their friend's neck.

The difference in time between all three actions taking place was milliseconds. Her hand crashed down on the man's neck, and his knees buckled from the blow. She felt the force of the one man's body as he wrapped his arms around her legs, simultaneously the second man converged at her from the other direction wrapping his arms around her waist. All four of them crashed to the ground. Maruch was on top of one man, and the man who tackled her at her waist was on top of her. The third one had fallen back and was not part of the pile of bodies.

The one below managed to maintain his hold on her legs as they fell, so Maruch began to wiggle, trying to get herself free. The second man briefly lost his grip, but with Maruch preoccupied trying to free her legs, he was able to grab one of her arms. By this time, the second man she had kicked was able to rejoin the foray and grabbed her other arm. The three men began stretching her limbs out, and soon she was outstretched on the floor wriggling her torso frantically as she tried to loosen their grip.

As she thrashed on the floor, she began to feel a sense of panic come over her. These men, who had directed their hatred for all Jews at her these last few years, had her trapped. She was completely at their mercy, and Maruch was certain mercy was not their strong suit. She didn't notice the fourth man begin stir, then slowly stand up. He walked over to where the three of them were. He stepped over her body so that he was straddling her, then looked down into her terrified but defiant eyes. Maruch didn't like what she saw in the man's eyes and began thrashing about with renewed vigor. The man towering over her kept staring at her, and then slowly a sinister smile spread across his face.

He didn't say anything, but Maruch's fear elevated to a level beyond what she thought was possible. Then he reached down and taking hold of each side of her blouse, ripped it open. Maruch screamed. The man on top cleared his throat to get her attention, then removed a small jackknife from his pocket. Seeing the knife, Maruch stopped screaming. She didn't know how far these people could go, but for the first time she feared for her life. He took the knife and slid it under each bra strap. Pulling it up in a smooth stroke, he cut each strap in turn. Roughly, he grabbed the bra and tossed it to one side. Now he moved down toward her waist.

Maruch was convinced he had decided to rape her. The thought of being raped by these men repulsed her, but she felt her only chance for survival and ultimately revenge would depend on her ability to survive this ordeal. She decided submission was her best chance at this point.

The man reached down and began to unbutton her blue jeans, then he unzipped the zipper. He took hold of a belt loop on each side of the tight-fitting jeans and pulled them down. Her panties came off with the jeans, so she was lying there with her jeans bunched up at her knees. He continued to tug at the jeans, trying to remove them completely, but in his haste the task became more difficult. He told the man holding her legs to change positions with him, so he could finish taking them off.

No one heard the door as it opened, then closed, or the footsteps of the man as he made his way down the steps to the front of the lecture hall where Maruch was being accosted. All of them were too engrossed at the thought of what they were about to do and were oblivious to the newcomer. Silently he approached the man removing Maruch's jeans. Just as the man finished pulling them off her feet, the intruder stepped into view. The would-be rapist held up Maruch's jeans like a trophy. The intruder was now within striking distance, so he clasped his hands together and brought them crashing down at the back of the man's neck. The force of the blow caused him to release his hold on the jeans. As he did, he fell forward onto Maruch. The sudden weight crashing down on her caused her to gasp for air.

As the first man fell forward, the intruder stepped to his left and kicked his foot up into the underside of the neck of the man who was holding Maruch's legs. He flew backward from the force of the kick, his head landing against the wooden podium with a crash. His whole body went limp, and blood started dripping out of his mouth.

By this time the two men holding Maruch's arms had released her and were running toward the stairs to get out of the lecture hall. In their haste they didn't think to split up. The intruder was able to stop them both by tackling the one, who was slightly in front of the other. The second one tripped over the two men lying on the floor in front of him. Pushing the second man off him, their unknown assailant gave the man lying on the steps beneath him a quick chop to the neck. He went limp.

There was only one man left, and he was scrambling to regain his footing to run. However, his panicked state was making that task impossible. The intruder stood up, grab the man's arm, and with a quick twist had it three-quarters of the way up his back before he could react. "If you're smart, you won't squirm too much, and I won't have to break it," he calmly stated.

Keeping the man in front of him, he proceeded down the steps, back to the front of the lecture hall to check on Maruch. Maruch had already regained her composure, retrieved her jeans and was in the process of tying her torn blouse around her. Considering what she had just gone through, she was amazingly calm. When the two men arrived, she glared at the only attacker to remain conscious. He was the same man that she had helped with a calculus problem in the library her freshman year, so long ago. Silently she approached him as if he were a long-lost friend. Putting her hands on his shoulders, it appeared as if she were about to lean over and give him a kiss, but instead she brought her knee up into his groin as hard as she could. He cried out in pain as his knees buckled. He was allowed to crumple to the floor. As he lay there, writhing in pain, Maruch just stared at him. Finally, she said, "The next Arab to try that with me will be dead."

She turned to face the man that had helped her, but he was disappearing through the doors at the top of the steps. She called out for him to stop, but he continued through the door. It closed behind him. She took off running, taking the steps two at a time, but by the time she got to the top of the steps and through the door, he was nowhere to be found. She rushed out of the building and frantically looked around but couldn't find him. She tore around to the back of the building as fast as she could, but there was no sign of him there either. He had vanished as mysteriously as he had arrived.

She stood for a moment looking out over the campus, wondering whom he was and where he had disappeared. Thankful though, that he had been there when she needed him...but sorry she hadn't had the opportunity to thank him properly for his help. A shiver ran up and down her spine as she thought about what those men had planned to do to her. She made two vows that evening; first, never to forget this man's face and to someday thank him properly for what he had done. And second, she vowed she would make all Arabs pay for what happened here tonight and what almost happened here tonight.

Sullenly, Maruch returned to her dorm room, mulling whether to report what had happened. Unsure of how everything would come out if she reported it to the police, she decided not to. Since the only witness she had to the attack was unknown to her and had disappeared, she decided it might be preferable to not say anything. There were five of them, and there was no telling what kind of story they might concoct. It would be her word against theirs, and that described a battle she feared she would lose.

It seemed like the incident made every news report within a fifty-mile radius of the school the next morning, but Maruch was glad she had decided against reporting it because three of the men ended up in the hospital. By not reporting it, she gave them a chance to make up their own story, and that is precisely what they did. They alluded, without actually saying it, to surprising a group of vandals in the lecture hall and chasing them away before they could do any damage to the facilities. However, the ensuing scuffle did result in some injuries to occur on both sides. Naturally, they didn't get a good enough look at the perpetrators to be able to describe them. Also, their injuries managed to be more serious than any the vandals had sustained in the fracas.

Maruch was responsible for putting two of the three men in the hospital, and what was amazing to her was she was actually proud of herself. She was truly pleased with herself because she realized she could be proud of that accomplishment. She never thought **SHE** would have ever been capable of that type of activity, much less be proud of it, but she was. These men had unleashed in her, instincts that she never knew existed. Now that they had surfaced, after being buried deep within her for so long, she knew they would never return to that part of her again. She had changed, for better or for worse was for someone else to decide. In either case, she knew the change would be permanent.

The first man that Maruch had attacked in self-defense sustained a concussion from his head hitting the concrete floor. The doctors felt his recovery would be complete, just slow. The second man Maruch put in the hospital was the one she had kicked in the groin. His damage, although not life threatening, would probably be permanent. The doctors already determined his chances for fathering children were very slim and told him so.

The man that helped her last evening was responsible for putting the third one in the hospital, and it appeared he was in the worst condition of the three. He was wavering back and forth between a coma and consciousness, and the news report listed him as critical. With each passing hour he remained alive, his chances for survival improved. But with each passing hour he remained in his vegetative state, the higher the probability he would have permanent damage. At hearing this, Maruch's thoughts drifted back to the man who saved her last night.

He had come out of nowhere. To Maruch, the odds of him being anywhere near at the time she was in need were astronomical. For whatever purpose, she reasoned, he was close enough to hear her scream. Otherwise, there wasn't any way he could have known what was going on. She thought about that for a moment, wondering why he would have been where he was. When he was. Finally, she shook her head in frustration as if she could shake the confusion out of her mind. There was no way she could deduce why he was there, and with the disappearing act he pulled, there was little chance she would ever find out. She decided it was Yahweh's plan and left it at that.

Her recollection of him remained vivid, possibly becoming clearer with time. He was blond, less than six feet, but built extremely solid. He was obviously in very good shape, she thought. He was clean-shaven, revealing well-defined, sharp lined features. Yet his face had an undefined softness to it that contradicted the sharp image. His actions indicated he was well versed in the art of self-preservation, and merely added to his already intriguing, yet dangerous mystique.

Maruch found herself, for the first time in her life, fantasizing about a man. She had always maintained an almost prudish approach to the opposite sex because she found them to be of little interest. It's not that she didn't like men; she just hadn't reached the point in her life where there was sufficient interest in them to supplant her interest in almost anything else. She felt the same way about other women. People were interesting, but not important enough to devote large portions of time to. She knew developing a close relationship with anyone, man, or woman, required copious amounts of time. Unfortunately, this man, who had entered and exited her life so quickly, was the first to stir within her the desire to know him better. She also knew that more would never come, so she was confident that her fantasizing was harmless.

She had just returned to the Star of David hotel from her supper when she saw him. Her first thought was that he couldn't possibly be the same man that had helped her that evening in the lecture hall at the University of California-Berkeley. But the reaction that her body had was as telling as her diary was as a prepubescent adolescent. He was standing at a public telephone, doing more listening than talking. He was very intent, but at the same time was well aware of his surroundings. So much so, that she perceived him to have reacted just the slightest little bit when his eyes panned across her.

She didn't want to appear obvious, yet she couldn't tear her eyes off him. Could it possibly be him? She kept asking herself as she worked her way across the lobby in an effort to get a better view. She found a half-sized sofa that was angled toward a window, but allowed her a view of the man without looking directly at him. She sat down and pretended to be waiting for someone, while watching him talk on the phone. After sitting there for a few minutes, she realized she no longer cared what happened to Toomas. Somehow, this stranger had replaced Toomas in importance, and she made no effort to change that.

The view was not actually better than when she first saw him upon enter the hotel. But it did offer her the opportunity to study him without being obvious. He was still as good looking as she remembered, but his face had begun to take on the character that can only be developed with age. He was dressed in clothes befitting a tourist, and she assumed that was why he was here. Although she had difficulty accepting that image of him because it was so contrary to the only way she knew him. Sitting there hypnotized by him, she lost track of time. She was surprised to see him hang up the phone, thinking he was done too quickly. He couldn't have been on for more than a few minutes, she thought.

She decided to do something she knew was foolish but was the only thing that came to mind. It would risk her cover, but she felt compelled to take that chance, nevertheless. If Ariel were to find out, he'd be furious, and ashamed, she thought.

Eric turned from the phone and left the lobby. He had just spoken to Jim and was disappointed to learn John's replacement wouldn't be here until sometime tonight. That left him in the unenviable position of trying to protect two Sheiks from two assassins. His contacts had confirmed the latest location of Jacque, and now they were trying to locate Manuel. Not that the information would do him much good, he thought. To the best of his knowledge, the whole consortium and the two Sheiks were staying at the Star of David hotel.

After he got outside of the hotel, he stopped and looked around. Spotting what he was looking for, he headed directly for it. It was an open-air restaurant, a sidewalk cafe. There was seating inside, but

Eric needed to keep track of the activity at the hotel, so he chose a small table near the storefront, underneath a canopy that provided the barest of protection from the late morning sun. The location offered an unobstructed view of the hotel lobby doors, except for the occasional pedestrians that could disrupt, but not completely block, his view of the door.

He sat down and ordered a cup of coffee. Then as the waiter started to leave, he called him back and asked him to bring some pastries, saying he expected to be here for a while. The waiter nodded, then traipsed off to another table where an older couple had just seated themselves. After taking their order, he headed back inside the cafe. Eric's mind was preoccupied with trying to devise a plan that might make his task possible, so he didn't notice that Maruch had followed him to the cafe. She was standing at the door to the cafe, debating her next move while staring at Eric. Finally, she decided, and with absolutely no confidence in herself or what she was doing, worked her way over to Eric's table.

She stood one table away, poised to speak, but unable to begin. Then the waiter returned with Eric's coffee and a basket of pastries. As he placed them on the table, Eric looked up at him briefly, and then glanced over toward Maruch. Giving no indication that he recognized her; he thanked the waiter and returned his attention to the hotel's lobby door.

Maruch summoned her courage, something she was unaccustomed to having to do, and approached Eric's table. Again, her voice left her, but this time Eric took the initiative. He kept his eyes trained on the lobby doors and the few people that were coming and going, then without warning asked her, "May I help you? You've been following me since my phone call inside the hotel lobby, so I would assume you have something to say to me. Either that or you're some kind of nut with an unhealthy interest in tourists."

She was taken back with his unkind remark and continued to stand there speechless as her thoughts went wild. She had spent many nights reliving her image of him and had subsequently elevated it way beyond realistic expectations. Now she was facing the per son she had idol-ized these many years, and he fell woefully short based on his opening remark. She briefly considered running away, but then quickly came to the conclusion that she was much too old for such adolescent behavior. Her humiliation, caused more by her perceived embarrassment from what he said than anything else, almost caused her to overreact by reading him the riot act. She waited to speak until she was able to gain control of her emotions. Eric, unaware of her anger, patiently waiting for her response, but kept his eyes on the lobby. "Guessing by your comment, I don't suppose you remember me."

Eric took his eyes off the hotel door and glanced up at her. He looked at her just briefly, then returned his gaze to the lobby doors, and said. "You're a little girl I met a long time ago. You were in trouble, and I helped you. That's all there was to it. I don't help little girls anymore."

She knew she should leave him there, alone to stew in his strange little ideas, but she couldn't. She needed to know why this man was there that night when no one else was around to help. She needed to know why he was willing to help her when no one else would have. But most, she wanted to know why he left without allowing her the chance to thank him for his help. "You left so quickly; I wasn't able to thank you for helping me. I have so many questions . . ."

"I knew you were thankful, so there was no need for you to tell me. You needed help, so I helped. Don't make more of it than it was," Eric interrupted her hoping to cut off her questions before she drew attention to them. Just what I don't need right now, he thought. I have the work of three men to do, and I run into someone I helped years ago. Eric knew he was being rude, but that was his intent. He would have liked to take the time to answer her questions, but he was not in a position to do so. He continued to watch the hotel doors, hoping she would take the hint and leave him alone. But Maruch was determined to learn more about this man, even if her first impression of him was less than flattering.

She couldn't quite understand or square this man's actions today with those of that fateful night. She was beginning to suspect that things were far different than what they seemed to be on the surface. Having gotten involved with covert activities under the direction of Ariel, her instincts were telling her that Eric was in a similar line of work. Her training began to take over. Instead of leaving Eric like he was hoping she would, she took a seat at his table. However, just before she sat down, she collared the waiter and asked him to bring a second cup of coffee for her. Taking a seat next to Eric, careful not to block his view of the hotel doors, she reached into the basket, uninvited, and helped herself to a small croissant. Then, as if to add insult to injury, she asked him. "Who are we trying to follow? The Sheik?"

Eric reacted to her comment by grabbing her by the arm and pulling her inside the restaurant. At first she resisted, but he explained to her that if she didn't come with him, he would kill her right there and now. Maruch could see in Eric's eyes that he was indeed serious and capable of doing exactly as he threatened. Without any resistance, she allowed him to guide her into the building. Once inside, Eric looked around. The place was not empty. In the need of privacy, he continued on, guiding her to the restrooms. He knocked on the men's room. Someone inside yelled back something about what he should do if he couldn't wait. Eric pulled her over to the women's room and knocked again. When there wasn't a response forthcoming, he opened the door and pushed her inside. Stepping in after her, he pulled the door shut behind him, then immediately locked the door. He walked over to the stall, bent down to see if anyone was inside, then returned his attention to Maruch.

"Who the hell are you, and what do you want?" he began. Then he added, "And you might as well tell the truth, because before the day's out I'll know everything there is about you."

Maruch's worst suspicions had been confirmed. She had hoped he was just a good Samaritan, but now she knew better. It was now her objective to find out, as he said, 'everything there is to know about him.' "I'm not in the habit of providing that information to everyone that demands it," she said defiantly.

Eric's attack was lightning quick. Even with Maruch's advanced training, by the time she could react, it was too late. Eric had her pinned against the bathroom wall, and his mouth was an inch from her ear. She could smell his breath, which was a mixture of halitosis from last night's supper, and the coffee he had been drinking this morning. In a whisper so soft she could barely hear him, he said. "You have mistaken me for someone who might care what happens to you. I'm not. What you don't understand is that right now I'd just as soon kill you as look at you. I don't have time to play word games with you right now. So, I want to know why you're so interested in me, and what exactly your doing here? If I don't start hearing an acceptable explanation soon."

He stopped talking, but brought a knife, which Maruch had not noticed he had, up to her throat. He held the point of it at the base of her neck, just above the curved bone at the top of the sternum. He slowly began increasing the pressure until she was sure he would puncture the skin any second.

"When I came into the lobby, I saw you on the phone. I knew I recognized you from somewhere, but it took me a moment to figure out where. Once I realized who you were, I really just wanted to meet you." Maruch wasn't sure if she was getting through to him or not, but at least the pressure on the knife blade was not increasing while she was speaking. "You may think it wasn't much, but I have always been very grateful to you for what you did for me that night. I was really just trying to thank you." Maruch's voice was pleading with Eric. "What I said about the Sheik was meant as a joke. I'm sorry if I offended you."

The last comment hit him like a sledgehammer. Was it possible that what she was saying was true, and in his paranoia after Steve and John's death, he was overreacting? Eric's mind was racing, could he have been overly sensitive to this woman's off the cuff comment, when in fact, all she was trying to do was be funny? He knew that was a possibility, but the risks were too great to take her word for it. He hadn't gotten much sleep last night and finding John dead this morning had him on edge. He had concluded that whoever killed John had to have inside information, and that made everyone he met a suspect. He had no reason to believe he could trust Maruch, but then she had given him no reason not to trust her either. She did have a good reason to follow him that had nothing to do with Steve or John. He relaxed the pressure on the knife to acknowledge the possibility she was telling the truth but didn't release her.

"I'm inclined to believe you," Eric said in a much less threatening voice. "But why are you here? Why are you at this hotel?"

Maruch expected the question, so she was prepared and somewhat relieved when he asked it. It meant she was improving her position with him. "I'm staying at the hotel. I'm a guest. What did you expect?"

"In that case, let's go to your room so we can talk more freely." Eric figured he was calling her bluff and was surprised when she readily agreed to his proposition. Changing his tactics he removed the knife, which had remained at Maruch's throat throughout the entire exchange. Then added. "That won't be necessary. I won't go into details about my actions just now, but I can assure you it was necessary. I'm sorry if I frightened or offended you. If you would like, we can go back to the table and start over." Eric was not convinced that she was the innocent bystander she was trying to pass herself off as, but he had no proof that she wasn't. He decided that if, in fact, she were simply offering her gratitude for his assistance that night, he could be gracious and accept. On the other hand, if she wasn't what she seemed to be, a more relaxed atmosphere might provide more information than his threats.

One item was very clear to Eric as they walked back to the table: She had maintained her composure much better than could be expected of a layman. As far as she was concerned, her life had been threatened, but yet she acted as if it were a common occurrence. The woman he helped that night had shown the signs of a person ready to panic. Today, that same woman gave no evidence that she could ever lose control, even at the threat of imminent personal danger.

The two of them returned to the table and the waiter delivered Maruch's coffee. They talked briefly about that incident in the past that marked the moment their paths crossed. Neither of them discussed why they were here, or what their plans were, and it was apparent the conversation had become very superficial. Maruch finished the cup of coffee, then excused herself and left. Eric wondered if his approach to this situation had been ill advised. As she walked away, he couldn't shake the feeling that she was not telling him the entire truth, and they would be seeing each other again.

As Maruch went in, Toomas walked out of the hotel doors. Eric watched from his seat at the restaurant as Toomas came through the doors and walked out to the edge of the curb. He stood there for a moment, looking as if he were drinking in the view, then nonchalantly turned to his left and started strolling down the street. He was acting innocently enough, giving the impression he was out for a morning stroll. No cares in the world, except trying not to get lost. With each building he passed, he would slow down, stop and peer inside at whatever might be in the window, then move on. His progress was slowly getting him to the corner and would take him out of view shortly if Eric didn't do anything. Although he was here primarily to keep an eye on the Sheik's activities in case Jacque or Manuel showed, he desperately wanted to follow the German and see what he was up to.

Toomas was at the corner when Eric decided to let him go. He wanted to return to the hotel lobby where he could continue watching for the Sheik. As he paid the bill, he looked up just in time to see Toomas round the corner. He brought his eyes back to the task in front of him, scanning the hotel in the process. It was then that he noticed Maruch come out the doors and quickly make her way straight to the corner, apparently following Toomas. His curiosity piqued, he continued to follow her with his eyes. As she neared the corner, she slowed considerably, approaching the corner at a more normal pace. At the corner, she took a wide berth as if providing herself the option of returning in the direction she had come, crossing the street or following the same direction as Toomas. It was obvious by her reaction; Toomas had increased his pace considerably once he rounded the corner. Maruch took off running, disappearing around the corner quickly. Eric made a mental note to talk to Maruch again.

This seemed to confirm his suspicions of her. They may have happened on each other by coincidence, but she was too interested in the consortium to allow her actions to go unquestioned. Whatever her interests, they would need to be subjugated to his own, he thought. It was clear to him she was involved in some manner, not necessarily with the consortium, but more likely with trying to stop them. If that were true, he couldn't risk her getting in the way at the wrong time and making his job more difficult than it already was.

Eric finished paying for his light breakfast and wandered out onto the sidewalk. His purpose for the day would be to monitor the Sheik's activities and possibly fine-tune his bearings on either of the assassins through his network of informers. He managed to make contact with Jim earlier, relaying the bad news about John. Jim still had not been able to get back to him confirming any replacement for John. During their conversation, they discussed the possibility of involving their Israeli counterparts and employing one of their people for the task, but it was left unresolved. This would reduce the time needed to get a replacement to Eric, because the traveling distance was negligible.

Both men also felt the chance of success would be significantly improved using a native of the area. During their conversation, Jim indicated he felt one of the reasons John was identified and neutralized so quickly was related to his nationality. If he had been an Arab or Israeli, he would not have been as obvious. Manuel or Jacque, whichever one took him out, obviously had little trouble locating or identifying John. The reason he was suspected in the first place was because he was a known American agent. Looking like an American but staying in out of the way hotels makes one easy to locate. A tourist he wasn't. And staying where he did actually raised everyone's awareness of him rather than providing him the obscurity he was seeking.

While mulling these things over in his head, Eric worked his way back across the street and was approaching the front door of the hotel, when he decided to walk to the corner. He walked toward the corner; the same one Toomas and Maruch had turned at, hoping to see them, but not really expecting to. At the corner he hesitated for a few seconds, but as expected both of them had disappeared. Satisfied, he returned to the hotel.

As he approached the door, he extended his hand to grab the door handle when Sergei burst out the door. Sergei preoccupied, and Eric immersed in his own thought, neither man noticed the other when their shoulders bumped. Eric was knocked back out of the way and against the wall of the building. He watched as Sergei, without turning to see who he had run into, continued on his way as if nothing happened. Sergei continued to the corner, turned, and headed in the direction both Toomas and Maruch had gone as Eric watched in amazement.

Eric decided Sergei's actions warranted an explanation, so he let the lobby door swing shut without entering and followed him. When Eric rounded the corner he was barely able to catch a glimpse of Sergei, as he turned left at the next street. Sergei was almost running, his gait equal to that of a slow jogger. Eric realized he would have to risk being spotted by running after him or lose him at the next corner.

Eric started running toward the corner, easily dodging the few people walking the street this time of the morning. At the next corner, he slowed down approaching it cautiously in case Sergei was suspicious and had begun watching behind himself. However, Sergei was already two thirds down the next street and seemed intent on where he was going, not where he had been. Eric began running again, but this street contained a few more people than the previous one, forcing him to spend as much effort going sideways as forward to avoid running into anyone.

Sergei continued straight for the next eight blocks, Eric slowly gaining on him with each passing street. When Sergei made his next turn, Eric had reduced the gap between the two men to just a little more than one hundred feet, and Eric no longer had to run; he was now able to keep up with Sergei by matching his pace. Eric finally felt comfortable with the distance that separated the two men until he made the next turn. As if he had walked onto the set of a busy movie studio during the middle of a shoot, the crowd exploded around him. He lost Sergei in the sea of humanity that filled the street.

Sergei had melted into the crowd. Eric frantically began searching the mass of bobbing heads, looking for any that might match Sergei's. As Eric studied the crowd, the crowd continued to move in what seemed like an infinitely random motion that created new patterns as quickly as old ones would disappear. The perpetual motion of the moving crowd was hypnotic. Eric fought the urge to stare blindly, increasing his concentration. As he studied the crowd, he saw Maruch's profile caught between two very ruthless looking Arabs. His eyes were now riveted to that section of the crowd as he tried to keep Maruch's image in view. Finally, two men moved, and he was able to see the side of Maruch's face clearly, albeit briefly, as the crowd quickly closed around her again. The two men were replaced with two women, then a man and woman, then two more women. But each time they separated enough; Eric would see Maruch.

Maruch did not appear concerned. She had positioned herself near a street vendor selling fruit so she could see the events taking place. Eric presumed she had maintained at least her visual contact of Toomas but was not sure. Eric briefly considered this turn of events, and then decided that Sergei was probably meeting Toomas here. He decided to work his way closer to Maruch and wait for either Toomas or Sergei to show themselves. Eric maneuvered until he was positioned just ten feet behind Maruch. Now his view was seldom interrupted. Then he noticed what she had been watching so intently.

There were three men standing up against the wall of a small rug shop. Toomas was in the center, Sergei, who looked as if he were still trying to catch his breath, was on the left, and a third man, who's back was to them, was on the right. There were occasional people walking into and out of the door of the rug shop, but for the most part these three men had found a secure place to talk. Neither Maruch nor Eric could risk getting close enough to the three men to hear their conversation. And no one in the crowd milling around close enough to hear was the least bit interested in what they were saying.

Maruch continued to watch the three men, while Eric began examining the crowd. While he was watching them talk, he sensed an impending danger. He couldn't be sure, but he thought it was centered on the third man; the one with his back to him that he had not yet been able to identify. Something else bothered him about what was taking place. Toomas and Sergei having secret meetings behind the rest of the consortium's back was not unusual, but the new player added a twist that Eric needed to understand. Who was he? What was his part in their plan? Who did he represent? Was he the third part in a triad, or representing a third-party Eric had yet to discover? As these questions raced through his head, he divided his attention between the crowd, the three men, Maruch and these questions.

Reacting, Eric took off. What he had just seen allowed him no time for precautions. He bowled over the first two people he bumped into. The crowd reacted to the disturbance by flailing out at each other, unaware that he was the cause. He continued to force his way through the mass of humanity, the whole time wondering if he would get there in time. To Eric, it seemed like it was taking hours, but within a few seconds he managed to cross the street and was scaling a vegetable stand. He used it to climb up on the roof of the building immediately behind it.

Maruch was the first to notice the disturbance in the crowd and started looking for its cause. When Eric jumped on the table containing the vegetables, her eyes projected his trajectory to the roof above. She was able to see the man just above Eric's outstretched hand as he started squeezing the trigger.

By this time Toomas, who had the best vantage point of the three men, looked up and saw what Maruch had already discovered. Grabbing the arm of the unidentified third man, he pushed with every last bit of energy he could muster. He sent the man reeling into a small table of throw rugs, then against the wall. The man and table crashed to the floor simultaneously just as the bullet passed through the area the man just vacated. It lodged in the wall of the store front, barely missing the store clerk. Toomas turned toward Sergei and dove directly at him. Both men hit the ground hard, missing the table of rugs to their right.

By now, Eric was on top of the vegetable stand. Hearing the retort of the first shot, he jumped straight up. He was able to grab the portion of the rifle barrel that extended over the edge of the roof. The marksman, caught completely off guard, was not prepared for the downward force Eric's handhold put on his rifle and lost control of it. Eric, the rifle barrel now in his hands, cleared the end of the stand on his descent and landed on his feet. Immediately he dropped the rifle and took off into the store.

Inside the store he quickly located a ladder attached to the back wall leading to a trap door that opened out onto the roof. Eric rushed to it. Taking the rungs two at a time, he climbed the ladder until he was stopped by the trap door. The latch was on the inside, which he just managed to release as he finished climbing the last rung. As he was pushing the door back, he began surveying the rooftop, looking for the man that just tried to assassinate one of the three.

Whoever had been on the roof was gone. Still, Eric pulled his body through the opening and stood up on the roof. He turned slowly in all directions as he looked for the man on the adjoining rooftops. Four buildings south of where he was standing, he saw a man climbing over the back wall. Eric took off running after the man, but by the time he was able to navigate his way over the three roofs in between, the man was gone again. Eric went over to the edge of the roof and looked over to the alley below. He was greeted to a scene like the one he had just left. The man had lowered himself into an alley filled with as many people as were on the street in front.

Eric looked down at the group of people in the alley below. There were two distinct types of people mulling around below. One type was obviously the user of any type of drug they could get and looked to be under the influence already. The second type had money. And were invariably accompanied by at least one, but more often two, very large and angry looking sidekicks, as they worked their way through the crowd looking for buyers. Eric looked for any sign of the man he was chasing. Not having gotten a good look at the man's face made the task impossible. Everyone he picked out looked as if he belonged right where he was. Eric briefly considered climbing down into the crowd to wander among them hoping to scare the man into making a mistake and giving himself away. But he decided against it when he realized getting caught up in that crowd could be deadly. Instead, he headed back to the roof with the trap door.

Before heading back to the trap door, he went to the front of the building to check on Toomas, Sergei and Maruch. From the roof he was able to assess the condition of each one and determine if the marksman was successful, while monitoring their actions for anything that appeared suspicious. In his haste to catch the man with the rifle, he hadn't taken the time to see if anyone had been injured in the initial attack. Now he was taking advantage of his vantage point to evaluate the extent of any damage by viewing the melee from above. He scanned the area immediately around the fruit and rug stands where Maruch,

Sergei, Toomas and the other man had been standing and was not pleased with what he saw.

There was no indication that any of them had ever been there. Whatever the reason, all four managed to disappear into the crowd. He continued his search by expanding the search area farther and farther away from the storefronts. He had reached the point where he was convinced, he wouldn't be able to find them when he noticed Toomas, then Maruch, a few feet behind him, turn the corner two blocks away. He wasn't able to locate Sergei or the other man in the discussion group.

Eric turned away from the front end of the building at the same time overheard someone being told, "The shots came from up there. I think I saw him still up there a few seconds ago." Eric realized whoever was speaking was obviously talking about him. This eliminated the possibility of leaving by the same method he had used to get here. He had no choice but to assume the voice was reporting what he had seen to someone in an official capacity. Eric didn't want to get tangled up with officials now or ever, but in this case, it could be worse than normal. He couldn't risk that his innocence would not be believed when he described the events to whomever. Nor could he afford the time required to explain his circumstances to anyone. Consequently, he hurried over to the trap door and closed it.

Looking around, he was able to locate some scrap wood that had been tossed up on the roof for who knows what reason. Eric was always amazed at what he was able to find on the many roofs that he had been on in his life. People were basically slobs or lazy, he thought. The result was all manner of garbage in the most unlikely places, like roofs. He took the wood and wedged it between the brackets that held up the door when it was opened and the door itself. Anyone trying to open the door from below would have a very difficult time, without the benefit of knowing why.

As he made his way to the back of the building, he heard voices as if someone began trying to open the door and found it was stuck. Eric looked over the wall at the end of the roof, saw a pile of empty boxes and jumped down near them. He was only eight feet up, so he was able to maintain his footing and quickly made his way to the end of the alley.

Out of the alley Eric headed straight back to the corner where he last saw Maruch and Toomas. He didn't expect to find them there, but he had to at least look. After verifying what he already knew, he decided to head back to the hotel knowing all three of them would have to return there as well.

10

-Then the Lord said to me, "Out of the north the evil will break forth on all the inhabitants of the land."

Eric had been moving from one location to another, constantly keeping the hotel's front doors in view. So far, his observations had yielded absolutely nothing. Since the incident this morning, all three men and Maruch stayed away from the hotel. Eric assumed the third man could be included in this conclusion even though he wouldn't have been able to recognize the man even if he bumped into him. As for Toomas and Sergei, there was the slim possibility they managed to get back to the hotel before Eric returned to start his watch. But with no evidence of Maruch, Eric felt this was unlikely.

He was terribly disappointed in himself for failing to keep track of at least one of the five people. He could rationalize his failure with the would-be assassin, and he could even accept losing Toomas, Sergei and the unknown third man. But the one that bothered him, and the one he wouldn't accept, was losing Maruch. His male ego somehow perceived this to be an unacceptable result. Granted he had been out of the business for a little while, but he still considered himself to be the best in the world. And the best in the world should have been able to keep the last person in the line, in view. And that person had been Maruch. If he would have kept her in sight, through her he could have kept tabs on Toomas for sure, and possibly Sergei and the third man. Instead, he spent the lion's share of the day moving from store to restaurant then back to the store again, watching a benign hotel door.

Activity at the hotel was modest. With the conclusion of the news conference yesterday, and the subsequent release of the excess tension in the crowd that accompanies such events, the city had very quickly returned to a more normal existence. This made the job of watching for the Sheik, or Oman 2, and either Manuel or Jacque relatively easy, but also very boring. The events of the morning with Toomas and Maruch had been an enjoyable respite from the day's activities, and Eric found himself thinking fondly of those events as the day wore on.

Eric's meandering brought him to a store that sold, bought, traded, or bartered in almost anything based on the looks of the potpourri of items strewn about the store. There was no discernible pattern to the way things were put out, but there did seem to be a main theme in the items as a whole. Predominantly the owner, by design or happenstance, had centered on a theme of metal containers. There were all sorts and sizes of metal containers. They ranged in size from the smallest incense bowls to large jug like containers that reminded Eric, in size only, of the old milk cans one often saw on farms in the Midwest.

At first glance, the owner didn't seem to employ any method for displaying the containers. However, at closer inspection it was obvious he had set the containers out based on the type of metal used in the construction. The larger ones, although Eric assumed they would be more expensive than many of the smaller ones, were placed nearer the street, and were mostly inexpensive metals. I suppose, Eric thought, no one would get very far trying to steal one of these. Taking hold of one of the largest containers and tipping it, he was surprised to find it was not that heavy. It was large, but the metal wall was actually very thin, keeping the weight reasonable.

No container made of anything more valuable than copper was displayed outside the shop's entrance. As Eric worked his way toward the counter at the back of the shop, pewter vessels were replaced with more copper, then silver, and finally gold. The size of the containers became smaller as well, with most of the gold items being reserved for the purpose of burning incense. There was one item that caught Eric's eye. It was a complete tea set, from cups to teapot made out of gold. Back home it was not uncommon for many households to display their silver tea sets, but this was the first time he had ever seen its gold counterpart.

Throughout Eric's inspection of the many shops and restaurants during the day, Eric would divide his attention between what he saw while browsing and the hotel, which he usually kept across the street to maximize his view of it. At most, seconds would pass between glances at the hotel. But that was all it took for Toomas to appear at the hotel door. Eric had just looked up during his inspection of the gold tea set to find Toomas taking the last few steps toward the front entrance.

Eric continued watching Toomas while he entered the hotel, then disappeared inside. He briefly considered going over to the hotel to maintain closer contact but decided to wait where he was and see if any of the other three people showed up. As he was considering these options, Sergei came into view. He also went directly to the hotel entrance and disappeared inside. If Maruch managed to follow one of them the whole time, she should be appearing at any moment, he reasoned.

Fifteen minutes passed without any sign of Maruch. The last ten minutes the shop owner had been staring at Eric as if he expected him to pick up something and bolt from the store at any moment. Eric decided he had overstayed his welcome, so, giving the owner a big smile and purposely displaying his empty hands, he left.

Out on the street, he started looking for a shop or building he had yet to enter. However, he soon realized he had visited every business establishment at least once and a few, two times. It was getting late in the afternoon, so he decided it might be appropriate to go to a restaurant. He turned toward the restaurant he and Maruch sat in this morning, deciding it was an acceptable alternative. Since he hadn't been there since early that morning, he reasoned, and the afternoon or evening crew was probably there now, it was unlikely he would be recognized.

Approaching the outside terrace, he was looking for an empty table when he spotted Maruch. She noticed him at the same instant but gave him no indication she did. He approached her and asked, "Maybe we can start fresh. I believe I might have been a bit harsh on you this morning, and I was wondering if you'd be willing to wipe the slate clean and start the process all over again?"

Maruch listened to him, but kept her eyes focused on the hotel across the street the whole time he was speaking. She continued staring at the hotel, waiting. Then choosing her words carefully, she spoke. "I am always amazed at how men want to wipe the slate clean, thinking all is easily forgotten and forgiven. I think they think it allows them the freedom from apologizing for rude or inappropriate behavior. I don't want you to mistakenly think that is the end result. You, and all men, must accept responsibility for your actions. Consequently, if you harbor any thoughts of joining me, you will make amends for this morning. I believe I have made myself clear enough on what it will take on your part to be invited."

Eric was taken back by Maruch's blunt response to his request. She was a very different woman. And he had to admit, right. "Your absolutely right," Eric began. "I apologize. First for my rudeness, which was inexcusable. And second, for not answering your questions this morning. You deserved better than that. Believe it or not, I happened to be passing by that night on the way back to my dorm room. Not being a regular student, I was always trying doors and going in if I found one open. I'm a curious sort, I guess." Eric sheepishly shrugged his shoulders as if to say it was an embarrassing habit he had and he was sorry.

"That night I tried the doors to the building you were in, and finding them unlocked, I went in. Once inside the building, I heard activity and decided to investigate. I wasn't sure what was going on, so I opened the door at the top of the lecture room and peeked inside. I happened to look in when you used that kick on one of the four men surrounding you. I stepped inside but stayed up by the door so I could observe without being noticed. The way you were handling yourself, I figured you wouldn't need any help, but I stuck around anyway. Once they had you on the floor, I decided it was time someone evened the odds a little bit. That's when I came to your rescue."

"Why didn't you stick around? You had to know I would want to thank you."

"Exactly. And you would probably want to know more about me than I was prepared to tell."

"Do you realize how many times--No, how much time in my life I've wasted wondering about who you were? And why you helped me? Or, why you were there in the first place? All because you didn't want to stay a little while longer."

They both stared at each other in silence. Both thinking this was not the way to make progress, but neither prepared to make concessions. It was obvious she was still angry with him, and his efforts to placate her anger were not very successful. Finally, Eric broke the silence, "I never gave it much thought--how much time you spent wondering about me, that is. It just never entered my mind that knowing who I was could be important to you"

"You forget. I was a vulnerable young woman, on my own, at a large University. Being accosted in a manner that was both demeaning and barbaric was terrifying."

"I didn't forget, I didn't know." Eric interrupted.

"I don't want to sound ungrateful, but you saved me from that." Maruch continued as if Eric hadn't said anything. "And, weird as it may sound to you, as time passed, I began to idolize you. When I saw you this morning, I was reduced to that scared, insecure, young woman that you saved. But you can rest assured--that feeling has passed. I appreciate what you did for me that night, but if I never get the answers to those questions, I no longer care. You may sit down if you'd like."

Eric was caught off guard by her sudden invitation. He'd come to the conclusion she wanted nothing to do with him, and his chances for changing her mind were extremely slim. However, he was intrigued by this woman's propensity to be unpredictable. Except for his wife, women had a tendency to become too predictable and too dependent on men: Traits Eric found to be a nuisance. Maruch seemed to offer a pleasant change from that. Eric made a mental note to arrange an accidental meeting with her once he had finished this assignment. She was worth getting to know better, and when he was through here, he'd have plenty of time.

"To demonstrate to you I'm not the ogre you have decided I am, I would like to take the time now to answer some of those questions. At least to the point my employer will allow me. I realize you said you weren't interested anymore, but I agree that you deserved those answers years ago. It was my mistake, and I would like to make amends, if you're willing."

Maruch continued staring over at the hotel entrance as if to punctuate her previous remark that she no longer cared about the answers or him. Eric felt the information he wanted from her was worth eating a little crow, so he provided them anyway. When he had finished, she knew why he had been there; to hear a series of lectures from one of the foremost speakers on life behind the iron curtain. The speaker was Gerhardt Shimman, a man that had lived there and escaped long before the wall came tumbling down.

Maruch found out who he was: Eric Dent. That he worked for the U. S. government and had happened onto her by pure chance at the time of the attack. He was only trying to be a Good Samaritan. There was nothing sinister about his actions, nor was there anything worth romanticizing about in the whole incident. He would have stayed around that night, but in his position, the news coverage was an unacceptable side effect of his actions. He figured, correctly, she would develop some reasonable explanation for the events, and no one would be the wiser. The only part of the equation that hadn't worked out very well, he added, was that the two of them were supposed to go their separate ways and forget the other one existed. Up until this morning, that is precisely what had happened, at least from Eric's point of view.

Eric stopped talking and looked toward the hotel doors while he let Maruch absorb this new information. Maruch sat motionless, staring at her empty coffee cup. She felt better about him after listening to his story, but she knew that feelings were often temporary. The two of them sat in silence, like two stone statues, staring: Her at the empty coffee cup, he at the hotel, neither one saying anything. It was time to reconsider each other, and words would only get in the way.

Maruch raised her head to look at the man across from her. She was still angry, but what he said was beginning to make sense to her. Her work with Ariel had taught her Eric's explanation was credible. There were many things that she did in her work, today, that would need the protection that only ignorance could provide. Often, she found it better not to explain her actions to someone, rationalizing her silence by saying it was for their own good that they didn't know more. It was possible and based on his actions this morning during his interrogation of her in the bathroom, very likely that his disappearance that night was justifiable.

Her eyes had drifted away from him and back to the empty coffee cup. Now, she looked directly at him, prepared to offer her acceptance of his story. But when she saw his profile, she stopped. She unexpectedly saw the same Eric she had envisioned so often in her dreams. She found herself thinking how good-looking he was for an American. Especially since he was an American that lacked any redeeming Jewish characteristics. Her memory of him that night at the University was a blur of action. It missed the details of a clear picture, but her imagination had filled that gap. When she recognized him this morning, he was seen through the eyes of someone admiring a hero, someone on a pedestal, not a flesh and blood person. For the first time since the incident, Maruch was able to actually see the man that interrupted her nightmare, not the hero. And she found she liked what she was seeing.

He was much softer than she remembered, or more accurately, the image her memory had created. She always thought he had the sharp features associated with rugged men, but in fact he didn't. It was more accurate to describe him as having a boyish appearance. Even sitting, it was apparent he wasn't as tall as she remembered either. She had presumed, probably because of the way he handled her attackers that he had to be six feet tall and close to two hundred pounds. But watching him sitting there drinking his coffee, it was obvious he wasn't an inch over five ten and couldn't weigh more than one hundred seventy-five pounds.

He was dressed very much like an American; blue jeans, light, long-sleeved shirt with the sleeves rolled up mid-way between his elbows and wrists and sneakers. His face was very clean-shaven, which made her remember what it looked like that morning. When his face had pressed up against hers in the bathroom, she distinctly remembered the stubble of an unshaven face. At the time, it added to the barbaric effect of his actions. His appearance now contradicted her memory of him from this morning. But it is a pleasant contradiction, she thought.

Her reassessment of him, partially because her anger at him had subsided with his explanations, and partially because for the first time she was seeing him without the added baggage of what he had done for her in the past, resulted in her positioning him as an equal. The myth of his heroism and his very real barbaric acts this morning was replaced with the realism of their equality.

"Maybe you are right, and we should start all over. I'll promise to forget the good and the bad of our previous two meetings."

"If you are sure, you can, I'd be happy to give it a try."

Extending her hand across the table, Maruch started, "My name's Maruch, it's a pleasure to make your acquaintance." She paused then added as an after thought, "and you're Eric?"

"Yes. Nice to meet you." There was another long, awkward pause before Eric added. "Now what do we do?"

"It appears we both have an unusual preoccupation with this hotel and it's guests. That might be an appropriate place to start. Maybe you could tell me why you followed me this morning, and whether or not you caught the guy with the rifle."

"I would imagine that you will then tell me why you followed the German, and what happened the rest of the day. Particularly after the sniper incident."

Maruch nodded her agreement, so Eric began. He was careful not to tell her too much but wanted to tell her enough to convince her he was being open. "First, you should know I wasn't following you. The German met a second man and that was the one I was following. In fact, if Sergei, the man I was really following, had not left the hotel in such a hurry, heading in the same direction as the two of you, we probably wouldn't be having this conversation."

Maruch sat expressionless as Eric continued. "I knew you were following the German and planned on talking to you about it when there was a need. When Sergei joined your little caravan, I decided it might be safer if I tagged along as well. After this mornings incident, I'm glad I did."

"Before you continue," Maruch cut in. "How do you know their names?"

"You know I work for the U. S. government, so the answer should be obvious. Getting back to my explanation: It was obvious to me that Sergei and the German were going to meet somewhere, and I wanted to know what was so important that they couldn't meet inside the hotel. It wasn't obvious to me why they felt they had to hide their meeting. I was hoping you could shed some light on that subject."

"I'm sorry to disappoint you, but after the sniper this morning, the three of them didn't get back together. Toomas didn't seem to have any purpose in mind after the meeting was disrupted. He spent the entire day traveling around Jerusalem with no apparent destination. It looked to me as if he was trying to kill time the rest of the day."

"You mentioned the three of them. Toomas and Sergei were two of them, but did you recognize the third one? From my vantage point, I wasn't able to see his face. Then the sniper occupied the rest of my time."

"He looked familiar, but I couldn't put a name to the face. I was only able to get a brief glimpse of his face when he reacted to the sniper. With the first shot, the three of them scattered. He went the opposite direction as Toomas, and I never saw him again." When she saw the disappointment on Eric's face, she added. "I'm sorry. Do you really think he's that important?"

"I don't know. The problem is one never knows what's important, until one can see the whole picture. At the moment, I'm still trying to see the whole picture. Could you make a guess?"

"Yes, but that's exactly what it would be, a guess," she added for emphasis. So far, they seemed to be exchanging information quite freely, but now Maruch was concerned about just how much information she could share with him. Ariel had warned her that a U. S. agent had been assigned, but he hadn't offered any advice as to how to deal with him if she were confronted. Although their group was not an official, sanctioned entity of the Israeli government, they were an often used, well-respected resource for the Israeli intelligence network. As a result, Ariel was kept well informed of the government's knowledge and intent on many covert activities. Israel had not been officially informed of any U. S. covert activities in this area, but their own network was well aware that the U. S. was active. Ariel simply passed that information along to Maruch when she was briefed about the assignment. Now she had the agents' names, and she could feed that back, through channels, to the government.

"You went after the sniper. Were you able to catch him, or her?"

"No. By the time I was able to get on the roof, he was climbing down into the alley a few buildings south. I went over to investigate, but whoever it was, had already disappeared into the alley crowd. I came back just in time to see you round the corner as you left. My timing was impeccable. I was able to lose everyone in the course of five minutes. After that, I came back here to wait for someone to show up. You and Toomas were the first ones to arrive."

"Why are you interested in these people?" Maruch asked.

"I was hoping you wouldn't ask. Simply put, we're a little concerned about Sheik Omani's rise to prominence. There isn't any rational explanation for it, and I'm supposed to monitor the situation and report back anything I can learn. We recently learned about the two men you saw this morning, Sergei, and Toomas. We aren't sure how they fit into the equation, but both of them are big money men, and we suspect they are, at the minimum, the source of the Sheik's financial backing. We are trying to determine if their involvement is restricted to financing, because we suspect there is much more to it than just that."

"You're just an observer, then. You're saying your main purpose is reconnaissance, so what do you do with the information once you have it?"

Eric wasn't sure whether she was convinced of his explanation at all, but he was hoping this ploy might buy a little time until he was able to get a better understanding of how she fit into the picture. "For the most part, you're exactly right. Where that explanation falls short is a recon assignment is restricted to reporting known facts: movements, contacts, conversations, and locations. That sort of thing. The reason I'm here is to draw conclusions based on that information and the intangibles that are often seen, but not understood well enough to be classified as a fact. In other words, I need to understand the motives for any activities I report and know how they affect behavior."

Eric allowed Maruch the chance to absorb what he had just told her. He felt his mixture of fabrication and truth might be just enough to keep her off balance. He continued to watch the hotel doors throughout their conversation because the frequency of people coming and going had increased dramatically as the evening approached. After what Eric reasoned to be sufficient time, he decided it was Maruch's turn to share information. He expected her to be less than completely honest with him as well but hoped to garner enough insight from what she said, to understand her motives. "If you're satisfied with what I have told you, maybe you could tell me why you're interested in the German," Eric began.

Maruch looked up from the coffee cup that she had been staring at for most of Eric's explanation. She wanted to watch the doors for any sign of Toomas, but she knew it would have looked foolish for both of them to be sitting there staring across the street. She had listened intently to Eric's explanation, knowing there were seeds of truth scattered throughout, but not exactly sure how to separate the facts from the fiction. Now it was her turn, and she couldn't just tell him she was following Toomas to find out why he hired an assassin to kill the Sheik. She didn't know if Eric was aware of that fact, and certainly didn't want to be responsible for informing him. It would have been best if she had been able to discuss Eric with Ariel before this conversation, but it was too late for that now.

Choosing her words carefully, she began. "The Israeli government is pleased with the direction discussions between the various factions have taken. However, they too, not unlike you Americans, are questioning the motives. Peace is certainly a worthwhile objective, but the destruction of our country under the guise of peace is a very real fear for most Jews. Consequently, we as a nation and a people, tend to be suspicious, almost paranoid. Particularly peace proposal generated by those that have no outward motive for continuing our existence."

"Our interest in Toomas is specifically related to that premise. As you said earlier, these two men, Sergei, and Toomas, have a relationship with Sheik Omani that we do not fully understand. It is my function to determine their motivation. Actually, Toomas' motivation. Until this morning Sergei was never included in any reports on Toomas," she lied.

"We need to determine if Toomas is in fact the controlling force behind the Sheik. We've made that assumption because there is no other explanation for his involvement, but it could be wrong. The Sheik, himself, could be the driving force, but we do not feel that is true either. The government has asked Ariel, us, to investigate and come back with a recommendation. By using us, the government can remain neutral until such time as they have enough information to make the proper decision."

"As you said to me---Then you, more or less, are on a recon mission too, since your primary purpose is information gathering."

"Yes. But our motivation is much different than yours. If we are wrong, Israel may cease to exist. For you, it is more out of a concern for your own economic welfare. The worst thing any American will experience is a reduction in their standard of living due to the increased cost of oil. Hardly comparable by my standards."

"I think you belittle our position, but I'll defer that discussion for another time. I have a proposition for you. It is difficult for either of us to fully observe every potentially vital activity on our own, but together, we can see twice as much. Would you be willing to share the load?"

"That's an interesting proposal. It would certainly enhance our knowledge base much quicker." Maruch was pleased with the idea. She had come to the same conclusion but held out little hope that she could convince Eric of its merit. "I would have to have authorization from Ariel before I could agree to that. Also, how would we know the other person was being completely honest and sharing all the information?"

"We wouldn't. But regardless, if the information were accurate, we would both realize a benefit. Agreed?"

"Alright. I'll raise the issue with Ariel and have an answer for you by morning. In the meantime, let's agree to do that for tonight."

Eric decided this would be the perfect time to leave, so he started to get up from the table. "Would you like to meet here, say ...six in the morning to have breakfast? We can review what happens tonight. At the same time, you can tell me what your Ariel decided."

"I'll be here waiting for you."

Eric planned on staying at the Star of David hotel tonight, but he didn't trust Maruch enough to share that with her. First, he had to retrieve his belongings. After leaving the restaurant, he went straight back to the two-bit hotel he stayed at last night. Before, he left the hotel this morning, he paid the hotel manager a little extra to store them 'til he returned. Now it was time to get them back.

- - - - -

He had the cab driver drop him off around the corner from the front of the Star of David hotel in case Maruch was still watching the front doors. Then, he headed to the back of the hotel looking for a rear entrance. He found what he was looking for and went in. Inside the hotel he located the public washroom, went in and locked the door. Removing the tweed jacket from his bag, the same one he wore in London, he began changing his clothes. He wanted to present the image of a nerdy tourist. To go with the jacket, he had purchased a pair of oversized black-rimmed glasses. Those combined with the tweed jacket and matching slacks, made him look like a throwback to the fifties. Wetting his hair down, he tried to comb it into a ducktail. Instead, it ended up looking like a haircut would be a good investment. As he gazed at his own image staring back at him from the mirror, he decided he failed to capture the look he was trying for, but the one he had achieved would certainly do.

Eric left the washroom and went to the front desk to check in. He'd made reservations under an alias, so he gave the name to the clerk. The clerk confirmed his reservation, then checked him into a room. The hotel had six floors and was assigned a room on the fifth floor. He refused the services of the bellman, and clumsily made his way to the elevator.

As he entered the elevator, another man got on with him. Eric averted his eyes from him in an effort to convey a sense of embarrassment. The other gentleman was dressed in typical flowing Arab robes with a portion brought up to cover his head like a hood. He stepped into the elevator and immediately positioned himself so Eric could not see his face. Eric watched as he pushed the button for the sixth floor. The elevator was no larger than a small closet and didn't have an inside door. One wall of the elevator sped past them on its way up to the fifth floor.

The two men rode silently together to the fifth floor, then Eric excused himself as he tried to squeeze past. As the man stepped back to let Eric through, his hood slid back slightly revealing just enough for Eric to recognize who it was. He was surprised and pleased to learn Sylvan, the Sheik's personal secretary, was the man he was sharing the elevator with. Eric made a mental note that the Sheik was staying on the sixth floor. This would save him a trip to the front desk to obtain this same information. The elevator stopped, so Eric stepped out, then turned to watch through the window as it moved off toward the sixth floor. Eric walked down the hall, found his room, and went inside.

As he sat on the edge of the bed, he thought about Sylvan in the Arab garb. He wasn't surprised to see Sylvan. But why was he dressed up? And, why did he have this nagging sense of Deja vu? It was possible that Sylvan was simply trying to blend into his surroundings, Eric thought. Soon, he rejected that idea since most people, even in Jerusalem, didn't dress that way. In fact, that style of dress often brought unwanted attention to oneself and Eric knew that was the last thing Sylvan would want. However, it did offer the wearer excellent protection from identification if the wearer kept the hood in place. At that thought, the light went on in Eric's head: Sylvan was the third man meeting with Sergei and Toomas this morning!

He reviewed the robes he had seen on the third man that morning. Every detail he could remember, matched what he just saw Sylvan wearing. Granted, there were very few differences available in this style of clothing, and identical robes were not unheard of. But the fact remained he couldn't remember **any** differences. Also, both men were approximately same size and build. Although Eric couldn't be absolutely certain, there were enough similarities to convince him Sylvan was the third man.

Eric considered what this meant. There were significant advantages for Toomas and Sergei if they had Sylvan on their side. Since their objective was to have the real Sheik assassinated, not Oman 2, it was important to be able to replace Oman 2 with the real Sheik at the appropriate time. Sylvan would be invaluable in that capacity. Due to Sergei's excellent work in producing Oman 2, just having Sylvan available to tell the difference between the two, would make him an important ally, Eric thought.

Eric was beginning to understand what these men were trying to accomplish. It was far from certain, and there were still some rather large gaps in his theory. With each increased bit of knowledge, he was becoming more convinced that not only must the assassination be circumvented, but also everyone involved in the conspiracy must be identified and stopped permanently. Otherwise, the cycle would begin anew. And the next time they would be even more difficult to stop.

- - - - -

Eric didn't care for the thought of having to stop them permanently. When he resigned from the Agency, he thought he was through with that part of his life. He wanted to put it as far behind him as he could, and that was his main purpose in finding and purchasing the land and cabin so far away from the East coast. So far away from the Agency. He'd been in most parts of the civilized world and decided the seclusion and serenity of west central Alberta would be the perfect antidote for his screwed-up life. And he had been right.

Up until Jim showed up that day, he managed to put everything pertaining to the Agency out of his mind and was actually starting to feel good about himself again. He lost a wife to this type of work and didn't think he'd ever be able to forgive the Agency for that. He began to enjoy living again, and he no longer hated himself. But the memory of the cabin in the woods of Canada was already beginning to fade. The positive feelings about himself were being replaced with the detached emotions necessary to allow him to do this type of work again. He knew it was necessary because this was the only way he could preserve his sanity. Slowly, he was allowing the old Eric back in control.

When he left the Agency, he just walked out. He didn't tell anyone where he was going, why he was leaving, or even that he was quitting. When it came time to give him his next assignment, no one knew where he was. Jim finally located him at his Uncle's cabin in northwest Pennsylvania. He managed to talk him into coming back long enough to go through the psychiatric debriefing analysis. That's when they, Jim, and Eric, learned that if he hadn't left when he did, there would have been serious repercussions. Eric had been on the verge of loosing it, and still was.

Because of his training and his amoral outlook on life, when he went, he wouldn't go alone. He had lost the only person that meant anything to him, the only person that could keep him in control, so everyone else was fair game. Particularly those he worked with at the Agency, but especially Jacque. And that was what Tom was hoping would happen. Jim, on the other hand, was the only person the psychiatrist could convince Eric's mental state was extremely delicate and volatile. Tom wanted to believe because of his obvious ulterior motives, but Jim really did believe. Fortunately that was enough. Jim was able to get Eric released the same day the psychiatrist's written report was issued. He personally handled the ton of paperwork normally associated with the resignation of a field agent.

When Eric walked out the door, three agents were assigned to monitor Eric's movements. Within twenty-four hours all three returned with the same explanation: Eric lost them. That was the last time Jim or anyone else saw Eric until a few days ago. He seemed to have disappeared from the face of the earth. Under the advice of the psychiatrist, Eric was allowed to remain hidden. Jim was advised that if Eric managed to get away without killing anyone, there was a slim possibility the healing process might begin. Eric might start his long journey back if left alone.

At the first hint there might be a conspiracy to assassinate the Sheik, the Agency tried to deal with the situation with their usual approach. Standard methods soon proved fruitless. Their intelligence network was not able to provide accurate, useful information. Frustrated, the Agency finally was forced to send in an agent. The man chosen was normally assigned to neutralizing an already identified threat. This was his first assignment requiring he establish the case before he executed the neutralization orders. If this failed, they would have to form an alliance with some third-party nation.

This new approach proved successful when they were finally able to establish the primary objective---assassinating Sheik Omani. When he was able to identify Jacque as the hired assassin, they fell into a false sense of security thinking they had the situation under control. Ultimately, it took the agent's death by Jacque's hand to convince them they were no more than spectators to the activity.

The death served noticed to the Agency that although their approach was good, replacing the agent with one capable of success would be extremely difficult. They had assigned their best covert agent who was an expert in neutralization. Unfortunately, he was not the most effective detective, and that cost him his life. Physically he could be replaced, but realistically his replacement would be signing his own death warrant. The dead agent was being groomed as Eric's replacement but was considered too inexperienced and unpolished to have reached that plateau. His funeral was confirmation of that fact. Now there was no one else even close to his level of expertise.

Tom and Jim argued at length about whether to search out Eric to request his assistance. The psychiatrist warned them that there was an excellent possibility Eric wouldn't allow them to get close enough to ask for his help. Jim wanted to leave Eric alone, but Tom insisted. Under the guise of National Security he argued, Eric must be offered the chance to help. He reasoned there was no one else the Agency could rely on to gather information and still have the capability to take out Jacque if or when the opportunity presented itself. No one had Eric's informal network. No one had Eric's natural ability to discover the little details that would allow the puzzle to be completed. And no one had the natural motivation to take out Jacque.

That was precisely what bothered Jim the most. He cared very much what happened to Eric and was concerned at the psychiatrist's warning, that what they were proposing for Eric might be too soon and he might blow up in everyone's face. But he was also concerned that Eric's mental state, and that same motivation, could cause him to lose sight of the main objective. If he does, he might go off in pursuit of Jacque at the expense of the assignment. The world could ill afford either result.

Jim wasn't convinced until the Agency lost their second agent, only one day later. This man was actually trained in the art of becoming a mole. He had infiltrated many organizations during his career at the Agency and was seldom called upon to perform anything more dangerous than sending a FAX. With the killing of the primary agent on this case, it was theorized that a non-threatening approach might yield the best results. They were wrong. Exactly twelve hours after he was given the assignment, he was found permanently sleeping in his hotel room. He hadn't even checked out of the hotel he was from his last assignment. Somehow, someone knew.

When Tom heard how quickly the second agent was identified and eliminated, he decided to locate Eric. The Agency enlisted the help of their entire network to find Eric Dent. Since Eric hadn't put any effort into hiding himself, but merely disappeared for the purpose of seclusion, he proved relatively easy to locate. Twenty-four hours after the initial request went out, a map pinpointing the location of Eric's cabin appeared on Tom's desk. He called Jim into his office to tell him they had found Eric.

"I'll be leaving this afternoon, and I'm putting you in charge during my absence," he began. "There's no need to tell you how important it is to stay abreast of the developments as they happen, and to keep me informed of anything that may affect my briefing of Eric after he accepts the assignment." Tom's back was turned toward Jim when he entered the room, so failing to see that Jim was not alone, he started talking immediately with the sound of the door closing. Tom's secretary had announced Jim's arrival over the intercom, but failed to inform Tom that the staff psychiatrist accompanied Jim. She mistakenly assumed that Tom had requested both of them to come to his office.

"I'll be checking in with you every two…" Tom stopped speaking as he turned around and saw Amos, the psychiatrist, standing next to Jim. "Hours. Every two hours. What are you doing here Amos? Unless I'm becoming senile, I don't remember asking you to tag along."

"Jim's been keeping me informed of your intent to get Eric back for 'just one' assignment. We thought it might be a good idea for the three of us to discuss what this may mean. You haven't forgotten what kind of shape Eric was in when he left, have you?"

"No. If that's all, we can consider the discussion over." Tom's expression said everything. He was both disgusted and put out with Amos' presence. There wasn't anything this pseudo-science could teach him about dealing with Eric, and he didn't like the idea of having to explain his actions to someone below him on the hierarchical scale.

"I can only assume you have some before unknown suicidal tendencies that I should be looking in to. I'm sure I've said this to you before, but if not, I'll say it to you now to be sure you heard it. Eric holds you personally responsible for what happened to his wife. You are only one step above pond scum, or Jacque, as far as he is concerned. I seriously doubt Eric would give you the chance to open your mouth before he blew you away."

"I can handle Eric," was all Tom was willing to say.

"I didn't say you couldn't. I'm merely informing you that in my professional opinion, you won't be given the chance to handle Eric. Eric would kill you long before you had the time to explain anything to him. I have notified your superior of my recommendation, and he concurred. You are removed from the responsibility of recruiting Eric for this assignment."

"Where do you…"

Amos interrupted him, "I have also recommended that Jim be the primary contact with Eric. Although I view the chance for success limited even for Jim, at least the chance of success, and survival, exists with him. Once again, your superior concurred and Jim has been given the assignment to contact Eric. If you have any questions or feel you might be able to change his mind, I called him just before we came over here. He is ready and available to listen to anything you have to say on your own behalf. The four of us can go right over. He's cleared his calendar until he hears from me. So, what's your position, Tom? Do we send Jim, or do we go talk to your superior? It's up to you."

Tom was always a very excitable person, and for that reason alone he had a permanent prescription for Tagamet. It was the only way to keep his inflamed stomach wall from exploding into a full-blown ulcer. He walked over to his desk, pulled open the top left drawer and pulled out a bottle of the stuff at the end of Amos' speech. Putting it to his mouth he took a swig, then put the lid back on the plastic bottle and returned it to his desk drawer. His frequent need for the medication had long ago caused him to give up the ritual of dispensing it in spoonfuls. A mouthful was just about the right dose to relieve his pain, assuming he took it before the pain actually started, otherwise time was the only medication that worked.

"Amos, you son-of-a-B. What the hell are you doing? I have no desire to hurt Eric or myself." Then changing his tactics in mid-stream, he calmly asked. "How 'bout if Jim and I go together?"

"No. It wouldn't work Tom and you know it. For whatever reason, Eric has decided you bear as much responsibility for his wife's death as Jacque, and that makes him irrational when he thinks of you. It is in everyone's best interest if you stay out of it."

Jim silently listened to the entire conversation between Amos and Tom. He thought he understood why Eric blamed Tom but wasn't entirely sure and continued to keep his thoughts to himself in the event he was wrong. He knew someday it would be necessary for him to intervene between Eric and Tom, or the hate might never stop. He saw what Amos couldn't see through the anger in Tom's reaction. He saw the hurt Tom felt every time he was reminded of how Eric regarded him. Jim knew it was not critical from a project perspective for Tom to brief Eric, but it was a need of Tom's. Tom knew, as with any assignment, this might be the last chance he would get to reconcile with Eric, but Amos made sure that would not happen.

Turning to Jim, Tom started explaining to him where Eric's cabin was. Taking a map of Alberta, he opened it and spread it out on his desk. Finding Red Deer on the map, he took his finger and traced a road that headed northwest out of the city until it came to an abrupt stop. "It's not shown on this map, but it will be on the one you're given. About here, there is an old loggers road. The gravel base is still there, but the road is succumbing to the local vegetation. I was told it's impossible to drive more than a couple miles on it before the brush gets too thick. I haven't been able to confirm that, so you're better off renting some horses right from the start and riding in. Eric's cabin is close to twenty-five miles back, so plan on a full day once you leave Red Deer. I've had Eddie prepare an executive overview that you can give to Eric to read. It'll help bring him up to speed on the whole situation."

Tom worked his way around the desk while giving the instructions for no apparent reason. Jim recognized it for another quirk Tom developed to help burn his excess nervous energy. Now he walked back around his desk to get Eddie's report out of the desk drawer and take another swig of Tagamet. "One more thing." He turned to look directly at Amos when he added; "I've taken the liberty of getting authorization for Steve Monroe to accompany you." Holding his hand up to keep them from interrupting, he continued.

"Steve not only accompanies you, but it is a requisite of Eric that Steve be allowed to stay with him as well. Eric is no longer a part of this Agency. His sudden and premature retirement has left a gaping hole in our network, and Steve has been designated the heir apparent. It will be Steve's task to gain as much knowledge and expertise during his time with Eric as he possibly can. We know Eric won't be back, and we also know we need him replaced. Steve will be his replacement. Eric will train him whether he likes it or not. Now, if either of **you** would like, you can verify what I just told you with my superior." As he said this, he picked up the phone and held it out for either of them to take.

"That won't be necessary right now, but I assure you I will verify what you're saying before Jim leaves." Abruptly Amos turned and left the room.

Tom looked at Jim, not sure what to expect from him. Jim was calmly evaluating this latest twist. He knew Tom didn't do anything without good reason, and although his explanation for requiring Eric to include Steve had merit, it wasn't his only motivation. Tom invariably held information back. It was second nature for him, and Jim was well aware of this fact. Maybe he had been in this line of work too long, or maybe he was just being smart. Jim knew he was only being given part of the picture and that was all he was going to get. If he needed or wanted more, he would have to get it elsewhere.

"Eric won't accept the deal without demanding something for himself. How much negotiating latitude are you willing to give me?"

"My only requirement is that Steve goes along. Everything else is negotiable. Just make sure you keep his demands within reason." As an after thought he added, "I've never known Eric to be unreasonable, and I don't expect he'll be unreasonable now. The difficult task will be getting him to help in the first place. When he left, he made it clear he was not the least bit interested in doing this type of work ever again. I don't imagine he's changed his mind."

Tom started folding up the map that he had laid out over his desk, a signal that the conversation was over. Tom never dismissed people; he just stopped talking to them. It was their responsibility to know when he was through with them. Jim waited until Tom finished folding the map as if he had something left to say. Then, without saying it, he left.

Jim wasn't the least bit convinced he would be able to talk Eric into helping them. He knew very well how adamant Eric was about distancing himself from the source of his troubles. He blamed the Agency much more than he blamed any one particular person, including Tom or Jacque, for taking Kathy away. Jim thought Tom might be aware of that, and it was why he was willing to risk confronting Eric.

Eric left the Agency because he was tired of doing things, he knew were wrong. Even though it had been his way of life for so long, he still had a conscience, and sometimes what he did still bothered him. With his wife killed as a consequence of his line of work, it gave him the perfect opening to leave. He was not extravagant by nature, and seldom had the extra time to spend his own money. Consequently, he accumulated a sizable bank account and portfolio. There was no incentive for him to keep working. He could do whatever he wanted for the rest of his life, and never have to face those moral conflicts again. Jim wasn't sure whether he should believe Amos, but this was the explanation he was given.

It was Amos' theory that Eric would consider Jim and Tom separate. He would associate Tom with the Agency, and the life he chose to leave. Jim, as his peer, would be considered an unwilling participant like himself. Regardless of whether Amos was right or wrong, the point that stuck with Jim was---Amos believed Eric had full control over his emotions. He was neither a threat to Jim, Tom, society in general or the Agency. Eric played the part of a hostile agent for the express purpose of quitting the Agency. Amos reasoned that Eric believed it was necessary for his superiors to think he had lost control and was dangerous. Eric believed it was imperative he be viewed as a direct threat to them, or they would never allow him to quit. With that in mind, he was a threat to Tom only to the extent that Eric thought it would be necessary to keep Tom convinced he was dangerous.

It seemed very complicated to Jim, because all he knew was there was no way Tom would get close enough to Eric to convince Eric of anything. Amos might be right, but he wouldn't want to be Tom if the theory was ever put to a test. That was why he was boarding the plane with Steve and heading for Calgary, and Tom wasn't.

- - - - -

Eric picked up the phone and started dialing Jim's number. It was time, he decided, to find out just where everyone stands. The phone rang just twice before he heard Jim's voice on the other end. Jim's voice sounded as if he had been up for some time. Eric couldn't hear any evidence of sleep left in the voice on the other end even though it was only five-thirty in the morning there.

"Hello, Jim here. Who's calling?"

"Hi Jim," was all Eric said.

"You're all right. That's good to find out. We got the report on John, and I was able to get a decision out of the top brass here. You may not like it, but it was the best they could do on such short notice. And after I thought about it, it made more sense than sending one of our own over there. It's their recommendation that you hook up with an agent from a fringe Israeli operation. This group is small, but very efficient. They don't belong to any official government office, but they're networked into the government through an older gentleman named Ariel."

"The whole group is made up of Israeli men and women, so they'll blend into the culture, the people, whatever, and we think that was the primary reason John ended up the way he did. I've some background information on them I need to tell you, but before I get started is there anything pressing you need to tell me?"

"No."

Jim waited a few seconds half expecting Eric to explain a little further, but he didn't. Jim provided Eric a ten-minute explanation of the Zealots. Who they were, why they existed, what their primary objective was and how they fit into the Israeli intelligence network, separate from the Mossad. He finished by giving Eric a brief history of the organization, and how they fit into the Sheik Omani puzzle.

"They consist of ten people, eight men and two women. All but Doshe and Ariel were originally U. S. citizens. Ariel and Doshe came from Germany, both having escaped from Nazi death camps. Those two men are the only ones in the group to have contact with the Israeli government. All assignments and recruitment take place through these two men. The Israeli government does not officially recognize them, but they supply equipment and financial support to the group. They also rely heavily on them for many of their covert needs."

"They were brought into this situation by the Sheik. About six months ago Sheik Omani contacted Ariel and began discussions about what it would take to carve out a peaceful existence between the two groups, the Zealots and Jihad Nadu's. Ariel listened, then told the Sheik he would get back to him. After the Sheik left, he contacted the government and ended up discussing the situation with the Prime Minister directly. Unknown to us, they devised a plan to trap the Sheik, or test his motivation. At this point, they're still not sure exactly what he's up to, but they did make the connection between the Sheik and Toomas. They have assigned an agent to track the German's every move, and that's the person we want to use as Steve and John's replacement."

"I think I've already met the agent tracking Toomas," Eric cut in. "She's a woman named Maruch."

"That's right. Please don't tell me you've already alienated her as well. Ariel has assured us she is literally the best, most ruthless agent he has. He alluded to something that happened in her past, then warned me to make sure you are careful around her until he's had the chance to brief her about you. Otherwise, you would probably need to be replaced. I didn't bother to explain to him it would more likely be the other way around, because he was quite adamant about you being in danger."

"You can relax. One of the reasons I called you was to advise you I had formed an alliance with her. I wanted you to be aware of it." Eric told Jim this simply to make him feel good, because until Jim brought up her name, he had no intention of telling Jim anything about his arrangement with Maruch. He still wasn't sure how Tom's relationship with Toomas fit into the picture, but until he did, everyone at the Agency was suspect.

"I'm glad to hear you were able to make friends with her. Although I must admit it comes as a surprise, and a welcome one at that. This assignment could use good news much more frequently. What kind of alliance did the two of you form?"

"At this point it's strictly informational. We share notes. She keeps me informed of Toomas' activities, and I keep her informed about

Sergei's movements. We both report back on anything else that we may consider important. Actually, it should prove to be quite helpful, assuming she can be trusted. It frees me to devote more time to locating Jacque. Since Toomas is in charge, what he does is important, and I need to know about it. This way Maruch removes that burden and I'm able to focus on other areas."

"Was she able to give you anything so far?"

"Not really. We mainly discussed something in her past that got her started in the business. Then a bunch of political mumbo-jumbos about why they, Israel, have more to lose if the Sheik is not on the up and up."

"Most Israelis think that way. Getting back to Maruch, do you think she's an adequate replacement, or do you want me to get someone else over there to help?"

"I thought you said the top brass made this decision."

"I did, but they're not the ones that have to rely on this person just to stay alive. You are. When you took this job, I told you I would look out for your interests. Say the word, and I'll go back to them and demand we send you help."

"No, Jim. It's all right. They're probably right that John's death was made easier by his nationality. It made him more obvious, especially staying in that local tourist trap I sent him to. I should have known better then to send him there. Steve, on the other hand, was another matter. He knew what he was doing, he was just beat by someone a little faster, a little better." Eric's voiced trailed off, a hint of caring evident in the tone.

"Do you know which one got him?"

"No, but Jacque's been very quiet so far, so I'm inclined to think it was Manuel. I can't be certain, but I think they were given different instructions."

"Care to venture a guess on those kinds of differences?"

"Nothing concrete, but I have a hunch. Manuel was hired after Jacque, but as far as we can tell, he's the person responsible for at least one attempt on the Sheik's life, namely bombing that commercial flight. Jacque's thorough and he's had enough time that I would have expected something from him by now, but nothing has his mark on it. Add to that, when Steve returned from Portugal after doing some background work on Manuel, it's a good possibility that Manuel followed him to Jerusalem. I suspect he was the one to kill Steve on the roof."

"You don't know that."

"No... I don't know that. But it's more likely it was Manuel, than Jacque. Also, up until I arrived in Jerusalem, my own sources hadn't had much luck locating Jacque. My first confirmed report has put Jacque in another city at the time. Any evidence I have is pointing to Manuel, nothing to Jacque. I don't believe they've been given the same criteria for the assassination, otherwise Jacque would have made a move by now." Eric added.

"It doesn't make sense to hire two assassins to kill the same man, then give them a different set of instructions."

"You wouldn't think so. But then I haven't been able to make much sense out of anything they've done so far. Off the subject a little bit, have you noticed unaccounted or lost periods of time in Tom's workday?"

"No. Why do you ask?"

"Nothing really. It just goes back to what you told me when I agreed to take this assignment. I wasn't able to figure out Tom's position with Steve, and I was just wondering if you knew anymore now, than you did then."

"Sorry."

"Alright. If you have nothing to add, I'll talk to you later." Eric hung up before Jim could respond. For some reason he was pleased to find out Maruch would be helping him. He felt secure in her ability to handle the situation, and he liked her motivation. He found people with strong emotional ties to their work tended to be more efficient, more dedicated, more reliable. And in the rare case, they were able to detach themselves from their emotion to become unusually effective. Maruch appeared to be this type of person. She had those strong emotional ties, yet she managed to assimilate her emotions into a rational approach to her work. She should prove to be very useful, Eric mused. He continued sitting on the edge of the bed considering how things had progressed since he first took this assignment.

His motivation was much like Maruch's, based entirely on an emotional reaction. But like Maruch, he was finding his irrational need to repay Jacque was being replaced with a passionate desire to resolve this sensitive situation. He was no longer obsessed with revenge because he was beginning to appreciate the serious nature of this assignment. His personal vendetta was being subjugated to a more important objective. And for the first time, he was able to function without thinking about his wife constantly.

That was probably the most debilitating result of his wife's death. He spent hours every day thinking about her, mourning her loss, blaming himself for her death. Then losing himself in her memory. Since her death, she controlled his life more than she ever did or could have when alive. He knew that, and now he was actually thankful that Jim had shown up that day. This was what he needed. He needed to immerse himself in his work again. He needed to get on with his life, something he hadn't done since he left for Canada after her funeral. He realized that Canada had been a mistake. It hadn't given him the peace he had expected, but rather kept the memory of her death fresh. Now, maybe he could start to move on, he thought.

Eric looked away from the phone. He'd been staring at it ever since he set it down. As he buried his wife for the last time, his mind wondered to thoughts of Maruch. He was curious whether Maruch had spoken to Ariel yet. He would have liked to talk to her tonight since their respective employers had modified their agreement. But the plan was set, so he would wait until they met at the restaurant in the morning as it dictated.

Looking at his watch, Eric decided it was still early enough to get a little sightseeing done. He was still puzzled why Sylvan would be meeting with Toomas and Sergei and wanted to see if he could get a better understanding why. Previously, all communication between the consortium and the Sheik was done directly with the Sheik. There didn't appear to be any reason for that to change, but it had.

Still dressed in the tweed jacket, Eric retrieved the glasses from the nightstand and left his room. He walked over to the elevator, pressed the up button, and waited for the elevator to arrive. He watched through the little window on the door as the cables first went up pulling a full car past his floor, then stopped for a short while. It changed direction and passing his floor again, continued on. This time there was only one man in the car. On a hunch, Eric decided to see who the occupant was and took off running.

Eric quickly reached the door in an alcove midway down the narrow hall. Opening the door, he started down the steps. Grabbing the handrails on both sides, he was able navigate each flight in two giant steps and was at the lobby floor in no time. He opened the door to the lobby just in time to see the flowing robes of the elevator occupant as he disappeared through the front entrance. Eric made a beeline to the front doors and stepped out onto the sidewalk in pursuit of the man.

On the sidewalk Eric looked right, then left, but didn't see him. Then glancing across the street, he repeated the motion. The man had crossed the street and was already one and a half blocks away. Eric sidestepped the sparse traffic as he hurried across the street. Once he reached the sidewalk, he started running again. While running he decided he would confront Sylvan at the first opportunity. That opportunity came at the next alley.

The man turned into a narrow opening between two buildings and Eric, now only a few feet behind him, followed him around the corner. As Eric turned into the narrow opening, he felt someone step out of the darkness to block his exit just as the man he was following turned around to face him, holding a knife in his right hand. Eric glanced back at the man blocking his exit and saw he too had a knife poised to strike.

The man in the robes spoke first, "It is a nice night for killing infidels, don't you think?" The man doing the speaking was barely visible in the darkness, but a sliver of light coming from a nearby window lighted his mouth. His illuminated mouth displayed the full effects of a difficult life. His half-rotted teeth were separated only by the gaps created by teeth that had already fallen out. Eric didn't answer, he was too busy concentrating on how was going to get out of this and hoped his silence would buy him some time.

"You don't look as dangerous as Jacque claims you are, but then maybe he never had you cornered before. I think his Christian beliefs cloud his view of how weak you really are." As the man finished his last sentence he lunged toward Eric. Looking into the face of his victim, he realized his knife had penetrated his companion's stomach. Eric had sidestepped his lunge and taking his attackers shoulders as he leaned into the spot Eric had been in, pushed him forward into his partner. His companion let out a soft grunt, and then slid off the knife unto the pavement, dead.

As the man stared at his companion in disbelief, Eric wrapped a wire around his neck. Then twisting him toward the building slammed him into the wall. The bloody knife dropped from his hand. "I want you to listen closely and repeat after me exactly as I say. If you make a mistake, the wire tightens. I'm not sure how many mistakes it will take before your dead, but I would concentrate on not making any if I were you. Do you understand?"

The man tried to speak, but the wire was already too tight, so he just nodded his head causing the wire to tighten even further around his neck. Eric loosened the wire a little, then began. "I have not forgotten my debt." Eric paused to give the man his chance to repeat the message. Eric noticed he had to loosen the wire a little more before the man could actually say the words; even then they sounded more like grunts than words.

As soon as he finished, Eric started again, "Regardless of what happens to the Sheik, I will not stop until you are repaid." Then pausing again, he gave his newfound messenger the chance to repeat what he had just said. He finished with, "Time does not heal all wounds." The man repeated the words, and as soon as he finished, Eric brought his free hand up and chopped him at the base of the neck. The man's knees buckled, and Eric allowed him to drop to the ground, the wire left dangling loosely around his neck as a reminder.

Eric pulled the man's limp body back into the space between the two buildings so no one passing by could see him. Then he retrieved the dead body and set him next to his companion. He searched both men for any possible clues but came up empty. As he walked away from the two men, he glanced back at them to review his handiwork. If it weren't for the blood down the front of the one man's robes, Eric thought, they would look like a couple of winos passed out from a night of hard drinking. Eric left the alley massaging his arm. His knife wound was healing slowly, and the recent activity simply aggravated it.

11

Eric returned to the hotel after the incident with Jacque's two friends and decided to get some needed sleep. With the loss of Steve and John on successive days, he hadn't had but a few hours of sleep in the last forty-eight hours. Before he actually dozed off, Eric considered what tonight's activities meant in the broader spectrum of both the consortium's plans and how well he understood those plans.

Prior to tonight's events, he actually started to question whether or not Jacque was really involved or if he was just being used by the consortium as a smoke screen for Manuel. Tonight's incident also served to relieve the uncertainty that was building inside him about whether the Agency had simply used Jacque's name to get him to take this assignment. With Jacque finally revealing himself, Eric was reassured, in a perverted sense, that Jacque was indeed involved.

This confirmed that the consortium did actually hire him, and they weren't putting on a complicated charade to protect Manuel. To some it might seem odd that Eric would even consider that possibility, but the intelligence community was an odd lot in that respect. They would often expend greater energy presenting a false image then they would accomplishing their original objective. And as far as the Agency was concerned, Eric knew they, meaning Tom, would use whatever motivation he could to entice Eric to help them.

It was comforting to know that he had finally generated enough concern in Jacque for him to react. This helped confirm that he was on the right track with the two-assassin scenario; otherwise, Jacque wouldn't have wasted his effort sending him the message tonight. Lately, it seemed most of his efforts were directed toward Manuel, but then Manuel was the only player actually doing anything, so he really had no choice. Eric's own network was watching Jacque, and he remained hidden behind the scenes quite well, making no overt moves toward the Sheik or Eric. Now that he finally did something, Eric could proceed confidently, pursuing his plans based on the two-assassin theory that was now validated.

Eric dozed off into a fitful sleep. His body was physically beat, but his mind wouldn't let him rest peacefully. He was preoccupied with thoughts about how to stop both Manuel and Jacque before it was too late. He sensed time was evaporating quickly, maybe too quickly. Maruch could provide him intelligence on events, but Eric didn't really consider her as a replacement for Steve or John when it came to taking out Manuel. He just couldn't believe that she was capable of neutralizing anyone. In his opinion, it would be his responsibility to take both men out. How? He didn't know. Manuel was actively trying to kill the Sheik already, and Jacque could start anytime now that the press conference had been held. With tonight's encounter, it was clear Jacque was sending him the message that it was time.

These thoughts and many others were not letting him fall into a deep sleep. As he opened his eyes and started to roll over again looking for that ever-elusive comfortable position that would allow him to truly sleep, he saw the glint of a knife as it reached the peak of its arc before starting down toward his chest. Eric's subconscious took over and he twisted, sliding out of his bed at the same instant the knife penetrated the thin mattress he had been lying on.

As fast as he hit the floor, he was back on his feet and diving over the bed at his attacker. His attacker, every bit as quick as Eric, had already started for the door. But he was unable to elude Eric, because Eric's dive was timed and angled to cut off the man's exit perfectly. Both men went crashing into the wall from the force of Eric's flying body, then in unison, slid to the floor.

Eric's right hand was caught between the wall and his attacker's body when it hit, causing a searing pain to slice through his arm. His arm immediately went limp, leaving Eric vulnerable to his attacker. The intruder, unaware of Eric's injury, scrambled to his feet and headed for the door. Eric pretended to pursue but allowed the man an easy exit not wanting to give away how badly he was hurt. As the door opened and light from the hall fell on the man's face, Eric saw that it was Jacque. He started to say something, then stopped. He knew there was nothing he could say to stop him, then watched as Jacque disappeared through the door. A soft, "damn," was all he could muster as Jacque slipped away.

Eric walked over to the nightstand next to the bed and turned on the light. He sat on the edge of the bed and began inspecting his hand to determine the extent of his injury. Methodically, he felt each bone and joint, then concluded it he just received a bad bruise. No bones were broken or dislocated, so he wouldn't require any medical attention. Getting up from his seat on the bed, he went over to the door to inspect it. He knew the only way into the hotel room was through the door because the outside wall wouldn't accommodate scaling it. Any foot or handholds were spaced too far apart to be of value for climbing.

After he inspected the door and found no evidence of a forced entry, he went back to the window. It was closed, not tightly and not locked. Opening the window, he stuck his head outside and looked down. He was right, there was no way a person could scale the outside wall from the ground up. Turning his head, he looked up to the roof. The window ledge was probably no more than fourteen feet from the roof. Eric decided to investigate.

On the roof, he started looking for something to secure a rope to that would allow a man to repel down the side of the building. There was only one item that would have worked, the chimney. Before he even got to the chimney, he could see the rope still attached. He untied it and started coiling it up as he followed it to the edge of the roof. At the edge of the roof was the excess. It was obvious it was thrown back up once Jacque reached the ledge of Eric's room. Looking down over the edge, Eric confirmed his window was below. Satisfied that he knew how Jacque managed to get so close to him without being discovered, Eric returned to his room.

He didn't like the idea that he'd come so close to the same fate as Steve and John. He was supposed to be experienced, but he made a rookie mistake by not confirming the window was locked. The lock wouldn't have stopped Jacque, but it would have served as an early warning device. He considered himself very fortunate to be alive, because Jacque does not fail very often. Unlike Manuel, Jacque's plan tries to account for all reasonable contingencies. He understands quality is more important than quantity. Whereas Manuel relies on quantity and isn't the least bit concerned about the quality of the job. That's why so many innocent bystanders are often maimed and/or killed in Manuel's work.

Eric secured his hotel room even though he knew Jacque wouldn't be back tonight. At the moment, it was as safe as it would get.

- - - - -

Eric saw Maruch shortly after he stepped onto the sidewalk into the bright sunlight. She was sitting alone at the same table they had sat at late yesterday. Eric watched as she got up to get something from another table. She was dressed in a decidedly western manner, light blouse, designer jeans and sneakers. She strode across the floor without effort, mesmerizing Eric with each step. She was truly beautiful, but until now, Eric had been unaware she was anything more than just another woman. She didn't have that untouchable, unreachable beauty that people tend to idolize. She was blessed with a very natural beauty that drew people to her, made them want to be around her.

That was precisely what Eric was feeling at the moment. Normally, he would have been irritated and would fight bitterly against assigning a woman to fieldwork. Especially on any assignment he was given. But when Jim informed him of the agreement with this fringe group last night, and he found out it included working closely with Maruch, he accepted it amazingly well. Eric wondered what Jim thought when he didn't argue with him about Maruch. But Jim, in his typical manner didn't say anything so neither did Eric.

Maruch was back at the table. Coming out of his trance, Eric realized she was waving to him. Why was she waving at him? Then he realized he probably looked like a fool standing in front of the hotel staring off into space. Somewhat sheepishly he looked around, but it was obvious no one was aware of him at all. Stepping off the curb he crossed the street making his way over to Maruch. When he got to the table, he decided to keep the conversation all business to cover up his obvious embarrassment.

"I assume you had a chance to talk with your superior. I believe you said his name is Ariel." Then taking a chair opposite her, he sat down.

"You act is if you didn't know we were given instructions to work together. Is that because you might not like the idea of working with a woman?" Maruch didn't appreciate Eric's pretense that he hadn't been informed she would be helping him, unofficially. She knew, and he knew, and there was no reason to pretend otherwise. She hoped he wouldn't be a typical American male, resenting her because of her sex.

Eric looked across the table at her and tried to decide how he should respond. This was the third time they were starting over, but it seemed each start was a repeat of their first. He didn't mean to offend her, but it was obvious he had again. His comment was just meant as an opening line to an inevitable conversation. Why, he thought, must every woman assign a hidden meaning to everything that is said? Choosing his words carefully, or so he thought, Eric replied. "We both know that our respective affiliations have come to a mutual understanding that it would be in everyone's best interest if you and I joined forces. There was no intended or implied dislike for working with women."

"That's good. I wish I could reciprocate, but I'm inclined to think men are a bit too moody for me. However, if Ariel says I'm supposed to help you, I will."

"Gee, I'm flattered." She may be good looking, but with an attitude like that I shouldn't have any problem keeping my mind on the job, he thought. "I don't mean to change the subject, but did Toomas do anything of interest last night?"

"No. Did Sergei or anyone else?"

"Something you might be interested in did happen, actually two things. Remember the third man in the meeting with Toomas and Sergei yesterday. I think I know who he was. I can't confirm it, but there is no other explanation. I was in that hotel last night," Eric pointed to the Star of David hotel, "and saw Sheik Omani's personal secretary, Sylvan, come in. He was dressed in robes similar to what the third man was wearing. Since he's a Frenchman, it made me question why? If I were a betting man, I'd bet he was the one with Toomas and Sergei."

Keeping the tone of the conversation businesslike, Maruch asked. "Do you have any theories as to why Sylvan would be meeting secretly with them?"

"Not good ones. Unfortunately, it may mean nothing; then again it may mean everything. Since these men are their primary source of income, it would be appropriate for them to meet periodically. For all we know, their meeting may have nothing to do with the plot to assassinate the Sheik. However, having an inside man would certainly be an advantage if one were trying to ensure the right person was killed."

"You make a good point. Sylvan may be a part of the conspiracy, and we should incorporate that into any model we generate."

"Precisely, we'll have to factor that possibility into our thinking. The second thing you need to be aware of, and I hesitate to talk about it here, but you need to know." Before he continued speaking, Eric leaned forward over his coffee. He put his elbows on the table, clasped his hands together and cradled his chin on the back of his hands. Following Eric's lead, Maruch leaned forward as well. They appeared to be two lovers enchanted with each other's presence. The image of two people in love that they were creating, served as an excellent disguise to the serious nature of Eric's information. The distance between the two of them was reduced to a few inches when Eric started speaking again.

"You're aware of Manuel." Eric stated this as a fact. Maruch nodded her head yes. "To date, he's the only one we can actually prove, within reason, has made an attempt on the Sheik's life. I'm convinced he was responsible for the downed Air France flight over Switzerland. I don't have any evidence, but I think he was responsible for Steve's death as well. Steve had just arrived from Lisbon after doing some research on Manuel. My guess is that he managed to pick up Manuel's trail and possibly tried to stop him during the Sheik's news conference."

"As far as John is concerned, it could be the handiwork of either man. The MO was not conclusive. The point I'm trying to make is, for the most part, Jacque has been eerily quiet up 'til now. But recently, his activity may have picked up."

"What do you mean, up 'til now?" Maruch interrupted.

"Last night I left the hotel, following Sylvan, or so I thought. The person ended up being a messenger from Jacque. He and his buddy tried to convince me to leave well enough alone. Instead, I sent one of them back to Jacque with a reply. Later last night, Jacque paid me a visit trying to punctuate his original message. It didn't work, because as you can see, I'm still here. That was the first overt action Jacque has taken. By itself it may not seem like much, but..."

Maruch interrupted his explanation again, "You're right it does not seem like much. There's no rule saying Jacque and Manuel must alternate attempts on the Sheik's life, or yours for that matter."

"Very good, Sherlock." Maruch had sounded a bit too condescending, so Eric tried to put as much sarcasm in his voice as he could. "You're right. No one has a monopoly on the assassination, but I think Manuel might be a decoy just like the second Sheik. And a little less controlled. Jacque was given instructions to wait until after yesterday's news conference as part of the deal. Manuel, on the other hand, was not given those same instructions. As far he knew, he was supposed to start when ready, and he did. There's no reasonable explanation for giving them each a different set of instructions, unless they're being used differently."

"What if they were? I'm not sure I see what difference it makes. They were both hired to do the same job, one simply started a little earlier than the other. I think you're making more out of this than there really is. After yesterday's news conference, the Sheik's death would be perceived as a breach of trust by all concerned. They have already achieved what they wanted, a stable political environment in the Middle East that hinges on the well being of the Sheik. They're in control. If the Sheik lives, and they control him as some have theorized, they control the Middle East. If he dies, chaos. Or more accurately, a Jihad against Israel. Because, as we both know, Israel will be held responsible by the Arab world."

"I think your tunnel vision is too restrictive. If what you say were true, there would be no need for a decoy. They could hire as many assassins as necessary to get the job done or do it themselves. They certainly wouldn't need such an involved plan if their only objective was getting Israel into a war. Keep in mind the consortium is made up of oilmen. Everything they do is most likely based primarily on greed or power, not hatred. Any hatred they have for the Jewish race is secondary."

"If you were Jewish, you would not be so quick to dismiss hatred as the prime motivation. Throughout history people would hide behind their greed as an excuse to kill Jews. It's always been easy for them to look at a successful Jew or even a poor Jew and say, 'It is because of him or them that I am poor.' They need a scapegoat for their own failures, and the Jewish people have always been easy targets and forced to fill that role because they were different. No, don't tell me it's based on greed or power, because those are just excuses to kill more Jews."

Maruch's viewpoint was totally foreign to Eric. Power and greed, mostly power, were the driving force behind the people that Eric usually dealt with. The thought that hatred could be a focal point of one's existence seemed hard to comprehend at first. But as he considered what she was proposing, he decided she could be right. History has taught us quite clearly there exists a natural hate in the world for the Jewish people. Since long before Christ they were being persecuted, captured, taken prisoner, made to be slaves, killed at will, almost any atrocity attributed to man had at some point in history been directed toward them.

Eric was beginning to realize for the first time in his life what all the fuss was about concerning the Middle East. It wasn't just about oil. There was a natural enmity of Arab for Jew, and the rest of the world condoned it. Now it made sense why Israel was always so demanding in negotiations, insisting on their sovereignty. Or, why they often struck first at war, seeming to be the aggressor. In reality they were merely defending themselves against a hostile enemy that would only be satisfied with their annihilation. They were paranoid, but rightfully so. Eric suspected he would be wise to start being more accepting and not so cavalier about Maruch's opinion. Her insight into the situation may yield unexpected benefits, and her perspective could prove to be very useful.

The two remained silent while they pondered what the other had said. Maruch was convinced she hadn't gotten through to Eric the difficult position this assassination could put the state of Israel in. She had come to expect little understanding from Gentiles, and there was no reason to think Eric would be any different. They've experienced life as a Jew, so they couldn't possibly appreciate its difficulty. Her only hope was that he wouldn't dismiss her arguments without at least considering them.

"I suppose…from your point of view," Eric was speaking very slowly. He chose his words carefully, trying not to offend her. "There might be reason to believe their motive is not so trite as greed or power. I really had not considered your option, but I have to agree with you that it is possible. Recognizing that my tendencies would be to ignore that, I'll rely on your opinion in that area."

Maruch was satisfied, although skeptical. Maybe he would include the elimination of Israel as a viable motive, but more likely, he's only giving lip service to her concerns. Odds are that when it comes time to walk the walk, he won't be there.

- - - - -

Sylvan managed to slip out of the hotel before Maruch established her observation point at the restaurant. The meeting with Toomas and Sergei had been disrupted by the sniper the day before, and they hadn't been able to get back together since. He had no idea who the sniper was, but the incident concerned him because it implied knowledge. The content of that knowledge could be catastrophic.

Neither Toomas nor Sergei stayed at the hotel that night, having checked out in preparation for the next consortium meeting. Sylvan received a phone call from Toomas early that morning requesting they reschedule the meeting and giving him directions to his new hotel. They were to meet in his hotel room, although the hotel was more like a boarding house. It was frequented mainly by Moslems that traveled a long distance to worship at the Mosque in Jerusalem and were not recipients of the oil-enriched wealth of their homelands. The accommodations were sparsely furnished and Spartan in appearance, but clean.

Sylvan arrived before Sergei, and the two men waited in silence for Sergei to get there. When Sergei finally arrived, he was fifteen minutes late and Toomas was visibly irritated with the Russian.

"You Bolsheviks always think the world waits for you. Some day you might be surprised to find out that isn't true." Without waiting for Sergei to respond, he turned to Sylvan and said, "How did the Sheik's replacement do? Is there anything that needs to be fine tuned, or modified? Mannerisms, twitches, anything at all that you can think of that you feel might give him away?"

Sylvan was prepared for this question. His answer was precisely what the three of them had worked so hard for, and he was pleased to be the one delivering it. "None whatsoever. This man has exceeded all my expectations. At times he seems more like the Sheik than the Sheik himself. He walks, talks, thinks, acts, in everything he does, he epitomizes Sheik Omani. I honestly could not detect anything that would give him away."

"Do you have a recommendation regarding when to put the wheels in motion? In other words, are we prepared to inform Jacque that he has the freedom to kill at his earliest convenience?"

"I would vote yes. I can't see any reason to delay any longer."

"Based on your report, I would have to agree." Toomas turned to Sergei and waited for him to state his opinion.

Sergei chose to sit at the small desk in the room, quietly sulking over Toomas' reprimand. While his head was down, he heard the silence fill the room until it became too much to ignore. Feeling their eyes burning into him, he looked up. Both men were staring at him, waiting for him to state his opinion.

"That is what we have worked for, so I say let's do it."

"Sylvan, it will be your responsibility to make sure the real Sheik continues to meet his public obligations. He expects not to have to expose himself to the public anymore, so you'll have to provide him with a good reason."

"I was planning on telling him the decoy needs to make some subtle adjustments in his delivery, and he needs a few more days to practice. I expect he'll accept that fairly easy, because no one likes the way they look when someone else portrays them. I suspect his ego will have the same problems."

"Sergei. Would you like to make contact with Jacque, and give him the go ahead to take out the Sheik?"

Sergei nodded his head yes. "Excellent." Changing topics, Toomas commented to no one in particular, "I haven't been able to track down yesterday's sniper, but I've been promised his name by tomorrow morning. However, I was able to get a fix on the man that stopped him. That was Eric Dent. He's finally surfaced, and I don't like where he chose to do it. First off, he managed to see the three of us together."

Turning to look at Sylvan he added. "Although with your disguise, I doubt he was able to recognize you. I would suspect he's still in a quandary about who the third person was. Still, we don't need to make it easy. I don't want the three of us to meet again until after the Sheik is dead."

Toomas looked at each man separately for a response, but none was forthcoming. "If we have to speak to each other, we should do it by phone. We can maintain security much easier on a phone, and there is less risk that someone will become suspicious if we're not seen together. In order for this to work, it's important that we check our messages regularly. Don't let more than four hours go by between checks. If one of us needs to talk to another, they call and leave an innocuous message with a time and phone number. Modify the phone number by adding three to each digit, individually. Don't carry anything over. In other words, a seven becomes a zero, a nine a two and a three a six."

Toomas paused to give either one of them the chance to speak, but neither chose to do so at this time. Toomas continued. "The person called returns the call from another phone, preferably a public phone, but minimally one that offers some privacy. Are there any questions?"

"Yes." Sergei was still upset about the way Toomas treated him when he came in, and it showed in his voice. "You were quick to criticize me this morning but aren't you the least bit interested in why I was late. Or has your superior, Aryan mind already figured that out?"

Toomas was glad to hear the Russian resort to sarcasm. It showed he really wasn't that angry. He was simply irritated that he hadn't been asked why he was late because he believed had something important to tell them. This was more like the Sergei he had come to know, not the man that sulked at being reprimanded. "I'm sorry Sergei. Yes, we want to know why you were late. I'm surprised though. Since when do you need a special invitation to tell us something? Normally, you're brimming with advice and counsel, giving it freely whether we want it or not. But today we must ask. So, consider yourself asked."

Center stage. This is what Sergei was always after. As much as he had come to enjoy Toomas, he still resented, just a little, the fact that Toomas was always in charge. The best way for Sergei to relieve that resentment was to surprise people, especially Toomas. In that way, he could rationalize accepting his number two position in the hierarchy by telling himself he was in control.

"As you know, both men that were assigned to help Eric were killed by Manuel."

"No, we didn't know that." Sylvan interrupted. "We knew Steve had been killed, but we hadn't even heard who is replacement was."

"That's alright. His replacement wasn't around very long anyway. In fact, the same night he arrived from Tel Aviv, he was killed. But that's not what I wanted to tell you. Things have gotten a little complicated. Eric has been assigned an Israeli agent that does not report directly to the government. And this is where it gets sticky. She," Sergei paused, enjoying the reactions of both Toomas and Sylvan at the realization the he, was a she.

"She is a member of the Zealots."

"Do they know what were trying to do?" Toomas interrupted. He was visibly shaken by the news. Normally Sergei's surprises aren't bombshells, but this one could be devastating. Everything they worked for hinged on being able to pull this off without the slightest hitch. Having used the Zealots to hire Manuel, and now finding out they're working with the government was a serious concern. "Have they made the connection?"

"They haven't made the connection yet. You can be sure they know we've hired two assassins, but they probably don't know why. If they did, you wouldn't be here right now." He was smiling when he said that to Toomas. "Don't forget, you and Doshe were the ones to hire Manuel. We needed their involvement then, now we've gotten more than we bargained for. However, before you get too worried, I should tell you they're scrambling. They don't know what's going on. They were approached by the Israeli government for assistance, otherwise they wouldn't have any idea what we were up to."

"What specifically do they know?" Toomas asked, not convinced at all that things weren't about to come crashing in on their plan.

"I can't be sure, but my sources say they know about Jacque and that he was hired through Jihad's group. They know about Manuel, for obvious reasons. They know about the consortium, and we have to assume they know the names of all its members, including us. I don't know if they have drawn any conclusions about the decoy. Or what theories they might have generated concerning him. I don't know what explanations they've come up with to explain why we've hired two assassins for the same job. I am confident though; they don't know about us yet."

"Why do you say that?"

"In reviewing the information, it became clear that they treated the consortium as a unified group. We all know if they understood our motivations, they would not be so quick to lump Toomas and me in that group. We are not simply greedy like the rest of them; we see a more beneficial end to this. A world that even your German predecessor could be proud of. Right Toomas?"

Toomas ignored Sergei's reference to Hitler. It showed Sergei's ignorance to assume that German hatred for the Jews could be defined by one man. What Toomas understood, but Sergei did not, was that the European world, including the western Soviet states, had a natural enmity for the Jew. It wasn't just a German predisposition, but rather a European predisposition to anti-Semitic behavior. Add to this, the natural religious hatred of all Arabs for the Jew. A hatred that dates back to before the Pharaohs of Egypt, and you have accounted for nearly half the world's population. Hitler was merely the modern-day icon of anti-Semitism.

"How long do you think it will be before they realize what we are trying to do?" Toomas responded to Sergei.

"That is difficult to say. Undoubtedly, our window of opportunity is shrinking quickly, but we may be far enough along that they can no longer stop us. If we keep the decoy out of the public eye, and allow Jacque and Manuel to do their work, there is little they can do to stop us before it is too late. A problem arises only if we have to use the decoy before we are ready, or Eric and his new friend are able to stop both assassins before one completes the assignment. That, I think, is highly unlikely."

"Why do you say that?"

"Eric has shown us he is quite rusty from his recent sabbatical. Two of his assistants have already been eliminated by Manuel. His new one, although she is an Israeli, is also a woman. If I were her, I would not want Manuel to find me. He is one sick individual, even by our standards. And what he would do to her before he killed her---would be a horrible thing to experience."

Sylvan and Toomas considered what Sergei just said. The thought of Manuel having time alone with any woman he was ultimately going to kill was gruesome. Manuel was one depraved man. He was the epitome of man given over to his own desires. If Satan could live inside a man, that man would be Manuel.

In an effort to shake everyone from their thoughts, Sylvan spoke up. "Let's not concern ourselves with what might happen to that little Jewish girl. I can ensure that the real Sheik Omani will handle all public appearances for the next few days. However, there is a limit to how much exposure he'll accept. It is imperative that this does not drag on too long. Otherwise, he'll start to get suspicious."

Now all three men retreated into their own thoughts. Each man lost in his own mind, contemplating what he, alone, could do. Each one thinking about how the events of the next few days would unfold. All three recognizing that if they could pull this off, the world would be changed forever---for the better.

- - - - -

Sylvan returned to the task of taking care of Sheik Omani. His first order of business was to inform the Sheik that he would have to handle the next public appearance because Oman 2 wasn't ready. He explained to the Sheik there was a problem with Oman 2's delivery, albeit minor, that Sergei had noticed and wanted to correct before they became pronounced. He told him they didn't expect it to take more than a couple days, but in the meantime, the Sheik would have to handle the next public appearance.

As Sylvan had predicted, the Sheik accepted this without question. He even managed to identify a couple of mannerisms that he felt were Oman 2's, not his.

- - - - -

Sylvan was sent ahead alone, while Toomas and Sergei took up separate positions and watched to make sure he wasn't followed when he left the hotel. Reassured they had maintained their secrecy; they left the hotel together. Only then, did Toomas and Sergei return to the Star of David hotel. The next scheduled meeting for the consortium was today, and it would not be unexpected for them to be seen together.

When they arrived at the hotel, they went directly to the meeting room. Everyone else had already arrived, so when Toomas entered, he chose one end of the room. Taking up his position, made that the de facto front of the room. All eyes turned toward him as he walked around the table and took his position. They were all eager to hear how Oman 2's performance was received.

The news media, specifically CNN, ensured that the whole world had the opportunity to view the event live. Consequently, everyone in the room had been able to see his performance. However, they recognized the pitfalls of accurately assessing Oman 2's performance from a TV screen. So, they were anxious to hear the report from Toomas and Sergei, since they were present for the event.

Toomas knew he had a captive audience, and purposely took his time as he was preparing to speak. At the end of the table, he stood for a moment, hands resting on the back of the chair. Looking over the faces of his four compatriots prior to delivering his assessment, he felt in total control of their destiny. Howard and Jason kept their eyes on Toomas, informing him they were ready, and he could start at anytime. Seymour, taking a more timid approach, was telling him the same thing. But rather than looking at Toomas, he kept his eyes on the sheaf of papers in front of him, fanning the corners, trying to give the impression he was not as anxious as the other two.

"Could you stop playing with your paper?" Sergei said, turning to Seymour. "It's a bloody bad habit of yours and it gets a tad bit obnoxious after awhile." Sergei tried to imitate the Englishman's accent, but it came out sounding more like a young English lad speaking a weak version of a strange dialect than anything else, and it was just as difficult to understand. Sergei often did this when he was trying to loosen up the group. They always seemed to enjoy his poor imitation of an English accent. The trick worked again. As soon as he finished speaking, everyone in the room started chuckling. Seymour stopped fanning the papers and turned his attention toward Toomas.

"We continue to make progress toward our long-term goal of influencing world oil markets." The use of the word "influencing" was intentional. He wanted to reassure everyone in the room they still shared the same objective, yet, in the event of a bug, he wanted to give the impression to the listener this was a business meeting, concerned only with business objectives.

"Sheik Omani has provided a stabilizing force here in the Middle East by initiating talks between the various factions that typically pursue radical approaches to the resolution of their problems. It is my contention, and my hope, that Sheik Omani proves successful in this endeavor. However, everyone here should be aware that the Sheik might not always act, as we would have him to. He is not our puppet, so his actions will not always reflect our position. In fact, it is not unrealistic to expect him to propose and in fact institute policies that are contrary to our way of thinking."

"In that vein, it might be appropriate to approach Sheik Omani in a spirit of cooperation and try to explain to him why his policies may not be appropriate. Open a line of communication with him that allows the sharing of ideas and the development of a mutually beneficial long-range vision for the future. Educate him on the finer details of global negotiations. Share with him our experiences, our goals and objectives, our needs and the needs of the world as we see them with a global perspective."

"The forum I am suggesting would also provide the opportunity for growth within a controlled environment for Sheik Omani…" The subtleties of Toomas' words were understood by everyone in the room. Toomas continued speaking, providing details about how this could be accomplished, but they were hidden in obscure references to the Sheik and the consortium. Anyone listening to the conversation live or over a tape would have a very difficult time interpreting the hidden meanings if they weren't well versed in the consortium's true objective.

In time, everyone understood the real Sheik Omani would handle the next public appearance. A significant risk to their plan was implied.

After Toomas was able to relay all the pertinent information that everyone in there needed to know, he opened it up for questions. He hoped and was rewarded that everyone would recognize the difficult position they were in and keep all questions superficial. With all members of the consortium brought up to date, the meeting was adjourned. Another meeting was scheduled for four days later at the Grand Hotel in Zurich. By that time, everyone thought, the world should be in shock.

- - - - -

Sergei was leaving word daily, with an unknown person, where he could be reached. It was through this source that all communications with Jacque had to be funneled. All Jacque gave him was a phone number, and he was required to call once per day to confirm his location with the person on the other end of the line. If his plans changed, he was to re-call the number and update the information. If there was a need to speak with Jacque, the request could be made through the channel, and an hour or so later he was expected to call back. He would continue checking back roughly every hour until Jacque left a message for him. Then he was expected to follow the instructions, which could mean a face-to-face meeting or a phone call.

Sergei was making his eighth call back when he finally received directions from Jacque. He was to remain in his hotel room and Jacque would contact him there. He hung up the phone and prepared to wait, but immediately there was a knock at the door.

"I don't need anything," Sergei called out, assuming it was housekeeping. The knock came again. This time Sergei got up from the lone chair in the room and walked over to the door. He placed his hand on the doorknob as if to open it, but before he did, he called out again. "I don't need anything," then waited for the response. Again, the knock came.

Sergei didn't like what was happening, but without a peephole, he had no choice but to open the door to see who was there. Sergei retrieved his pistol from his briefcase, then returned to open the door. Pressing himself to the wall, he let the pistol hang in his left hand resting between his thigh and the wall. Slowly and as quietly as possible, he turned the doorknob and began opening the door a crack to see who was there. He was hoping to catch the person in the hall off guard, but before he could see anyone, the door flew out of his hand and crashed against the dresser.

Then Sergei felt the grip of a man's hand as it reached around the doorframe and started squeezing his neck. He tried to raise the gun with the intent of shooting the hand, but as he did, he felt the grip of a secondhand clamp around his wrist. That was followed by a sharp pain as his hand was slammed against the corner of the doorframe. He dropped the gun.

By this time his attacker had cleared the doorway and was in full view, but Sergei had closed his eyes as he tried to keep from passing out from the loss of oxygen. Suddenly he felt himself hurtling across the room, tripping over the bed as he fell to the floor. As he was falling, he heard the door close, then everything became still.

His first thought was that his attacker had left, but he knew that was unlikely. He had fallen face down between the bed and the wall, so he had to twist his head and body around to see directly behind him. When he did, he was looking into the smiling face of Jacque.

"Monsieur," Jacque began with a very faint French accent. "You have been trying to get a hold of me, then you greet me this way. What is wrong with you? Do you have some strange death wish? If so, please tell me out right and I will solve that problem. Now, what is it you want?"

Sergei slowly began pulling himself off the floor. He moved as if he had been brutally beaten, finally managing to climb on to the edge of the bed. Looking at Jacque he asked very softly, "why couldn't you have said, 'It's me'. At least I could have recognized your voice and saved myself this abuse."

"You and many other people can recognize my voice. I could just as easily have said 'shoot me' for all the good it would do announcing my own arrival. No, it is better you suffer some pain than I should die to spare that pain. Agreed?"

Sergei stared blankly at Jacque while he sat rubbing his neck. He tried rubbing away the feeling of Jacque's hand squeezing the life out of him, but he could still feel the pressure of Jacque's fingers on his throat. "I suppose." He paused long enough to rub his wrist for a little while, then started again.

"I probably would have been better off. No, I definitely would have been better off relaying the message through your service, but I felt it was too important to entrust to a voice I had never seen over the phone. It's official; we would like you to complete the assignment. I have a tentative schedule and can provide you updates as I become aware of them through your channel. We would like the job completed as soon as possible." As he finished speaking, he handed Jacque the Sheik's itinerary for the next two days.

Jacque took the sheet of paper and immediately started reviewing it. When he finished, he folded it and started putting it in his pocket when Sergei interrupted him. "I think it would be better if you copied it or memorized it. I don't want anything on you that could possibly lead back to me."

"If I were an amateur', that would be understandable, but I am not. However, you are the customer, and as the American's used to say, 'the customer is always right'." Jacque retrieved a piece of paper from the desk and began transferring the information.

"We haven't had an update on Eric recently. Could you tell me what is going on?"

"I suppose. Eric has formed an alliance with an Israeli girl named Maruch. She is a formidable opponent and will greatly enhance his position. Both her information network and her physical skills are valuable additions."

"Eric has managed to avoid the few obstacles I have put in his way, which I have decided to stop doing. They have been providing him with unintended practice sessions, and he is beginning to refine his skills. He is also getting close enough that he has become more than just a casual nuisance. His own network has been reestablished to a limited degree, and my movements will no longer be hidden from him."

"Will you have to take care of him before you deal with the Sheik?"

"I suspect I may end up doing just that. But now that I have the go ahead to pursue the real quarry, it is not so important as it used to be, except from a defensive posture. Now he'll have to go on the offensive to stop me."

"Do you have any idea why he might have joined forces with the Israeli woman?"

"I suspect she's a replacement for the two men he lost. I would imagine she'll be assigned Manuel." Jacque waited for Sergei's reaction. He enjoyed the expression on Sergei's face when it finally dawned on him what Jacque had just said.

"What are you talking about?" Then thinking better of what he asked, quickly added. "We would have told you about Manuel, but it was for the good of the cause that we kept you in the dark. This way if Eric somehow managed to capture you, you couldn't tell him anything you didn't know."

"Both of us knew about Manuel within hours of the time you decided to hire him." Jacque smiled wryly as he watched Sergei squirm to get out of his predicament.

"We didn't know you'd find out that quickly. Believe me. We thought we were doing what was best for everyone."

"I see." Jacque said as he walked over to where Sergei was sitting on the bed. He sat down next to Sergei and just stared at him. Sergei became very uncomfortable with Jacque sitting so close, his own eyes began darting around the room, trying to avoid Jacque's stare. Both men sat silently, Jacque staring and Sergei trying to avoid eye contact. With each passing second, the tension built inside Sergei until he couldn't stand it any longer. He stood up ready to yell at Jacque to say something, but before he could get the words out of his mouth, he noticed Jacque lifting a pillow towards him. Confused, he stood motionless, then heard a soft pop. Everything went black. Sergei's legs involuntarily took two steps backwards before they lost balance and crumpled to the floor. Jacque took the pillow off the gun and started removing the silencer.

The bullet entered in the center of Sergei's forehead, his panicked expression frozen in time. It would take a mortician's fine work to remove it, thought Jacque.

Jacque got up from the bed and walked over to where Sergei lay on the floor. Taking hold of Sergei's shoulders, he dragged him around to the side of the bed. He pulled the covers back, then lifted Sergei and placed his body in bed. Next, he carefully pulled the covers up, covering Sergei's entire body and face. Jacque spent the next thirty minutes cleaning up the remnants of Sergei's mess.

The bullets Jacque used were designed to essentially explode on contact with almost anything. Consequently, the victim did not suffer the typical exit wounds and subsequent splattering of human debris associated with typical bullets. The mess consisted of limited amounts of blood, a slightly disarrayed room and the powder burned pillow. But being the professional he was, he made sure there was no trace of him being there.

It was not Jacque's intention to cover up the killing, but simply to delay its discovery. With the room straightened up, he slid the burned pillow under Sergei's head. Looking around, he was satisfied. To the casual observer it would not be apparent anything unusual happened. Then taking a piece of stationary from the drawer in the nightstand, he scribbled 'do not disturb' in Hebrew on it and slipped it between the door and the door jamb as he closed the door on his way out.

- - - - -

Toomas approached the building as the sun began to dip below the horizon. He'd flown to Tel Aviv on word that Manuel returned there after his failed attempt on Oman 2's life during the news conference. Both Sergei and he were upset that Manuel would have even tried anything. He was told very clearly not to do anything during the news conference. If he'd been successful, it would have wreaked havoc on their plan, possibly destroying it completely. They were very fortunate that Steve managed to circumvent the attempted assassination. They can't rely on good fortune in the future, Toomas thought as he knocked on the door.

Toomas had been to Tel Aviv just once before in his life. Early in the development of his business, he met a man at the airport, between flights, to discuss an oil shipment that was coming from Iraq. Never having been anywhere in Israel before, he took an extra day just to be a tourist, taking in the sights of the city.

He was warned by the desk clerk at the hotel to stay away from this part of the city. He was told it was a meeting place for a small, but radical, contingent of Arab residents. They did not welcome anyone they didn't know, particularly those who were obviously not of Arab bloodlines. At the time, Toomas followed the clerk's advice and stayed clear of the area. Now he found himself nervously knocking on a door in the heart of that same district he was warned to avoid. He was never more aware of his German nationality than he was right now. There was no mistaking him for an Arab, and he was fearfully aware of that fact.

He didn't hear any activity inside after his first knock, so the second time he increased the force. He looked around nervously, convinced that at any moment a band of Arab vagabonds would come out of nowhere and make him regret he had come here. But in fact, that didn't happen. He was startled when the door finally opened without warning and a particularly gruff person asked, "What the hell do you want?"

Toomas was momentarily caught off guard, then managed to compose himself and speak just as the man started closing the door. "I was told I could find a man called Manuel here."

The man stopped, and then slowly reopened it. He looked at Toomas as if he were contaminated with some unusually grotesque substance, then waved him inside. Toomas stepped into a narrow hallway as the man closed the door behind him. Extending his arm over Toomas' shoulders, the man silently motioned for Toomas to start down the hall.

Toomas tentatively started walking forward, then crumpled to the floor. The man behind him calmly slid the gun back into the waistband of his slacks. He reached down and grabbed Toomas under his armpits. He turned Toomas' body around then slowly started backing down the hall. When he came to the third door, he kicked. Moments later someone opened the door, so the man continued to drag Toomas' limp body into the room.

Toomas woke up tied to a chair. As the fog started fading from his mind, he remembered what happened. As he started walking down the hall, someone hit him on the back of his head with an extremely hard object and he blacked out. With that thought, he tried to reach behind to the back of his head and feel how bad it was because with each passing moment of consciousness, his headache was becoming more painful. That's when he realized he couldn't move his arms or hands. At first, he continued trying, but slowly he came to the realization his hands were tied behind his back.

He looked around the room to see if there was anything he could use to free himself. If he found something, he was sure he could maneuver himself over to it. As his eyes panned the room, he noticed the man lying on the bed. Until now, he assumed he was in the room alone. Of course, there was no reason to have expected that, but when no one noticed right away after he regained consciousness, he jumped to that conclusion.

He couldn't make out the man's face. From this angle he could only see the boots and lower half of the dungarees the man was wearing. The man's face was partially blocked from view like the rest of his body. He briefly considered sliding his chair across the room to get a better view, then quickly decided against it. He decided if he were going to risk making that much noise, he would do it trying to escape, not identifying his captor. He returned to searching the room for anything that could help him get untied. Soon he was rewarded by locating a kitchen knife sitting on the dresser.

Slowly Toomas slid the chair, or more accurately, dragged the chair across the room as he inched his way over to the dresser. He'd extend both feet as far as they could reach, but since they were strapped to the legs of the chair just below his knees, that amounted to a few inches. After both feet were extended, he'd start dragging the chair to the feet while lifting his body off the chair as much as possible to reduce the drag. The scraping of the wooden legs against the floorboards still made too much noise for him to feel comfortable. With each slide, he'd pause and look over at the sleeping man to make sure he was still asleep.

Thinking this method would ultimately wake the man lying on the bed, he decided to change his approach. He pushed back with his feet until he was balancing on the two rear legs of the chair. Then, pushing off with his right foot and leaning back toward his left side, he was able to get the chair temporarily balanced on the left rear leg. He allowed the chair to naturally spin toward the left side, then he carefully broke the chair's fall with his feet. This allowed him to move more quickly while making very little noise on his way to the dresser.

With the landing of all four legs on the floor, there was a distinct bump, but it was erratic and soft. Each time he managed this awkward maneuver, he would stop, look over at the man on the bed, verify he was still asleep, then continue. He would alternate twisting on the left rear leg, then the right front leg in order to control his progress toward the dresser.

Finally, after what seemed like an interminable amount of time, he was at the dresser. However, he had become so intent on getting there that he hadn't considered how to retrieve the knife once there. With his hands bound behind his back, the task looked impossible. He sat there emotionally drained at the prospect that his effort was in vain.

While staring at the knife, he considered the height of the dresser. He leaned forward to estimate it when he realized he could reach the knife with his chin. He stretched out further, caught the knife under his chin and started sliding it toward the edge. Before he allowed it to drop to his lap, he stopped to make sure of his next move.

Getting the knife in his lap would leave it as useless as it was sitting on the dresser. He still had to get it into his hands before it would be of any benefit, and even then, there was no guarantee he would be able to maneuver it well enough to actually cut the ropes off. Toomas thought for a moment, then twisted until he could pull a drawer partially open.

He was pleasantly surprised when he discovered a spare blanket inside the drawer. Leaning over, he caught the knife with his chin and slid it off the dresser. He carefully directed the knife until it fell on the blanket inside the open drawer. Turning his chair around until the back of the chair was against the open drawer, he leaned back and caught the knife between his fingers. Sliding his fingers along the blade, he faced the blade outward, then slid it to the corner of the drawer and pushed the drawer shut until it pinched the knife.

Carefully he started rubbing the rope binding his hands against the exposed blade. As long as he kept the pressure relatively light, he was able to cut without the knife slipping out of its position. He continued working carefully, painstakingly slow. Periodically he would stop to position the knife, then continue cutting the rope.

While he worked the knife, slowly cutting through the rope, he watched the man lying on the bed for any signs of movement. There were none. In fact, the longer he stared at the man, the more he was convinced the man wasn't even breathing. By the time he came to this conclusion, the blade had cut through the second wrapping of rope, and he could feel it loosen from around his wrists.

With this newfound knowledge about the man on the bed, his fear began to heighten. He had no idea who he was, or why he would have been killed. Or even why they were in the same room together. Regardless, the thought of their fates being the same caused Toomas to increase the force of the rope against the knife. "Shit," he said disgustedly. The increased pressure against the blade had caused it to twist in the drawer, then fall inside.

He leaned back in the chair and reached into the drawer. As he did, he could feel the ropes around his wrists give some more. He stopped trying to grab the knife and started working his wrists in an effort to further loosen the ropes. Up and down, then side to side. Soon he could feel the rope loosen more and his adrenaline seemed to increase exponentially with each incremental increase in movement. Without warning, the ropes fell off completely. He couldn't bring his arms around, because his upper body was still secured to the back of the chair with another rope, but now his range of movement was drastically increased. He reached into the drawer, and with his added flexibility was able to quickly locate the knife and retrieve it. He brought it around to his front and began cutting the ropes, careful to keep the blade between his chest and arms. Needing to rest much less frequently than before, he was able to cut through the ropes binding him to the chair in a very short time.

Now all that remained was freeing his legs. Directing the knife to the ropes at his legs, he proceeded to cut through them as quickly as he could. No longer concerned with the man on the bed, his concern was redirected to the possibility the person responsible for this might return and catch him before he was able to escape. With all the ropes cut and removed, he started to stand. The lack of circulation to his limbs left them weak and numb, so he fell back into the chair.

He rubbed his legs furiously trying to hasten the blood flow on its way through his legs. He tried to stand up a second time and this time was rewarded for his efforts. His legs were still shaky, but at least he was able to stand and walk. His first inclination was to beat it out of there as fast as he could. But he resisted the temptation and walked over to the man lying on the bed. He looked at his face and was shocked to see it was the man that let him in and, he presumed, the one that knocked him out.

There was a mat of dried blood at the base of the man's neck; Toomas knew how he had died. He checked the man's front pockets, then reached under the man's hip, trying to feel if there was anything in his back pockets. He was disappointed to come up empty but not wanting to risk staying around any longer, he started for the door.

Toomas approached the door carefully. There was always the chance that someone was guarding the room from the outside. He put his ear to the door and listened. Nothing. This was the only way out of the room, so he started turning the doorknob very slowly, hoping it wouldn't have any squeaks. He stepped to the side of the door, then opened it a crack. Looking outside, he was pleased to see the hall was empty.

Cautiously, he opened the door the rest of the way, and then stepped into the hall. Quietly he made his way down the hall to the door leading outside. Again, he opened the door slowly and verified it was safe on the other side before venturing out. It was pitch black outside, the moon obscured by an overcast sky, and there were no working streetlights in either direction. Toomas stepped outside into freedom. Just then, he noticed the silhouette of a man round the corner ahead and turn in his direction.

Toomas desperately wanted to turn and run, but he knew that would draw attention to himself and that was last thing he needed. As he pressed his body back against the wall, he decided there was no choice but to wait it out hoping the man wouldn't notice him cowering in the shadows. As the man approached, Toomas feared he would be recognized. He had this premonition-like feeling that the two men had met before. Finally, the man was close enough that Toomas could make out who he was. "Pssssst," Toomas whispered, "Manuel."

Manuel stopped and turned, staring in the direction of the voice. After a few seconds, he started walking toward him. Stopping just inches away from Toomas he said, "Where were you? We were to meet here hours ago."

Manuel was so close Toomas could smell the rotten mixture of alcohol and cheese on his breath. Still, it was so dark he could barely make out Manuel's mouth moving as he spoke. "It's a long story. Is there someplace where we can go and talk?" Toomas asked.

He didn't notice Manuel's hand motion indicating he was to follow, but when he heard Manuel start to walk away, he followed anyway. Manuel walked past the door to the building Toomas had just escaped from and continued down two more doors. This building looked identical to the previous two buildings from the outside, reminding

Toomas of similar districts at home. Toomas walked into the building while Manuel held the door for him, unaware of what just occurred.

Inside the building, there was a small entryway and a well-worn wooden stairway leading up to his left, and another door directly in front of him. He waited for Manuel to step inside, then started up the stairs as he was directed. At the top of the stairs was a small platform and a door on the left side. Manuel motioned for Toomas to go through the door.

Inside the room, Manuel spoke again. "Now where were you? I expected you hours ago. You're lucky I even came back here."

"I must have made a mistake." Toomas began. "I was in the building two doors down from here. At the time, I didn't realize I entered the wrong building."

"I thought you might have double crossed me because I was attacked and tied up. Now that I see I was at the wrong address, it's obvious you had nothing to do with it."

Toomas continued to tell Manuel what had happened, oblivious to Manuel's obvious lack of interest. Manuel busied himself with different things in the room until he positioned himself slightly behind Toomas. Toomas could still see him, but he was at the edge of his peripheral vision. Regardless, Toomas had become enthralled in telling the story of his ingenious escape and was unaware of what Manuel was doing. Blissfully, Toomas continued talking.

Manuel kept moving around until he drifted slowly out of Toomas' view. This room was very much like the one Toomas had escaped from. It had a dresser, a bed, a small table and four wooden chairs haphazardly scattered about. Manuel worked his way over to what would be the kitchen area. He spied the hot plate in the corner of the counter, but quickly rejected that as a possible weapon. At the other end of the three-foot counter was a filthy water stained porcelain sink. Underneath the counter near the sink was a drawer and below that a small cabinet for storing foodstuffs.

Manuel pulled the drawer out, but instead of retrieving any eating utensils, he removed a large hunting knife. The kind you would expect to find strapped to the waist of an experienced hunter. Manuel held it in his hands for a moment as he evaluated its utility. It showed the signs of use, the intricate carvings on the handled nearly rubbed smooth from handling. With his index finger Manuel felt the finely honed blade, then smiled. It was razor sharp, just as he requested.

Toomas had just gotten to the part where he recognized the man on the bed when Manuel interrupted. "I hope you didn't set up this meeting to bore me with stories."

Toomas stopped speaking in mid sentence and turned to face Manuel. Manuel was holding the hunting knife in front of him; slowly turning it over and over as he carefully examined it. Toomas noticed the knife and a twinge of fear went through him, then he realized Manuel had no motivation to harm him and he relaxed again. "Ja, it would be best if I told you why I'm here."

"First, there is a slight change in plans." Toomas paused to give Manuel a chance to say something. When he didn't, Toomas continued. "When you were hired, we gave you a time limit to complete the job. That's been changed." Again, Toomas paused expecting Manuel to say something. But again, Manuel stood mute.

"It's imperative that the job be completed within the next 96 hours. If you can't complete the task by then, we will have to consider the contract null and void." With each word he spoke, he was gaining confidence around Manuel. He added that last statement as a direct result of that budding confidence, but when he looked at Manuel, he started regretting it. Manuel simply stared at Toomas intent on not giving any indication of how he viewed his new instructions.

Toomas reached into his pocket and removed a piece of paper, as he did, he added. "I assumed your task would be made easier if you knew the Sheik's schedule for the next four days. This itinerary, although subject to change, is compiled with the intent of knowing his location every minute of the day." He handed it to Manuel, then continued. "As you can see, it's very detailed. Do you have any questions?"

Throughout Toomas' speech, Manuel wandered about the room nonchalantly, fidgeting with the hunting knife as he moved from place to place. When Toomas offered him the itinerary, he took it and walked over to the only window in the room. The sun just completed its rise above the horizon and was now shining brightly through the window. Manuel looked over the itinerary, then turned to face Toomas. "Is that all?"

"Ja."

"Then you may go. The sun is up, it should be safe now."

Without hesitating, Toomas turned and started for the door. Manuel made him nervous and putting distance between the two of them was his best solution to the uncomfortable feelings. As he was opening the door, he felt a sharp pain in the middle of his back, then he passed out. Manuel walked over to him as he lay on the floor face down with the knife firmly planted in the middle of his back. He knelt down and felt for a pulse on Toomas' neck. Satisfied, he slowly removed the knife, and then dragged him over to the bed kicking the door shut at the same time. He threw Toomas on the bed, then taking the knife slit his throat. He went over to the sink and washed his hands and the knife. He set the knife back in the drawer where he found it, then left.

- - - - -

After Toomas and Sergei left the hotel, Seymour, Jason, and Harold got back together in Harold's suite. They waited in silence for Sylvan and the Sheik to join them. Harold was the first one to hear the knock at the door and quickly got up to see who was there. He put his left eye to the peephole and saw the Sheik and Sylvan standing in the hall. Harold let them in then went to the sofa and sat down next to Seymour.

Jason was seated in a lounge chair at the end of the sofa. The chair was turned to help form a semicircle with the matching chair at the other end of the sofa. A coffee table separated the two lounge chairs and was directly in front of the sofa. The Sheik took his place on the other lounge chair, while Sylvan started looking around the suite for a place to sit. He disappeared into the bedroom for a moment, then returned with a desk chair in tow. He set it directly across from the sofa completing the circle.

"Did any of you notice if Toomas and Sergei have left?" Harold asked the question of everyone in the room but directed it specifically toward Jason. He was assigned the task of confirming their departure and nodded his head in response.

"Good." Then turning to Sylvan, he asked. "I assume Oman 2 is ready to take over for the Sheik." Again, there was no answer, just a nodding of the head.

"To bring everyone up to date, I personally gave both Jacque and Manuel the instructions to terminate Toomas and Sergei. They have been paid in advance, and I have been assured that by morning, the task will be complete. Any questions?" He looked at each person in turn, offering them a personal invitation to speak. But no one took him up on the offer.

Turning back to Sylvan, Harold returned to the topic of Oman 2. "Did Oman 2 give you any indication that Sergei had spoken to him recently? Any indication that Sergei was preparing him to be removed from his role?"

"Non, Monsieur."

"We can not be sure what Sergei may have told Oman 2 in preparation of reversing roles." Looking at Sheik Omani, "It was their objective to have you be the one assassinated, and Oman 2 would permanently replace you."

Turning back to Sylvan he continued. "It's up to you to make sure he doesn't do anything to jeopardize our position. If you even suspect he might be the least bit aware of our plans for him, let one of us know."

"What should I do if he requests to speak with Sergei?"

"That will be a problem. Try putting him off by telling him Sergei is contacting Manuel and is unavailable. If that doesn't placate him, explain to him we can't take the risk that someone might see the two of them together. Reassure him that everything will be done in four days, and once it's over he'll be able to go anywhere, see anyone, do anything he likes. If he doesn't want to accept that, let me know. He's the critical part of the plan right now, so we have to keep him mollified."

Redirecting the conversation to Jason and Seymour he asked, "How have the negotiations progressed?"

"The term negotiation implies a give and take methodology. We've come to an agreement, but the Palestinians didn't give anything as far as I'm concerned. They just took." It was apparent from his tone of voice Seymour was still disgusted at the way the Palestinians had approached the negotiations.

"How so?"

"The opening proposal called for Solomon's Temple to be built on the same sight as the original and to specifications identified in the Old Testament. Only the temple would be built, no outside courtyard would be included, effectively keeping the size to a minimum. They wouldn't even consider it."

"They demanded the dimensions of the Temple be restricted to those identified in the Pentateuch, and even then, without the outside courtyard. It was their contention using the dimensions of Solomon's Temple would bring the building to close to the Temple Mount. We discussed it at length, but they wouldn't accept any variation from the original Temple's size minus the courtyard."

"How do you think it will be received by Israel?" Sheik Omani cut in.

"The Israeli government was being much more reasonable in their approach to the whole issue and has already agreed."

"Yes, with good reason." Jason explained, "At first glance it might appear they're getting everything they wanted out of this. Jerusalem stays under their control. They get to rebuild their Holiest of Holies. And they give up something they won in a war that has caused nothing but problems for them ever since."

"But most of their population believe they have the right to the Jordanian land they won in the war. It's not just the spoils of war to them. They believe God gave them that land, and now they'd be giving it to a bunch of Palestinians that have no right to be there. Hostile Palestinians at that."

"The government doesn't see it that way though, and they're the ones we negotiate with. Also, they're the ones that have to explain this to their own people, we don't. They've already put in place the framework needed to relocate all those that choose relocation over the alternative."

"What's the alternative?"

"Remaining settled in the West Bank, after it becomes a Palestinian state. It's an option we don't expect many to choose, because they would be put under Palestinian rule."

"Once King Hussein gave permission for the West Bank land to be used as a bargaining chip, it provided Israel, and the Palestinians an avenue for peaceful resolution that heretofore never existed. The Israeli's understood this immediately, and with some rather intense negotiations, eventually so did the Palestinians."

"What was the general reaction when you suggested the news conference focus on the fanatical groups, at the exclusion of the heads of the various states?" Harold asked.

"Surprisingly it was very positive. Without exception, they felt it promoted the most unified image and added a level of acceptance that could not be achieved with formal government involvement. However, without exception they are all planning to attend."

"What framework will be used for governing Jerusalem? You said it would remain under Israeli control, but it will be surrounded by this new Palestinian state which can be expected to be much more hostile than Jordan ever was. It will share borders on three sides with the Palestinians. Not an ideal situation for a Jewish holy city, or for Jews in general"

"Just as Berlin existed inside East Germany," Jason answered, then explained. "The theory is to pattern Jerusalem similar to the divided Berlin, although without the wall. Arabs will be allowed a narrow access route to the Temple Mount policed by Arabs. Under no circumstances can Israel block that route. The area immediately around the Temple Mount will also be designated Arab land, although still under the authority of the city government."

"It sounds as if the most important details have been worked out to everyone's satisfaction. Have you scheduled the news conference?"

"We originally estimated the news conference could take place tomorrow, but we want everyone to be comfortable with what was negotiated first."

"Will that be sufficient notice to ensure that everyone that needs to be there will make it?"

"Not really. What we wanted do, if you think it's acceptable, is set it up for the day after next. Say…1:00 in the afternoon. That would give everybody enough time to get here and allow the networks time to set up during the morning."

12

-Slaves rule over us; there is no one to deliver us from their hand.

Maruch agreed to meet Eric in her hotel room at nine that evening. It was almost ten o'clock, and she still hadn't arrived. Eric was up from his chair every couple minute pacing. He'd sit, try to watch the television, CNN, never really achieve interest, then get up again and start pacing the room. He was becoming obsessed with her absence.

He spent the day trying to get a fix on Jacque and was finally rewarded for his efforts late that afternoon. He located where Jacque was staying and was able to search the room while he was out. It was apparent Jacque was not too concerned, because he had not bothered to booby trap the room in any noticeable manner. Eric assumed he took the precaution of setting up a benign alarm system so he could determine if anyone had entered the room while he was away, but his lack of any more serious attempts to protect his privacy left Eric somewhat surprised.

During his search for Jacque, his own network unearthed the heretofore unscheduled and still unannounced, news conference set for tomorrow. Eric was convinced that the real attempt on the Sheik's life would take place during that news conference. He could not confirm which Sheik would be at the news conference, but at this point it didn't really matter. As far as the rest of the world was concerned, the Sheik's assassination would completely destabilize the already precarious peace that existed. Whatever the circumstances, if they weren't able to stop both Manuel and Jacque in time, the consortium better hope they can control the mob after it happens.

That and the nagging fear that Manuel had been successful once again were causing Eric to be unusually tense. This morning Maruch agreed to simply locate Manuel, then return to her hotel room and wait for him to arrive. He thought she had understood when he explained to her the importance of approaching this problem from the assassin's point of view. Every point he made was followed by her nodding her head in agreement. Now he was beginning to think she simply did that to pacify him.

His approach, which he still firmly believed was the best, was to intercept the assassination while it was in progress. Neither man would be as vulnerable as he would be when he was concentrating on the kill. Since it was their objective to ensure that the Sheik, fake or otherwise, not be assassinated, he felt increasing the chances for success by maximizing their element of surprise was best. The last thing either of them wanted was to attack prematurely, risking failure, and losing their advantage.

However, as he continued his pattern of pacing, then sitting, he was becoming increasingly concerned that Maruch might not have adhered to that plan. There was no reasonable explanation for her not being here now, except if Manuel had discovered her. And Eric didn't want to dwell on that thought.

He walked over to the small window and standing to one side, looked down at the street below. He mused about the insignificant activities of those he was watching, entrenched in their own world, oblivious to the chaos that was being planned for their lives. As he mulled these things over, he heard a key unlocking the door to the room. Silently, he hurried to the door and positioned himself behind it as it swung open. Looking through the crack between the door and hinge, he was relieved to see it was Maruch. Adding to his relief, she looked fine.

Waiting for her to clear the door, he clenched the doorknob and quickly closed the door behind her. Not surprised at his presence, but annoyed at his actions, Maruch gave him a questioning stare.

"You're sixty-five minutes late." Eric stated as if that were enough to indict her on some trumped up charge.

"You're right, I'm sixty-five minutes late. Now if you'll relax, I'll explain why." She matched Eric's stare until he waved his hand signaling her to explain.

"I was able to track Manuel to his hotel, a grimy place close to the Temple Mount. It was obvious he chose it for its location, because he has a perfect view of the open area between the Wailing Wall and the stairs of the Temple Mount. There's an excellent chance he could work right out of his room. Depending, of course, on how the final arrangements work out for the news conference."

"The reason I'm late is a little more interesting," she continued. "Late this afternoon he left his room. I figured it was an excellent chance for me to look around, so I did. Before I was able to finish and get out of his room, I heard him coming down the hall. I couldn't exit through the door, and it was three stories above the street, so I did the only thing I could do. I hid in his room."

"Just inside the closet there was a little nook in the wall. If one stood inside the nook, and the person using the closet didn't look around inside, you could hide there. Manuel didn't use the closet for his clothes, but he did open it just a tad to check it when he got back. Fortunately, he just looked straight inside and didn't see me. Regardless, I didn't have any choice but to wait for him to go to sleep or leave again." She stopped talking and waited for Eric to respond.

"And?" Eric asked expecting her to continue; surprised she decided to stop there with her story.

"And…he did leave again. That's when I came back here."

"That's it. He left and you came back here. Can't you be more specific on the details?"

"If you mean did I learn anything while I was in his room, the answer is yes. He had a copy of the Sheik's itinerary for the next four days. Three, now that today's almost done."

"Let me guess. Tomorrow afternoon there is a tentative news conference scheduled for the Sheik."

"You're right. How did you know?"

"I found a similar schedule in Jacque's room. I've been able to get confirmation that the news conference has definitely been scheduled. In other words, it's no longer tentative. Getting back to the note for a minute, could you tell where he might have gotten it? The one in Jacque's room was definitely in his own handwriting. I'd have recognized it anywhere," he added needlessly.

"It was written on stationary with the hotel's letterhead, so I would assume he wrote it. I wouldn't recognize the handwriting," Maruch answered a little puzzled at the question. "Why do you ask? You know they got it from the consortium. What difference does it make who actually wrote it."

"I had people keeping tabs on both Sergei's and Toomas' movements and was recently informed both men have disappeared. They suspect they were killed but haven't been able to locate the bodies." "They didn't have to die to disappear." Maruch responded incredulously at Eric's comments. "Let's face it, their part for the next few days is unimportant. The Sheik will be most vulnerable at the news conference, and the assassination would get the best coverage available at the same time. So, we can be reasonably confident, one, if not both men, will make their move tomorrow. Sergei and Toomas probably went underground in anticipation of the fireworks. Consequently, our efforts need to be directed entirely toward stopping the assassination, not locating Sergei and Toomas. There will be plenty of time for that-- after we stop the assassination."

Eric considered her point and decided it was valid, although he wasn't ready to reject the theory of their death solely on her logic. "You're right. Neither of them is necessary anymore, nor they may have chosen to go underground. And if you're right, we, as you said, should concentrate on Manuel and Jacque. Still, it's a possibility we should factor into our thinking." Eric decided to drop the point since it was not critical to the issue at hand.

"If I know Jacque, he'll head out fairly early in the morning to run through his plan a couple times looking for any weaknesses. He's never satisfied until he's certain of its success. If possible, I want to be ready to intercept him before he's ready."

Eric continued explaining to Maruch what he envisioned would happen tomorrow. As he talked, Maruch was finding it difficult to focus on his rambling dialogue. It wasn't that she wasn't interested in what he was saying, because she was. But instead of listening to what he had to say, she found herself staring at him, watching him talk. She was mesmerized by the way his mouth formed the words and the facial expressions he chose to emphasize certain points. She became transfixed, not by what he was saying, but rather by her enjoyment in watching him say it.

Unknown to her, Eric was finding himself in much the same position. He was providing her information that was useless to her in her assignment, but he couldn't stop himself. Neither one of them understood what he was talking about or why. They momentarily lost their focus and were concentrating on each other. Eric's speech had become as much a cover-up for his own feelings as an excuse for Maruch to watch him. In either case, it was accomplishing what they both wanted, A delay to his departure.

They continued like this for some time, he is talking and she listening, neither of them able to bring the conversation to a close. Eventually, Eric ran out of things to say, and the silence quickly enveloped them. Both wanted to continue but couldn't find the words to say. It was not natural for them to feel this way in the midst of a crisis, they reasoned. Except the needs of the human experience were seldom dictated purely by the circumstances one finds oneself in. And Eric and Maruch were painfully aware of this fact.

They were not in the position to develop a relationship because everything they started could end tomorrow and they both knew this.

The futility of investing their time and effort in something that most assuredly would be temporary, was not consistent with the way either of them had lived their lives up to this point. Instead, they should be directing their efforts toward stopping the assassination.

It was this thought that seemed to strike them at the same time. Embarrassed, they turned their eyes from each other, suddenly self-conscious of what was happening. Eric got up from his seat and started for the door. Maruch did the same. Neither spoke.

At the door, Eric stopped and turned to face Maruch. Maruch looked up just in time to keep from bumping into him, stopping inches from him. Their eyes met, Eric looking down ever so slightly into her eyes, and she is looking up into his. It seemed natural and expected that he should lean forward and kiss her on the forehead. She responded by raising her arms and wrapping them around his shoulders and returning his kiss with one of her own.

Unaccustomed to their newfound passions for each other, they parted slowly. Maruch started to speak, but Eric touched her mouth with his finger as if to say it was best left unsaid. Then they released each other, and Eric was gone.

Maruch was disappointed, yet happy, that for the moment, nothing else happened. She was not ready for something like this, and she knew it. She was certain it could only lead to bitter disappointment. Their paths had crossed, not out of the natural occurrence of events, but rather the unnatural occurrence of a sinister plot. Although, he seemed open to new ideas and concepts much different from his own, he could not possibly accept her Jewish way.

For him to understand and accept her view of life, which had been founded on a constant struggle for existence in a society that could only see evil in her heritage, was more foreign to him than anything he had ever experienced or even read about. He could not possibly appreciate the racism that she dealt with daily, because his knowledge base would, at best, be founded on the black experience in America: A poor substitute. An experience that was relegated to pockets of history in various regions of the world, and centered in the United States, but no comparison to Jewish experience. Black racism derived its strength from the perceived superiority of one race over another. A fact that could be combated because it was founded in the false belief that there was scientific justification for that superiority. That was not true in the case of the Jewish race. The enmity was not founded on some perceived scientific fact, but rather jealousy or pure hatred.

Blacks never suffered the attempts of some to destroy their race, but the Jew had. Blacks had never been rounded up, based solely on the basis of race, and summarily executed en masse, but the Jew had. Blacks had never had their cultural and religious center under siege, then captured and finally destroyed, but the Jew had. No people had been so uniformly hated throughout time for no rational reason as the Jew had. No, Maruch reasoned, Eric could not possibly understand what loving her could mean. It was best that it ends before it was allowed to start.

- - - - -

Eric moved through the early morning haze so carefully it was scarcely disturbed as he passed through the moisture hanging in the air. He spent the night perched on a chair at the window of a room directly across the street from Jacque's room. As the first light of the day began to chase the darkness away, Eric decided to reposition himself closer to his quarry and moved to the street. He briefly considered making his move on Jacque last night, but respecting Jacque's sense for self-preservation, he decided his best chance would be when Jacque was preoccupied. That preoccupation would be greatest in the last minutes before his attempt on the Sheik's life.

A light came on in Jacque's room, marking the beginning of what might prove to he the most critical day in his life. Eric concluded, right or wrong, that the bombing of the Air France flight was a diversionary tactic of some sort. Most likely to divide Eric's attention and cause Sergei and Toomas to tip their hand. It was clear that the intended target could not possibly have been on that flight regardless of who it was. At that point, Oman 2's final evaluation was still in the future. The resulting confusion and media attention caused the police around the world to concentrate on terrorist groups and their motives. The Sheik was not considered a target, effectively removing the authorities from the equation.

Add to this the fact that Steve, a top-flight agent, albeit somewhat new, who should have had the element of surprise in his favor, was killed too easily. There was no indication that any type of struggle preceded his death. It is unlikely that Manuel could have escaped without injury, unless he was waiting, prepared to spring a trap on Steve. It is more likely that he set Steve up by preparing a fake assassination, giving himself the upper hand. If he were caught in the act, he would not have been able to kill Steve so neatly, Eric surmised. He knew this was the day, and it was up to Maruch and himself to make sure it was like any other day in Jerusalem: Hot, dry, and boring.

The light went off in Jacque's room, so Eric prepared for Jacque to come out of the building. They were maybe a mile from the Temple Mount, on a narrow side street, just off of Jericho Rd. With the narrow streets and the buildings so close together, it was going to be difficult to follow Jacque without exposing himself. As Jacque came out, Eric slid back into the alcove of the entryway he was standing nearby. Once outside, Jacque turned left heading toward Jericho Rd. Eric waited for him to get a safe distance ahead, then took off in the same direction.

At Jericho Rd. Jacque turned right making his way toward the Temple Mount. Eric continued to follow at a distance; thankful Jacque chose a main thoroughfare, which allowed him the luxury of increasing the distance between them, while still keeping him in sight. As they worked their way toward the Holy Places that captured the imaginations of such a wide variety of people, Jew, Moslem, and Christian alike, the activity on the street steadily increased. It grew to the point that on a number of occasions Eric almost lost Jacque, something he could ill afford to do.

Before Jacque reached the entrance to the Old City, he turned off Jericho Rd. onto a side street. Eric hurried to the corner afraid he would lose Jacque, but as he looked down the street, he was able to make out Jacque as he disappeared around a bend in the road. Eric picked up his pace, so he was almost running. A few people stopped to stare as he hurried past them, but for the most part they passed him off as an out of place tourist.

At the bend, Eric slowed his pace to a quick walk until he saw Jacque head into a tall building on the right. Eric immediately slowed to a normal walking pace. As he approached the building, he looked for any other entrances and was rewarded by spotting a side entrance. During his review he wasn't able to determine what the building was used for. There were no markings or signs on the outside of the building to provide Eric any insight into what he might be entering. Regardless, Eric knew he would have to follow Jacque inside. This may prove to be the best time to stop Jacque. If he could neutralize Jacque before the news conference, he might be able to get to Maruch in time to help her. He decided the side entrance offered the best choice and was pleased to find the door unlocked.

Inside there was almost no light. While Eric waited for his eyes to adjust to the low light, he removed his pistol from it's resting place inside the calf holster. While he was doing that, he heard someone move. He paused to listen, but everything was still again. By now his eyes were adjusted to the low light and he was able to make out the general shape of the room he was in. It was a small vestibule size room with three exits into other areas of the building. None of the exits had doors on them.

He approached one and looked through it into a hallway. The doorway on the wall directly opposite also opened into a hallway. The third doorway, across from the entrance to the building, led into a large, completely empty room. Staring into the room, he could barely make out another doorway in the center of the wall on his left.

He considered for a moment the layout out he had just seen. A large room bounded by a hallway on one side with a doorway at the front of the building. If Jacque came into the room, he would have to exit into the room Eric was presently standing in. Eric decided to follow the hallway on his left that led toward the front of the building. As he started down the hall, he heard something again but couldn't be sure where it was coming from. The sound was simply too muffled and too far away.

The hallway went straight for twenty feet, then turned right. Ten more feet, and it opened into a vestibule like room identical to the one he just left, including the three doorways. The door on his left led outside at the front of the building and could only be locked manually from the inside. The one directly across from it opened into the large empty room. Eric's eyes were completely acclimated to the low light by now, and he could clearly make out the doorway across the room on the right wall that led to the vestibule he just came from.

Eric looked through the last doorway and was not surprised to see it led to another hallway. Again, he could hear something, only this time it was clearly coming from the hallway he was about to enter. He stepped through the doorway and made his way to the corner. He pressed himself against the wall, then slowly brought his head around the corner until he could see down the hall. Halfway down the hall was a staircase leading up to the second floor.

There was no one to be seen, so Eric started down the hall toward the stairs. If Jacque heard him coming now and appeared at the top of the steps, he would make a perfect unobstructed target. He shook the thought from his mind, then continued to the stairs. He positioned the handgun at chest level pointed upward, poised to aim and shoot. Moving forward slowly, he relied on instinct to take over when necessary. At the steps he paused again to listen for any sounds. Now it was clear that someone, Jacque, was upstairs moving around.

Eric started up the steps, carefully testing each one with his weight, listening for any creaks. If the step started to creak, he would place his foot in a different location and try again. If he couldn't find any spot on that step that wouldn't creak, he would try the next one up. After fifteen steps he came to a landing with a door on his right. By this time Eric was able to determine the sounds he was hearing were on the next level up. He assumed the next level was the last level, but it was too dark to make out if the stairs ended at that point.

Knowing errors of omission resulted in premature death in this business; Eric pressed his ear to the door. He slowly twisted the doorknob, then quietly pushed the door. It moved a fraction of an inch before it stopped. The door was obviously locked. Eric knew there was no way to be sure it was empty, so he proceeded with renewed caution. He moved away from the door and started his climb to the next level. Progress was painstakingly slow, but with each step, he was confident he was getting closer to Jacque.

Eric would pause at each step, listening for any indication that Jacque might hear him coming up the steps. After another ten steps, he began to suspect the top floor contained more than one room because the sounds coming from the other side of the wall were too muffled for a single wall. Eric finished his climb of the last five steps, finally reaching the top platform. Again, there was a door on his right. But previously unknown to him because he couldn't have seen it until now, was a half door that led through the wall directly in front of him. Eric considered it's significance for a moment then tried the door on his right.

He twisted the doorknob slowly. When he had turned it as far as it would go, he gently pushed the door and was rewarded to find it was unlocked. He was pleased at this because the previous door was locked with a deadbolt. He learned long ago there was no way to unlock them quietly. He would have given up the element of surprise breaking open a locked door, something he could ill afford to do with Jacque so close.

He opened the door just a crack and looked inside. This offered no clues to what was inside. He continued to open the door until he could squeeze through the opening and stepped inside. The room was considerably smaller than the one on the first floor, but it was just as empty. He made his way to the only other door in the room and started the process all over again. When he opened that door, he was surprised to learn it was an empty closet. While he was evaluating this new information, he heard a noise on the other side of the wall. He paused, listening to the sounds to see if they would give any clues to what was happening on the other side. When they stopped, he returned his attention to the closet.

He looked carefully at the walls of the closet again but could not see even a hint of an opening. He stepped inside the closet and started feeling the far wall when it suddenly dawned on him: This was an outside wall. The trap door at the top of the steps probably opened onto the roof. Jacque was outside getting setup right now. He looked at his watch and was surprised to see it was already 11:30. The news conference was scheduled for one, so he still had plenty of time, but time was slipping past faster than he expected.

Eric quietly made his way back to the stairway. Carefully, he started to push the trap door open, but it caught on something, and he stopped pushing. There was nothing he could do from this side to dislodge the door except push harder, so he did. Gradually he increased the force against the door until it gave way. Eric hung on desperately to the door, trying to keep it from slamming open, and managed to stop it just before it hit the wall. In his desperation to keep hold of the door, he lost his balance and fell to the roof. As he fell to the roof, he let go of the door and it slammed against the wall.

He relaxed and allowed himself to fall as soon as he realized there was no stopping it. He hit the roof, rolled, and came up with both hands on his pistol, ready to fire at anything that moved. It was silent. Eric knew Jacque was here, and now Jacque knew he was here as well. But his advantage was lost by the trap door, because now Jacque knew where Eric was, giving him the upper hand. Eric quickly evaluated his position and his alternatives. He dove for a vent just as a bullet hit the roof where he had been crouching.

Eric looked back at where he suspected the bullet came from and saw the glean of shiny metal as a pistol was pull back from the roof above the trap door. He continued to watch the spot where he saw the gun disappear and was pleased to see it reappear for a moment, confirming Jacque's location. For the next two minutes, there was nothing. No movement. No reappearance of the gun. And no hint of Jacque. Eric knew he just regained a small advantage, even though he was considerably more exposed than Jacque. He knew that sooner or later Jacque would have to make the first move. For the first time during this whole escapade, Eric could afford to wait for something to happen. As long as he stayed here, Jacque couldn't do anything.

It became a waiting game and eventually Eric would be rewarded. Jacque moved down the roofline to a protrusion off the roof that would offer him a limited amount of protection. However, in order to go on the offensive, he would have to lean forward enough to expose the upper portion of his body and that was exactly what he did. Eric waited for a clear shot at the left center of Jacque's chest, then fired. He heard the cling of the lead as it ricocheted off the gun, then saw the pistol drop to the roof.

Jacque noticed Eric poised to shoot just before Eric squeezed the trigger. He recoiled in time to keep from getting hit but did not get his hand out of the line of fire soon enough. Eric watched as a bloody hand tried to retrieve the pistol before it fell to the roof below. Most people would gain some level of comfort in knowing they wounded their adversary, but Eric knew from experience that Jacque was every bit the same formidable opponent wounded or not.

Eric decided this was his chance. He got up and started running toward the ladder to the upper roof. As he approached the ladder, he saw a shadow on the roof directly in front of him rise up to twice his size. The shadow seemed to take flight, then Eric realized what was happening and fell to the side. Jacque timed and aimed his jump to land square in the middle of Eric's back, but Eric's evasive move resulted in both men glancing off the other with no clear advantage.

Eric tucked and rolled, coming up with his gun pointed at Jacque. But Jacque was prepared for that move and Eric felt the sting of Jacque's foot as it landed on his hand and watched helplessly as the gun flew, skidding along the roof surface, then drop off the eave. Eric went on the offensive, trying not to let Jacque enjoy his newfound equality.

Twisting and turning Eric brought his right foot up in a high arc that ended against Jacque's face. Initially, Jacque's head snapped back, but he allowed the rest of his body to absorb the remainder of the blow and was able to retain consciousness as he fell to the side. His left hand hit the roof first in an attempt to take control of his body, but this was the hand that had taken the bullet. It immediately gave out under the weight of his falling body.

With Jacque lying on the roof, Eric went for the kill. Jacque had collapsed face down on the roof, and Eric targeted the back of his neck. Just as the side of Eric's hand came crashing down to where Jacque was, he managed to roll to the side causing Eric to miss. At the same time, he rolled he lifted himself slightly off the surface of the roof with his good hand, then pivoted his whole body toward Eric's legs. He caught Eric just as he straightened up, midway between the ankle and knee. Eric crumpled to the roof.

Jacque jumped up prepared to attack again, but Eric had already regained his footing. Jacque made one last desperate lunge at Eric, fearing the battle was already lost. He was losing too much blood from the bullet wound, and he knew he was weakening from the loss of blood. Compounding his predicament, Eric was successfully countering every move he made and suffering almost no damage. If he wasn't successful this time, the battle would be lost. So, he lunged with every ounce of energy his weakened body could muster.

Eric sidestepped Jacque's futile attempt and with his shoulder knocked Jacque to the roof. Jacque lay on his back dazed and hurt. With lightening speed, Eric hit Jacque just below the Adam's apple with his extended fingers. Jacque gurgled momentarily, then exhaled for the last time. It was finished.

Eric didn't feel the exhilaration he expected to feel from winning. In the past he would have enjoyed the rush of adrenaline that accompanied the battle and final defeat of his opponent. But now, as he knelt next to Jacque's lifeless body, he was filled with emptiness, a hollow, depressing lack of emotion. No comfort in the joy of victory was forthcoming. No fulfillment in having stopped a hired killer. In completing his assignment. No pleasure in gaining revenge for his wife's murder. Eric was a different person and was only beginning to realize that now.

They say that once one reaches adulthood, values and personalities become as permanent as stone. That changing one's viewpoint is as difficult and unlikely as returning to one's childhood. Only a truly traumatic experience can effectively change that value system. Eric lived that trauma for the last eighteen months, and its effect was never more evident. What he used to enjoy, now caused him to feel like a pariah.

Slowly Eric came out of his funk and started searching Jacque's body. He didn't really know why or what he was looking for, but he felt compelled to do it. While flipping through Jacque's passport, he couldn't help but reminisce at the names of various locations he spotted. As he closed the passport in anticipation of taking it with him, a piece of paper slid out from between its pages. He set the passport down and taking the paper unfolded it. As he read the words a tear formed at the corner of his eye, something that had not happened since he was seven. He read.

Eric,

If you are reading this paper, it is only because I am dead. I have regretted few things in my life but separating from you and accidentally killing your wife are two I truly do regret. I am sorry she died. It was an accident. If I could have known she would be there, I would have stopped it. I am sorry mon amie.

Jacque

Folding the paper again, Eric placed it back inside the passport, then slid the passport into his pocket. He dragged Jacque's body over to the wall and propped it up against the wall as if Jacque were sitting there, thinking. It painted the proper picture of Jacque, Eric thought. He approached everything as an exercise in learning, and now he would finally have the time to think things through completely.

He retrieved Jacque's gun from the roof above, then said good-bye to his old friend and left. Back down on the street, he walked around the corner of the building and located his own gun that had fallen to the ground during the struggle. It was time to find Maruch and help her if there was still time. Eric looked at his watch. It was five to one. The news conference was about to start.

- - - - -

Sheik Omani changed from his flowing Arab attire to a decidedly western look. Never one to settle for the mundane, he was wearing a seven-hundred-dollar suit and the latest in power accessories. The image he was trying to present to any that might see him or think they recognize him, was one of conspicuous and inappropriate, wealth. He had every intention of viewing the news conference from the audience, and this was how he planned to get away with it. Sylvan had tried to talk him into watching it from the hotel room, but he would have none of that. He wanted to evaluate firsthand how the people reacted to his pronouncement and his own assassination. He felt it might give him an advantage sometime in the future. Even though they would be taping the whole thing on four different stations, and he would have ample time to review that perspective at his leisure, he still wanted to feel firsthand the excitement.

"Sheik," Sylvan began as soon as he entered the room. "I have arranged for a bodyguard while you are out and about today. We will not take the risk that something happens to you during the news conference, particularly after the assassination. No one knows for sure how the crowd will react. If they riot, we'll need someone to make sure you get out of there safely. I reviewed this with Harold, and he agreed. He said you either accept the bodyguard, or I'm to use whatever force is necessary to hold you in your room." Sylvan paused long enough to allow everything to sink in, then asked. "What will it be?"

Sheik Omani was not surprised by this demand. If the truth were known, he was expecting it. He knew they couldn't risk something happening to him. He was still an integral part of their plan, even if he wasn't going to be Sheik Omani for the next few days. Resigned to the inevitable, "I can accept your bodyguard." He said.

"Good," was all Sylvan replied as he left the bedroom to answer the door. A few seconds later, he returned with a huge Arab in tow. Pointing at Sheik Omani he said to the Arab, "This is the man you are to protect. I expect both of you back here no later than three this afternoon. Do you understand?" Sylvan was looking directly into the Sheik's eyes when he asked this last question.

The huge Arab simply answered, "yes," oblivious to the undertones of the conversation.

Continuing to look at Sheik Omani, Sylvan asked. "It is getting late. Is there anything else I can do for you before I leave?"

The Sheik just shook his head no.

The huge Arab shook his head no as well, but no one was watching him. Sylvan was already on his way out the door.

- - - - -

Maruch did not sleep very well after Eric left. It wasn't just her concern for his well being that made sleeping difficult; it was also her concern that they would somehow fail in stopping the assassination. She was not convinced that Eric fully understood the importance of this assignment, although she felt confident, he would not allow anything to interfere with his efforts. For her, the importance of succeeding was founded in her Jewish nationalism. Eric, on the other hand, didn't have that to rely on. He would have to get his inner drive from some other passion.

Once up, Maruch wasted little time traveling to Manuel's hotel. The night before she'd briefly contemplated renting a room there and staying the night but decided against it because she was afraid it would have affected her sleep. As it turned out, her sleep was affected regardless.

The hotel was on the outside, northwest corner, of the remnants of the old city's wall. She decided to work her way through the already thickening crowd to the Temple Mount steps to evaluate firsthand the line-of-sight Manuel would have from his hotel room. When she reached the top of the steps, she was surprised to find out that Manuel would not have a clear view of them. The window of his hotel room barely reached above the wall and now a temporary structure inside the wall completely blocked off the view of the Temple Mount steps. Consequently, the window in his room offered him no visibility whatsoever. Maruch reasoned the newfound obstruction was probably needed by the news media in their effort to cover the press conference.

Maruch took the opportunity to look around from the Temple Mount steps and made mental notes of the various buildings that could be used by Manuel. There were only four on the west side, and near as she could tell, just two on the east side. She panned the perimeter again but came to the same conclusion. Satisfied, she started making her way back to the hotel. She hoped Manuel had not left the hotel yet, but she knew that was unlikely. Once he realized he could no longer use it for the assassination, he would start looking for alternatives.

In the time Maruch spent inside the city walls the crowd had grown considerably. As she worked her way through, she was impressed with the wide variety of nationalities she encountered. Contrary to accepted thought in the western world, Jerusalem was probably the most international city she had ever been in. No matter which direction she looked, there seemed to be people of all nationalities mingling together, giving life to the city like blood pulsing through veins.

Granted Arab and Jew were predominant, but white Anglo-Saxons were scattered throughout the crowd in a fairly large number as well. Europeans and North Americans blended together making identification impossible without hearing them speak. They were obviously interested not only in the ruins representing their own Christian faith, but also historical artifacts that were typically revered singularly by Muslim or Jew.

Blacks in business suits walked beside their brothers in African native dress. Orientals representing a base from Mongolia to Japan, Korea to Micronesia, all speaking languages that Maruch could not discern any difference between. Those of Spanish or Latin descent were represented as well, although their variation in speech was as wide ranging as Italian to Spanish to English. Indians from both Americas and Southwest Asia, cultures worlds apart that shared the same name. Rare is the city that can claim a cultural interest as broad based as Jerusalem has, she thought.

She exited the walls of the old city and turned west heading toward the hotel. As she approached the hotel, she saw Manuel and stepped to the side just beyond the stream of pedestrians to watch him. He came out the front door and immediately turned in her direction. She waited for him to pass, then stepped in behind him. She maintained a slightly slower pace, allowing the crowd to build the distance between them. When she was satisfied she could follow him undetected, she picked up her speed to match his.

Maruch was surprised to follow him back into the old city. She expected he would have already made his choice of buildings, but it was clear by his actions he had not. Maruch held back as she saw him make his way up the Temple Mount steps. Manuel was not allowed access to the very top steps because the construction crew had included it in the area cordoned off for the temporary stage, even though the stage was be erected to the side of the Temple Mount. An area roughly ten times the size of the stage had been included in the restricted area, creating some rather interesting traffic patterns in the crowd milling about.

Manuel accepted his limitations and started looking around like Maruch had earlier in search of his alternatives. Within a few minutes it was clear he had found what he wanted as he started down the steps. She waited for him to pass and again slid in behind to follow him careful to allow the crowd between them to build up providing adequate cover. Manuel returned to the hotel and disappeared inside. Maruch waited out front, confident he would reappear momentarily and head to his new location.

The first few minutes went by without Maruch giving it a second thought. After fifteen minutes, she was beginning to question why it would be taking him so long and started making plans to go inside. At thirty minutes she couldn't wait any longer and started for the front door of the hotel.

Inside the hotel, she went to the front desk, gave the clerk a description of Manuel, and handed him a fifty shekel note. The clerk checked, then came back and told her what room he was in and pointed to the stairway. After Maruch disappeared up the steps, the clerk picked up the phone and made a short call.

When Maruch reached the top of the steps she hesitated. Looking around the corner, she peered down the narrow hallway to see if it was empty. The hallway was barely thirty inches wide, and the floor was made of six-inch-wide wood floorboards with a worn out and faded purple runner down the center. She placed her first foot in the center of the hallway and started to shift her weight to that foot. The floor started to groan. She moved her foot to another spot and tried again.

She tested each step before she would fully shift her weight to that leg, slowly working her way down the hall.

Manuel's room was the last one on the left. She passed two doors on each side of the hall, and there was one more on the right at the end of the hall. She pressed her ear to the door of Manuel's room. Nothing. She removed a piece of wire she had taped to her side under her arm and started to work the lock. Before opening the door, she re-taped the wire to her side.

Carefully she twisted the doorknob to the left when it encountered resistance she pushed the door to open it. It wouldn't open. Carefully, she twisted the doorknob to the right. Again, when she felt resistance, she stopped turning and pushed gently against the door. It started to open. She was at the mercy of the hinges now. There was no way for her to stop any creaking, but she didn't have to. Just before the door was open wide enough for her to squeeze through the opening, the hinge began a high-pitched squeak. Maruch stopped momentarily, then burst through the door. If she couldn't enter silently, she would need to startle Manuel as much as possible she decided.

Inside she found what she feared most but least expected. Manuel sat at the window, facing the door with a rifle lying across his lap. He raised the rifle and pointed it at Maruch as she came to a stop at the foot of the bed.

Manuel tossed her a dirty piece of cloth. "Cover your mouth and tie this behind your head. Or open your mouth and die," he added. He smiled at his last comment, showing her a mouth full of yellow and black, half rotted teeth.

Maruch did as she was instructed, then Manuel got up from his seat and started walking over to her.

- - - - -

Eric thought it would be quicker entering the court from the south side and cutting across diagonally to the opposite corner rather than walking all the way around the perimeter, but shortly after he was inside, he realized he had made a mistake. The crowd inside was unbearable. It was worse than anything he had ever experienced before. The mass of humanity stretched as far as he could see, and once inside it, it seemed to take on a life of its own.

He had only ventured into the crowd a few layers deep when he realized he'd made a mistake and tried to turn around. Try as he might, he couldn't even change directions! He was being forced deeper into the crowd and there was nothing he could do. He tried to find the stage, but the best he could do was see the top of the dome on the Mosque. Resigning himself to the crowd's wishes, he allowed it to slowly carry him to its center, nearer to the Dome. As he was carried further into the depths of the crowd, he noticed he was able to begin making out what the speaker was saying even though he still could not see who it was.

He looked at his watch. It was already quarter after one. It should be Sheik Omani speaking he thought, but he could tell by the voice it wasn't. He listened to the speaker as the crowd continued to move him closer. Soon he realized it was the mayor of Jerusalem's voice, and he was in the middle of his introduction of the Sheik. The introduction went on for another fifteen minutes, or more accurately the Sheik's life story went on for another fifteen minutes. The mayor never had this many people attend any function he was involved with before, and he had every intention of staying in front of the audience as long as he could.

During his drift in this sea of bodies, Eric noticed a subtle current had developed that carried people more quickly toward the center. Eric decided to concentrate his efforts on getting into the flow of that current in the hope it would propel him toward the stage. He began applying increasing amounts of pressure to the people around him in the direction he wanted to go. As he did this, he realized not only was he moving more quickly, but he actually could take control of his destiny, and when necessary, move against the crowd.

Eric continued this approach, and was finally rewarded by catching the current, and accelerating his progress substantially. Shortly he was able to make out the stage. The mayor was standing at a cluster of microphones near the center of the stage. Behind him were five chairs, his empty one was in the center bracketed by the other four. Sheik Omani was seated immediately to the right of the center chair. Next to him was Doshe, representing the Zealots. To the left of the mayor's empty chair were Jihad Nadu and Jerome Bechard. Far to the right of the stage, near a curtain, was Sylvan. Eric assumed Sylvan was standing next to the curtain because it led to a stairway off the stage.

By this time Eric found himself directly in front of the stage, a mere twenty feet away from the front of it. At this point he felt himself start to circle back away from the stage. He was slowly being carried, in a human eddy current, away from the stage and back toward the direction he came from. Looking around, he saw a similar movement in the crowd, but rotating in the opposite direction, maybe ten feet away. Recognizing this for the opportunity it was, he began to press toward it. He applied the lesson he learned earlier: the proper pressure applied to the bodies around him would cause them to part, allowing him to move in a specific direction.

Progress came painfully slow, but eventually he managed to break from the current carrying him away from the stage and started making progress toward the one heading in the direction he wanted to go. Without warning he reached a point between the two crowd currents, like the eye of a storm, and came to a complete stop. He could see where he wanted to go, but he no longer was moving toward it. He looked back at where he had been and noticed he was centered exactly between the two currents.

Realizing he had to try something drastic to jar himself loose, he jammed his elbow into a man standing next to him. This innocent bystander was appropriately disturbed, and blindly lashed out at no one in particular. Shortly, the small stable area of people trapped between the two currents became the center of activity. Although the area itself still could not move, people inside this small island of humanity began to exchange positions with each other. Eric used this opportunity to move to the river of people he was trying to join. As he stepped into the current and began moving away from the crowds natural center, he looked back at the disruption he had caused, and was amazed to see it was already back to normal. Once again, the people in the center were motionless, being held in place by the river of bodies coming at them from both sides.

Eric realized he was running out of time and began pressing harder against the crowd trying to increase his speed. There was nothing to prevent Manuel from shooting the Sheik while he waited for the mayor to finish speaking, he thought. Every little while he would glance back at the Sheik as if his watchful eye could somehow protect him. The crowd never did thin as he expected it would, but suddenly he burst through an opening and found himself outside the outer court walls.

Eric looked around to get his bearings, then began searching for the hotel Maruch said Manuel was staying at. Once he located it, he started running. As he approached the hotel, he scanned the side of the building that would offer Manuel his shot and noticed three windows. Eric assumed each window would equate to a room for rent and he would have to check out all three to find Manuel.

His first stop was at the front desk. "I would like a room with a view of the Temple Mount," he began. The clerk gave him a quizzical look making it clear he had no idea what Eric was saying. Eric thought for a moment, then began to pantomime his request in hope that he could communicate this way.

Eric removed a bundle of bills from his pocket, waved it in front of the clerk, then pretended to sleep by laying his head on his hands. The clerk nodded his understanding and started opening a drawer to get Eric a room key. Eric hit the counter hard with his open hand to regain the man's attention. He looked up a little startled, but motioned for Eric to continue. Next Eric put his hand above his eyes to protect them from the sun and pretended to be looking at something far away. Then he stopped, turned to face the direction he thought the Mosque was in, extended his arms and acted as if he were going to pray.

Eric looked up at the clerk and was disappointed to see a blank stare. The clerk looked directly into Eric's eyes and waved both hands as if to say, no more, then reached into the drawer and removed a room key. He motioned for Eric to show him the money again, and when he did, he removed what he needed, and showed Eric one finger. Eric interpreted that to mean one day then started looking for the way to the room. The clerk used Eric's trick to get his attention by slamming his open hand on the counter. When Eric looked, the clerk pointed the way to the stairway.

Eric hurried over to the steps and began climbing, oblivious to any creaks. He'd spent less than ten minutes with the clerk, but by getting a room he'd managed to narrow Manuel's location down to two rooms. Now the somewhat more difficult task of selecting the correct room out the remaining two was left. At the top of the steps, Eric stopped to listen for any sound that might give Manuel's location away. But the persistent hum of the crowd outside the building was drowning out any normal movement or conversations.

Eric carefully evaluated the hall. There were three doors on the left side of the narrow hall, and a fourth door at the far end on the right. He looked at his key, a 204 that had originally been pressed into the surface was barely visible. 200 was the room number on the first door. He moved to the door and pressed his ear to it. There was no sound whatsoever.

Wanting to be absolutely sure, he picked the lock and started opening the door. As he did this, he removed his gun, and prepared to fire at the first sign of movement. He looked into the empty room and immediately started memorizing the position of everything in the room. He figured this information would be valuable when he located Manuel. The window was just to the left of the bed; it was a typical 1940's style wooden double hung window. Walking over to it, he noticed the window opened directly to the outside. Nothing was in the way, no screens, or storms. This would make an ideal location to shoot a high-powered rifle from, he thought. Manuel made an excellent choice.

He stood at the window for a minute and watched the proceedings going on down on the stage. Sheik Omani had replaced the Mayor of Jerusalem, and it appeared he was in the middle of introducing Jerome Bechard of the Christian Liberation Front. Although there was a speaker not more than one hundred feet in front of him, it was facing the crowd and the sound was too distorted for him to understand what was being said. Eric moved the bed stand, then leaned out the window and looked down the outside wall for the windows of the two remaining rooms. The one he had rented and the one Manuel, and probably Maruch were in. Approximately twenty feet of wall separated each window, but from this angle, he could not see if the next window was open. Since his room key put him in room 204, and he was in 200 right now, he expected Manuel would be in the next room.

Eric pulled himself back inside and looked around the room again. There was a cheap picture on the wall opposite the window with a small writing desk below it. A plain table lamp with a dust encrusted cloth lampshade the sole item on the top of the desk. The single bed had matching bed stands against the wall on both sides. It was safe to assume Manuel would move the bed stand to give him clear access to the window, just as Eric had done when he wanted to lean out the window a moment ago. With the room's layout etched in his mind, Eric could plan his entrance.

On the left wall as he entered the room was another door. Eric walked over to it and opened it to look inside. As expected, it was the bathroom. There was enough room for a small shower stall and the commode, but nothing else. He walked back to the bed and removed the sheet. He took one last look around the room, then returned to the hall.

Quietly he stole down the hall to next the room. As he was passing the door, he glanced at the room number expecting to see 202, simply wanting to confirm that fact. 204 was the number he read. Leave it to an Arab to screw-up the simplest things, he thought. He decided to keep going and check the number on the last door. He was not surprised to see it read 210. Must have got them on sale, he reasoned, and returned to the center room.

He patiently picked the lock. Once inside, he headed straight over to the window, opened it and looked down the wall to the room Manuel should be in, then looked up to the eave. He went to the bed and removed the sheets like he had from the last room. Satisfied, he left the room. Instead of going to room 210, he went to the door on the right side of the hall and tried it. It was unlocked. He opened the door and found what he expected; stairs leading up. There was no light in the stairwell, so it became pitch black when he closed the door behind himself.

He climbed the stairs as quickly as he could, but each one had it's own special squeak, and it took some time to find a safe place to step. At the top, he tried opening the door and discovered why the last one was unlocked. With his experience at picking locks, he knew not being able to see anything wouldn't be a problem. Five minutes went by, and he still hadn't unlocked the door. Every time it felt like he had unlocked it, he would try the door only to find out he hadn't.

He decided there must be a deadbolt lock as well and started feeling the edge of the door, from the doorknob to the top. Six inches above the doorknob he found the problem, a latch. After unlatching the door, he opened it and immediately had to cover his eyes from the bright sunlight. After his eyes became accustomed to the sun, he checked the door and was somewhat relieved to find it had a lock and he had not wasted his time picking it. It also had the latch that was all.

Eric closed the door, then walked over to the edge of the roof. He located the window to the room Manuel was in and leaned over the edge to see if the window was open. It was. Straightening back up, he walked back over to where he threw the sheets on the roof. He picked one up and started tearing it in one-foot-wide strips the length of the sheet. He did this to all four sheets, then started tying them together. He did this until he had a rope four sheets thick and about twenty feet long which he secured to the hinge on the door. He tested it, then started working his way down the wall, careful to hang on to the excess.

As he neared the window, he could begin to make out sounds of movement inside the room. He stopped, holding himself just above the top of the window and listened. There was definitely a struggle going on inside the room, but it certainly wasn't a conventional one. Deciding he may not have a more opportune time to interrupt, Eric prepared to drop in. He looked down at the open half of the double hung window---It was four feet below and if he timed it perfectly and had equally perfect aim, he could pop right through the window.

Eric gathered up four feet of the sheet, then slowly started easing himself down. The surface of the building was very similar to stucco, giving him excellent footing. At the very edge of the window frame, he prepared to push off and swing down through the window, then stopped. The footing on the edge of the building had given him another idea. Figuring the struggle would be in the open area of the room, he scaled over the wall to the side of the window, opposite the bed, and started letting himself down again. He wasn't ready for what he saw through the window.

Inside, Maruch was tied to the bed, each arm extended to a corner of the bed and secured there. Her blouse, although still on, was wide open and her bra had been ripped open. A gag had been stuffed in her mouth, effectively keeping her from making more than just grunts for sounds. Looking down her body, he saw Manuel struggling to remove her pants, but Maruch's legs were flailing wildly making the task very difficult. He had gotten them down to the middle of her thighs but was having trouble getting them any further. It was obvious she was not giving up the fight, but Eric knew if he hadn't shown up Manuel's goal would have been reached sooner or later. It was only a matter of time before he succeeded in raping her. Then he would have killed her, something he probably would have enjoyed more than the rape. Just at that moment, Manuel looked up and saw Eric outside the window.

Neither man wasted any time. Eric pushed off and plunged through the open window. At the same time Manuel dropped Maruch's legs and turning toward the desk reached for the rifle he'd set on top of it. Manuel knew the rifle was a mistake the second he picked it up. It wasn't like a handgun that he could just point in the general direction, fire, and afflict some measure of damage on his opponent. The rifle, being longer, and more accurate, would cause him to lose precious milliseconds in his reaction to Eric's attack.

Fortunately, Eric was right in his assumption that the bed stand would be moved, and he was able to slide through the window and hit the floor without any problems. As his feet touched the floor, he added to his momentum by springing forward and dove for Manuel's feet. As he dove, Manuel raised the rifle to where Eric had been and fired. The bullet passed over Eric's back and lodged in the plaster wall behind him. Before Manuel could redirect the rifle, he felt his feet being pulled out from under him and he crashed to the floor. The rifle harmlessly exploded a second time. Manuel relied on brute force, which gave him the advantage in wide-open areas. But Eric based his attacks on his speed, timing and finesse giving him the advantage in the confines of the hotel room.

With Manuel down, Eric scrambled to his feet removing his gun at the same time. Manuel was not ready to concede defeat and kicked up from his position on the floor catching Eric just below the kneecap. Eric's leg gave out and he fell to the floor dropping his gun in the process. A wide toothless grin broke across Manuel's face, because like an animal, he could smell the kill. He walked over to Eric who had grabbed his own leg and was lying on the floor in pain and kicked him in the side. Eric let go of his leg and grabbed his side, then realizing what was happening, started to crawl toward the bed hoping to find some measure of protection underneath it.

Manuel watched as Eric made painfully slow progress toward the bed, and then walked over to where Eric's gun lay on the floor and picked it up. As he turned to face Eric again, he felt a sharp pain in his neck. He reached up to touch it but found the handle of a knife instead. Instinctively he removed it from his neck. Now he saw blood pulsing out in front of him. Confused at what happened, he turned to see Maruch sitting on the bed. He thought to himself 'that was odd,' just before he passed out and fell to the floor in a heap.

Maruch jumped off the bed and picked up the knife. She grabbed Manuel's arm and felt for a pulse. It was there but getting weaker with every beat of the heart. She knelt down, hanging onto his arm, waiting for the pulse to stop, ready at any moment to stab him again, and again, and again if he moved at all. He died with Maruch holding his arm, and a knife hanging in the air above him.

She looked over at Eric, who had managed to crawl halfway under the bed, then dropping the knife, she fell back against the wall. They'd managed to stop the assassination, but not without exacting a huge toll on themselves. Still, they'd stopped it.

"Well, you are not here to listen to me," the mayor of Jerusalem said into the cluster of microphones at the front of the stage. "It is this man," he turned and pointed at Sheik Omani, "that you have come to hear. So, without taking up any more of your time, I present to you, Sheik Omani, the creator of the last peace settlement this region will ever need."

Instead of breaking into a loud, raucous roar as would be expected from a crowd of this size at the Sheik's introduction, the crowd went eerily silent. They had come to hear Sheik Omani tell them of the negotiated peace settlement, and they didn't want to miss a word. Their lives were filled with the constant struggle for survival in an area that had been effectively without peace since man arrived. And it was finally time for that enmity between neighbors to end.

Sheik Omani began by introducing his guests just as he had done at his most recent news conference. First, he called up Jerome Bechard. He presented him to the crowd and offered him the opportunity to speak. Jerome declined the offer, then simply waved to his followers. As he did so, he stepped forward until he was even with Sheik Omani on the stage, taking up his position on the Sheik's right side.

Next, he introduced Jihad Nadu. Jihad remained seated for a few seconds after his introduction. He wanted the full impact of his presence to sink into the minds of his followers; those that were physically here and those that were watching at home on television. Finally, he stood up and crossed the short distance of the stage to the Sheik. Sheik Omani offered him the chance to speak to his followers, but like Jerome, he too declined, choosing to wave instead. Then, making his way to the right of Jerome, he took up his place next to him. As he did, Jerome extended his hand in a symbol of cooperation and unity. Jihad took his hand, and before Jerome could react, he pulled Jerome close. Then leaning forward, greeted him with a kiss. There was a single, loud, uniform, almost orchestrated gasp from the crowd, then silence.

Now it was time to introduce Doshe. Up to this point the news media had been disappointed. They expected an unruly and anxious crowd, one wound so tight that it could explode at any moment. But what they got was just the opposite. Instead, this crowd remained well controlled, essentially quiet except for the sounds of feet shuffling, bodies bumping and that persistent low hum that is present with any large crowd of people no matter how quiet they are.

Following Jerome and Jihad's lead, Doshe waved to the crowd, and then walked over to where they were standing to join them. Again, Jerome extended his hand in greeting, but like Jihad before him, Doshe took the hand and pulling Jerome toward him, greeted him with the traditional kiss reserved for friends and allies. Then he turned toward Jihad who was waiting with open arms. Doshe stepped forward opening his arms, and the two men embraced and kissed each other on their cheeks. The crowd erupted. Finally, the news media was getting what it hoped for, or so it thought.

But instead of the crowd turning violent, they were cheering and shouting, clapping their hands over their heads in celebration. They were pleased with what they were seeing. For the first time in their memory, leaders of all the factions that laid claim to this spot as uniquely holy, were coming together in a peaceful setting. This is what each of them had hoped would happen some day, but never expected it could. The coming together of the de facto leaders in a peace initiative that would allow the masses to stop fighting a war they never wanted in the first place.

This is what separated Sheik Omani from the rest of the world when it came to acting as a mediator: He recognized that the general public was seldom, if ever, the root problem. They were usually ready and willing to trade a peaceful coexistence for almost any reasonable request. It was the leaders of the world, the ones that seldom lost their lives in the fight for their beliefs that were so willing to go to war. They were the ones, like spoiled children, that couldn't or wouldn't accept compromise. And they were the ones that always determined if peace could ever exist in the Middle East. But not today.

Sheik Omani knew this. So, what he had done, with the help of the consortium, was first provide economic pressure, then, through his own power of persuasion, applied social pressure. Between the two, he had forced the leaders to approach the negotiations with the same objective: Resolution of their economic crisis to the equal benefit of all parties.

What the consortium had done was simply reduce purchases of crude oil for their refineries from the troublesome countries. Within a relatively short three months, the contracts reduced the flow of crude oil from the Middle East by fifteen per cent. And with each passing week, the spigot was being turned off a little more. The world as a whole did not actually feel anything, because the consortium had planned for this event and made appropriate plans to protect them from it. Between the reserves they had built up over the last five years and the increased production from their own wells, they easily made up the difference. Their long-term planning would allow them a twenty-five per cent reduction in crude from the Middle East, to last as long as a year, without throwing the rest of the world into an oil shortage.

Once Sheik Omani was able to demonstrate he had the power to hurt them economically, and the guts to use it, it was easy to convince them the true desire of their hearts was peace.

Getting the Israelis and the Christians to agree required different tactics. Neither of them was as dependent on the sale of crude oil to maintain their economic and military strength as their Arab counterparts were. Both, however, relied heavily on purchased refined petroleum products from the consortium. Up until the time the Sheik approached them about the peace proposal, they were not aware of the consortiums strength or how much they actually relied on the consortium's refined products. They too, had to be convinced of the Sheik's willingness to use the economic power at his disposal.

Systematically the purchase contracts from Lebanon, Israel, and the Palestinians were shorted. They were always supplied, but in a slightly reduced quantity. If any of these groups were able to purchase more on the open market, the consortium, through their intelligence network would confirm the purchase, then reduce any shipments by an equal amount. By the time Sheik Omani came around to discuss his peace initiative, there was little need for discussion. All parties concerned felt obligated, for the good of the cause or their country, to negotiate.

Once the negotiations were complete, all that remained was selecting the best representatives for the news conference. At that time, the peace agreement would be explained to the rest of the world. This is where the consortium, with the help of Sylvan and Sheik Omani, demonstrated how well they understood the Middle East. Conventional wisdom would have brought together the heads of state from all the countries in the Middle East, Southwest Asia and northern Africa that were affected, in an attempt to demonstrate unity. Negotiations would commence, but then end abruptly because one side or another would explode at a perceived slight. But these were not the true representatives of the common man, and Sylvan and the Sheik were aware of this.

They knew governments could not ultimately control how the people would accept the news. Those who control the government often trade their own security for the ideals of the people. It becomes an exercise in protecting themselves at the expense of those ideals and the average citizen. The populace, as a whole, has a basic understanding of this, and would not willingly compromise their religious goals without a strong commitment from leaders they respected. Government leaders did not qualify.

In deciding on the three men they had finally chosen, they captured the essence of the three different religions, without conceding to the more radical factions. All three men represented a middle ground between conventional beliefs and more zealous splinter groups. They provided acceptable representation to most people and did not alienate members of faction groups on the fringe. As a result, there was confidence they could control the reactions of the greatest number of people through these three men.

Sheik Omani stood at the cluster of microphones and looked out over the crowd. As far as he could see there were people. Every square foot inside the old city walls was occupied. He continued to look at the crowd, scanning from side to side, quietly drinking in the adulation of the audience. Although each man, woman, or child there, might claim they were here to catch a glimpse of their respective leader, Sheik Omani knew they were here to see him.

- - - - -

Eric was the first one to stir. Although he was still physically exhausted, his desire to watch Sheik Omani address the crowd renewed his spirit enough to get up. As he did, Maruch's eyes opened, and she looked over at him. A smile crossed her face as she realized they were safe. "Is the Sheik alive?" She asked.

"Listen...That sound you don't hear is a riot averted."

Eric stood next to Maruch and taking her hand helped her to stand up. "I..." his voice stopped as her mouth covered his. They kissed long and hard. Not a passionate, lover's kiss, or a prelude of things to come, but rather a kiss that expressed their mutual happiness for the other's survival. When they stopped, it was as if they had transferred an unknown energy force into each other, rejuvenating their tired bodies.

Eric began again, "I think Sheik Omani is about to speak." They walked over to the window, arms around each other's waist, relaxed, and content just to watch. They stood at the window through the introductions. First Jerome. Then Jihad. And finally, the Israeli Doshe. When Jihad and Doshe embraced and greeted each other with a kiss, the crowd gasped in unison.

By now the fog had cleared from Eric's head enough that he found himself, much like Sheik Omani, although for drastically different reasons, scanning the crowd. The crowd's reaction to the kiss was a subtle warning that they were not completely in tune with what was happening, and it triggered Eric's investigative nature. Now he was searching the crowd for anything or anyone that looked even remotely out of place. That feeling of contentment he'd been enjoying just a moment ago was replaced with an overwhelming feeling of impending danger.

Maruch sensed the change in Eric, and while looking at him realized why. She, too, started searching the crowd for anything out of the ordinary. Suddenly the crowd reacted to something that happened on the stage and they both turned to see what it was. Sheik Omani had slumped to the floor of the stage. Sylvan was rushing forward from his position at the back of the stage, followed by four burly looking men dressed in white robes that had burst through the curtains at the first hint of trouble.

As Jerome, Jihad and Doshe surrounded Sheik Omani, shielding him from the eyes of the crowd, Sylvan stepped to the microphone. "Stay calm! Stay Calm!" He raised his hands in an effort to motion the crowd quiet and to allow him to speak. "It is God's responsibility to punish, and man's to endure."

As he continued to speak, Eric searched the perimeter of the crowd for any sign of the assassin. Out of the corner of his eye, he caught an unusually active part of the crowd and began studying their movements closely. It looked like they had someone on the ground and were kicking him. Without saying a word to Maruch, Eric bolted from the window, ran down the hall, taking the steps three at a time, then rushed out into the street.

Eric pushed his way through the crowd that had grown so large; it had spilled outside the walls of the old city. This far back, they still had no idea what was going on. They were completely unaware that Sheik Omani had been shot. The crowd offered little resistance to Eric as he worked his way to the spot in the crowd where he saw the commotion.

As he continued to work his way closer, he could hear Sylvan explaining to the crowd that the Sheik would be alright, "…as a messenger of God, God would not allow him to die…" He was frantically explaining to the crowd that this would have no impact on the peace initiative that the Sheik was presenting to them today. As proof, he offered the words of each of the representatives. Jihad stepped to the microphone first since Palestinians appeared to outnumber everyone else by at least two to one.

Eric didn't listen; he had reached the perimeter of the crowd where he observed what appeared to be kicking. This part of the crowd resisted Eric's initial attempts at penetration, but ultimately Eric worked his way through. As he neared the center it was obvious, they were still kicking whoever was on the ground. He grabbed one of the kickers by the shoulder and muscled his way in.

At the center of the activity lay a bruised and bloody, motionless body. Next to the body was a rifle. Eric knelt down to pick up the rifle but stopped when he realized the people were still kicking the obviously dead body. He yelled one of the few Arabic words he knew, meaning stop, at the crowd. As if on cue, they all stopped. Rather than pick up the rifle, he reached over to the body, which was curled up into the fetal position in a feeble attempt at survival and turned it over to look at the face. Unfortunately, the fury of the crowd around this man had caused them to kick with such hatred, that the face was no longer recognizable. The police, Eric thought, will have an impossible time trying to identify this one.

Looking around on the ground, Eric found some newspaper that had been discarded. He used it to keep his hands from touching the rifle as he picked it up to examine it. He was looking for any identifying marks or unique attributes of the rifle that would provide even the remotest clue to its owner. But it had none. While he did this, the crowd in the immediate vicinity just watched, seemingly hypnotized by his actions. When he was finished, he laid the rifle back on the ground next to the body and began searching through the man's clothes. He found a scrap of paper tucked inside a pocket of the robe, and carefully removed it. Keeping it in the palm of his hand, he took extreme care to ensure that no one watching him could see it.

He continued to search the body but found nothing else. As he stood up, he slid the paper into his pocket in the same motion. He was relieved when no one said anything to him. He looked at the crowd, who continued to watch him in silence, then spoke. "Does anyone here speak English?" He asked the sea of faces staring blankly at him.

A Jewish man that looked to be in his fifties pushed through the edge of the crowd and haltingly said. "Yes, I can speak a little."

Eric removed his U. S. government I. D. card and showed it to the man. "I've been investigating this conspiracy for months," he lied. "I would like to ask just a couple questions. Would you be willing to help interpret?" Befuddled, at first the man acted as if he didn't understand what Eric was saying. But finally, he relented, and haltingly nodded his head.

"Good. Did anyone see the man talking to anyone else?" Eric asked.

The man looked at the crowd, and then repeated the question in Hebrew. Someone else picked up on the question and repeated it a second time in Arabic. Everyone Eric could see shook their head no.

"Did the man say anything?" Eric asked his next question.

Once again, the man repeated the question and after a short pause a second voice could be heard translating it into Arabic. A number of people started to speak at once, then one voice seemed to take control and override the rest. The man's response was translated first to Hebrew, then the older Jewish gentleman translated it to English. "He is credited with saying 'Death to the infidel, Mohammed has spoken.' That was all."

The interpreter added to the explanation, "The man yelled out something I could not understand, but this person tells me this is what he said. I believe him, although I don't know him from Adam and he's obviously an Arab. As soon as the two shots were fired, and we realized Sheik Omani was hurt, we reacted. Unfortunately, we overreacted. Sheik Omani was offering us true peace for once, and we feared this man might have destroyed it by killing him. It was a natural response." The man shrugged his shoulders as if to say, we goofed, I'm sorry.

Eric managed to get to the assassin's location very quickly because he knew exactly where it was. Having seen the commotion from the hotel room, it gave him a distinct advantage over the police. Now the Jerusalem police were about to arrive, so it was time for him to disappear.

The first policeman to arrive, without hesitation, picked up the rifle and started examining it. The next two policemen rolled the body of the assassin on its back and started rummaging through his clothes. It wasn't until the last one arrived that some semblance of investigative skill was evident. He yelled at the three policemen, who were busy destroying any clues they might have found on the body and rifle, to stop what they were doing. But judging by the looks on their faces, he knew he had arrived too late. They'd be lucky to be able to lift fingerprints off the rifle after these buffoons were through, he thought.

He asked the crowd what happened and received a torrent of responses making it impossible to hear or understand any of them. By this time, Eric was already breaking free from the pressing crowd and could see the front door to the hotel where he left Maruch.

13

-You will repay them, O Lord, according to the work of their hands.

Sylvan was able to keep the crowd calm while his four cohorts attended to Sheik Omani. As they started to carry the Sheik to the back of the stage, Sylvan called the three leaders to the microphones. Turning away from the microphones and speaking in a soft but forceful voice, Sylvan began. "Quickly, each of you need to address your people and convince them Sheik Omani will be alright. If you don't, Armageddon will begin right here and now."

The three men looked at each other, then Jihad spoke. "How can I convince them of that, when I am not convinced, myself?"

"I promise you, and you can promise them: Sheik Omani will return to speak to them, in person, by Sunday."

"And if he doesn't?"

"If he doesn't," Sylvan paused for effect. "You'll get a three-day head start on the rest of the world, 'cuz you can be sure all hell's going to break loose if he dies."

The three men looked at each other again. Then slowly Jihad stepped to the microphone and began to speak to the crowd, haltingly at first, but as his confidence grew and his voice strengthened, he saw that the crowd would listen to him. As he spoke, his voice gained the authority that his comrades in the fight for a Palestinian homeland had come to associate with his leadership.

"Today, . . . you have witnessed an act against Mohammed. But Mohammed's revenge is swift and decisive. That man, who perpetrated this abomination against the Sheik, is no longer with us." A roar of approval went up from the crowd, feeding Jihad's confidence. "Mohammed has chosen Sheik Omani to bring peace to his Holy land, and he will not allow any mere mortal to destroy what he has wrought. Sheik Omani will be back." The crowd voiced its approval again at what Jihad said, drowning his next statement. "I have been instructed to inform you, by Mohammed's command, that Sheik Omani will return."

Jihad realized after he finished, that the sound of the crowd's most recent reaction precluded them from hearing his last statement, so he repeated it. "I have been instructed to inform you, by Mohammed's command, that Sheik Omani will return." Contrary to Jihad's expectation, the crowd went silent.

As if on cue, a lone voice from the crowd cried out, "How do you know this? Did Mohammed speak to you personally?"

"I will stake my life on it. Sheik Omani will present himself for your review, no later than Sunday." As the words left his lips, Jihad was convinced he would regret his outburst. But Sheik Omani managed where everyone before him had failed, he tried to reassure himself. First, he united the entire Arab world behind a single leader, himself. Second, he negotiated an acceptable peace treaty between all Arab nations and Israel at the expense of neither. Finally, he was able to redefine all three factions through leaders that did not represent governments---Probably his single biggest accomplishment. By aligning the governments behind men like himself, the Sheik successfully negated the impact and vagaries that countries, more often than individuals, brought to the negotiating table. If anyone could make this miracle come true, Jihad believed Sheik Omani was the man. Now all he could do was wait and see like the rest of the world.

"Sheik Omani did not bring us here to fight, but to live. The three of us pledge to return to this stage, with the Sheik, and finish what he started here today. In order for any of us to do that, we must have your cooperation." Doshe and Jerome, seeing the crowd's hesitant response to Jihad's plea, stepped forward. Each man took hold of one of Jihad's hands and raised it above their heads in a show of unity. They managed to get the result they wanted: The crowd began to regain control of itself, content to wait on the three of them.

The three men conferred for a minute, then each, in turn, stepped to the microphone directing their comments exclusively to their followers. After all, three had completed their statements, the crowd began to disperse. Somehow, they managed to avert the start of a Holy war on the steps of the Temple Mount. None of them were exactly sure how it was accomplished, but each was satisfied at that final result. As they prepared to leave the stage, they realized they had no idea where to go, or worse, if confronted by the media, how they could respond.

Doshe was the first one through the curtain at the rear of the stage, and he almost bumped into a news reporter from CNN. The reporter recognized Doshe and seized on the opportunity to get his idea of an exclusive. He stuck the microphone into Doshe's face and asked, "Isn't it true that Sheik Omani's death would effectively negate the peace accord that he has negotiated with all the parties? And if so, would war be the logical result?"

"If it is, you're in a war zone right now," was Doshe's quick response. Doshe's covert activities and precarious relationship with the Israeli government had put him in many difficult situations during his lifetime, ultimately preparing him for times like this where his response could determine the action of nations. So, thinking better of his gut reaction to the questions, Doshe began to explain his thinking more compassionately.

"First, anyone that believes Sheik Omani is dead is sadly mistaken. Second, no individual is so valuable that peace in the Middle East hinges solely on the beating of their heart. And finally, as you said yourself, this peace initiative was worked out to the satisfaction of all nations involved, and it adequately addressed the religious needs of the Christian, Moslem, and Jewish people. Therefore, there is no reason to believe, whatever the outcome of this brutal attack on Sheik Omani, that peace must be sacrificed. If you don't believe me when I say we speak as one, ask them." Doshe turned and pointed to Jerome and Jihad who quietly stood behind him as he answered the reporter's question.

The reporter moved to step past Doshe, but Jerome didn't wait for him to repeat the question or start a new one. "Jihad and I are in complete agreement with what Doshe have said. And I believe if you ask any government representatives, they will mimic his response. Now, if you'll excuse us, we'll be on our way."

As the three men worked their way through the crowd of reporters to the side street outside the old city where their ride was supposed to be waiting, they were bombarded with more questions. "Are you going to the hospital? Or will you be waiting elsewhere for word on Sheik Omani's condition?"

"In case it was not obvious, we were preoccupied when the Sheik was taken away, so until we are informed of his location, our news of his condition will have to come from the likes of you." Jihad spit out the last few words making it clear to the reporter his distaste for the profession.

The reporter, although very young and still relatively inexperienced, had already encountered more than his fair share of snide, hurtful remarks from a public that placed his job on an equal plane with that of a used car salesman, simply ignored Jihad. He continued to ask questions until he was separated from his cameraman in the crowd, and his cameraman called out to him. He turned just in time to have the microphone yanked out of his hand and then watched as it disappeared under a horde of feet. He turned back toward the three men, again just in time to watch them disappear into the crowd. He yelled after them, "They took him to the University hospital." Then sighed deeply and turned his attention back to the cameraman.

The three men rode in silence on the way to the hospital. Each one buried himself in the thought of how they, and the rest of the world, would react if indeed the Sheik does die. Up until now, they were too preoccupied with all the activity that was happening around them to give that thought any serious consideration. However, the long, slow ride through the throngs of people still congregating in the streets was giving them ample time to consider how they would be affected.

Jihad was convinced that the identity of the assassin would dictate the response. If he was Jewish, there would be no alternative. The entire Arab world would be forced to come down hard on Israel. Terrorist activities would be stepped up in preparation for the final annihilation of the state of Israel. War would be the end result, and enough Jewish blood would flow through the streets of Jerusalem to make Hitler proud. On the other hand, if the assassin was an Arab, it would mean the Arab unity that he was led to believe existed---was a lie, and the Sheik---was a farce.

Doshe was most concerned with what conclusions Ariel and the Israeli Prime Minister might come to. He knew both men were levelheaded and extremely careful in their dealings with the media, but almost anything they said would be misconstrued and/ or misrepresented. The news media will be hounding all high-level government officials of every country involved, in the hope that one of them will slip up, say something that creates an incident, and build on it until this crisis has turned into overt hostilities. In general, he was most concerned with what was purported to come from the Israeli government, because he knew that irrational statements made by Arabs would be dutifully ignored, but the opposite would not be true.

He was still lost in thought when the car drove up to the emergency entrance of the University hospital. Jihad was the first one out of the car and inside the hospital door entrance, followed closely by Jerome, then finally Doshe. Inside they quickly located the nurse who was acting as the day's receptionist. But before they were able to ask where Sheik Omani had been taken, a voice behind them said, "He's in surgery, and the doctor will notify us as soon as they know more."

As if choreographed, the three men turned around at exactly the same instant to confront Sylvan. "I was able to have a few words with the doctor that made the initial diagnosis upon the Sheik's arrival. He was, as I expected, very hopeful that the Sheik would be fine. It was his belief that only one of the bullets had hit anything vital but was confident he could save the Sheik. He felt the loss of blood had been kept to a minimum, which greatly enhanced his chances. He assured me that as soon they knew more, I would be told."

Just then a man, who didn't look very far removed from puberty, walked around the corner dressed in a blood-stained surgical gown and called for Sylvan. All four men hurried over and formed a semicircle around him, leaving his backside to the door he came in as his only exit. The young man seemed unimpressed with the conglomeration of important personalities that surrounded him and asked which one of them was Sylvan.

"I am," Sylvan responded.

"And who are the rest of these people? News media?" Without waiting for an answer, he added, "you'll have to go. We have a hospital to run, and we can ill afford the interruptions you'll cause. If you will be so kind as to wait in the waiting room at the front of the hospital, someone will brief you as soon as something newsworthy happens." Then as if to dismiss them he waved his hand and turning to Sylvan, grabbed his elbow and began. "Maybe we should go to my office where you'll be more comfortable, and I can brief you in private."

The two men, one more boy than man, started through the door and down the narrow hospital hall that had brought the doctor to the emergency room admissions where Sylvan was waiting. Jihad, who was unaccustomed to having anyone walk away from him before he was properly dismissed, was the first to react.

Following them through the door, "Doctor, or whatever you are, I am Jihad Nadu, and you will inform me of the Sheik's condition." Then he added, "This is not a matter up for discussion. If you question my resolve, I am sure you have coworkers that can brief you on who I am. They will assure you; I have a long and painful memory."

The inflection in Jihad's voice caught the young doctor's attention. It was obvious even to him that he was dealing with someone who felt very strongly about what he was saying. He adjusted his manner, turned to Sylvan and asked if these men were to be included in the briefing. When Sylvan answered yes, the young doctor apologized for his oversight and invited all of them to his office.

Office was a misnomer for the room they found themselves in. It was a perfect ten by ten box, with a standard size desk, two filing cabinets and every possible inch of wall space masked by overflowing bookshelves. This man was nothing if not well read when it came to medical literature. His diplomas came into view only after everyone was in the room and the door was closed, which was no simple task. Hung precariously on the backside of his door and partially covered by a lab coat that should have been sent to the cleaner's weeks ago, were a series of framed diplomas.

The Doctor walked around his desk, sat down in his chair, then motioned for Sylvan to sit across from him. Next, he started rustling through some papers on his desk, oblivious to his guests. After a few minutes he found what he was looking for, read the document, then looked up at the four men. "You'll have to excuse me, I don't intend to make you wait, but it is important that I verify the circumstances for Sheik Omani's visit to our fine hospital." Pausing, he looked at each of the four men, as if to say he was talking only to him.

"The Sheik's injuries were more severe than the admitting doctor originally thought. He was shot twice: once in the head, just behind the jawbone, and the second, just below the rib at the base of his heart on the left side. I don't know which bullet hit him first, but I pray it was the one near the jawbone. That one almost completely severed the brain stem from the rest of his body, which would have allowed the second bullet to kill him mercifully, without pain."

"You mean he's dead?" Doshe asked incredulously.

"When I left the operating room, they were repairing the body in preparation to sending it to the morgue."

As the four men stood there in shock, the door to the doctor's office burst open and a nurse shouted. "Doctor come quickly, the Sheik is alive." Momentarily she stopped, stared at the men in the doctor's office, then started again. "Quickly, they need your help. They've been able to remove the bullet from his heart, but they're afraid to touch the other one."

The doctor pushed Jihad into the hall, and out of his way, then took off running down the hall. He disappeared around a corner, and the excitement was replaced with an eerie silence. The four men just stood there, frozen in time, staring silently at the corner the doctor had disappeared around.

No one was quite sure who said what to whom to get them to move, but hours later they were all sitting in the hospital cafeteria waiting for word of the Sheik's condition. Throughout the time they waited, conversation was nonexistent. As they sat staring at each other, lost in their own thoughts, the silence became overbearing. Jerome gave in to his discomfort and finally broke the silence.

"I know we are all thinking about it. The question, so here goes; what do we do if the Sheik dies? I doubt any of us," then momentarily he stopped, looked at Sylvan, then started in again. "I don't mean to be cruel Sylvan, but I doubt any of the rest of us are as concerned with his death the same way you are. We are most concerned with how it might affect our own plans. I want everyone to know that I think the Sheik's plan was good, and we are still willing to honor the peace pact with the rest of you. If you are so inclined."

Doshe looked up from the cold cup of coffee he had been staring at for the last fifteen minutes. True, he'd spent the last four hours trying to determine how the Sheik's death would impact the tenuous peace package that had been put together from the Jewish perspective, or at least those aligned with his beliefs. But up until Jerome voiced his reaction, he really hadn't decided for himself what their group's reaction should be. He was too busy trying to figure out how everyone else would react and preparing for that event. By asking the question, Jerome reminded Doshe that this issue was not a singularly Jewish problem, but an entire Middle Eastern problem.

"You raised a good question, Jerome." Then addressing everyone at the table, including Sylvan, he continued. "We can not afford even the slightest appearance that the Sheik's death will cause the peace initiative to unravel. We've already wasted precious time sitting here mulling over the situation for the last four hours. I propose, as a group, we call a news conference and reaffirm our personal commitment to the Sheik's plan. I think it's important that we do it immediately, and Sylvan, you need to be there to represent Sheik Omani."

As the four men started to get up from the table, Jihad voiced what all of them were silently praying without respect for their varied religious heritage. "May Allah spare the Sheik."

- - - - -

"Tension in the Middle East rarely reached this level without producing a war. Inside sources confirmed that widespread troop mobilizations were occurring, not only with U. S. forces, as would be expected, but all U. N. forces stationed from Europe to Viet Nam. The belief is that the rumored death of Sheik Omani, which has neither been confirmed nor denied by authorities, will ultimately result in the war Sheik Omani had so earnestly spent his life trying to avoid."

"The news conference, held by the leaders of the three religious factions that Sheik Omani hand picked, in conjunction with Sylvan, the Frenchman that has served as Sheik Omani's right-hand man, did little to relieve tension in the area. The news conference was held almost five hours after the attempted assassination leaving some to question the reason for the delay. Although some local University professors are crediting that effort and their continued show of unity as the reason peace has been maintained to date. Questions persist concerning the time delay and the lack of information surrounding the Sheik himself."

"For the most part, government representatives in nearby countries have echoed the remarks the four men made during the news conference. It would appear the fragile coalition continues to exist in spite of the lack of confirmed information on Sheik Omani's condition. Or possibly, as one Middle East expert put it, 'It's holding together because of the lack of information.' He went on to explain that the lack of confirmed negative information concerning the Sheik's condition might be suspending the reaction of the masses. However, it was his contention that if the ultimate news of the Sheik is worse than expectations, particularly if his rumored death proves to be true, the resulting war would best be described as the **Armageddon** so often referred to by religious experts when talking about war in the Middle East"

"U. S. President Harris has said that the U. S. was committed to peace in the Middle East and has urged the U. N. to take immediate action to ensure that stability be maintained. He has formally requested a vote on U. N. Resolution 1666A authorizing the deployment of multinational forces to maintain peace in and around Jerusalem. King Hussein of Jordan, Assad of Syria, Hussein of Iraq, Mubarek of Egypt and Fahd of Saudi Arabia have all agreed with the wording of the resolution and have added their voice to President Harris' request for a quick and unanimous vote."

"Around the World in thirty minutes, this is CNN news. We will continue to keep you apprised of the latest developments as they occur. It is now hour thirty of the Sheik Watch."

Jason pressed the power button on the remote control, and the screen went blank. "They can commercialize anything. Hour thirty of the Sheik Watch, indeed," he added in disgust. "You'd think we were in the middle of another hostage crisis at the embassy."

"That young doctor you were able to secure for this work, how confident are you that he can keep his mouth shut?"

"I'm not. He came from a very poor background and just because we invested in his education for the last four years with the agreement he would pay us back someday with a favor, doesn't mean he'll come through. Today's the day. As soon as we switch the dead Sheik with the live Sheik and the Doctor makes his announcement about the miracle, his usefulness is over. We've made plans to have every person that comes in contact with the dead Sheik to be dealt with. He might have an accident on the way home after the news conference."

"I don't think its necessary for everyone to be killed, only those who know."

"And how do propose we make that determination?" Jason asked sarcastically. "Should we debrief them like the CIA? Don't be ridiculous. We can't afford the risk we would expose ourselves to if we missed anyone. It is simply good business."

"I suppose. I can see your point, but it does seem just a tad drastic. What's the timing?"

"Tomorrow morning. More people believe the Sheik is dead than believe he's still alive, so we can do it anytime. But come morning it will have been three days, and the message will be clear."

"The world will have peace for the first time in recent history, and one of the few times throughout history. We will have essentially seized control of the world's oil supply, and no one will be the wiser. And by carefully manipulating both, we can swiftly wrestle the last bit of control of the world's economy from Japan and the U. S. Hitler, Napoleon, Caesar and Nebuchanezzar never understood that true power was in the monetary system. And today's money is defined by oil."

"I think we've all heard this before, so please don't bore us with it again. How many times do I have to remind you, we invited you to join us, not the other way around? We know how the plan works."

"I'm sorry." Jason explained. "But the idea was so good, I keep reviewing it over and over again. Savoring it and making sure there are no flaws."

"Whatever happened to our friend Eric?" Howard cut in determined to change the subject initiated by Jason.

"He did the excellent job we expected him to do. Unfortunately for him, he never discovered he was stopping a ruse. We waited until the last possible minute to hire the actual assassin, so he has no idea what is happening."

"We had him followed," Jason continued. "He was personally responsible for the termination of both Jacque and Manuel. An act most governments around the world will praise heartily. His Jewish girlfriend was given the opportunity to entertain Manuel while Eric dealt with Jacque. Then, she continued entertaining him until Eric was able to rescue her from her perverted prey. Which, I am sure, left a lasting impression on the girl. Manuel was alone with her for almost fifteen minutes, and he can do an awful lot of damage to a girl's psyche in that amount of time."

Howard continued to probe, not convinced he would be rid of Eric. "How long did we keep the tail on them? And do we know what happened to them after the assassination?"

"I have to admit that is a bit distressing." The smile left Jason's face as he realized his satisfaction might be short-lived. "The tail managed to follow Eric to an area near the assassin. If you remember, the assassin's body was found in the middle of an angry crowd. Eric was able to get inside the group that had surrounded the assassin, but our tail had difficulty following him. By the time he reached the now dead assassin's body, Eric was nowhere to be found. He hustled back to the hotel where the girl had been left, but by the time he got there she was gone as well."

"You have no idea what happened to Eric and the girl after that." Howard was simply stating an observation. He was visibly upset with the outcome, but he knew it was not the fault of anyone in the room. Consequently, his disgust was not directed at anyone in particular, and no one in the room interpreted it that way either. "Have you made any effort to find out where he is or what he is doing?"

"Our network has been alerted to notify us if he or Maruch turn up anywhere. But we have not received any word so far."

"He may not be a concern to us anymore but keep the network alert. In the event he decides to cause us problems, we will need as much warning as possible."

Seymour, who had been silent throughout the conversation so far finally decided to add his opinion to the discussion. "As a student of Eric's career, I feel uniquely qualified to speak on this subject. Remember the background reports we received from Tom on those who might fit our requirements." Both men nodded, acknowledging they understood what documents Seymour was referring to. "Eric's history was one I read over and over again before making the final recommendation to this group. An underlying theme to Eric's life might best be described as: His need to complete a task. This need was his only negative point."

Seymour paused, allowing the two men to absorb what he had just told them. "I'm sorry, your mythical methods have once again left me wondering." Emphasizing each word, Howard continued. "What in the hell are you talking about now, Seymour?"

Ignoring Howard's outburst, Seymour continued spinning the pencil on his hand as he continued with his explanation. "From early childhood Eric demonstrated a proficiency for bringing any task he started to a natural conclusion. That is not to say he always finished as originally planned. But rather, when confronted with an unexpected obstacle, Eric always managed to overcome that obstacle. And usually in an innovative and unique way I might add. Regardless, he was able to complete his assignment. As he grew older, and the obstacles became more formidable, Eric developed the ability to modify his objective to reflect the new information. His new objective would incorporate everything he knew, and the modification would not compromise the originally intended results."

"I don't mean to be rude," Howard said as he interrupted Seymour again. "But in case you don't remember, the reason you were supposed to read these people's history, was to save the rest of us from that very task. If we're going to be spoon fed Eric's childhood," Howard paused for emphasis. Then slowly, carefully enunciating each word, he added, "Don't you think that defeats the purpose?"

This evoked a chuckle from Jason, but Seymour just stared blankly back at Howard as if to say, 'If your done, I'd like to continue.' "Never mind," Howard gave in. "You're going to tell us what we don't need to know regardless, so go ahead."

"Thank you. As I was saying before, Eric has the uncanny ability to achieve his original objective regardless of the odds. He carefully and intelligently modifies his methods, while maintaining his direction. Now to my point, Eric knows neither of the two men he killed was the assassin. In a relatively short period of time, I suspect, he'll figure out that Jacque and Manuel were simply diversionary in nature. Then he'll begin looking for the people that hired the third assassin. Ultimately, that information will lead him back to here. We may become his new objective."

"Wait a minute. Are you proposing that Eric is going to come after us? That he'll try to neutralize us." Jason was visibly upset.

"No. No. You misunderstand. Remember, I said he modifies his objective."

"I think coming after us would qualify as modifying his objective."

"His objective, if you remember, was to stop the assassination. He didn't do that. The next best thing would be to stop our plan."

"What are you trying to say?" The light bulb was beginning to flicker in Howard's head, and he wasn't sure he liked what he saw.

"Eric could still screw up everything if he could assassinate the real Sheik."

"He wouldn't take that risk. He knows the whole region is on the brink of war right now, and the only thing that's stopping it is the uncertainty of the Sheik's condition." Jason countered.

"War hasn't broken out. People are beginning to accept the fact that Sheik Omani might be dead, and the talk of war is less today than it was yesterday. Eric sees this as well. And if he believes he can stop us by eliminating Sheik Omani, he'll do it."

"That assumes he knows the real Sheik is still alive."

"I think we have to assume he knows that."

- - - - -

The young doctor stepped up to the podium thinking the cluster of microphones sticking up from the backside of the podium, with their tangled cables, cascading to the floor, reminded him he was better at understanding the workings of a ganglion than a news conference. After today, he thought, his debt would be paid. No more sleepless nights wondering what payment for his soul the devil might want. Now he knew. He knew what he was doing wasn't ethical. Ethical, hell, it was illegal, he thought. And if he's caught, ...he didn't want to finish the thought.

But these were important men. Powerful men. Men that he didn't want to owe anything else to. Besides he was a doctor, and these were political issues. He was supposed to worry about diseases not politics. He was just a doctor doing the best he could. It will all be over with in a few minutes, he thought, and then took a deep breadth.

Up to the time they made the request, he hadn't even heard of Sheik Omani---which, looking out at the sea of faces staring back at him, was a good thing. Because if he had known how important this man was, he could never have agreed to do this, he thought. But it's too late for that now. Doctor Denison cleared his throat, and as if on cue, all sound ceased.

He wanted to run from the room. This was unreal. It was like a nightmare. No, it was a nightmare. He hated public speaking; yet here he was getting ready to speak to the whole world. He cleared his throat again, and it was obvious the audience was already getting impatient. Veteran news people don't care how frightened the speaker is; they have a job to do. And in that self-righteous belief, they will disregard all that is kind and force the issue. A voice from the center of the crowd yelled out, "Doctor, is Sheik Omani alive? And if not, did he die from the assassin's bullet or complications from that wound?"

The question jolted Doctor Denison from his fear, and he inched up closer to the microphones on the podium. Leaning forward, he peered into the crowd trying to see exactly who asked the question. Then with a newfound confidence he began, "I'm sorry, I didn't catch your name."

"Leonard Doyle, UPI."

Looking to the back of the crowded room, Doctor Denison spotted what he was looking for. "Security," he called out. A ridiculously large man, leaning against the back wall, raised his finger identifying himself to the doctor. "Good. Good. Would you be so kind and remove Mr. Leonard Doyle from the room? And before anyone else repeats his mistake may I add: This news conference is for your benefit, not mine. I will not tolerate any outbursts whatsoever. I will not answer any questions from the audience. I am here to make a statement regarding

Sheik Omani's condition, and that is all. If you are looking for debate, you have come to the wrong place."

- - - - -

Seymour watched as the waiter set the tray on the table by the window. As he walked with the waiter to the door to his hotel room, he pressed a ten shekel note into the waiter's hand and thanked him again. Carefully he locked and reattached the security chain before returning to the table to eat his brunch.

He looked at the food on the tray, and although it wasn't of the quality he was used to, it was adequate. Before he sat down, he remembered the newspaper and retrieved it from the bed. As he walked back to the table, he passed the TV and turned it on. Switching the station, he located CNN, and left it there. The news conference was only a half hour away, and he didn't want to miss it.

He sat down at the table and briefly glanced out the window at the street below. Then removing the front section from the paper, he folded it in half and set it on the table next to the tray. Returning his eyes to the street, he started looking around again. Movement out of the corner of his eye caught his attention, and he turned his head toward it to get a better look.

At first, he wasn't sure what he was seeing. Then, as he looked more carefully, he realized he was looking at the barrel of a rifle sticking out of a window across the street and pointing toward the sidewalk. He tried to make out the face of the person holding the rifle, but the morning sun was not high enough yet, and he was standing in the shadow caused by the window frame.

Transfixed, Seymour continued to watch the play unfold before him, leaving his food and coffee to get cold, untouched. This should be interesting, he thought. Suddenly the man in the window leaned forward far enough and the sun lit up his face. Seymour recognized the assassin and froze. His mind kept telling him to move away from the window, but his body wouldn't move. Slowly the barrel of the rifle changed direction and Seymour, frozen in time by the realization of what was happening, stared helplessly at it.

Most of the blood splattered on the carpet behind Seymour as the bullet exited his skull. The force of the bullet caused his head to snap back, and the front legs of his chair were lifted off the carpet. Then, as the chair fell back to the floor, Seymour's body went limp, and his head fell forward. It landed neatly on the folded newspaper next to the tray. Blood began to seep into the paper, blending with the letters of the USA Today's headline.

SHEIK OMANI DEAD OR ALIVE?

Today's news conference should

provide the answer. Dr....

- - - - -

Dr. Denison watched as the security guard made his way through the crowd of reporters to Leonard Doyle. Len, as he was called by his friends, was still very shocked by what was taking place. He had always been criticized by management for playing everything too close to the vest. But here he was, about to be tossed out of the most important news conference of his career. And for what? Being the first person to ask the same question everyone else was prepared to ask.

"Sir." The security guard was looking down at the seated reporter, hand outstretched, as if to say, 'it's time to go now.' Len suddenly felt very old. He reached for the hand and was assisted out of the seat. The guard motioned for him to go first, and Len started for the rear of the room. Halfway back he stopped, turned, and looked back to the podium at Dr. Denison. He wanted to say something to the Doctor. He wanted to say something profound, something to make the Doctor realize he was wrong sending him away. But the words failed to come. Everything he thought of seemed too petty for words. Defeated, shoulders slouching, Leonard Doyle left the room.

During the removal of Leonard Doyle, Dr. Denison busied himself fiddling with the papers in Sheik Omani's file. He thought the file gave him an added appearance of authority. As he waited, he began to formulate his opening statement. A couple minutes passed after Len was removed, but Dr. Denison still hadn't started the news conference.

Finally, the doctor, realizing the room had been silent for quite some time now, looked up from the papers. Once again, he was faced with a room full of reporters waiting to record his every word. Only this time, there was no Leonard Doyle around to delay the news conference any longer.

"Gentlemen. Ahhhh, sorry. And women. I will try to keep the technical aspects of this report as simple as possible. Therefore, I will not be giving you a detailed medical report on what has taken place, but rather a layman's report on the history, progress and the prognosis."

"As we all are aware, an assassin's bullet, actually two bullets, found their way into Sheik Omani's body approximately sixty-seven hours ago. After careful examination of the wounds, the emergency room doctor made the determination there was nothing he could do for the Sheik. Any effort he made to save Sheik Omani's life would hasten his demise. As luck would have it, I happened to be in the hospital, and the attending physician asked for my assistance."

"At that point in time, approximately four hours after the wounds were inflicted, it was our medical opinion that the Sheik would die. We were certain the only thing we could for him was to keep him comfortable until the end. One bullet had lodged just below the heart. Although this was serious, it was the other bullet that we focused on. The second bullet had severed two-thirds of the brain stem. It was at this point that Sheik Omani was put on 'subsistence life support."

Dr. Denison paused and looked up at his audience. Up until now, he had kept his eyes focused on the papers in front of him. But as he spoke, he became more comfortable and was now able to gather up enough courage to look at his audience. Those who were finished writing were watching him, while the rest were furiously trying to get every word down on paper as potential quotes in their yet to be written articles.

"Um…as I was saying. We put Sheik Omani on a subsistence life support and began the arduous task of removing the bullets. It was done as a precursor to his ultimate autopsy, and in preparation for this news conference to announce his death. However, that is why you are here, but not why we are here. Sheik Omani is, in fact, very much alive!" Dr. Denison let the audience absorb this news and react accordingly to the unexpected announcement. After the noise had subsided somewhat, he started in again. The crowd of reporters immediately was silent, no one wanting to miss a word. Now, Dr. Denison was given their undivided attention.

"There are times, documented throughout history, when the medical profession has to acknowledge that their contribution to a problem is nonexistent. This is one of those times! We, in the field of medicine, and I speak on behalf of the entire hospital staff, have done nothing to warrant such a recovery in Sheik Omani. There is no medical explanation that can be put forth to explain his survival. Based on everything we know; Sheik Omani should be dead. This is the most significant medical phenomenon I have ever been associated with."

"The latest prognosis is for a complete recovery with no lingering effects. Our last MRI showed no serious damage from the two bullets we removed." Dr. Denison held up his hands to stop the barrage of questions that were waiting for him. "As I stated at the beginning of the news conference, I will not be taking questions. So please, keep them to yourself, or you will be dealt with in the same manner as Mr. Doyle. Thank you."

"Sheik Omani has requested that he be allowed to address you, and that his address be broadcast to as many people in the world as possible. I cannot meet his request. That is up to you, the news media. In my professional medical opinion, there is no reason why he can't do this. He is preparing to discuss this with you at 2:00 P. M. this afternoon, exactly seventy-two hours after he was shot. He felt the timing was important."

"That is all. This news conference is now over." With that statement Dr. Denison gathered up his papers and left the room.

- - - - -

Jason smiled as Dr. Denison's face on the screen was replaced with a picture of the room. A few people remained seated, busily finishing the last sentences before heading for a phone to call in their report. The rest were trying to squeeze through the single door exit at the back of the room to start their search for phones. The announcer continued the broadcast by commenting on the havoc that the announcement created. Then he began to ramble on, trying to explain how the world would react to the news of the Sheik's miraculous recovery. It was obvious he had been instructed, through the microphone at his ear, to continue the broadcast until the studio was ready to take over the feed.

The camera continued to pan the room, but Jason had seen enough. He started to walk over to the TV to turn it off, but then decided against it and made his way to the bathroom. He walked into the bathroom, stepped up to the toilet and spread his robe. A sound caught his attention, and he stopped to listen. Cocking an ear toward the door, he waited to hear the sound again. As he listened, he thought he heard something again, but the noise from the TV was making it too difficult to be certain. He should have turned the TV off before he came in, he thought. Deciding he could wait, silently he walked toward the door.

From his vantage point he could see the hotel room door, and almost three-quarters of the room. Thinking he was being unusually paranoid, he stepped out of the bathroom. He saw movement from the left side, but it happened so quick he couldn't muster a defense. Pain exploded on the left side of his face, and the force of the blow caused him to stumble forward. As he did, the attacker moved behind him. Suddenly his neck began to feel as if it were being severed, his head destined to roll away.

Jason reached around behind him clawing at his attacker, but his assailant was able to keep his body just out of reach. Turning his attention to the wire, he desperately tried to grab at it. Instead, his hands came back coated with a warm, slippery substance. He looked at his hands, detached for a moment, from the reality of the grotesque picture he was watching. Finally, the reality of what was happening sunk in, and he began to panic. Why would they do this to him? It had to be Howard, he thought. He wants complete control, and he'll do whatever it takes to get it, he decided.

Needing to confirm his suspicions, Jason began turning his head to one side to see his attacker. As he did this, the wire cut further into his neck. The pain was excruciating, but he continued until he saw the face. In his shock, Jason tried to speak, but nothing came out. All he could do was mouth the words, "why you?" Then everything went blank. The assailant allowed Jason's body to slump to the floor when he passed out but continued to tighten the wire around his neck. It was another two minutes before the body gave a nerve induced final kick. Loosening his grip on the wire, he allowed Jason's body to fall limp to the floor. Then flipping the body over he put his ear to his chest and confirmed the kill.

- - - - -

"We have not been able to confirm this report, but we have received word that a terrorist bomb has exploded and decimated the cafeteria at the University Hospital. I repeat. We have an unconfirmed report that a terrorist bomb has exploded and decimated the cafeteria at the University Hospital."

The announcer put his hand to his hear to reposition the microphone, then started in again. "I have just received word; we have confirmed the bombing. It was restricted to the cafeteria at the Hospital, but it was over the lunch hour, and considerable loss of life is projected. We go now to the scene outside the hospital. Jane, what is happening right now?"

The announcer's face was instantaneously replaced on the screen by a middle-aged woman standing on the sidewalk in front of the hospital entrance. "Well Bill, the scene around here, as you can see, is mass confusion. The police have already cordoned off all entrances and are funneling everyone through the emergency entrance after they have been thoroughly searched and undergone an initial interrogation. The remaining entrances are heavily guarded, and no one has been allowed inside. Everyone trying to enter the building is searched and interrogated as well."

"No word as yet about who might have been killed, or who the target was. There is speculation the bomb was a retaliatory strike by Palestinians for an incident that occurred last week involving the death of two of their members who worked in the medical field."

"Excuse me, Jane. I don't mean to interrupt, but the question on everyone's mind is: Could this in anyway be related to Sheik Omani? And was he in any way threatened or hurt by this terrorist act."

"Bill, the consensus here is that the event is independent of the Sheik, except for the more newsworthy location. It is believed the University Hospital was chosen specifically because the eyes of the world are focused here at this moment. Whoever was responsible wanted the world as the audience, not just Israel."

"How soon can we expect a report on the casualties?"

"We have been told no information will be released until all the bodies have been identified. Just a minute Bill." A second person briefly entered the cameras view, and then the feed was cut.

"We will return to Jane in just a moment. The leading economic indicators were released today, and they show the economy continues to expand at a robust 4.2 per cent for the year. The price of oil, which shot up to thirty-eight dollars a barrel shortly after the news of Sheik Omani's attempted assassination was released, has continued it's downward trend. It now stands at thirty-one dollars and forty-seven cents for West Texas light sweet crude."

Sylvan and Sheik Omani continued watching the CNN report, waiting, in silence, for more information on the bombing. Sheik Omani continued to pick at the bandages placed over the entry wounds made by the bullets. He insisted the bandages be made as small as possible to minimize their appearance, but regardless of their size, the adhesive still made his skin itch.

He wanted the public to be aware of the bandages, but only as a second thought. He was adamant that the public's attention is not drawn to them. He wanted them to believe he has miraculous healing power, but not to forget the terrible thing he suffered on their behalf. No greater suffering has been experienced by any man than this, he thought. Then, not able to contain himself, he began to chuckle out loud.

Sylvan turned to him and asked, "What's so funny?"

"I was just thinking how gullible the news media, no, the world is. If they only knew that these wounds were done while under local anesthesia."

"And by a very dead surgeon no less," Sylvan added.

"We don't know he's dead yet."

"Watch the news," Sylvan pointed to the TV screen. "Jane's back."

"Bill, we've just received confirmation there was an important name among the list of those killed inside the cafeteria. A man, who's face the world has become very familiar with recently, Dr. Denison. The surgeon credited with saving Sheik Omani's life. Other, less prominent names are being leaked, but this one will truly rock the world."

"Excuse me, Jane. Has Sheik Omani made any comment about this tragedy? Is he aware the man who saved his life is now dead? Do we have any idea what is going through the Sheik's mind right now?"

"Bill, I feel confident saying that if Sheik Omani is aware of this insidious turn of events, his remorse, his sense of loss would be unequaled right now..."

"I'm sorry to disappoint Jane, but I couldn't care less about Dr. Denison," Sheik Omani responded to the reporter's feeble attempt at melodrama. "When will people learn?" He asked rhetorically. "These reporters are just actors, paid to play a dramatic role at six and ten every night. Or, in the case of CNN, every thirty minutes," he added. "They wouldn't know what I was thinking anymore than I know what the good doctor was thinking just before the bomb made his widow a very rich woman."

- - - - -

"Due to the bombing this morning, security at the hospital has been extremely tight. Only communication crews were allowed into the building, and they were given limited and controlled access for the sole purpose of setting up the audio and visual feed to Sheik Omani's room. That is where he has chosen to address the world in just a few minutes."

"Originally, it was thought the news media would be allowed into the room and be given the opportunity to question the Sheik immediately after he makes his statement. However, that is not the case. Since we won't be allowed direct access to the Sheik, two-way communication feeds are being installed. The logistics of two-way communication are considerably more complicated and limits the media's control of the news conference. Even once we've completed the two-way communication capability, there is no method for determining who can ask what. Typically, the person being interviewed controls the questioning by controlling who's allowed to speak. But today that is not possible. Trying to anticipate this, we have drawn straws for the first twenty questions. If the Sheik allows more, we will continue to draw straws. The first question will come from Bruce Schaver, ABC."

"It appears the news conference is about to begin, so we will switch to the video of the room now. Possibly we can catch Sheik Omani as he makes his last preparations before addressing the world. The man, that only three days ago, was presumed dead---A result of this act by a crazed radical."

"We will switch on the audio feed in just a moment, so we are able to catch every word. As you can see, he appears to be reasonably healthy at this point. A very pleasant change, I might add, over how he looked a scant three days ago. I've just gotten word our audio is ready. We go live to Sheik Omani as he addresses the world from his private room inside University Hospital."

- - - - -

Howard missed lunch in his panic. He'd made phone calls to both rooms and was surprised that neither man answered the phone. Assuming they were indisposed or out at the time of the phone call, he decided to go get a newspaper. Knowing no other language than English, he was particularly pleased the hotel gift shop carried USA Today. It was hardly the in-depth look that he was accustomed to, but it did provide accurate top-line reports.

On his return to his room, he detoured by Jason's room. When he knocked on the door, it gave ever so slightly, enough that Howard noticed. He pushed the door, and it slid open a crack. The door hadn't latched the last time it was closed, he thought. Somewhat apprehensively, Howard pushed the door open more as he called out, "Jason."

No one answered, so Howard pushed the door completely open. Jason's prone body came into full view. Howard could tell immediately Jason was dead, but he still wanted to go through the motions of confirming it. He glanced back down the hall to see if anyone was watching. Satisfied he was alone; he stepped inside and closed the door until he heard the door latch behind him. Once inside the room, the unmistakable stench of death began to fill the air.

He walked over to the body and kneeled down. Taking hold of a wrist, he felt for a pulse. The body was still warm, but as expected, he couldn't find one. He put his finger up to Jason's nose, nothing. Howard looked at the wound around Jason's neck and began to feel nauseous. The wire, which was still lying on the floor underneath the body, had cut deeply into Jason's neck. The blood that had oozed out of the wound after he was already dead had created a small puddle on the carpet. A layer of skin had already formed on the surface of the puddle, but the telltale indent of dried blood had not yet taken shape. Verifying in Howard's mind, just how close he had come to walking in on the murder in progress.

With that realization, Howard stood up. Then calming himself, he reasoned he may have passed the murderer on the way to the room. Howard stood over Jason's body as he tried to regain his composure. He knew that panicking would only make him more vulnerable, so it was imperative he deals with the situation just as he would a business deal gone sour. There was no sense sticking around here, and even less notifying the authorities. The last thing he needed was an investigation that involved him, he thought.

His next order of business was to make sure he left no evidence that he'd been in the room. Then leave. Retracing his steps in his mind, the only thing he touched was the door handle when he came in. He retrieved a hand towel from the bathroom, and on his way out, carefully wiped off the doorknob. That done, he could return to his room, taking the towel with him. No one was in the hall when he left, and he was able to get back to his room unseen.

Inside the room, he pressed the door closed and quickly attached the security chain. He knew it offered no real security, but still, it made him feel a little safer. He walked over to the phone and dialed Seymour's room number. After the tenth ring he set the phone back in its cradle and collapsed in the seat next to the window. He took a couple deep breaths, then nonchalantly looked out the window. At that moment it dawned on him; he might be next! He scrambled to the floor, then crawled out of the way of the window. Carefully, he made his way over to the lounge chair.

Now what should he do? Jason's dead. By whom, he had no idea. They, the three of them, had gotten rid of Toomas and Sergei, but that had always been the plan. They never fit the overall plan of the consortium. Too fanatical, they reasoned. They were used for their resources, nothing more. They were expendable, and they were expended.

This was different. This was eerie. Jason, Seymour and he had planned this thing for over ten years. There is no way Seymour could have fooled them that long, and he couldn't believe Seymour had been bought either. The only logical conclusion was that Sylvan and or Sheik Omani ordered the killing. If that were the case, he feared the reason he couldn't get an answer from Seymour was because he was too late.

But what possible motive could they have? They didn't control any oil, so without the three of them, there was little Sheik Omani or Sylvan could gain, particularly financially. Neither of them was noticeably anti-Semitic or anti-Arab, so there was little evidence supporting a motive based on hatred or revenge. After spending an unknown amount of time racking his brain for the answer, he finally gave up. Power and money were synonymous, so if they weren't after money, he reasoned, they weren't after power either. At best they would gain some minimal leverage over, critical, but very unstable countries. They wouldn't have the necessary influence to ensure control. Whatever their plan, it was obviously fraught with erroneous assumptions.

Howard moved back toward the window. For what he could see, there was little evidence a marksman was waiting to put a bullet in his head, so he began making plans to leave his room. It was imperative he confirms his suspicions concerning Seymour, and he knew hiding until it was safe was not an option. He had little choice, but to find a way into Seymour's room. So, he left the relative safety of his room and went down to the front desk.

As he neared the front desk, he settled on the direct approach. He hadn't seen the girl before, so there was no fear she would recognize him. "Excuse me ma'am." The girl behind the desk, looking as if she belonged in school not working for a living, looked up. "I mistakenly allowed the door to close, then realized the key was still on the table. Does someone have a master key they could use to let me in. It will only take a moment, just long enough to retrieve my own key."

The girl gave him a quizzical look, then held up one finger, said something in Hebrew, and walked away. Howard stood at the desk looking awkward, not quite sure what he was supposed to do. The last thing he wanted was for her to discuss this with anyone else. They might decide to investigate and find out he is not the man registered into the room. Howard briefly considered walking away, but before he did, the girl returned with an even younger looking man in tow. As she walked up to Howard, she said something to the young man, then pointed at Howard.

"What can I do for you?" He asked through a thick Hebrew accent. It was obvious he was born and raised in Israel. Most people have some remnant of their original language evident in their accent, but it was obvious by his accent, this was his homeland and Hebrew his native tongue. "Sarah can not speak any English, otherwise she would have been very happy to help you. She is a recent immigrant from the Russian province of the old Soviet Union, consequently, she feels woefully inadequate when helping foreigners. The hotel management is committed to helping immigrants, and in this industry, exposure is the greatest teacher. In a year Sarah will speak fluent Hebrew, and an understandable English. In the meantime, she is supposed to solicit help whenever she needs it."

Regaining his confidence, Howard repeated his story. The young man listened then asked for his room number. He moved down the counter a bit, then tossed a key toward Howard. "Just drop the key off here on your way out."

Howard took the key, thanked them both profusely and left.

A cold chill slid up and down his spine as he prepared to open the door. He was afraid of what he was going to see, but after looking into Jason's blank eyes and seeing the pool of blood that had continued to grow even after his death, Howard knew he could handle whatever lay on the other side of the door. Or more accurately, knew he would have to handle it.

Howard slipped into the room as quickly as possible, closed and latched the door. Before turning around, he paused to get his composure. Then, for added privacy, he attached the security chain. After doing that, he started thinking the killer might still be in the room, so he spun around quickly, as if by doing so he could catch the intruder by surprise. There was no one there.

This room was of a slightly different design than Jason's and his. The opening to the other room was further to the right, blocking his immediate view of the room itself. Sunlight was streaming through the archway leading to the sitting room. It reflected off the tiled floor of the entryway, producing an eerie pattern of shadows and light on the wall. He stared at the pattern for a moment and saw Seymour's dead body in its ink spot like image. A precursor of things to come, he thought.

Gathering his courage, he stepped to the opening. He was prepared to find Seymour dead, but the sight still left him cold. For a moment he just stared at the body, transfixed by it's total lack of movement. Normal bodies, no matter how relaxed, will show the subtle movement of the chest going up and down as air enters and exits the lungs. It was painfully clear; Seymour would move no more.

Howard walked over to the body, head lying on the table, to look at Seymour's face. The bullet left a small, clean hole in the center of his forehead. But what caught Howard's attention was the look on the dead man's face. It was one of acknowledged terror. An odd expression for one who died so suddenly, he thought. Then he realized; Seymour must have seen his killer just before the bullet hit. He must have turned toward the window, saw the assassin as he took the shot and concluded accurately what was about to happen. The whole event taking just enough time to paint the perfect picture on his frozen face of how he felt about dying. He knew he couldn't stop the inevitable. A terrifying thought, Howard concluded, as a cold shudder passed through his body.

He searched the room, not quite sure what he was supposed to be looking for, but confident he was doing the right thing. After a few minutes he came to the realization he was not increasing his knowledge by looking at blood stains and gray matter sprayed about on the carpet and walls. He was ill prepared to become a detective and his lack of understanding of what the clues were trying to tell him made it clear he was out of his league. But since there was no authority, he could turn to, he continued his search.

He carefully assessed everything in the room but found his attention being drawn to the shards of glass on the floor. It didn't take Sherlock Holmes to realize the bullet passed through the closed patio door, but it should have taken a deaf Sherlock Holmes not to hear the subsequent shattering of glass. Judging from the lack of reaction from the hotel's staff, either no one had heard the noise, or they didn't bother to report it or investigate it.

Gingerly, Howard stepped through the glass on the floor jockeying for a better view of the buildings across the street. The view added little useful information from which to draw conclusions. There were a number of buildings and more than a few windows from which the assassin could have fired the rifle. There were no obstructions or evidence elevating one window location over another except, possibly angle. Not having the expertise to reenact the assassination, or evaluate the angle based on the entry wound left Howard as ignorant now as when he came into the room. No, he thought, when he came into the room, he only had expectation that Jason might be dead. Now he had proof staring blankly back at him from the table.

It was time to leave. He'd learned as much as he could here, which sad to say was very little. However, standing around staring at Jason's dead body would do neither of them any good. As he worked his way back through the glass toward the entry, he decided he had but two choices. First, he could confront either Sylvan or Sheik Omani about the killings. How he would do that was not immediately obvious to him. But he was curious, and it was an option.

The second choice was much more palatable, and it may be his last chance at survival. He and his band of businessmen had expended an excessive amount of money on this project. If the project was successful, they would have become the three richest men in the world. A worthwhile investment, he reasoned. However, any good businessman would recognize this project was on the fast track to failure. One does not invest in failures, he reasoned, they're financial sinkholes. The only rational approach at this point, from a business perspective, was to kill the project. Besides, he thought, it might yield the added benefit of his own survival---At this point, the most important benefit.

As he approached the desk, he called to the girl that had gotten him the key to Jason's room. When she looked up at him, he threw the key unto the counter, said "thanks," and kept walking. He'd already made up his mind; he was not going back to his room, nor was he going to confront Sylvan or Sheik Omani. His only objective from here on out was to literally disappear. He had access to his money through any of a number of accounts, which would be the first order of business once he landed in New York. He also knew some of the finest plastic surgeons available in the States, and within a week, he should be unrecognizable even to his mother. Except for his height and weight, he won't look anything like he does now. Howard continued planning his self-directed witness protection program as he rode in the taxi on the way to the airport.

Howard paid the driver a healthy tip, then headed straight to the ticket counter. Wasting no time reading the schedule behind the ticket counter, he approached a waiting agent. "I need to get back to New York as quick as possible. Could you check to see what carrier has the earliest available seat out?"

The agent nodded then started typing on the keyboard in front of her. A few minutes later she looked at him over the VDT and said, "We have our last flight leaving for New York in a little over two hours. Otherwise, you will have to wait until tomorrow for the next flight, or you can try another carrier."

"No other airline has a flight leaving for New York before that." The inflection in Howard's voice made the statement sound more like an accusation.

"Well sir, there is a flight that takes off five minutes before ours, but I assumed you were concerned with a larger time savings. However, if you insist, I can certainly put you on that flight if you'd like."

Suddenly, Howard realized he was probably coming across rude and demanding, leaving a lasting impression on her. If he is being followed, and this girl is questioned, she will undoubtedly remember him, he thought. That's the last thing he needed. He wanted to blend into the crowd, not draw attention to himself. "I'm sorry," he started in again. "Things have not gone well for me on this trip. My luggage was stolen, I lost the contract, and now all I want to do is get back home. No fuss, no muss, just get back home and relax." he lied.

"I didn't mean to take it out on you. Your flight would be fine. If you have any first-class seats left, I'd prefer one of those. If not, business class would be acceptable. However, coach I can't handle." As he finished, he removed his wallet and started rifling through his credit cards. Finding a credit card, he removed it and set it on the counter sliding it toward the girl.

The ticket agent looked up briefly, and then returned to her typing. Howard started looking around the ticketing area for anyone that might look suspicious. As each minute passed, he became more and more confident he would be able to leave this holy hell of a city without incident.

"Sir," she paused, waiting for him to look at her. "If you would sign here, and here, then I can issue your seating assignment with the tickets. The total cost from here to New York will be just over twenty eight hundred dollars." She returned to her typing while Howard quickly read the documents, then signed them. "Now," she said returning her attention back to him. "I need to see your passport. And how many bags did you want to check?"

"No bags." He replied as he pulled out his passport and handed it to the agent. She confirmed it, then picking up the tickets, boarding pass and receipt, returned everything to Howard. "I'm truly sorry your stay here has been so horrible, but I assure you---That is not normal. I hope you decide to come back again so we can have a chance to redeem ourselves."

"I don't expect to do be doing that anytime soon, but thanks anyway."

"The gate is down to your right, through security and passport control. After passport control, it is the second concourse on your left. They'll begin boarding about a half-hour before departure." Then looking at her watch she added, "And that should be in another hour. Have a nice flight."

Howard did not wait to hear the last bit of explanation; he had already left and was approaching the security station. He showed the guard his tickets and passport. Taking the hand-held metal detector, the guard motioned for Howard to raise his arms by pointing the detector at him, then up. Howard did as he was instructed and the guard ran the detector along the underside of both arms, and then continued down his torso and legs, to his feet. After he completed checking both sides, he stuck the detector between Howard's legs and cracked it back and forth against both of them to get Howard to spread his legs even more.

He brought the detector up the inside of one leg, then down the other. Waving the detector at Howard's chest and stomach, he finished the front side and motioned for Howard to turn around. The guard completed the search by checking Howard's backside then motioned for him to leave. Throughout the whole ordeal, the guard never uttered a word. He'd become so accustomed to this task; he was able to perform it while his mind was completely detached from what he was doing. He relied on the buzz of the metal detector to rouse him back to consciousness as he would an alarm clock to wake him in the morning. If the detector would buzz, he was quick to jump into action, never missing a beat.

Howard began to relax now that he was so close to being out of the city. He knew he would remain a target, at least until he could have his features altered. But he felt safer now that he was putting distance between himself and whoever was killing the consortium one by one. He continued walking down the concourse until he came to his gate furtively glancing at anyone that came near.

There were only a few people in the waiting area, but he knew many others were roaming the halls and shops of the airport wasting as much time as possible while waiting for the flight to board. He evaluated each face of those in the waiting area, and one by one manufactured a reason why they weren't the hired killer. After finishing up his evaluation of the last person in the immediate area, he decided this might be the best time to use the restroom. He wanted that out of the way so he could assess as many of the passengers as possible, before boarding the plane. As the departure time grew closer, more and more people would be arriving at the gate, making it difficult, if not impossible, to evaluate everyone for their potential threat. The plane, he thought, would be an excellent place for the assassin to corner his prey, and Howard wanted to minimize that threat as much as possible.

Howard's paranoia caused him to view every face he passed as that of a potential assassin. As he entered the washroom, a balding, middle aged man came out. In Howard's rush to get out of the man's way, he crashed into the wastepaper basket in the corner, almost tipping it over and drawing a curious look from everyone within ear shot. The bald-headed man gave him a funny look but kept walking. Howard watched as the man's body was replaced by the door, as it swung shut.

The bathroom was small, with two urinals and two stalls. Howard bent over to see if anyone was in either of the stalls and was pleased to find both of them empty. After he finished relieving himself, he went over to the sink to wash his hands. Standing at the sink, he stared at himself in the mirror. He looked exhausted. Maybe he could get some sleep on the plane, he thought. Bending over he turned on the water and started scooping with his hands, splashing it on his face.

He didn't hear the door open or the pronounced click as the door was locked from the inside. The sound was drowned out by the rush of water in the sink, and his mind was distracted by the refreshing feeling he was getting from the water splashing against his face. By the time

Howard's sixth sense told him something was about to happen, it was too late. An arm wrapped around Howard's dripping face, positioning Howard's mouth in the crook of his arm effectively muffling any screams. At the same time, he pressed a stiletto into the soft flesh of Howard's back in the approximate location of his heart. Howard fainted, then died without making another sound.

The assassin was surprised Howard went limp so quickly, almost losing his hold on him. He repositioned his hands under Howard's armpits and dragged him over to one of the stalls. He pushed the door open and dragged the body inside, setting it on the seat. Pressing his fingers to Howard's neck, Eric could feel a faint pulse. He was ready for this. Killing someone in public without regard to who sees what was difficult enough, but when it must be done without creating a scene, the task becomes almost impossible.

Eric removed a piece of wire from his pocket and wrapped it around Howard's neck. He pulled it tight and twisted the ends so it would stay in place. Within minutes he would either suffocate or die from the knife wounds.

Eric unraveled a large wad of toilet paper from the roll hanging on the wall. As he removed the knife from Howard's back, he pressed the paper into the wound. It immediately stuck to the blood soaking into Howard's shirt and started absorbing it. Taking some more paper, he cleaned off the blade of the knife. With the knife clean, he held it for a moment admiring its simple but deadly design. Sliding his fingers across the blade, he was impressed anew with the strength and sharpness of the plastic knife. When he finished admiring it, he returned it to its plastic sheath on his calf.

Eric quickly looked around the bathroom to make sure there was no evidence of what happened. Then returning to Howard he checked for a pulse one more time and was pleased to find there was none. He reached inside the front of Howard's shirt looking for his passport and was rewarded when he found it hanging on a chain around Howard's neck just as he suspected he would find it. Finally finished, he locked the door to the stall from the inside, then slid under the door to get out.

He unlocked the bathroom door and left. Outside, people were mulling around, walking back and forth past the bathroom door oblivious to the activities that had just taken place behind it. Calmly Eric turned toward the terminal and started walking toward it.

Once he was back to the main terminal, he found another bathroom and went inside. Inside one of the stalls, he sat down and removed Howard's passport. He opened the passport, looked at the picture, then set it down on his lap. Removing his wallet, he found a picture of himself and compared it to the one in Howard's passport. He carefully cut the photo to a slightly larger dimension than Howard's. Next, he removed the release paper on the back of his picture and carefully pressed it into the passport directly over Howard's picture.

He held the passport at arm's length to review his work. There was no evidence of tampering and the picture adhered tightly to the page, effectively masking Howard's picture underneath. Satisfied, Eric left.

- - - - -

"Here are your tickets to Montreal, with a connecting flight to Calgary, Manitoba, Mr. Davies. Now, if I could see your passport, please." Eric handed the ticket agent the passport and waited. The ticket agent looked at Eric and the new picture of Howard, then handed the passport back to Eric and said, "Everything looks to be in order. The gate is to your right, through security, then the first concourse on the left. I hope you enjoy your flight."

Eric picked up his carry-on bag and started for security. Passport control was just in front of security, so Eric had to stop there first. The guard barely looked at the picture before he let Eric pass. The next guard took Eric's bag, sent it through to be x-rayed, then began his metal detection routine on Eric's body. When he was satisfied Eric wasn't carrying any concealed weapons, he waved him through.

Eric continued on toward the gate. When he arrived, he found a seat close to the gate door and sat down. The seating area was beginning to fill up as the long line at the check in desk dwindled down. Eric pulled out a copy of USA Today and began reading, careful to keep an eye on the crowd.

Shortly, the agent's voice came over the loudspeaker announcing the start of boarding. Eric folded his newspaper and patiently waited for the agent to announce the boarding for First and Business Class. When his turn came, he joined the line of people that had anticipated the announcement and were already in line waiting to board. A few minutes passed as Eric worked his way to the front of the line, then past the agent, and finally made his way to his seat. Sliding into his seat, he started relaxing the moment he sat down, and looking forward to a restful flight home.

-Whom do you surpass in beauty? Go down and make your bed with the uncircumcised.

Eric's flight landed at 2:00 AM. He should have arrived at seven the evening before, but a series of delays put them woefully behind. First, the flight from Jerusalem landed fifteen minutes earlier than scheduled at Heathrow. But the flight scheduled to leave from their gate hadn't left yet. This caused the first half hour delay before they could even start deplaning. Then, during the inspection prior to takeoff on the next leg to Montreal, maintenance noticed two of the tires needed replacing. Naturally, they could only find one replacement in stock. It took better than an hour to find another carrier, with an acceptable replacement, that was willing to let them buy one.

This set them back three and a half hours, just in time to get fogged in. The plane had already left the gate, so they waited for a half-hour on the tarmac before heading back to the gate. Another half-hour went by inside the terminal before they were allowed to re-board. By the time the whole incident had run its course, they had lost five hours. The result put Eric into Montreal well after his connecting flight had left. He was finally able to get to Calgary, but it was two in the morning.

Eric didn't waste any time getting his luggage and leaving. One of the benefits of getting in at this hour of the morning was not fighting crowds for your luggage. He headed straight out to the parking lot, spotted his Toyota 4-Runner, and quickly loaded his bags into the back. Hopping behind the wheel, he was off. In a relatively short time, he would be home again, and that thought alone, rejuvenated his overly tired body for the long drive. For the first time since he started this trip, he was able to relax.

- - - - -

The sun had risen completely above the horizon by the time he pulled up to his cabin. As he unloaded the Toyota, he stopped for a brief moment and stared at the cabin he called home. As he stared at it, he realized it was just this type of feeling that probably inspired the expression 'Home Sweet Home.' Right now, that sparsely furnished cabin looked as good as it ever would.

Shaking the cobwebs from his head, he returned his attention to unloading the Toyota. Once everything was out of the vehicle and in his hand, he headed for the cabin. As he walked, he heard the unmistakable sound of voices. He stopped to listen. It sounded like a television program, except he couldn't hear the generator running, so there shouldn't be any electricity available to power it. Whoever was there, assuming there was someone here, obviously was not concerned about being discovered, Eric thought. Either that, or his uninvited guests weren't expecting anyone else.

Eric was too tired to expend any energy sneaking up on anyone, so he continued to the front door and set down his bag next to the cabin. Then walking over to the window, he peered inside. "What the hell is she doing here?" He asked himself. Inside the cabin, sprawled comfortably on the sofa, was Maruch. Five feet in front of her was a battery-operated television perched on a kitchen chair. Leads from the TV led to a battery and transformer underneath the chair.

Eric shook his head in disgust and started back to the front door. Whatever she was doing here might as well be dealt with head on, he thought. Without stopping, Eric picked up his bags sitting by the front door and headed into his cabin. When he entered the cabin, he expected Maruch would act somewhat surprised, but instead she just looked up at him from her place on the sofa.

"If I'd have known when you were coming, I'd have fixed you breakfast."

Eric stepped inside, letting his bag drop to the floor as he kicked the door shut behind him. He walked over to the TV and turned it off. "There's a generator and plenty of gasoline out back, why didn't you use that?"

"I figured since I was here uninvited, I shouldn't be a freeloader too. So, I brought my own supplies."

"Where's your vehicle? I didn't notice any outside." Without waiting for a response, Eric walked back into the kitchen and started stoking the stove with wood. After he had enough inside, he stuffed some paper in between some of the wood then lit it. The wood was dry and soft and started almost immediately. Eric closed the door, went to a cupboard, and retrieved an opened can of coffee. He was making the coffee when Maruch walked in.

"I hid it back up the logging road a little way. I figured you wouldn't be expecting anyone, so I didn't go overboard hiding it. I guess it was adequate, based on that question."

Eric finished getting the coffee ready and set it on top of the stove to start heating. The stove was already generating plenty of heat, and it was beginning to warm the already stuffy kitchen. He turned to look at Maruch and replied, "If I was supposed to be impressed, I'm not."

"Aren't you curious why I'm here? Or did you just figure that since your assignment was done so was our partnership? You forgot one thing in that line of reasoning---partnerships end like they started, by mutual agreement. And my government has not agreed yet."

"I'm not overly concerned with what you or your government think. But I don't imagine that's going to stop you from telling me anyway."

"Your assignment was to stop the assassination." Eric opened his mouth to interrupt, but Maruch motioned for him to be quiet. "More accurately, I should say you were assigned to stop Jacque and Manuel from assassinating the Sheik. You did that. With your task complete, and based on our intelligence information on you, the only logical place for you to head was back here. Simply put, you were done. Now everything was someone else's problem. Right so far?"

"Yeah."

"You disappeared after examining the body of the actual assassin. At first, I accepted it, thinking you were trying to discover what was going on. I thought you'd try to contact me later that day, but you didn't. That made me a little suspicious, so I contacted Ariel and Doshe. They had an interesting theory you might be inclined to hear. In fact, that's why I'm here."

"Do tell." Eric's voiced dripped with sarcasm. Ignoring Maruch, he walked over to the now percolating coffee and watched as it burst against the glass top, then filtered back down to the grounds to extract a little more flavor.

"I should warn you: Their theory, like yours or mine, is constantly being modified as more information becomes available. But I suspect you already know that. They thought, based again on our intelligence on you, that you considered your job done and you were washing your hands of the whole ordeal. Based on that thinking, I was sent here, on behalf of my government, to in effect debrief you. Nothing more, nothing less."

"I was able to get a late flight out the same day Sheik Omani was shot. When I arrived in New York, a fax was waiting for me. I had left Jerusalem without any more information other than your cabin was located in Alberta. I came through New York in case your government decided to provide more accurate information...and I wanted to make it as easy as possible for them to find me," she added as an after thought. "The fax was simply a map to your cabin with the admonition from somebody named Jim to be careful on my vacation. What do you think he meant?"

"I don't know, maybe you should ask him. I can give you his phone number if you'd like."

The aroma of the coffee convinced Eric it was ready. He found two cups in the cupboard and poured Maruch a cup as well. "You take yours black, right?" He said as he handed her the cup. "Be careful, it's very hot." As Eric started walking back into the front room, he asked. "Should I start the generator or is this battery still good enough to run your TV?"

"The battery has plenty of juice left if that's what you're worried about. But if you're looking for something to do, go ahead and use the generator."

"No sense wasting my fuel then." He said as he turned the TV back on and plopped down onto the sofa. "You'll forgive my lack of manners. But remember, you weren't invited, and I'm extremely tired from the trip. Now, it's obvious you're trying to lead up to some bombshell that you're anxious to drop on me. But, under the circumstances, it probably wouldn't have the desired effect anyway. I'm just too tired to care. Understand?"

Ignoring his pleas, she returned to the reason she was here. "What do you think Jim meant when he said be careful? He knew we were working together, so why would he warn me to be careful."

"Jim tends to worry. He was just being cautious."

"All right." Maruch accepted the explanation temporarily, not because she believed it, but because she suspected that was the best she would get out of him for the moment. "I was surprised I got here first," she started into her explanation again. "But I figured you might have some errands you wanted to take care of before you came home. When you still weren't here after the first day, I began to suspect that wasn't the reason. I kept track of the news, but there was nothing there that would explain your delay. At least not at first, so I went back to town to check in with Doshe. He couldn't help much either. It seems you simply disappeared. Your people claimed to have no idea where you were. Believe it or not, I was actually getting worried about you." Maruch's embarrassment at this last comment was obvious. She didn't like the thought that she actually had feelings for this Gentile.

"There was little I could do from here, so I told Doshe I was going to return to Jerusalem and try to find out what happened to you. Fortunately, he was able to talk me out of it."

"The third day after Sheik Omani's assassination, the news media went wild. With the bombing of the hospital cafeteria, someone was able to eliminate the only people that could tell the world exactly what happened in that operating room the day Sheik Omani was shot. The news media didn't make the connection, but we did." Maruch paused to evaluate the reaction on Eric's face, but there was none to evaluate. He continued to alternate his attention between the TV and Maruch's explanation. It was obvious he was looking for something on TV, and she was distracting him, but it was not clear exactly what he was listening for.

Maruch continued her story. "The 'accident,' as the media called it, convinced me it was time to talk to Doshe again. This was when I learned the good Doctor and the medical staff were not the only recipients of bad luck that day. He informed me the last three members of the consortium were found dead as well. Two in their hotel rooms and one at the airport. Howard was also missing his passport."

"Whoever stole Howard's passport used his identity to fly to Montreal later that day. The trail ended at Montreal, or at least that's what the killer wanted everyone to think." Pausing during her explanation, she nonchalantly moved to the center of the room to take a position that would block Eric's exit. Meanwhile, Eric remained transfixed on the TV. As she passed the TV, she picked up her gun. It was sitting on top of it, just where she left it shortly after coming in from her walk earlier that day.

She raised the gun pointing it at Eric, then asked. "Why did you kill Howard? I'm going to assume you were responsible for the rest of the killings as well." Then, almost pleading she said, "I'm at a loss Eric to explain what's going on, especially your actions since the assassination. They're inconsistent with the Eric I thought I knew. Granted, I didn't have much to base my perceptions on, but in this business, one gets proficient at judging people accurately, or they die from their mistakes."

Eric, oblivious to the gun pointed directly at him, continued to watch the TV. Obviously frustrated at not seeing what he was waiting for, Eric got up and walked over to the TV. He looked at the back, then reached down and picked up a cable that was lying on the floor. He connected it to the TV and adjusted the station. Maruch watched Eric as he connected the cable to the TV, assuming it was for an antenna and would improve the reception. But when she heard the familiar words, 'Around the world in thirty minutes,' she realized the antenna was really a satellite dish.

"Peace in the Middle East, that's today's big story. I'm Anson Diakus reporting for CNN. After the miraculous raising from the dead, as some have begun to refer to Sheik Omani's brush with the hereafter last week, the Sheik has managed to solidify his support throughout the Middle East. The initial shock and tenuous political situation throughout the region have been replaced with dancing in the street. As the world prepared for a possible start to World War III just forty-eight hours ago, an expected result of the Sheik's assassination, that fear turned to euphoria with the news the Sheik lives. Word of his recovery and his subsequent address to his Arab and Jewish brothers has brought about the most dramatic turn of events ever recorded." "From Qadaffi and Hussein, two of the most radical political leaders in the world today, come these words. 'Sheik Omani deserves our prayers and support as he seeks to serve Allah.' Likewise, Mubarek of Egypt, leader of the strongest moderate Arab state, has 'urged unilateral support for Sheik Omani's peace initiative.' On the Jewish side, a similar story is heard. The Israeli Prime Minister along with Orthodox strong man Yakim Shanet have requested Israel, as a nation, support a united Jewish state in the Sheik's peace initiative. Add to this the initial pleas of the three; Jerome Bechard, Jihad Nadu and Doshe and a picture of unity not seen in the family of man since before Cain and Abel, comes into focus."

"Sheik Omani, wounds still evident by their trappings and his somewhat restricted movement, is being carried through the streets of Jerusalem in the cities' most elaborate celebration of peace. The Sheik makes frequent stops along the way to speak to the crowds made up of almost equal numbers of Jew and Arab. Sheik Omani is often greeted with the sight of uniformed men clasping hands in celebration together. These same men, wearing uniforms that a few days ago would have identified them as mortal enemies, are now greeting each other with a kiss."

Looking up at Maruch, Eric started in. "It was for this reason," he pointed at the TV, "that I did what you attribute to an Eric you didn't know. It was for peace: A concept Ariel, Doshe, Jim and Tom don't understand. And even if they did, they still wouldn't want anything to do with it. It's for those people on the TV, the ones you and they claim to want to protect, but then do everything in your power to destroy. It's for them, not you, not Tom, not Jim, Doshe or Ariel that I did these things. I killed in order to end the senseless killings between men and governments. I killed so that others may live. Have you or any of your so-called friends thought that this should have been your goal?" Eric asked rhetorically.

"Yes, but how do you know that will be the end result?" Maruch asked wryly.

"I'd say this is pretty good proof that I made the right decision," he said pointing at the TV screen again. "When I worked for the Agency, I was always told that what I was doing was for the good of the country, even the world. But I could never see any good come out of it. This time, the good is here for the world to see. I have proof that what I did contributed to this end. What do you have?" Eric paused to give Maruch a chance to respond.

"They're friends today, but tomorrow we die. There can be no peace between Jew and Arab. And I don't say that out of hatred for Arabs, I think you know that" Maruch countered. "Six thousand years of enmity can not stop and be healed overnight. They will not stop hating Jews anymore than Jews will start trusting Arabs. And no man, no matter how convincing, can ever achieve a permanent peace between the two. The Messiah, which Sheik Omani is not, is the only person that will be able to resolve this issue permanently, and I suspect he is still many years in our future."

"Maybe you underestimate Sheik Omani. Wasn't the Messiah supposed to set up His kingdom on Earth? Who's to say that both Jew and Arab cannot be a part of this kingdom? You both claim the same heritage. And it's justifiable, since ultimately the same parents conceived both lines. Maybe this is the way God intended it to be. Maybe it's His intention that both Jew and Arab are equally His chosen people."

"You can't be serious. You talk like you believe this man might really be the Messiah." Eric's expression frightened Maruch. Then she added, "Eric, please tell me you don't believe that."

Eric wasn't sure how to respond. True, he didn't actually believe that Sheik Omani was the Messiah. For that matter, he wasn't convinced God, if there is one, concerned himself with the things of men. Therefore, to jump from that level of ignorance to argue Sheik Omani was the Messiah was beginning to look foolish, even to him.

"You misunderstand what I'm telling you. I don't profess to understand the prophecies of Judaism anymore than Mohammed. And I certainly don't mean to imply that recent events are a part of them. All I'm asking you to do, is look at it from a less critical eye." Pointing at the TV, he added, "Look at your own people in Jerusalem. When was the last time you saw Jewish children laughing and playing with their Arab brothers? When was the last time they could walk the streets without fear of reprisal for some forgotten incident in the past? I really think Sheik Omani has accomplished something good here. I really think I helped." Then, as an after thought he added, "for once. And I'm not going to concede to you or anyone else that what you're seeing on TV right now shouldn't have happened. It should. And I'm responsible. You should be thanking me, not criticizing," Eric added emphatically.

"I wish I could tell you you're right, Eric. But in my heart, I know you are wrong." Silence created a bigger separation than mere distance ever could as they considered each other's position. If they had remained on different continents, they wouldn't be farther apart. Maruch was more disappointed than Eric, because she felt as if she had lost someone dear to her. Eric, on the other hand, was disappointed that Maruch couldn't grasp the great thing he had done for the world. Typical, he thought. Always being sorely misunderstood. He finally contributed positively to the world, and he wanted to believe that at least she would appreciate his effort.

Finally, Maruch broke the silence. "When did you switch over? Was it before I was brought in?"

"No. No. It wasn't until after the assassination. The assassin used a Russian made rifle, so I naturally started my search at Sergei. Even though he was dead, there was a possibility that our intelligence failed to pick up the fact that he hired a third assassin. I made a few calls, including one to a friend of mine in Russia named Joseph. I don't know how he knew, but he told me Sylvan and Sheik Omani needed to meet with me. I was surprised he included Sheik Omani because all the news reports at the time were reporting his death. He assured me Sheik Omani was not dead."

"He went on to explain to me that Sylvan and Sheik Omani were never a part of the consortium's conspiracy to control the world's oil supply. They allowed the consortium to create the Messianic image of Sheik Omani, but now they wanted the consortium eliminated. They wanted all ties to the consortium severed, and the best way to do that was to have the remaining members of the consortium killed. They convinced Joseph their only objective was peace, and now Joseph was trying to convince me. I might add he presented a very convincing argument that no one has been able to refute."

"After my talk with Joseph, I was determined to make contact with Sylvan to hear their plans firsthand. As I left the phone booth, a man handed me a handwritten note from Sylvan. He was requesting a meeting and asking me to meet him at the Star of David hotel within the hour. It was at that meeting that he convinced me to help them."

Maruch moved over to the sofa and sat down next to Eric as she listened to his explanation of what happened next. Eric described his conversation with Sylvan, and for the first time she began to understand how Eric could believe he would be doing what was right by helping them. Sylvan presented a very convincing argument for their position and it was easy to see why Eric joined their cause. As Eric continued to replay Sylvan's message, Maruch found herself nodding agreement at many of his points. Slowly, she was being won over to his worldview. The arguments that Ariel and Doshe had given her were looking less and less convincing. She was beginning to see the way: Sheik Omani's way. Or was it Sylvan's way? Not that it mattered, because it was now Eric's way. And it might just be the best way.

Eric, sensing her change in heart, slid over on the sofa, and put his arm around her shoulders. She leaned back against him, letting his arm cradle her. It was the first time in very many years that she actually felt safe. Eric continued his description of the world according to Sheik Omani as Maruch rested her head on his shoulder. The sound of the TV faded into the background and Maruch, hypnotized with the talk of a world at peace, quietly placed her pistol on the floor. She was safe, and there would be no need for this thing anymore, she thought.

- - - - -

"I wish there had been a way to fake my death without the need for scars," Sheik Omani said as he carefully removed the bandages from his chest and head. The doctor's wounds were healing nicely, and the permanent scar tissue was already developing, but Sheik Omani was growing tired of the discomfort.

"I think you'll agree, the pain was worth the payoff," Sylvan responded to the Sheik's complaint.

Stepping out of the bathroom Sheik Omani replied. "That's easy for you to say, since you didn't have anyone trying to imitate bullet holes in your body." Sheik Omani lifted the last bandage from his chest and stared at the wound. It was still a little tender, but for the most part the pain wasn't nearly as bad as he pretended it was. He picked at the scab, removing bits and pieces around the edges, but the center held tight. It still wasn't ready to come off.

Sylvan turned on the TV and sat down to watch the news. He never tired of seeing himself on the news, even if he was always playing second fiddle to the Sheik. They were in control of the heart of the Middle East now. And soon they, by virtue of their stranglehold on the Middle East, would control the whole world.

Sheik Omani walked over to the recliner sat down and pushed it back until he was almost parallel to the floor. "How long do you think it will take before we can annihilate Israel?" Sylvan asked the Sheik.

"It's hard to say. Maybe three or four years.

Author's Note

It was never the intention of the author for this novel to be perceived to be anything more than a fictitious representation of Scriptural prophecy in a modern-day setting. Since prophetical interpretations vary greatly, arguments could be made that the storyline incorporates inaccurate details regarding the Antichrist and end times. I will not debate this point.

With that said, it was the intention of the author to present a theoretically feasible and plausible scenario that incorporates the technological capabilities of today's society. And, to demonstrate how those capabilities could be used to promote the interests of a person or group at the expense of humanity. That is why all the events were written with a critical eye toward whether they were realistically achievable within man's limited capabilities. Eric Dent, the oil consortium, Sheik Omani, and Sylvan had similar, albeit not identical, goals, and all were willing to sacrifice humanity to achieve those goals within those constraints.

When the Antichrist comes, he will have at minimum paranormal and possibly supernatural capabilities. The restrictions that were placed on the characters in this novel will not be placed on him. Prophecy is clear that he will be able to rally the world, en masse, around his person and his initiatives. It is your choice whether you are prepared.

Regards,
Brendon F. Ribble

About The Author

He is Brendon F. Ribble, a tenacious author from Florida. He is happily married with 3 daughters. Early of his times, he was able to invent 20 things national and many are international and the reason why he has lots of patents. The reason behind the book was made because he loves reading the bible every day and God finds ways to motivate him spread the words.